Information Technology

Tomorrow's Advantage Today

Stephen Haag

Daniels College of Business
University of Denver

Peter Keen

International Center for Information Technology

McGraw-Hill Companies, Inc.

New York • St. Louis • San Francisco • Auckland • Bogotá
Caracas • Lisbon • London • Madrid • Mexico City • Milan • Montreal
New Delhi • San Juan • Singapore • Sydney • Tokyo • Toronto

For Pam and Indy. They are my family, my life,
and my truest and dearest friends.
—Stephen Haag

For all my friends in St. John, U.S. Virgin Islands—
two hurricanes this year . . . still paradise,
With love and thanks,
—Peter Keen

McGraw-Hill

A Division of The **McGraw·Hill** Companies

Information Technology:
Tomorrow's Advantage Today

1 2 3 4 5 6 7 8 9 0 BAN BAN 9 0 9 8 7 6

ISBN 0-07-025447-8 Text
ISBN 0-07-844295-8 Text and *IT Tutor* CD-ROM

Sponsoring Editor: Frank Ruggirello
Associate Editor: Rhonda Sands
Editorial Assistant: Kyle Thomes
Production Supervisor: Richard DeVitto
Project Manager: Elm Street Publishing Services, Inc.
Cover and Interior Design: Cloyce Wall
Compositor: Elm Street Publishing Services, Inc.
Illustrations: Precision Graphics
Printer and Binder: Banta Company

Library of Congress Catalog Card Number 95-80842

As authors, our goal is to reflect our passion for and philosophy of teaching Information Technology (IT), and our belief that the student is at the center of the educational process. We believe that good teachers make a personal difference in students' lives and careers, and that the pace of change, jargon, and complexity of the IT field too often lose students and lose personal relevance to them. Every page of our book is aimed at bringing student, teacher, and Information Technology together.

Objective of the Book

Information Technology: Tomorrow's Advantage Today is designed for a one-semester introductory course in which the goal is to give students a foundation in the concepts of information technology and their applications to business and other disciplines. There is no technology prerequisite.

We have made every effort to create a concise text that is independent of any particular hardware or software platform, giving the instructor the flexibility to combine the book with any available software tutorials, or to use it as a stand-alone text in a conceptual course.

A more subjective goal is to stimulate the interest of students in the dynamic and exciting field of information technology and to encourage their sense of discovery about it throughout their academic careers and beyond.

Themes of the Book

The main theme of this book is *The IT Advantage*. Throughout the text we emphasize the advantages of information technology to students— in their personal lives, their careers, and to organizations they may become a part of. As we help students understand the advantages of IT, we approach the material from several points of view:

- We introduce students to information technology, *how it works,* and *issues relating to the use and development of IT*.
- We emphasize *people* as the primary component of any IT system.
- We show students the many examples of *information technology in their every-day lives,* and we encourage them to discover more of it; to experience as much as they can.
- We look at the *personal advantage* that IT can provide.
- We look at the *business advantage* that IT can provide.

▶ We emphasize that we live in a *networked society* and that, within that society, knowledge and use of IT are essential to future success.

▶ We emphasize that the networked society is a *global society*.

The last two points of view are given special attention:

Today's students are the most diverse group ever to enter college. It is more important than ever for them to understand the power of modern IT tools to break down barriers to culture, business, and language. We live in a networked society. We believe the Internet is an especially useful vehicle for illustrating this point. For this reason, we introduce the Internet in Chapter 1, discuss it in some depth there and in other parts of the text, and provide content-related Internet assignments at the end of every chapter's exercise set.

We believe it is critical that students understand that the networked society is a global proposition. To underscore this point, we have chronicled the success of many foreign, domestic, and transnational firms and their use of IT as an instrument of success and as a competitive weapon. We have devoted an entire chapter (Chapter 9) to what it means to be a "global citizen." After reading Chapter 9, students will understand the nature of today's global economy, how businesses are using IT to operate worldwide, and how IT can work to their personal advantage in an increasingly international landscape.

Discovering IT

These boxes are short assignments that encourage students to think critically about IT in every-day life. They focus on getting students out into the real world to see IT in use. Instructors will find these useful teaching tools for bringing home the practical applications of IT.

Personal Advantage

Personal Advantage boxes focus on using IT to become a more productive human being. Many contain success stories of individuals who have improved their quality of life through the use of IT, while others encourage students to apply IT to their own situations.

Today's Business Advantage

In these sidebars, students will learn how IT is being used effectively in the workplace. The IT applications and strategies of such companies as Club Med, Avon Products, AT&T, Chrysler, American Airlines, Blockbuster Entertainment Corp., Dell Computer, and many more are profiled throughout the text. In all, students will read about more than 150 businesses and their use of IT.

Tomorrow's Business Advantage

For many students, the business world and full-time employment are several years away. Between now and then, the IT landscape will change dramatically. Technologies that seem futuristic today will be tomorrow's standard. *Tomorrow's Business Advantage* sidebars encourage students to develop an entrepreneurial sense of how they might use today's innovations to their advantage in tomorrow's business community. Students will find exciting such topics as DBMSs that can speak any language, virtual reality on the Internet, genetic software, and many more.

Current Business Examples

It has been said that any book on Information Technology is out of date before it comes off the press. While this may be true in the strictest sense, we have taken steps to provide students with the most up-to-date business technology possible. For example, this paragraph is being written three months before the book is due to be published. We added our most recent example to the text discussion this morning. For another, our World Wide Web site http://mgh.willamette.edu/mgh/ will regularly provide technology updates to augment examples and discussions in the text. With well over 150 examples, many of them international in scope, this text is quite a resource for students.

Now You Can . . .

This section at the end of each chapter is tied to chapter objectives and summarizes the practical outcomes realized by students from what they've learned. This emphasizes what students are able to *do* as a result of learning the chapter material.

Cruising the Net

To encourage use of the Internet, we have included an overview of "Net" concepts in Chapter 1 and exercises requiring the use of the Internet at the end of each chapter. (These exercises occur at the end of extensive exercise sets, so they can be skipped if your school does not yet have an Internet connection.) These exercises will help students find more information about the chapter topics, learn about the Internet, and learn where to find relevant information on the Internet.

Working in a Group

At the end of each chapter we have included projects designed to be completed by groups or teams of students. Group projects are an excellent vehicle for motivating students, fostering peer teaching, and gaining good experience for an increasingly team-oriented workplace. The *Instructor's Manual* includes tips for leading students through group projects and for evaluating their work.

Custom Binding Option. The book can be used comfortably in any computing environment. To give you additional flexibility to create the course of your choice, the book may be custom bound with any of the following McGraw-Hill software tutorials, giving you a complete concepts and applications course in one spiral-bound volume, at an affordable price:

Operating Systems	**Database**
Windows 95	Access 2.0 Windows
Windows 3.1	dBASE 5 Windows
DOS 6.0	Paradox 5.0 Windows
Word Processing	**Integrated Software**
Word 6.0 Windows	Works 3.0 for Windows
WordPerfect 6.1 Windows	
WordPerfect 6.0 Windows	**The Internet**
WordPerfect 6.0 DOS	Internet
WordPerfect 5.1	
	Office Integration
Spreadsheets	Office Integration
Excel 5.0 Windows	
Lotus 5.0 Windows	**Presentation Graphics**
Lotus 4.0 Windows	PowerPoint 4.0
Lotus 2.4 DOS	
Quattro Pro 6.0 Windows	**Programming**
Quattro Pro 5.0 DOS	Qbasic
	Visual basic

State-of-the-Art Course Management System

A state-of-the-art book requires a state-of-the-art support package. A World Wide Web site @ http://mgh.willamette.edu/mgh/ provides regular technology updates to augment examples and discussion in the text. To help you create the best possible learning and teaching environment, we have provided an integrated package of teaching supplements, appropriate for any classroom environment:

Instructor's Manual

The *Instructor's Manual* offers a complete set of tools for developing the structure of your course. It includes suggested outlines for 10-week quarters, 15-week semesters, 8-week summer sessions, and 5-week summer sessions. You'll also find detailed outlines for each chapter with suggestions for how and when to use the transparencies and transparency masters, teaching strategies for getting students involved and excited, and tips for including the book's pedagogical aids into your teaching. We also include solutions to all questions in the text.

Test Bank/Computerized Testing System

Our Test Bank contains more than 1,200 true/false, multiple choice, fill-in and short answer questions. Two short, pre-formatted quizzes are also included for each

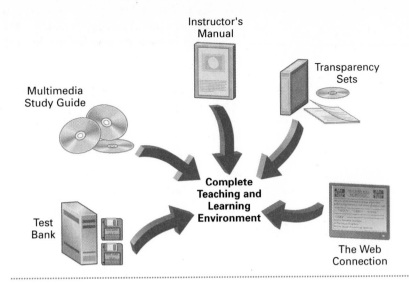

chapter. A computerized version is available, and may be administered over a network or may be used in more conventional disk or printed formats. The computerized version is available for DOS or Windows.

PowerPoint Presentation on CD-ROM

More than 200 four-color electronic transparencies have been created for this package and are contained on a CD-ROM that is packaged with the Instructor's Manual. They can be easily copied to disk format. Many of the transparencies are adapted from art in the book, while others offer students a new way of viewing IT concepts.

Multimedia Study Guide

Patricia Fox's *The IT Tutor* is an interactive multimedia CD-ROM available to students that allows them to actively explore state-of-the-art IT concepts by simply clicking a mouse. The CD includes interactive presentations of major topics in the book, animations and video clips that bring abstract concepts to life, self-tests with immediate feedback, and interactive games and exercises designed to give students an active and visually exciting way to learn. An additional benefit of *The IT Tutor* is that, by putting the learning control in the hands of the student, it stimulates a sense of discovery and feeds a growing interest in the exciting world of information technology.

Acknowledgments Many people contributed to the development of this book. Without all of these people working together, it would not have been possible.

We would like to thank the crew at McGraw-Hill. First, there's Frank Ruggirello, our editor, the man who brought the two of us together, and the man who really made it all happen. Frank's expertise in project management provided the real foundation for completing this project. Without his consistent prodding, critical eye for detail, and quest for quality, we would not be writing these acknowledgments today. Thanks, Frank, for giving us this opportunity and for seeing it through to the end.

The others who had their hands on this project at one time or another include Rich DeVitto, Kyle Thomes, Debra Yohannon, Natalie Durbin, Kris Johnson, Jeff Rydman, and Rhonda Sands. There are probably many more people in the background but their names never came across our desks. To all of you we extend our heartfelt gratitude.

Patricia Fox, Trident Technical College, and Dr. Maeve Cummings, Pittsburg State University, helped us greatly. Pat developed the Multimedia CD-ROM Study Guide, and her expertise shows in the quality of that material. Maeve acted as our consultant on Chapter 9 and wrote much of the material.

Our gratitude is also extended to helpful reviewers of the manuscript. We had the best. They include:

Peter Aiken
Virginia Commonwealth University

Lynda Armbruster
Rancho Santiago Community College

Gary Armstrong
Shippensburg University of Pennsylvania

Harvey Blessing
Essex Community College

Bruce Brown
Salt Lake Community College

Eli Cohen
Wichita State University

William Cormett
Southwest Missouri State University

Ray Crepeau
Western Carolina University

Jack Cundiff
Horry-Georgetown Technical College

Richard Fenzl
Syracuse University

Joey George
Florida State University

Harry Glover
Georgia College

Kaye Greene
Bentley College

John Grillo
Bentley College

Joe Hagerty
Raritan Valley Community College

Jack Hogue
University of North Carolina–Charlotte

Wade Jackson
University of Memphis

M.B. Kahn
California State University, Long Beach

Ken Kozar
University of Colorado

Marilyn Kletke
Oklahoma State University

Skip Lees
California State University, Chico

David Letcher
Trenton State University

Diane Marshall
University of Alaska, Fairbanks

George Novotny
Ferris State University

Herb Rebhun
University of Houston, Downtown

Martin Richards
University of North Texas

Bernard Straub
Trident Technical College

Anthony Verstraete
Pennsylvania State

Don Voils
Palm Beach Community College

Connie Washburn
Dekalb College

Fred Wells
Dekalb College

From Stephen Haag. . .

My work on this project has been supported literally by a cast of thousands. To Phyllis Crittenden and the many others at Elm Street Publishing Services, Inc., I extend my gratitude. I would also like to thank the faculty of the Department of Information Systems and Management Sciences at the University of Texas at Arlington, who guided me through my Ph.D. work and impressed upon me the seriousness of providing a quality education to those who seek it.

I have friends all over the country as well who supported me throughout this process. To my friends—John and Marsha Semple, Diane Cole, Pat Jaska, Pat Hogan, J.D. and Judy Ice, Maeve Cummings, Fran and David Stevens, Ray and Cindy Raab, and Jim and Sarah Wood—my sincere gratitude for your support.

My family has provided consistent, undying emotional and spiritual support. My brothers and sisters—Carla, Rodney, Jerry, and Christi—each put up with my unending discussions and conversations about this project. My parents (Carl and Iona) and my adopted parents (Homer, Marilyn, Al, and Fern) really could not care less how successful this project is—they only care about me.

Most important is my wife, Pam. Throughout these last two years, Pam has been my greatest supporter, my most critical reviewer, and always my source of strength. Pam, a million thanks is a million too few. I owe you for the rest of my life and will gladly spend the rest of it proving that to you.

S.H.
October 1995

From Peter Keen. . .

Over the years a number of people and groups have helped to shape my thoughts and experiences as an educator. I will always be thankful to Arthur Taylor, then Dean at Fordham University School of Business, who gave me the fullest freedom, encouragement, leadership, and scope for innovation I have found in any university. Also at Fordham, Linda Jo Calloway, a superb colleague and a leader in developing the highly innovative IS program at Fordham. I have much to thank her for. Eduardo Perez, my colleague at the University of Stockholm and a prodigious innovator in the fusion of technology into all areas of education. For the past year Eduardo has taught me much about teaching, and I thank him for it. Jim Gannon of the Royal Bank of Canada has been a creative and challenging friend, who has stimulated and applied much of the work of which I am most proud. Jim has been the bridge for me between the education of students and the new realities of careers in an ever-changing world.

This book was begun at a time of great personal turbulence for me and appears at a time of personal peace. I don't have space to thank the many people who helped me during that transition, but I will never forget them.

Finally, my love and thanks to Sherry for quite literally, everything.

P.K.
October 1995

Brief Contents

Contents

Information Technology: What It Can Do for You

2

Software: The Intellectual Interface

3

Input and Output Devices: The Physical Interface

4

The CPU and Internal Memory: The Processing Engine

5

Storage Devices and Databases: Organizing Your World

6

Communications and Connectivity: Living in a Networked World

7

Building IT Systems:
The Tools You Use and Your Role

8

Information Technology in Business: How Organizations Use IT

9

Reaching the World through IT: Information Technology as Your Passport to the World

10

Putting It All Together:
Careers, Social Issues, and Horizons

1

Information Technology:

Your Objectives for This Chapter

1 Define information technology and understand why you should study information technology.

2 Describe the seven building blocks of an information technology system. **3** Identify the difference between data and information and the qualities of good information. **4** Describe important competencies, including a knowledge of information technology, that can help you obtain a personal advantage. **5** Describe how information technology helps an organization obtain a business advantage. **6** Describe the Internet and the three types of servers—FTP, Gopher, and Web—you can find on the Internet.

It's the year 2006—you're up early one morning to get a head start on the day. Your integrated home management (IHM) system—which consists of your computer, television, telephone, fax machine, VCR, stereo, and home environmental controls—has already turned on the coffee machine, printed a list of concerts in your town for the weekend, confirmed your airline reservations, and is displaying a message that you need to call Shannon. While sitting in the comfort of your favorite reclining chair, you say, "Call Shannon and send airline information." Your IHM system calls Shannon and sends her a copy of your flight schedule. On your television screen you see Shannon and your flight schedule, and the two of you discuss when Shannon will pick you up at the airport.

Sound farfetched? Not at all! In the near future you will have computer-controlled home systems that will respond to voice commands. You'll also be connected to every home, business, school, and government institution across the country (see Figure 1-1). Working with easy-to-use interfaces and equipment including fax machines, videoconferencing, presentation graphics, and interactive televisions, many of you will probably even *telecommute*—be an employee of a business but work at home instead of going into the office. Did you know it's estimated today that almost 8 million American workers already telecommute?[1]

Integrated home management systems and telecommuting are just the tip of the iceberg. The changes that are going to occur in the next few years will undoubtedly affect your personal life and your career in ways no one can imagine. What's behind all these changes? It's *information technology,* and you're reading this book to learn about information technology, what it can do for you, and how you can use it to help you in your career. We welcome you to this most exciting and fascinating field.

Why You Should Study Information Technology

Information technology (IT) is a set of tools that helps you work with information and perform tasks related to information processing. That set of tools includes such computer-related items as a printer, a keyboard, CD-ROM, and multimedia applications that let you hear, see,

---

Figure 1-1

Getting Connected

Ⓢ omeday, information technology will connect the entire United States, and most of the world! From your home, office, car, or even a public bus terminal, you'll be able to communicate with anyone. The information you send and receive will be in the form of pictures, sound, and video as well as letters and memos.

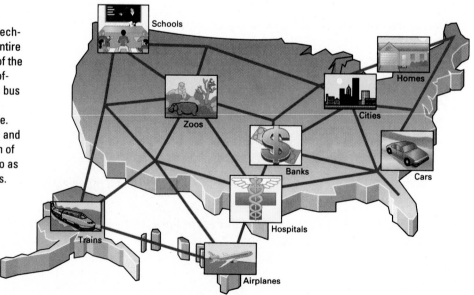

---

and read about various topics, home budgeting software that helps you maintain your checkbook, and the Internet that lets you find information all over the world and communicate with people everywhere.

Basically, IT is a valuable set of tools because it benefits you immediately and directly. Let's stop for a moment and talk about why IT is important to you. We think your knowledge of IT is important because:

- IT is everywhere.
- IT can help you be more productive.
- IT is exciting and changing.
- IT will enhance your career.
- IT will give you a world of opportunity.

Information Technology Is Everywhere

To say that IT is everywhere is almost an understatement. Right now, IT systems are at work handling tasks from the most mundane to the most unbelievable. Some of these tasks include:

- Assigning social security numbers (over 6 million per year; that's about one every five seconds)
- Transferring billions of dollars around the world every minute
- Helping doctors diagnose diseases and recommend treatments
- Letting families "virtually" view their new home before it's built
- Helping pet stores track customer sales so that customer preferences can be identified
- Processing millions of payroll transactions and generating paychecks for thousands of people

Multimedia applications on CD-ROM are great for hearing, seeing and reading about various topics.

But on an even more personal note, IT is literally in every area of your life. Think about the tasks you perform every day and the products you use. VCRs, televisions, automobiles, telephones and telephone answering machines, and even refrigerators all have IT in them. You see, IT is everywhere, and it's a part of your life you cannot escape. The best thing to do is become an active participant in the excitement of IT; you've already taken the first step by reading this book.

Information Technology Can Help You Be More Productive

IT has been created with you in mind. Think about a term paper for your history class. Using IT, you can increase your productivity at an unbelievable rate. Today's word processing software can check your grammar, style your bibliography, and even correct your spelling *while you type*.

Writing term papers is only the beginning. You can also use spreadsheet software to do homework for your finance class, presentation graphics software to create presentation material, the Internet to find research material for your term papers, and database management system and statistical software to identify sales trends for your marketing class. The list is almost endless.

What about banking? Using an automatic teller machine (ATM) card, you can make transactions around the world anytime, day or night. It doesn't matter what

Box 1-1

IT Is Everywhere!

Ⓓid you know that microchips are replacing dog tags for identification? That's right. And it's also being done in zoos for rare animals. People use handheld scanners to read a digital number from the microchip. The digital number is then fed into a computer that displays the animal's name, medical history, and other information.

In dogsled races like Bear Grease in Minnesota (a 500-mile preparatory race for the Iditarod), and the Iditarod, the consummate dogsled race in Alaska, a small microchip about the size of a grain of rice is implanted between the shoulder blades of each dog. In doing so, the race veterinarians can verify that each dog has gone through the appropriate medical examinations.

Race officials use the microchip to make sure the dogs that finish the race are the same ones that started. Finally, breeders and buyers of the dogs use the microchips after the race to make sure the dog is the one that won or made a strong showing at one of the races.

Companies are also exploring the possibility of using microchips for human beings. Someday, you may have a microchip implanted somewhere on your body. This chip will contain information such as your social security number, name, place and date of birth, driver's license number, and medical history.

currency you need or which country you're in, that small ATM card does it for you. And behind all of it is a worldwide IT system. Today, you can be in Cancun, Mexico, and get $20 in Mexican pesos or check your account balance—even if you bank in Portland, Oregon.

Information Technology Is Exciting and Changing

Did you know that microcomputers have only been around for about 15 years? In 1978 Apple sold the first Apple II microcomputer, and in 1982 IBM sold the first IBM PC. Since then, IT has progressed by leaps and bounds (see Table 1-1). CD-ROM systems first became commercially viable in about 1992—now you can listen to your favorite CD on your system while performing other tasks. You may even be able to connect your system to cable TV and use video capturing and editing software to record shows. Then you can change the way the shows are recorded by flipping, omitting, or adding frames, varying the background music, or adding your own on-screen captions.

IT systems are great for typing term papers, preparing monthly budgets, and scheduling appointments, but you don't have to stop there. Today, you can use your IT system to order pizzas, obtain the most up-to-date football scores, find out what's happening with the weather worldwide, and tune up your car engine. When you look at that computer in front of you, let your imagination run wild. Think of your IT system as a gateway to possibilities you've never seen before. And don't worry—if IT can't do it today, it will probably be able to do it tomorrow.

Information Technology Will Enhance Your Career

Your ability to use IT is important to you because it translates into a job skill, and it's a skill that all employers are looking for. Today IT skills are similar to reading,

Information Technology: What It Can Do for You

arithmetic, and communication skills; you have to have them to get a good job. This will be even more true in the future.

Find some friends who have prepared résumés and are looking for jobs. On almost all their résumés, you'll probably notice a section called "Computer Skills" or "Information Technology Skills." The simple fact is, if you don't possess certain skills, you can't get a job. IT skills are among the most important and sought after skills, because employers want people—like you—who can use IT to be more productive and make the company better.

Information Technology Will Give You a World of Opportunity

Finally, IT will provide you with a world of opportunity. You can take that statement to mean two things—IT can open a lot of doors for you, and IT will literally open the world to you. Both are correct and equally important, but the second is the newest and holds the most opportunity. IT tools such as the Internet and the World Wide Web now make it possible for you to virtually travel the world over, communicate with people all over the world, obtain information all over the world (perhaps from the Louvre in Paris or the Vatican library), and learn about diverse and interesting cultures.

If you've ever dreamed of studying and hearing the animals on the Serengetti, shopping in Hong Kong, exploring the Great Barrier Reef, or simply learning about interesting tourist spots in North Dakota, IT can take you there. What's really great is that you don't have to worry about getting the appropriate vaccinations, having a passport, or buying a plane ticket—you can sit in the comfort of your living room and use IT to see the world. (See Figure 1-2).

Table 1-1		

The Fast Progress of Information Technology

❶n 1982, IBM introduced the IBM PC for about $2,500. This basic system performed 330,000 instructions per second. Today, you can spend half that amount to purchase a system for your home capable of performing over 100 million instructions per second. If other industries had progressed in similar fashion over the last 14 years, you would be able to . . .

Purchase a set of automobile tires for $100 that would last 12 million miles.

Purchase an automobile that would get 8,800 miles to the gallon.

Purchase a ticket for an around-the-world airline flight that would last only six minutes. No in-flight movie on this trip!

Purchase a home for $10,000 that would occupy 440,000 square feet.

Purchase a one-pound T-bone steak for . . . well, at that price, they'll just be giving away T-bone steaks.

Interview one or two people employed at a company you want to work for. Find out what IT skills they think are important and how they were able to obtain those skills. Do you think the skills apply to everyone or just people interested in your area?

All these great opportunities and many more are available to you through IT. All you have to do is learn about IT and how to use it, and how to take the greatest advantage of it.

What Is Information Technology?

Information technology is a set of tools that helps you work with information and perform tasks related to information processing. Included in this set are seven building blocks (see Figure 1-3). Together, we call these building blocks an IT system.

1 *Input and output devices* that you use to enter information and commands and to receive (usually by hearing or seeing) the results of your requests. Input and output devices include a mouse, a keyboard, a screen, and a printer.

2 *Software,* or the set of instructions that are used to perform a particular task for you. Software includes word processing, budgeting, payroll, and communications.

3 *Communication devices* that connect IT systems and people all over the world. Communication devices include modems, satellites, and coaxial cable (similar to the cable you use to connect your TV to your VCR).

Figure 1-2

Information Technology and Opportunities around the World

Information technology can take you around the world while you sit in the comfort of your living room.

4 The *processing engine* contains two components: the central processing unit and the internal memory. The central processing unit executes the software to perform a particular task for you, while the internal memory is a temporary storage area for software and information.

5 *Information* you work with. Today, you can work with information in a variety of forms—text, sound, video, and even movement.

6 *Storage devices* that permanently store information and software. Storage devices include CD-ROM, tape, and disks.

7 Finally, and most important, *people.*

When most people think about IT, they think about the computer in front of them—a printer, a keyboard, disks for storing information, a screen, and perhaps a telephone modem for communicating. Although all are components of an IT system, you must look at yourself and others and realize that people are the most important building block. Without you, an IT system really is nothing more than a computer—an expensive piece of electronic equipment that takes up space and gathers dust. In this book, we'll often use the term *computer* when referring to these physical components of IT.

You should view a computer the same way you view your car. Your car is just a car, but when you get inside and start driving, your car becomes your transporta-

---

Figure 1-3

Building Blocks for an IT System

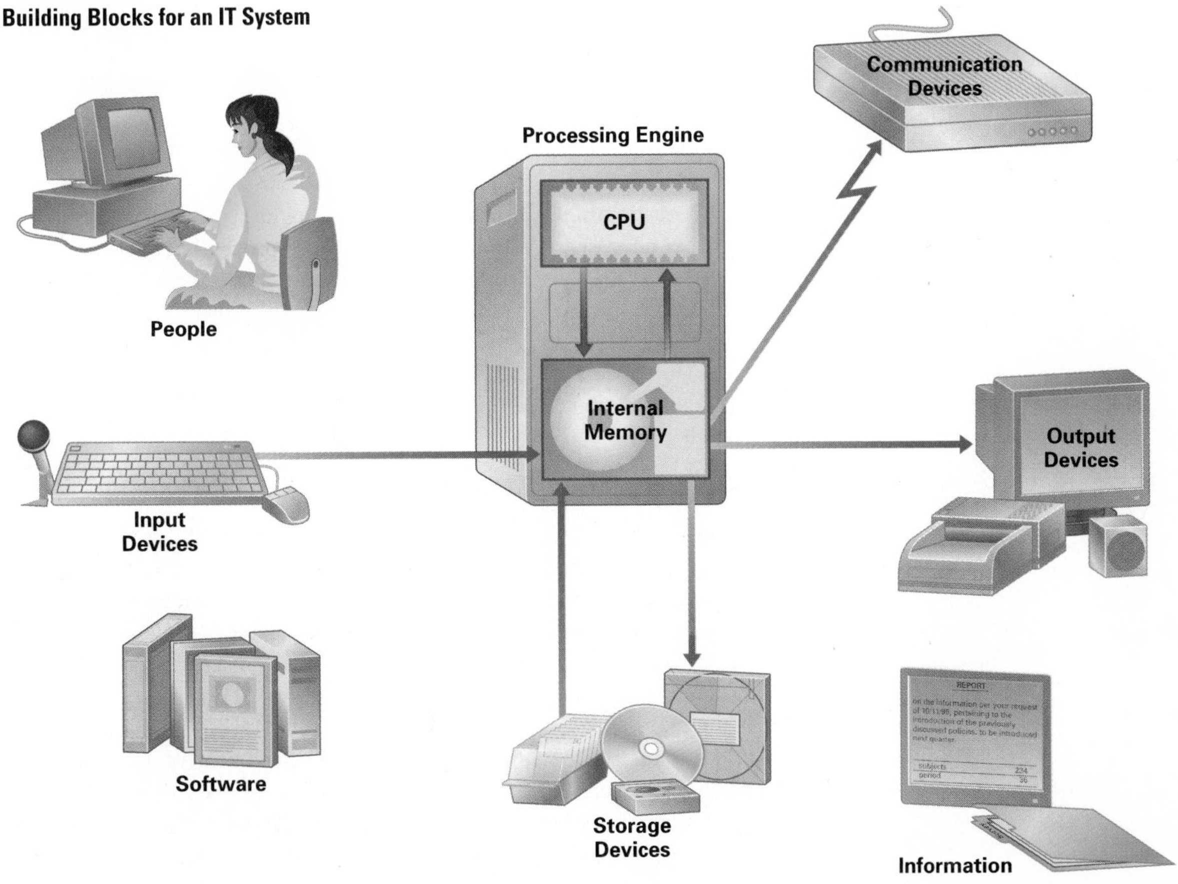

Communication Devices

Processing Engine

CPU

People

Internal Memory

Input Devices

Output Devices

Software

Storage Devices

Information

---

tion system. Without you behind the wheel operating the foot pedals, steering, and deciding where you want to go, your car is just a piece of equipment. Your car can't do anything on its own and neither can a computer. That's why you are the most important building block of your IT system. You, and you alone, transform your computer into a fully working and beneficial IT system.

So, as you read this book, don't think, "I'm going to learn about computers." Rather, say to yourself, "I'm going to learn how I can use my IT system to do better in school, prepare to get a really great job, and do things in my personal life and career that I've never been able to do before." After all, you don't want to just learn about IT, you want to learn what your IT system can do for you. Let's take a closer look at the seven building blocks of an IT system and see what they do.

Input and Output Devices

Input and output devices provide you with the physical interface to your IT system. That is, input and output hardware devices allow you to enter information and commands and to receive the results of your requests. We use the term **hardware** for these devices because they are part of the physical building blocks of your IT system.

Input devices help you capture information and commands. Examples of input devices include a keyboard, a mouse, and even your telephone and a microphone for speech recognition. **Output devices** let you receive the results of your requests. Output devices include screens and printers that let you see results and speakers that let you hear speech, music, and other types of sound. In Chapter 3, we'll explore different kinds of input and output devices and what they can do for you.

Software

Software is the set of instructions that your central processing unit executes to perform a particular intellectual task for you. Software, then, provides the intellectual interface to your IT system because it is the set of instructions or procedures that the central processing unit follows when performing tasks for you.

For example, you can write a term paper using word processing software, send messages to other people using communication software, schedule appointments and create a budget using personal information management software, learn to play the guitar using educational software, and create presentations that include color, sound, and video with presentation graphics software. In Chapter 2, we'll look at these types of software as well as many others.

Communication Devices

Communication devices are the hardware connections between different IT systems. In Chapter 6, when we talk about IT systems that are connected, we'll refer to them as *networks*. Communication devices include switching stations that direct information throughout a network and the electronic pathways over which information travels, including microwaves, coaxial cable, and optical fiber.

You already use communication devices in other areas of your life. Think about making telephone calls. Your call travels over cable through a lot of switching stations to get to its final destination. In a sense, when you travel by plane, you're also using communication devices, except that you are the one traveling instead of information. The plane is essentially the pathway over which you are traveling, and the airport acts as a switching station where you arrive, get off one plane, and board another to get to your destination.

Box 1-2

Rolling on Down the Highway

Imagine a day when you can communicate with people anywhere in the world and access any information you need anytime just by having access to IT. You'll no longer have to go to the library to find research material; instead you'll work efficiently from home, accessing large databases located all over the world. You'll no longer use the telephone to talk to people; instead you'll see them on your screen while you talk. That super network of the future is the Information Superhighway, and the Information Superhighway is rapidly approaching.

Not only will you be able to see people while you talk and access information for your term papers, you'll also be able to obtain special information like sports and weather updates, stock prices, and airline flight departure and arrival times. You'll even be able to buy, sell, and advertise products, order pizzas, and purchase gold futures on the Japanese stock market.

Well, the future is here, and it's up to you to take advantage of it. There are already many computer networks (also called online services) that give you most of these capabilities. One network gaining attention from both business and the public as the model for the future Information Superhighway is the **Internet**, or the Net for short. The Internet is basically a network of networked computers that lets you communicate with people all over the world and obtain information from all over the world.

The Net as we know it today started in the 1980s with the creation of a standard method for connecting computer networks at various research and educational institutions. Initially, access to the Net was limited to researchers and educators in the sciences—computer sciences in particular. Today, millions of people around the world use the Net every day to communicate with each other and to access available resources. Business and government agencies alike are increasing their efforts to make information available through the Net. One reason for this increased interest is a powerful software tool called the World Wide Web (WWW), or the Web (see Figure 1-4). The Web wipes out some of the technical and geographic hurdles that have been limiting most users from using the Net for anything more than electronic mail. The Web also makes it easy for anyone to publish information that others can access.

Figure 1-4

Sample Web Page

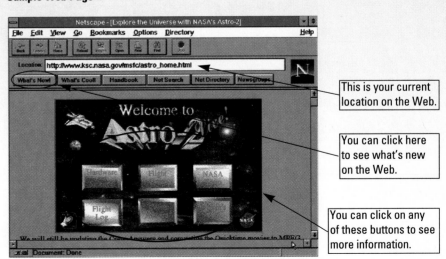

This is your current location on the Web.

You can click here to see what's new on the Web.

You can click on any of these buttons to see more information.

Box 1-2 cont.

Today, you need to use a Web browser program to access information on the Web. There are a number of Web browsers from which to choose. The most popular is Netscape, which is available for several platforms, including Macintosh and Windows. Although the ease of use and type of access to information depend on the browser you're using, you can usually begin cruising the Web with a simple click of the mouse. Eventually, access to the Web will become an integral part of every IT system.

How the Net Works

Whether you're trying to communicate with someone or access information, you need to know the address of that person or information resource. Just as the U.S. Postal Service identifies each building by an address, each computer on the Net is identified by an Internet Protocol (IP) address. An IP address is usually displayed as a series of four numbers separated by periods (called "dots"). For example, 158.104.1.1 is the IP address of a computer at Willamette University in Salem, Oregon. However, since many people have a hard time remembering numbers, especially large ones, there is a name, called *domain name,* associated with each IP address. The domain name has several parts separated by dots. The last part is an abbreviation for a geographic or administrative domain, such as "au" for AUstralia hosts, "edu" for EDUcational institutions, "com" for COMpanies, or "gov" for GOVernment agencies. Before the geographic or administrative domain is the name of the institution or the organization. Before that is the subdomain (if it exists) within the institution, getting progressively more specific, until finally reaching the name of the individual computer. The same computer at Willamette University has the domain name jupiter.willamette.edu, meaning that it is the computer named jupiter at Willamette University, which is an educational institution. Another example of a domain name is che1.chem.wm.edu, a computer named che1 in the Chemistry Department at William and Mary College.

When you want to send messages to another person, you need to find out that person's e-mail address. The e-mail address is usually the user account followed by an @ sign and the domain name of the host computer on which the account resides. Let's say that you have a friend named Steve Brown who has a user account "sbrown" on the Internet host "phoebe," located at University of Nevada, Reno, with domain name "unr.edu." His e-mail address would be sbrown@phoebe.unr.edu.

Figure 1-5

**A Partial List
of Newsgroups**

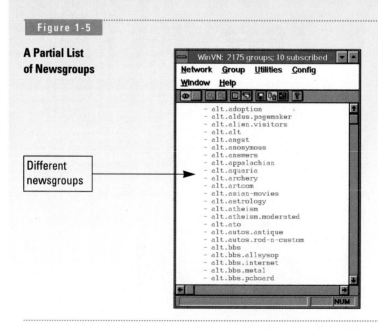

Different newsgroups

Box 1-2 cont.

When you want to access a resource on the Net, you specify the domain name of the computer that offers the service. Sometimes you also need to specify the service desired. For example, if you want to access WWW resource at the White House, you specify www.whitehouse.gov as the desired resource when you run the Web browser program.

What You Can Do on the Net

Besides being able to communicate with other people on the Net, you can also communicate with other people who share your interests, join newsgroups, and access resources. If you want to exchange e-mail with other people who share your interests, you can subscribe to mailing lists. There are mailing lists for practically every subject—from rock climbing to Zen Buddhism. When a message is sent to the mailing list, the message is distributed to everyone who has subscribed to that list. Be careful, though; some mailing lists generate hundreds of messages a day!

Another way to communicate is through Usenet newsgroups (see Figure 1-5). These are subject-oriented electronic bulletin boards. There are literally hundreds of newsgroups from which to choose. A news reader program is used to read messages on newsgroups or to post messages for others to read. Be warned, however, that the content of a newsgroup may not be apparent through its name. Also, most newsgroups are not moderated, meaning you can't be sure of the content or language used in the messages. You may find some fantastic discussions, but you may also find some to be ridiculous, and even offensive.

There are several ways to access resources on the Net. One way is to log in to a remote computer. Some computers, such as the ones holding library catalogs, are freely accessible, while others require you to obtain an account before you can log in and use the available services. Still others have a specific log in name that gives you limited access.

Internet host computers that are set up specifically to make information available to others are called *servers*. The computer that holds resources in the World Wide Web format is called a *Web server*. Other types of servers include *FTP* and *Gopher*. Just as you use a Web browser such as Netscape to access the Web server, you need to use a special FTP program such as Fetch or WSFTP to access an FTP server, and a Gopher program such as TurboGopher or WS_Gopher to access a Gopher server.

Figure 1-6

An FTP Server Screen

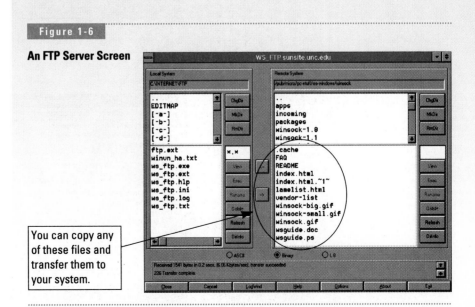

You can copy any of these files and transfer them to your system.

Box 1-2 cont.

▶ An FTP server is an archive of documents and files (including software) that can be transferred to your computer. On some FTP servers, you find an index of contents. Many FTP servers are named ftp.<domain name>, such as ftp.sumex-aim.stanford.edu (see Figure 1-6).

▶ A Gopher server lets you access information in a menu-driven format (see Figure 1-7). That means your options are displayed as a menu on the screen. When you make a selection from a menu, further choices may be displayed. By following a series of menus, you will eventually arrive at the resource you are seeking. Many educational institutions publish their Campus Wide Information Systems (information about their own campus) on Gopher. You'll also find many library catalogs on Gopher. Gopher sites, too, are often identified as gopher.<domain name>, such as gopher.micro.umn.edu.

▶ The Web, on the other hand, uses a hypertext. That means that in a display on the screen, certain words are underlined, or a button may appear (see Figure 1-8). When you select or click underlined words or buttons, a new display appears. A hypertext is almost like a footnote. Whereas a footnote tells you the name of the reference material (which you can go and look up), a hypertext will display the actual document being referenced. Using a Web browser program, such as Netscape, you specify which Web location you'd like to access. The Web location is often preceded by the letters "www," such as www.yahoo.com.

Often, when an Internet resource is listed, its URL (Uniform Resource Locator) is given. A URL is a technical description of exactly where the document is found on the Net and what kind of document it is. You see, one of the interesting things about a Web browser is that it can also access other types of servers, such as an FTP or Gopher servers. By specifying the URL, the Web browser program is able to distinguish which type of document you are trying to access.

Server	URL Format	Example
FTP	file://<domain name>/<path name>	file://ftp.uu.net/ls-1R.Z
Gopher	gopher://<domain name>	gopher://mtv.com
WWW	http://<domain name>/<path name>	http://cuiwww.unige.ch/w3catalog

Figure 1-7

Gopher at gopher.micro.umn.edu

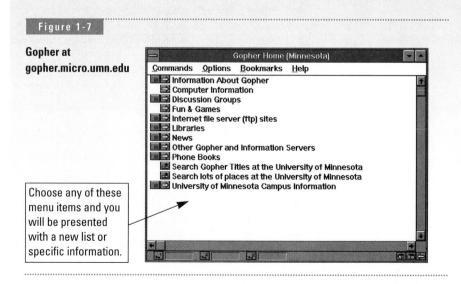

Choose any of these menu items and you will be presented with a new list or specific information.

Information Technology: What It Can Do for You

Box 1-2 cont.

How You Can Get Connected

If your school or business has a network that is already on the Net, you have it made—at least while you're at work or school. Just talk to someone about obtaining an account and gaining access. All you have to do is learn how to use the Net tools for the platform available to you.

If you don't have access to a network already on the Net or you don't happen to be at work or school when you want to access the Net, you have three basic choices: dialing into the network at your school or work where you have an account, connecting to an online service that has a gateway to the Net, or connecting directly to the Net through an Internet service provider. Each of these three choices requires that you have an IT system at home and a modem—a special device that lets computers talk over phone lines.

Dialing into the Network at Your School or Work Where You Have an Account

If this option is available to you, it is the least expensive way to get connected. There are two ways you can connect. With one method, usually text based, your personal computer acts as a dumb terminal for the Internet host computer at your school or business. You can log on to the computer and use whatever Internet tools are available to you on that host computer. Another method allows your home computer to act as if it is hard-wired onto the network, giving you the same type of access you may have at school or at work. Ask someone at your school or work about telephone access. You may find that some institutions charge a nominal fee or limit the number of hours of connection time.

Connecting to an Online Service That Has a Gateway to the Net

Most online services now provide access to the Internet, including CompuServe, Prodigy, America Online, Delphi Internet, GEnie, The Microsoft Network, and Interchange Online Network. You have to be careful, however, because many services that boast access to the Net only let you exchange e-mail with Internet users and read newsgroups. The services that do provide full Internet access, including the ability to prowl the Web, have their own Web browsers, which you must use. Don't forget that these services offer other features besides access to the Internet, which may affect your decision regarding which service to purchase.

These online services charge access to the Net by the hour, just as they do other services. For example, at the time of the writing of this book, Prodigy charged $9.95 per month for up to 5 hours of connect time. At the time, the charge beyond that limit was $2.95 per hour. Some services will even charge you a fee for the e-mail you accumulate. If you subscribe to a mailing list with heavy traffic, the cost can be substantial.

Figure 1-8

www.willamette.edu

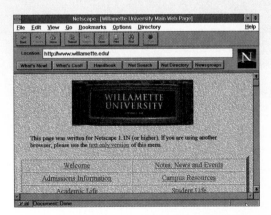

Box 1-2 cont.

Connecting Directly to the Net through an Internet Service Provider

If you want Internet access, without all the extra features of a commercial online service, you can do so through an Internet service provider. You can get more hours of access for less money. The access may be text based or with full graphics and multimedia capability. The latter type of connection will cost you more. Also, some of these services will require you to use their software. If you choose to use an Internet service provider, you'll need to shop around and find the best price and capabilities.

In Chapter 6, we'll look at IT networks, their characteristics, different types of switching stations, and many other interesting topics. How you use IT to connect and communicate with other people is the most exciting and rapidly changing aspect of information technology; it is the part of IT that is connecting every home, business, school, and government institution throughout the world. Today, we call this the Internet, which is the foundation for the soon-to-come and far reaching Information Superhighway (see Box 1-2).

The Processing Engine

The **processing engine** contains two components—the central processing unit and the internal memory. The **central processing unit** (CPU) is the hardware that executes the software to perform a particular task for you (see Figure 1-9). So the CPU is responsible for performing all calculations and processing information associated with such tasks as preparing the payroll, generating graphs, and helping you find movies that you want to watch. The CPU is also the hardware component

Discovering IT

Online service providers give you a variety of features and options and also differ in how they charge you to use those features. Fill in the table below to show the fees for various features of the different online service providers.

Basic Features	Compu-Serve	Prodigy	America Online	Delphi Internet	GEnie	The Microsoft Network	Interchange Online Network
Monthly Fee							
Hours Free per Month							
Additional per Hour Charge							
Fee for E-Mail Messages Sent							

in your IT system responsible for coordinating the interaction of all the other hardware devices (see Figure 1-10).

While the CPU is at work, it temporarily stores information and software in the internal memory. The **internal memory** is hardware that takes the role of a notepad where the CPU holds information and software with which it is currently working. In Chapter 4, we'll take a closer look at the CPU and internal memory in your processing engine.

Information

Next to you, information is the most important building block in an IT system. After all, the term *information technology* implies that you are using *technology* as a set of tools to work with *information*. That's a good way to view information technology—as a set of tools for working with information. If you think about it for a moment, carpenters have tools for working with wood, plumbers have tools for working with plastic and metal pipe, so why shouldn't you have tools for working with information? This is especially true when you realize that over 80 percent of the American work force today is considered to be "nonmanual labor."[2]

Just as it is important to know how your tools work (your IT system), it's also important to know something about what you're using your tools to work on—information. Let's consider the scoring statistics in Table 1-2 on page 20 for a basketball team and define two very important terms—*data* and *information*.

At first, you might think these terms mean the same thing—but they don't. A piece of **data** is a known fact with a singular meaning, while **information** is a fact known as a result of presenting data in a more meaningful way. Many times, information is data that have been processed in some way. Consider the number of field goal attempts by Joshua Havel (50). This piece of data has a singular meaning; it tells you how many field goals Joshua attempted and nothing else. Now, consider Joshua's field goal percentage (60 percent). This is information because it tells you the relationship between field goals attempted and made by Joshua.

There are many ways to transform data into information, and your IT system can be a big help. If you consider the table again, you'll notice that it is sorted by average points per game. This method of presentation tells you more information—who scores the most and least points per game. You could also total the average points per game column to obtain even more information—the average points per game for the whole team. You could obviously do all these things without your IT system, but not nearly as fast.

IT is an important set of tools because you use information all the time to do things and make decisions. This will be especially true for you as you work in the business world and make business decisions. Information, however, is only useful if it possesses certain characteristics or qualities. Qualities of good information include relevance, timeliness, completeness, and accuracy.

▶ **Relevance:** Perhaps the most important characteristic of good information is that it is pertinent to what you are trying to do. For example, if you were the manager of a music store, the number one hit single would be relevant information, while yesterday's high temperature would not be.

▶ **Timeliness:** As with other assets, information can spoil or become obsolete. Have you ever heard someone say, "I wish I had known that before I made my decision"? Think about the battle of New Orleans in the American Civil War—it was fought three weeks after the war was over!

▶ **Completeness:** Information that is complete tells you everything you need to know. Creating an average from a list of numbers is a good example. It means

Figure 1-9

The CPU Is Small But Powerful!

The CPU is the real computer; it is the hardware part of your system that performs such tasks as arithmetic and sorting. This Pentium chip easily fits in the palm of your hand, but it can process more than 100 million instructions per second!

nothing though if you don't know other things like the range, median, mode, and standard deviation.

▶ **Accuracy:** Information that is accurate tells you the correct story. Although the standard deviation of a list of numbers may be important to you, it will be

Figure 1-10

How Hardware Works in an IT System

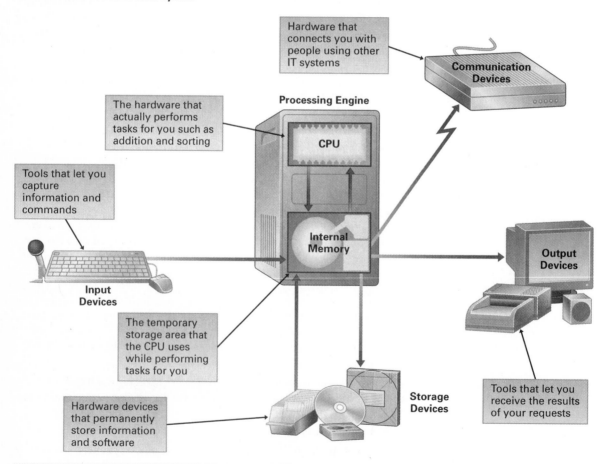

Hardware that connects you with people using other IT systems

Communication Devices

Processing Engine

The hardware that actually performs tasks for you such as addition and sorting

CPU

Tools that let you capture information and commands

Input Devices

Internal Memory

Output Devices

The temporary storage area that the CPU uses while performing tasks for you

Storage Devices

Tools that let you receive the results of your requests

Hardware devices that permanently store information and software

We Are in the "Information Age"

Society has gone through many stages. In history texts, these stages are called *ages* or *revolutions*. In the last two centuries, we have passed through the agricultural and industrial ages and are now in the information age.

The *agricultural age* lasted through the late 1800s. During that time, the acquisition of land and the production of food were society's primary concern. It was a time when land was power—those who had the land were the people who had the power.

The *industrial age* began in the late 1800s and lasted until the 1960s. Rapid technological advances in mechanization and mass production factories characterized this period. It was a time when capital (plant assets and equipment used to produce large volumes of goods) was power—those who had the capital were the people who had the power.

IT brought about the current age—the *information age.* Today, most people in business do not build things with their hands; they build things with their minds. That is, today we work with information to create knowledge. If you think about it for a moment, bankers, lawyers, accountants, marketing specialists, stockbrokers, and countless others work every day with their minds and information technology to convert information into knowledge.

That is why today's employee in business is called a *knowledge worker*. That's also why you're getting an education—because today's business environment wants people who can work with, manipulate, and assimilate information and knowledge. Here's an interesting list of the role of IT in business:[2]

 ▶ **In the last ten years, businesses have invested over $1 trillion in IT.**

 ▶ **Since 1990, spending on high-tech equipment has accounted for over 35 percent of economic growth in the United States.**

 ▶ **More people work in the area of IT than in the automobile industry.**

 ▶ **Investments in IT account for almost half of what business spends on equipment—this doesn't even include software.**

 ▶ **Exports of IT and related services more than double that of aircraft (the previous biggest U.S. export).**

of little use, not to mention that you may make the wrong decision, if you calculate it incorrectly.

Storage Devices

Storage devices are the hardware components that permanently store information and software. In fact, many people refer to storage devices as *permanent storage devices.* Storage devices include videotape, CD-ROM, magnetic disks (the most popular type of storage device), and magnetic tape (similar to cassette tapes) for backing up information. Storing information with your IT system may seem trivial to you, but consider the fact that a single CD-ROM disk can hold the equivalent of 300,000 pages of printed text. That's a stack of pages over 100 feet high! In Chapter 5, we'll look more at different types of storage devices.

Table 1-2

**Defining Data
and Information**

Name	Field Goals			Average Points per Game
	Attempted	Made	Percentage	
Wes O'Neal	212	91	42.92%	23.37
Phillip Brooks	145	83	57.24%	16.89
Bobbie Russells	120	60	50.00%	14.44
Joshua Havel	50	30	60.00%	12.75
Will Thole	60	25	41.67%	10.32

The fact that Will Thole made 25 field goals is **data**. It tells you only one thing; therefore, it has a singular meaning.

Joshua's field goal percentage and average points per game are both **information** because they tell you something about the data for Joshua.

People

The last building block in an IT system is people. The other building blocks of IT systems have been created with people in mind. Think about an ATM as an example of an IT system. ATMs were designed so that you could do your banking without going to the bank. If people don't use ATMs, banks will stop providing them. Always remember—you are the most important building block of an IT system.

The people component of an IT system not only includes you as a user of IT but also a host of other people. Some of these people include IT specialists who develop systems, people who maintain the hardware, and IT management individuals who are responsible for making sure an organization has the right IT for the job. Throughout this book, we'll explore the various roles and responsibilities of these individuals, and in Chapter 10 we'll discuss how to pursue a career in the field of IT.

How You Can Classify Information Technology Systems

As you read through this book and study IT systems in the real world, you'll notice that there are a number of different ways you can classify or group IT systems. It's like music, which you can classify by type (easy listening or rock 'n' roll, instrumental or vocal, solo artist or group, recording label, and so on). When you learn about a particular IT system, it may help you to consider how it, too, can be classified.

Some IT systems are called **embedded IT systems** because they are built into another product. For example, the IT system in your VCR lets you program recordings, and the IT system in your car controls the electronic ignition. Many IT systems are also called **dedicated IT systems**. ATMs are a good example; they are designed for you to do only banking-related transactions. No matter how hard you try, you'll never be able to write your term paper using an ATM.

When you look at IT systems from within a business, you can classify them according to the function they perform and the level of the business they support. For example, IT systems by function include accounting systems, manufacturing systems, radiology systems (in a hospital), and human resource management systems. IT systems by level of support include transaction processing systems that

Box 1-4

It's 10:00 P.M. Do You Know Where Your Information Is?

All good things have a bad side. IT is no different. What's good about IT is that you can be in Florida on vacation, you can get sick, and your family doctor can electronically transmit your medical history to Florida within seconds. What's bad is that other people can intercept that same information while it's traveling electronically.

Also, if you have medical records at a hospital, it's entirely possible that someone can "break into" the hospital's IT system and steal your information. When others steal or intercept your information, they are invading your privacy. That is, they are invading your right to keep information about yourself confidential and share it with only those people whom you want to have it.

Invasion of privacy falls into the broader category of ethics. **Ethics** are the standards or set of principles that help guide behavior, actions, and choices. And, unfortunately, many people today use IT to commit unethical acts. Some of these acts are against the law, such as breaking into another computer system, but some are not.

What you always need to remember is that IT does not commit unethical acts—people do. IT is just a tool they use, much the same way people use IT to perform good acts such as doctors using IT to diagnose diseases and cities using IT to give you instant access to 911 operators if you need emergency medical care.

help nonmanagement employees perform day-to-day activities such as recording customer orders, and executive support systems that support the information needs of senior management. In Chapter 8, we'll look closely at IT systems by their level of support in a business.

Finally, you can also classify IT systems by their size—not necessarily physical size, but rather how much information storage is available, what capabilities the system offers (fax, sound, and so on), speed of the CPU, and how many people can work on the system at one time. Categories by size include portables, workstations (often called personal computers or microcomputers), minicomputers, mainframes, and supercomputers.

Portable and workstation systems are designed for use by one person. **Portables** are small, battery-powered systems that you can take with you wherever you go, while **workstations** fit easily on a table or desktop. Workstations are the more powerful of the two, with information storage exceeding 2 billion characters, CPU speed over 100 million instructions per second, and interactive CD and full multimedia (including video) capabilities. Portables, on the other hand, are not as powerful as workstations. For example, portables cannot typically store as much information or process information as quickly as a workstation. You will, however, find that portables have similar capabilities in areas such as faxing and multimedia. You can also power a portable from a standard 110-volt outlet to conserve the battery.

Minicomputers and **mainframes** are larger systems usually found in business environments where many people have many information processing requests at the same time. These systems can hold hundreds of billions of characters of information, and some even have CPUs measured in terms of billions of instructions per second. The last category, **supercomputers**, are high-speed special purpose systems designed to perform billions of instructions per second in a research environment. These systems are not typically used to process business transactions but rather mathematical and scientific data such as seismographic and aerospace calculations and geodata analysis. Figure 1-11 on page 24 shows how much money Americans are spending on information technology.

If you think everyone will take advantage of IT, think again. Many people are still hesitant to embrace new technologies; remember, people by nature resist change, even if it's for the better. You, however, are different. You have taken a positive step toward learning about IT and getting the most out of its use. That is, after all, your goal—to learn about IT and get the most out of its use. When you reach your goal, you will have a definite *advantage* over people who resist moving into the new generation of IT.

Reaching your goal amounts to taking three simple steps (see Figure 1-12 on page 25). It's like climbing a set of stairs on your way to the top. Your steps include:

1. Learning how IT works
2. Learning how to use IT for your personal benefit
3. Learning how to use IT for the benefit of the company you work for (or the business you own)

When you take these three steps, you will achieve your goal.

Your first step toward the top is to learn how IT works. Don't worry about many of the technical details of the internal workings of IT. Focus rather on the building blocks of IT, their role in an IT system, and their purpose. After all, you use a telephone every day, but whether you understand how the inside of a telephone works is not important.

Your second step is to take your IT knowledge and learn to apply it to your personal life; we call this **personal advantage**. Applying IT to your personal life includes using word processing software to write neat and well-organized term papers, using presentation graphics software to prepare professional-looking, colorful slide presentations, knowing how to decide on the printer that will meet your needs, and using the Internet to find information about topics that interest you.

Your third step is to be able to make good decisions regarding the use of IT in a business setting. Whether you work in a bank, an automobile assembly plant, a clothing manufacturing company, or an accounting office, you'll find IT there, and you must be able to use IT in the best possible way. If you can do this, you will be helping your organization gain a **business advantage**. Businesses today are looking for individuals, like you, who can apply their IT knowledge to keep the organization ahead of its competitors.

This book is designed to help you reach your goal. In each chapter, we introduce you to certain IT concepts to give you a good understanding of how they work. Following these discussions, we present tips, describe pitfalls, and offer helpful suggestions as you learn how to use IT for your personal benefit and the organization's benefit. We also tell you how individuals and businesses are using IT today and how they plan to use IT tomorrow. Let's take a closer look at personal and business advantages and see how IT can help.

Personal Advantage and Information Technology

Everyone wants to get ahead in life; the simple fact is, though, unless you win the lottery or inherit millions from a rich aunt or uncle, getting ahead (and staying there) amounts to a lot of preparation and work. By reading this book and studying other disciplines, you are building an important set of competencies or skills. These competencies will help you get the job you want or perhaps even help you succeed in working for yourself.

Box 1-5

Information Technology in the Home

Over 30 million workstations and portables exist in homes today. In 1994 alone, nearly 7 million systems were sold for use in the home. No one really knows how many will be purchased in the coming years. Here's how IT has found its way into our homes:

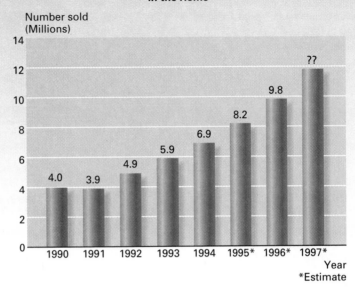

Information Technology in the Home[3]

Some competencies that you should focus on in your studies include:

▶ Interpersonal communication—the ability to communicate with others, including presentations to groups, one-on-one interactions, and the appropriate use of physical gestures.

▶ Interpersonal relations—the ability to relate to and work with people in different situations.

▶ General business knowledge—an awareness of how all areas of business work.

▶ Specific business area knowledge—a thorough understanding of a specific area of expertise.

▶ Problem solving—the ability to recognize a problem, state it correctly, and find the best possible solution.

▶ Flexibility and adaptability—being willing and open to change and recognizing the need to change and when to change.

▶ Vehicle for business advantage—being the person who makes things happen in the organization so that a business advantage can be realized.

Finally, we believe that an important skill for you to have is that of information technology knowledge. This skill includes not only knowing how to use information technology but also when to use IT and what IT is best in a given situation.

Figure 1-11

Spending Money on Information Technology

How Americans spend their money on IT is closely correlated to the projected worldwide shipment of computer systems for the years 1995 through 1997. In 1994, America spent $137 billion on information technology. In 1998, that figure is expected to grow to $179 billion.[4]

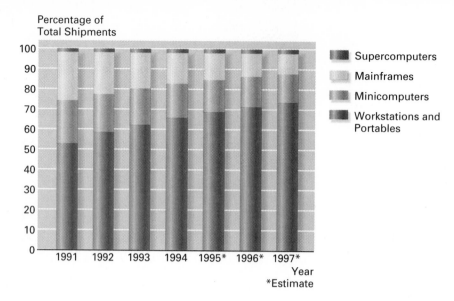

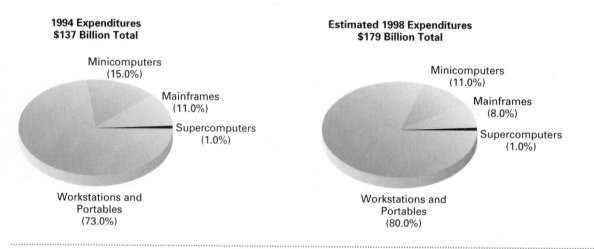

1994 Expenditures
$137 Billion Total

Minicomputers (15.0%)

Mainframes (11.0%)

Supercomputers (1.0%)

Workstations and Portables (73.0%)

Estimated 1998 Expenditures
$179 Billion Total

Minicomputers (11.0%)

Mainframes (8.0%)

Supercomputers (1.0%)

Workstations and Portables (80.0%)

Having the right IT knowledge can also help you with your other skills. For example, you can use IT to create presentations (interpersonal communication), learn about fields of study (general business and specific business area knowledge), decide how best to invest your money (problem solving), recognize trends in the marketplace that require change (flexibility and adatability), and do a better job so your business does better (vehicle for business advantage). In short, your knowledge of IT may determine how successful you will be.

Business Advantage and Information Technology

Just as you must possess certain competencies or skills to gain a personal advantage, businesses must also have certain skills to survive in today's ever-changing world and stay ahead of the competition. Through IT, businesses can gain an advantage in the marketplace by (1) doing things right, (2) doing the right things, and (3) doing new things. These skills are efficiency, effectiveness, and innovation (see Table 1-3).

Being **efficient** means doing things in the right manner—doing things as inexpensively as possible and in the least amount of time. For example, most retail establishments like supermarkets and music stores use IT systems equipped with scanners to read product bar codes that represent the price, tax status, and applicable discount. This makes the checkout process much faster for you, and it also reduces the number of checkout clerks needed.

Being **effective** means doing the right things or making the right decisions at the right time. Consider a music store—the scanning system used for efficiency in the checkout process also updates the inventory system automatically. This automated inventory system helps the store manager know which tapes, CDs, and LPs to reorder based on how quickly they're selling. Let's face it, if you went into a music store and couldn't find what you were looking for because they were sold out, you would simply take your business elsewhere.

Finally, **innovation** means doing new things—offering new services, offering new products, and reaching new customers. Parcel delivery tracking software, digital pagers, and pay-per-view events are all examples of innovation that have result-

Figure 1-12

Obtaining Complete Advantage through Information Technology

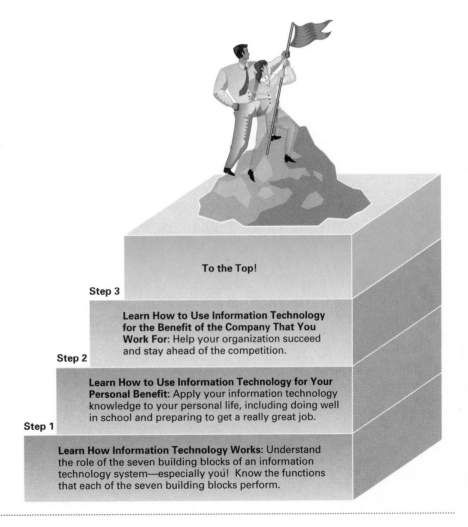

To the Top!

Step 3

Learn How to Use Information Technology for the Benefit of the Company That You Work For: Help your organization succeed and stay ahead of the competition.

Step 2

Learn How to Use Information Technology for Your Personal Benefit: Apply your information technology knowledge to your personal life, including doing well in school and preparing to get a really great job.

Step 1

Learn How Information Technology Works: Understand the role of the seven building blocks of an information technology system—especially you! Know the functions that each of the seven building blocks perform.

Table 1-3

Characteristics of Business Advantage

Business Advantage Characteristic	Definition/ Objective	Examples
Efficiency	Doing Things Right	• Product scanning in stores • Touchtone telephone registration • Electronic filing of tax returns
Effectiveness	Doing the Right Things	• Deciding how much inventory to carry • Disease diagnosis in the medical industry • Determining optimal routes in the trucking industry
Innovation	Doing New Things	• American Airlines' SABRE system • Home shopping networks • Digital pagers

ed in a business advantage. FedEx was the first parcel delivery company to offer its customers their own parcel tracking software. Instead of calling FedEx to find out the status of a parcel delivery, customers use this software to connect with the FedEx IT system and find out for themselves where their package is.

FedEx's parcel tracking software is an example of using IT for innovation in offering new services. Digital pagers, on the other hand, are just one of literally

Discovering IT

Hotels such as Marriott and Hilton are putting IT in the hands of their customers. Once in your room, you can order pay-per-view movies, review your bill, and check out without ever stopping by the front desk. You can even see a list of local events just by pressing a few buttons on your TV remote control. For hotels, is putting IT in your hands an example of efficiency, effectiveness, innovation, or a combination of the three?

Figure 1-13

Using Efficiency, Effectiveness, and Innovation to Obtain Business Advantage

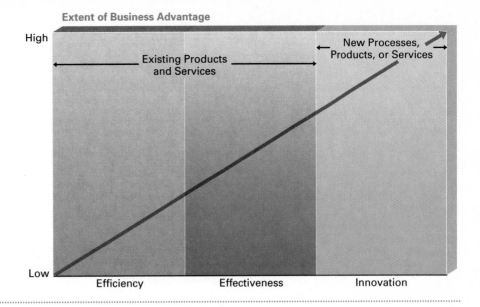

hundreds of examples of using IT for innovation in offering new products. That is, digital pagers, cellular phones, TV satellites, and numerous other products would simply not be possible without IT to support them.

Pay-per-view events on cable television are an excellent example of using IT to reach new customers. Today, you can order concert events, boxing matches, football games, and wrestling events and watch them in the comfort of your home. Just a few short years ago, you would probably have spent a lot of money on airline tickets and hotels traveling to watch some of the same events.

As you have probably already guessed, businesses attain the greatest advantage when they possess all three skills—efficiency, effectiveness, and innovation (see Figure 1-13). First, businesses must be efficient in what they do. Second, businesses must make sure that what they are doing is right (effectiveness). Finally, businesses must constantly seek new ways to bring new products and services to the market and reach new customers (innovation).

Information Technology is exciting, fascinating, and promises to change every day. You have taken a positive step toward success in your future by deciding to learn more about IT and read this book. As your studies introduce you to IT and what it can do for you, here are some important things to keep in mind.

In An Information Technology System, You Are the Most Important

An IT system is composed of seven building blocks: input and output devices, software, communication devices, the processing engine, information, storage devices, and people. Although all seven building blocks are necessary, you are the most important. The other components have been created with you in mind and would not exist if it were not for you.

Today's Business World Revolves around Information

The business world today revolves around information. People who work with their minds outnumber those who work with their hands by a four-to-one margin. Your IT system is a set of tools for working with information. This makes it vitally important for you to learn about IT and what it can do for you while you work with your information.

Information Technology Can Be Your Advantage

In both your personal and business life, IT can be your advantage on the road to success. Whether it's for interpersonal communication like writing letters, budgeting your money at home (problem solving), identifying new services or products, or reaching new customers, IT can help you do better. You will have a definite advantage if you learn how to use IT, when to use IT, and what IT is best for a given situation.

Now You Can . . .

1 Define information technology and understand why you should study information technology.

▶ *Information technology* is a set of tools that helps you work with information and perform tasks related to information processing.

▶ *Why you should study information technology:*

IT is everywhere

IT can help you be more productive

IT is exciting and changing

IT will enhance your career

IT will give you a world of opportunity

2 Describe the seven building blocks of an information technology system.

▶ *Information technology* is a system of components that includes:

Input and output devices that you use to enter information and commands and to receive the results of your requests.

Software, or the set of instructions that are used to perform a particular task for you.

Communication devices connecting IT systems and people all over the world.

The processing engine that contains the central processing unit, which executes the software to perform a particular task for you and the internal memory—a temporary storage area for software and information.

Information you work with.

Storage devices that permanently store information and software.

Finally, and most important, *people.*

3 Identify the difference between data and information and the qualities of good information.

▶ *Data* are known facts with singular meanings.

▶ *Information* is a fact known as a result of presenting data in a more meaningful way.

▶ *Qualities of good information:*

Relevance

Timeliness

Completeness

Accuracy

4 Describe important competencies, including a knowledge of information technology, that can help you obtain a personal advantage.

▶ *Interpersonal communication*—communicating with others.

▶ *Interpersonal relations*—getting along with others.

▶ *General business knowledge*—knowing about things around your area.

▶ *Specific business area knowledge*—knowing about things within your area.

▶ *Problem solving*—making the right decision.

▶ *Adaptability and flexibility*—being able to and recognizing the need to change.

▶ *Vehicle for business advantage*—helping your organization stay ahead of its competitors.

▶ *Information technology knowledge*—being able to use your IT knowledge to help develop other competencies.

5 Describe how information technology helps an organization obtain a business advantage.

▶ *IT can help a business be more efficient*—do things right.

▶ *IT can help a business be more effective*—do the right things.

▶ *IT can help a business be more innovative*—do new things such as offering new services, offering new products, and reaching new customers.

6 Describe the Internet and the three types of servers—FTP, Gopher, and Web— you can find on the Internet.

▶ The *Internet* is basically a network of networked computers that lets you communicate with people all over the world and obtain information from all over the world.

▶ An *FTP server* is an archive of documents and files (including software) that can be transferred to your computer.

▶ A *Gopher server* lets you access information in a menu-driven format. That means your options are displayed as a menu on the screen.

▶ The *Web* uses a hypertext format. That means, given a display on the screen, certain words are underlined, or a button may appear. When you select or click on the underlined words or buttons, a new display appears.

Key Terms

Business Advantage

Central Processing Unit (CPU)

Communication Device

Data

Dedicated IT System

Effective

Efficient

Embedded IT System

Ethics

Hardware

Information

Information Technology (IT)

Innovation

Input Device

Internal Memory

Internet

Mainframe

Minicomputer

Output Device

Personal Advantage

Portable

Processing Engine

Software

Storage Device

Supercomputer

Workstation

Self-Test

1. The seven building blocks of an information technology system include:

   A.

   B.

   C.

   D.

   E.

   F.

   G.

2. _____ is the set of instructions that your central processing unit executes to perform a particular intellectual task for you.

3. What type of devices do you use to enter information and commands and to receive the results of your requests?

4. _____ are the hardware components that permanently store information and software.

5. The processing engine is composed of what two components?

6. _____ are IT systems that are built into other products.

7. _____ are IT systems that are designed to perform only one function or related set of functions.

8. Facts with a singular meaning are called:

   A. Information

   B. Omnimedia

   C. Data

   D. CD-ROM

   E. Software

9. Qualities of good information include:

   A.

   B.

   C.

   D.

10. A business advantage in innovation can be obtained by:

    A.

    B.

    C.

11. _____ are small, battery-powered systems that you can take with you wherever you go.

12. High-speed special purpose systems used primarily in a research environment are called:

    A. Portables

    B. Workstations

    C. Minicomputers

    D. Mainframes

    E. Supercomputers

13. _____ means doing things right while _____ means doing the right things.

Short-Answer Questions

1. Why is it important to study IT?
2. How do data and information relate to each other?
3. What are the hardware devices in an IT system? For what are they responsible?
4. How can businesses use IT to get ahead and stay ahead of the competition?
5. How can IT help you develop your personal competencies?

Discussion Questions and Projects

1. In an IT system, people are the most important building block. Order the remaining six building blocks from most important to least important. Justify your ordering.

2. Consider the following statement: "One person's data is another person's information." Why is this statement true? Can you think of an example that supports this statement?

3. Throughout this chapter we've identified many different ways that businesses are using IT for efficiency, effectiveness, and innovation. What are other ways that specific businesses are using IT to help them get ahead and stay ahead of the competition? If you think of an example in the area of innovation, be sure to identify whether it's for offering new services, offering new products, or reaching new customers.

4. The Information Superhighway is going to allow us to send information back and forth to each other. This information may include personal letters and business correspondence. How do you think the postal service will be affected by this? Will the postal service go out of business? How will the postal service have to restructure how it works?

Cruising the Net

1 Locate online Internet training material using either Gopher or Web. Describe what you located. (Hint: you can connect to the Web page at http://www.clark.net/pub/global/learn.html)

2 When using search tools on the Net, you are often required to do a "keyword search." What is a keyword search and how do you perform such a search?

3 Connect to the Web page for the Internet Organization at http://info.isoc.org/. Follow the link "Internet Service Providers of the World." Give information on providers in your area.

Solutions to Self-Test (1) input and output devices, software, communication devices, the processing engine, information, storage devices, people—p. 8; (2) software—p. 10; (3) input and output devices—p. 10; (4) storage devices—p. 19; (5) central processing unit, internal memory—p. 16; (6) embedded IT systems—p. 20; (7) dedicated IT systems—p. 20; (8) C—p. 17; (9) relevance, timeliness, completeness, accuracy—p. 17; (10) offering new services, offering new products, reaching new customers—p. 25; (11) portables—p. 21; (12) E—p. 21; (13) efficiency, effectiveness—p. 25.

Working in a Group

1. Perform a survey in your classes. Find out: How many people own their own IT system? On average, how long have they had their IT system? For what do they use their IT systems? How many people are planning to buy an IT system within the next year? For those who don't own an IT system, find out why.

2. Let your imagination run wild while you think about this. If you could build your dream home of the future (say, in the year 2010): What would it look like? What role would IT play in the functioning of your home? Do you think homes of the future will use IT the way you have described your home? If no, why not?

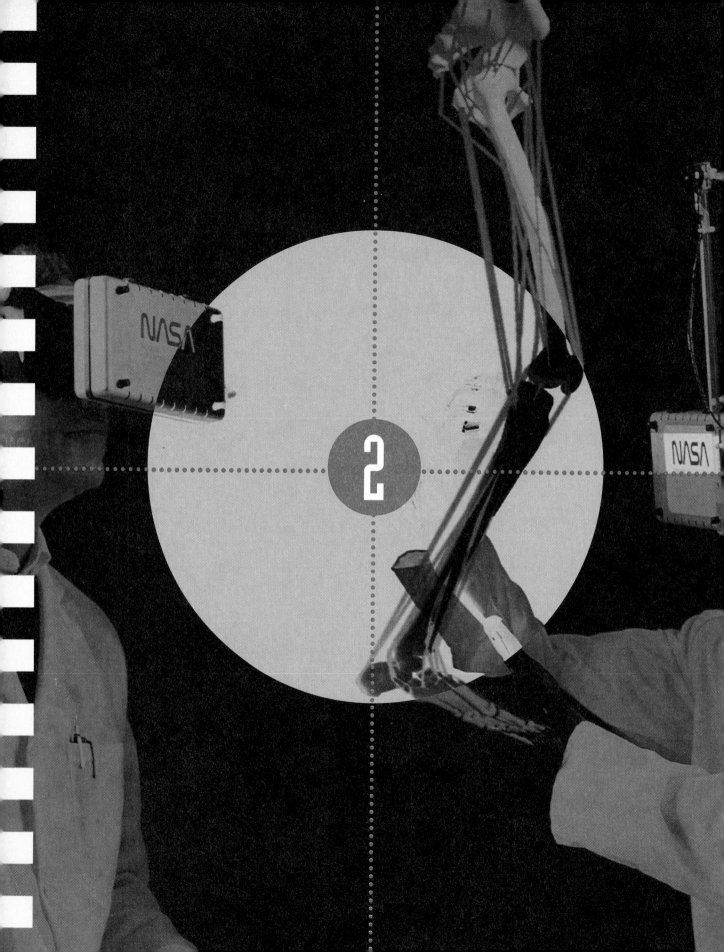

Software:

The Intellectual Interface

Your Objectives for This Chapter

1 Describe the role of software in an IT system.   **2** Describe the difference between application and system software.   **3** Describe the categories of application software.   **4** Identify which types of personal productivity software can help you perform different tasks.   **5** Explain the responsibilities of system software and identify different operating systems.   **6** Understand the guidelines for purchasing application and system software.

Let's design a robot. Sure, everyone needs a robot—especially in the morning. The robot will help you make coffee, boil an egg, and unload the dish washer. A key to the success of the robot will be to "program" it or tell it what it needs to do. The set of steps that you generate for the robot to perform is called *software*. And writing software is no simple task. Consider the following set of steps:

1 Pick up the coffeepot.

2 Fill it with water.

3 Go over to the stove.

4 Turn it on.

5 Place the pot on the stove.

6 Wait until the water boils.

7 Get a cup from the cupboard.

8 Add two spoons of instant coffee.

9 Pour the water in.

10 Stir and take the cup away.

11 Turn off the stove.

For the robot to perform tasks, you must tell it what to do by programming it with software.

Unfortunately, this won't work. Look at step 1. What if the coffeepot is not in its usual place? The robot doesn't have your common sense; it'll either stand waiting for the nonexistent pot or generate an obscure message like "ABEND: ERROR Type 071," which really means, "I don't know what's happened. I can't continue." Similarly, step 2 fails if the pot's already full. The robot needs instructions such as, "If the pot's already full, skip step 2 and go on to step 3."

There are many different ways of programming steps; this example is artificial, but you get the idea. This is also an example of application software—a set of instructions that performs a particular task for you. You could also add other software for tasks such as boiling an egg and unloading the dishwasher. Each of these applications is far more complex than our human common sense realizes, but you could do a good job of laying out the steps if you had a week or so.

How about laying out the steps to handle all these tasks at the same time—that is, make coffee while boiling an egg and unloading the dishwasher? Give up? This requires system software, the software that manages the processing of applications and controlling of how everything on your robot works together. System software is by far the most complex—it takes hundreds of people years and millions of lines of code to produce system software. Just one error in logic or coding can cause disaster. For example, one day in 1991 the entire air traffic control systems at Kennedy, LaGuardia, and Washington National came to a screeching halt for over six hours, leaving them paralyzed. The problem was caused by a single line of code in the roughly 8 million lines that handled phone calls in a relatively new telecommunications system.

So that's our focus in this chapter—software, and, more practically, application and system software. **Software**, as a building block for an IT system, is the set of instructions that your CPU executes to perform a particular intellectual task for you. We say that software is the "intellectual interface" to an IT system because the software tells the CPU what steps are necessary to perform intellectual tasks for you—for instance, writing memos, creating three-dimensional color graphs, and generating payroll checks.

The two types of software we'll explore in this chapter are application software and system software. Application software and system software act as layers between you and the CPU (see Figure 2-1). **Application software**, the software layer closest

Figure 2-1

Your Focus in This Chapter: Software

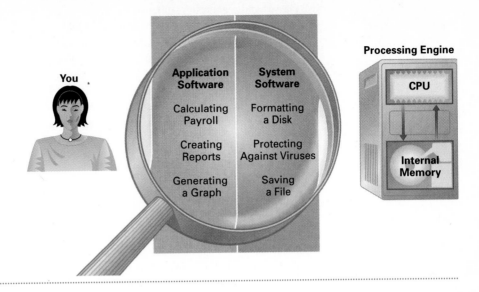

to you, helps you solve specific problems or perform specific tasks like writing a term paper and preparing a financial report. **System software**, the layer of software closest to the CPU, coordinates the interaction of all the hardware while you use the application software. For example, when you print a report, the system software takes care of such tasks as making sure the printer is ready, verifying the printer has paper, and sending the report to the printer along with printing instructions.

Application Software   Application software makes it faster and easier for you to do routine tasks. These tasks may be of a personal nature—preparing a monthly household budget and keeping track of your CD collection—or they may be tasks that businesses undertake such as processing customer orders and sending out bills. You can divide application software into the following categories:

- General business management
- Industry-specific
- Custom-developed
- Education
- Personal productivity
- Groupware
- Specialized software tools

General business management software automates specific functions that businesses perform every day such as payroll, project management, accounts receivable, and inventory control. Some businesses, however, need special application software to help them perform tasks specific to their particular industry—we call this **industry-specific software**. For example, a dentist's office may use special software for scheduling patients, examination rooms, and dental hygienists.

Many businesses find that general business management and industry-specific software still cannot do everything they want it to do. In this case, a business may choose to write its own application software—this is **custom-developed software**.

For example, a university may write its own application software for scheduling classes and registering students.

Education software helps you learn about a specific topic or area of interest. As an example, Microsoft's ENCARTA software is a multimedia encyclopedia that you can use to learn about such topics as the battle of Bunker Hill, the ancient city of Pompeii, and the art of conjuring magic.

The last three categories in the list of application software—personal productivity software, groupware, and specialized software tools—are the categories we want to concentrate on in this chapter. Let's take each and see what they can do for you.

Personal Productivity Software

Personal productivity software is designed to help you do things that you could probably do manually. For example, before workstations and portables became widespread, businesspeople and students would handwrite or type reports and correspondence. Today, an IT system with word processing software helps you to create, edit, and print high-quality documents much faster and easier than working with a typewriter. Below, we've listed the categories of personal productivity software and identified what they can do for you.

Personal Productivity Software	What's Your Advantage
▶ Word Processing	Create high-quality documents that consist primarily of text
▶ Desktop Publishing	Create more elaborate documents than with word processing, such as menus, advertising flyers, newsletters, and books
▶ Spreadsheet	Work with information in cells and specify (with formulas and functions) how the contents of the cells relate to each other
▶ Information Retrieval and Management	Store, retrieve, and update information by logical association, such as key word, term, or subject
▶ Presentation Graphics	Create high-quality presentations of material including transparencies, handouts, on-screen presentations, and even slides
▶ Communication	Send and receive information electronically to and from another person
▶ Personal Information Management	Manage information relating to contacts, schedules, tasks, and finances

Word Processing Software. **Word processing software** helps you to create, edit, save, and print documents that primarily consist of text (for example, letters, memos, and term papers). With word processing software you can do not only basic editing but also advanced imaging and writing. Basic editing functions include such functions as inserting a word in a line, moving text from one place to another (sometimes called *cut and paste)*, bolding, and varying the size and style of writing (see Figure 2-2 on page 41).

Advanced imaging and writing functions let you do things such as add graphics, photos, and tables and use bullet points and multiple columns (see Figure 2-3 on

Software: The Intellectual Interface

Box 2-1

Purchasing Application Software

Most of the application software (including personal productivity software) that you will probably need can be purchased at a computer store or any store that sells computer-related products. Software of this type is called *packaged* or *off-the-shelf*. Besides determining what kind of software (for example, word processing) will help you be more productive, here's a list of other things to keep in mind.

Software Suites
Many software manufacturers today offer "suites" or "bundles" of application software. A *software suite* is a collection of software applications (usually word processing, spreadsheet, presentation graphics, and DBMS) that work together in an integrated fashion. There are two advantages to buying a software suite. First, the cost of a software suite is cheaper than if you purchased all the software packages individually. Second, it's easier to transfer information among different types of application software in a suite. Popular software suites include:

Software Included	Microsoft Corporation Microsoft Office Professional	Lotus Development Corporation Lotus SmartSuite	Novell Corporation PerfectOffice
Word Processing	Word	Ami Pro	WordPerfect
Spreadsheet	Excel	Lotus 1-2-3	Quattro Pro
DBMS	Access	Approach	Paradox
Presentation Graphics	PowerPoint	Freelance Graphics	WordPerfect Presentation
Communication	Mail		Groupwise
Personal Information Management		Organizer	InfoCentral

Version Numbers
Each time a software manufacturer provides new software, the software is given a version number. For example, "6.0" in WordPerfect 6.0 is the version number. This means that it is newer than versions with smaller numbers (for instance, 5.2) but not as new as versions with higher numbers. Make sure you always buy the most recent version.

When You Bring It Home
Once you buy a software package, you must install it on your IT system. To do so, you simply follow an installation process. The *installation process* is described in the instructions accompanying the software. These instructions tell you how to load the software onto your system.

Common User Interface (CUI)
Most application software today also has a *common user interface* (CUI). This CUI format is used by software manufacturers so that similar commands appear in the same place no matter what package you purchase. This helps you learn new software quicker and easier.

Other documentation will also be provided with the software. First, you will find *registration material*. This is a form that you fill out and send back to the manufacturer. That way the manufacturer can notify you when new versions or products become available. There will also be some material that

Box 2-1 cont.

describes the type of *support* the manufacturer provides. For example, some manufacturers provide a toll-free number you can call if you have questions or problems.

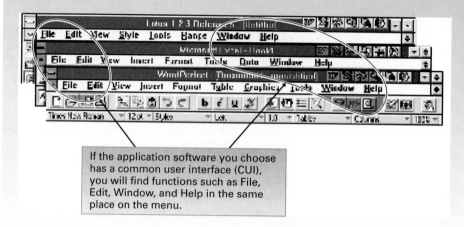

If the application software you choose has a common user interface (CUI), you will find functions such as File, Edit, Window, and Help in the same place on the menu.

Privileges

Finally, the documentation will tell you about your *privileges*. When you purchase software, you have really only purchased the right to use the software. That privilege rests solely with you. You have not purchased the right to make copies of the software for your friends or family.

page 41). All of these capabilities help you increase the effectiveness of your written communication skills. Table 2-1 lists some popular word processing packages.

Desktop Publishing Software. Sometimes you may need to create a document that is more elaborate than one easily created by a word processing package. **Desktop publishing software** extends word processing software to help you create documents that need special features not provided by a word processing package (see Figure 2-4). For example, books—just like this one—are created using desktop publishing software. Desktop publishing software gives you advantages over word processing software, including the use of sidebar notes, picture sizing and moving, and the use of color shading behind text.

In reality, the distinction between word processing software and desktop publishing software is fading rapidly. For example, both types of software will let you add pictures, draw your own freehand pictures, and use different styles and sizes of type. Desktop publishing software, however, still gives you more control over how information is formatted and printed.

Table 2-1

Popular Word Processing Packages

Package	Manufacturer
Ami Pro	Lotus Development Corporation
MacWrite Pro	Claris Corporation
Word	Microsoft Corporation
WordStar	WordStar International Corporation
WordPerfect	Novell Corporation

Figure 2-2

Some Basic Word Processing Software Features

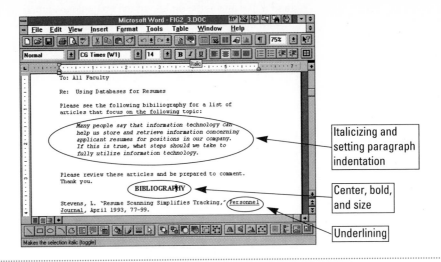

Italicizing and setting paragraph indentation

Center, bold, and size

Underlining

Figure 2-3

Imaging and Writing Capabilities in Word Processing Software

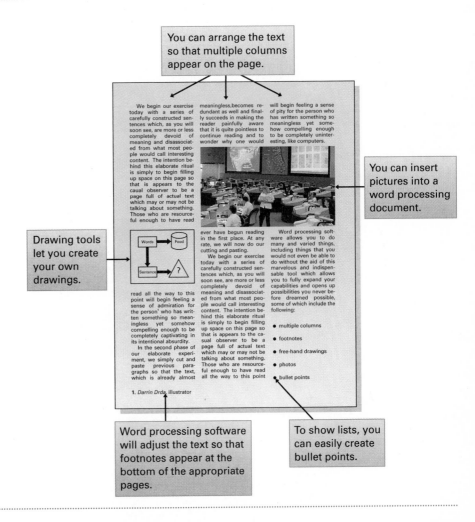

You can arrange the text so that multiple columns appear on the page.

You can insert pictures into a word processing document.

Drawing tools let you create your own drawings.

Word processing software will adjust the text so that footnotes appear at the bottom of the appropriate pages.

To show lists, you can easily create bullet points.

For instance, you can use word processing software to create text that's enclosed in a box with a background color of light blue. Desktop publishing software, though, will give you the capability to start the color of light blue at the top of the box, then fade it to white at the middle of the box, and eventually bring out the color red toward the bottom of the box. Desktop publishing software will even let you change the orientation of the box so that it (and the text inside) prints up and down the page while the surrounding text prints across the page.

Table 2-2

Popular Desktop Publishing Packages

Package	Manufacturer
CompuWorks	Wizardworks
Corel Draw	Corel Corporation
FrameMaker	Frame Technology
PageMaker	Aldus Corporation
PagePlus	Serif
PFS: Publisher	SoftKey International
PhotoShop	Adobe
Publish It!	Timeworks International
Publisher	Microsoft Corporation
QuarkXPress	Quark
Ventura	Corel Corporation

Figure 2-4

Desktop Publishing Software

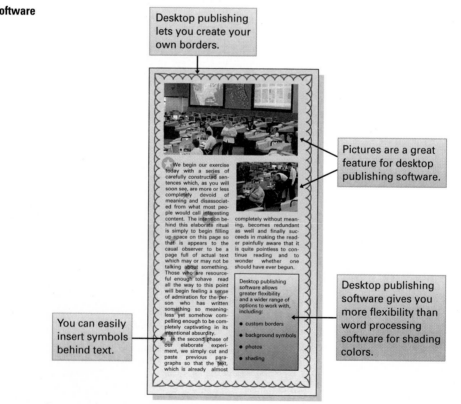

Desktop publishing lets you create your own borders.

Pictures are a great feature for desktop publishing software.

You can easily insert symbols behind text.

Desktop publishing software gives you more flexibility than word processing software for shading colors.

Software: The Intellectual Interface

Spreadsheet Software. Have you ever tried to budget your expenses for a month or year? You probably started with your income and then estimated your monthly expenses. After finding that your expenses exceeded your income, you probably began reducing some of your expenses and perhaps cutting out some altogether. During the whole process, you undoubtedly found yourself constantly erasing and recalculating.

To make these tasks easier, you can substitute spreadsheet software for your pencil, paper, eraser, and calculator. **Spreadsheet software**, which works with columns and rows, lets you enter and change information in *cells* (the intersection of a row and column) and specify how the cell contents relate to each other. With spreadsheet software, you use *formulas* and *functions* to define these cell relationships.

Consider the spreadsheet in Figure 2-5. The information in column D (Avg. Income/Member) represents column B divided by column C for each family. For the Jones family, you could enter the value $10,000, but what happens if you find that the Jones family has 10 members and not 5? That would require two changes—the 5 to 10 in cell C4 and $10,000 to $5,000 in cell D4.

With spreadsheet software, however, you would enter a formula (B4/C4) in D4 that represents the mathematical relationship between cells B4 and C4. Now, whenever you change the contents of B4 or C4, the value of D4 automatically changes. (See Table 2-3 for popular spreadsheet packages.)

Information Retrieval and Management Software. While spreadsheet software lets you define the relationship between information by physical location using cell

Figure 2-5

Spreadsheet with Formulas and Functions

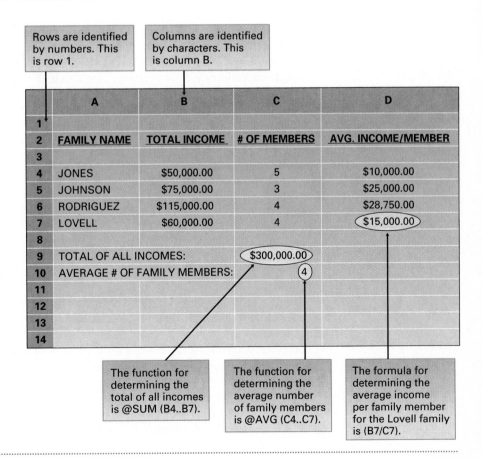

Rows are identified by numbers. This is row 1.

Columns are identified by characters. This is column B.

	A	B	C	D
1				
2	FAMILY NAME	TOTAL INCOME	# OF MEMBERS	AVG. INCOME/MEMBER
3				
4	JONES	$50,000.00	5	$10,000.00
5	JOHNSON	$75,000.00	3	$25,000.00
6	RODRIGUEZ	$115,000.00	4	$28,750.00
7	LOVELL	$60,000.00	4	$15,000.00
8				
9	TOTAL OF ALL INCOMES:		$300,000.00	
10	AVERAGE # OF FAMILY MEMBERS:		4	
11				
12				
13				
14				

The function for determining the total of all incomes is @SUM (B4..B7).

The function for determining the average number of family members is @AVG (C4..C7).

The formula for determining the average income per family member for the Lovell family is (B7/C7).

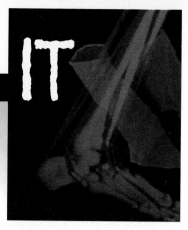

addresses, **information retrieval and management software** lets you store, retrieve, and update information by logical association. When we say logical association, we're referring to such things as key words, terms, and column names. The two major types of information retrieval and management software are database management systems and hypertext.

PERSONAL ADVANTAGE

Chris Dow

❝If opportunity knocks and you don't have the necessary skills, you can't open the door!" exclaims Chris Dow, a senior graphics design major at the University of Minnesota at Duluth (UMD). Chris was approached last year about designing a cover for a book—he had the necessary desktop publishing skills and was able to open the door.

The book, Introduction to Computer Literacy, 2nd edition, is published by McGraw-Hill through its College Custom Series and program titled Students Writing Textbooks for Students. The College Custom Series usually allows faculty members to design their own course material and publish it as a book.

At UMD, however, the Department of Finance and Management Information Systems (MIS) lets the MIS student organization write the text. "Our book covers DOS, Windows, WordPerfect, Lotus 1-2-3, Access, and e-mail," says Alyssa Shann, this year's club president. "A faculty member works with us to make sure that we cover all of the necessary material and that it is of the highest quality."

The first year the MIS Club wrote the book they allowed the designers at McGraw-Hill to create the book cover design. When the second edition was due, the MIS Club decided to do something different. "If this is to be a student book project, then the book cover should be designed by a student," Alyssa said.

That's when they found Chris. "If I hadn't known desktop publishing, they would have given the project to someone else," Chris pointed out. "It was probably the greatest thing to happen to me while I was in school—the opportunity to design a cover to go on a published book."

Chris has received requests from time to time from McGraw-Hill and other book publishers to design more covers. "At this rate, I may not have to go to work for a company. I might just open my own graphics design shop and go into business for myself."

Chris is part of a growing number of college students who understand the need to know as much as they can about IT. His knowledge has helped him succeed in a big way.

Box 2-2

Other Great Features of Spreadsheet Software

Spreadsheet software packages provide you with many basic capabilities, including formulas, functions, number formatting ($, %, and so on), spell checking, and text formatting (like centering and underlining). There are also other great spreadsheet features that will save you a lot of time and help you do a better job.

▶ **Sorting: Spreadsheet software allows you to sort information. You can specify multiple fields for sorting and whether the sorting should be done in ascending or descending order. Sorting will help you order information for presentation purposes.**

▶ **Regression: Regression is a statistical process that attempts to explain causal relationships between pieces of information. For example, many businesses use regression to determine the extent to which advertising helps increase sales. Regression is quite mathematically complicated, but, with spreadsheet software, you can do it in a matter of seconds.**

▶ **Matrix Manipulation: Matrix manipulation is also a complex task. Again, with spreadsheet software you can multiply matrices or invert a matrix in a matter of seconds.**

▶ **Graphing: "A picture is worth a thousand words," so sometimes the best way to understand numeric information is to see it graphically. The accompanying graph was built from the spreadsheet information in a short time with only a few clicks of the mouse.**

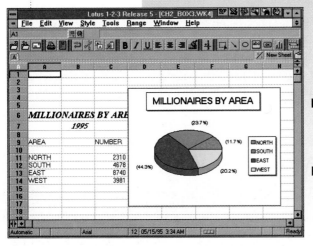

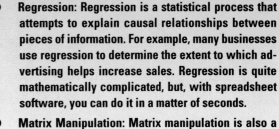

Database management system (DBMS) software is designed to help you create, store, and manipulate a *database*—a collection of two or more related files of information. In a database, each file contains *records,* and the records contain *fields*. Fields contain specific pieces of information such as name, address, and salary. You can even set up fields in a database that contain pictures and sound. In Chapter 5, we'll look more closely at database management systems and databases, so let's consider a short example here—your CD collection. As you can see in Figure 2-6 on page 47, your database has two files, your CD file and your FRIEND file.

Table 2-3

Popular Spreadsheet Packages

Package	Manufacturer
Claris Resolve	Claris Corporation
Excel	Microsoft Corporation
Lotus 1-2-3	Lotus Development Corporation
MacCalc	Bravo Technologies
Masquerade	Night Diamonds Software
Quattro Pro	Novell Corporation
WingZ	Informix Software

At first, you might think, "How are my CDs and friends related to each other?" Well, if you look closely at the CD file, you'll notice that there is a field called LOANED_TO. In it, you will find the name of friends to whom you have loaned your CDs. Suppose you were in the mood for country music and wanted to listen to the Silver Spoons. If you queried your database, you would find out that you had loaned your only country CD to Teresa. You could then query your database to find out Teresa's phone number (which is located in the FRIEND file).

Besides doing simple queries to look at a specific record, DBMS software offers you other ways to easily retrieve and manipulate your information. You could, for example, use the query "DISPLAY ALL FOR CATEGORY = 'R&B'" to see all of your CDs in the Rhythm and Blues category or "DISPLAY ALL FOR LOANED_TO = 'STEPHEN GREEN'" to see which CDs you have loaned to Stephen Green. You can also do other tasks such as:

▶ **Create Quick Reports:** A quick report lets you print all the records or a subset using a query. The DBMS will use the field names as column headings and produce your requested information.

▶ **Create Customized Reports:** DBMS software allows you to customize report formats. Customizable features include page numbers, report titles, and foot-

PERSONAL ADVANTAGE

Letting Spreadsheet Software Help You Buy a Car

Ⓢpreadsheet software is a great personal productivity software tool because you can change information in a spreadsheet and instantly see how those changes affect other information in the spreadsheet. In Chapter 8, you'll see that spreadsheet software is actually an example of a *decision support system*—an IT system that helps you make decisions.

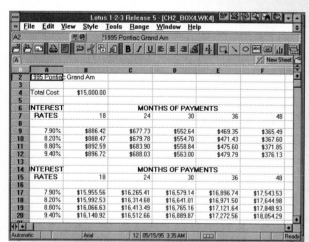

Suppose you wanted to buy a car and were considering the following questions:

1. **How expensive a car can I afford?**

2. **How many months should I take to pay off the car?**

3. **How will interest rates affect my decision?**

4. **Based on the loan amount, interest rate, and number of months, what will my total payments be?**

This is an important set of questions that you should consider when buying a car. The accompanying spreadsheet can help you make your decision.

If you create this spreadsheet, you can easily go in and change the cost of the car (cell B4), any of the number of months (cells B7 through F7), and/or any of the interest rates (cells A9 through A12). The keys to this spreadsheet are in cells B9 through F12 and cells B17 through F20. In the first set of cells is a function that determines your monthly payments; for cell B9 it is @PMT(B4,$A9/12,B$7). In the second set of cells is a formula that determines the total amount of payments; for cell B17 it is (B$7*B9).

What would you choose to do?

Software: The Intellectual Interface

Figure 2-6

Your CD Database

All information (*fields*) relating to your Lost Forever CD makes up a *record*.

CD File

CD_NAME	GROUP	PRICE	CATEGORY	PUR_DATE	LOANED_TO
Go Lucky	Happy Reds	$14.95	R&B	9/13/83	Stephen Green
Win It All	No Names	$7.95	R&B	12/14/81	
Where Are You?	Happy Reds	$12.95	R&B	7/14/94	Stephen Green
I've Got It All	The Moods	$8.95	Rock&Roll	11/23/92	
Me and You	Silver Spoons	$11.95	Country	9/19/87	Teresa Gilbert
Lost Forever	Young Town	$10.95	Rock&Roll	6/23/90	

FRIEND File

FRIEND_NAME	FRIEND_PHONE
Stephen Green	555-1687
Magry Kuo	555-4365
Teresa Gilbert	555-4999

These two files are logically related because a name that appears in LOANED_TO in the CD File must also appear in FRIEND_NAME in the FRIEND file.

ing information calculated from various fields. Using the customizable report feature, you can create high-quality, professional-looking reports.

▶ **Perform Calculations:** Similar to spreadsheet software, a DBMS lets you use formulas and functions to obtain summary information from a database. You can specify calculations when creating reports as we stated previously, or you can use them in the form of a query. For example, "DISPLAY AVERAGE PRICE FOR ALL WHERE GROUP = 'HAPPY REDS'" will let you see how much you paid, on average, for the CDs recorded by the Happy Reds.

▶ **Do Sorting:** Sorting allows you to specify the ordering of records in a file. This is particularly useful when creating reports. For instance, you might want a printout of your CDs in a customized report alphabetically by GROUP. (See Table 2-4 for a list of some popular software packages.)

Hypertext software lets you create, manage, and retrieve modules of information—in the form of text, pictures, sound, and even video—by logical association such as information topic, key word, and author. In HyperCard, the most popular hypertext software for the Mac, a module of information is called a *card* and related groups of cards are called *stacks*.

To see how HyperCard works, let's suppose you're writing a term paper about various types of application software. After some research in the library, you'll probably find yourself with 50 (or more!) articles that address some aspect of application software. You would create different cards for summaries of each article and perhaps pictures of different application software screens (see Figure 2-7). An example of a stack would be all cards relating to word processing software

For the cards containing popular software packages for each type of application software, you could specify the software type (for instance, word processing) and the key term *Vendors*. Now, using HyperCard, you could ask to see all cards with the key term *Vendors*. HyperCard would present you with a new stack (the Vendors stack), which contains the software vendors for all types of application software.

As you can see, hypertext software allows you to organize text, sound, and picture information in such a way that it can be easily retrieved by any number of logi-

---

Table 2-4

Popular Database Management System Packages

Package	Manufacturer
Access	Microsoft Corporation
Alpha Five	Alpha Software Corporation
Dbase	Borland International
FoxPro	Microsoft Corporation
Lotus Approach	Lotus Development Corporation
Paradox	Novell Corporation
Superbase	Computer Concepts
Visual Express	Computer Associates

Figure 2-7

Hypertext Term Paper

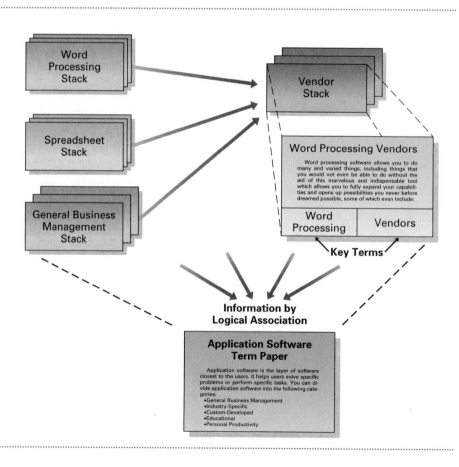

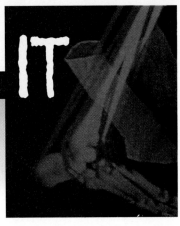

Music stores keep a database of the CDs they sell. They obviously use their database to keep track of more information than you would as an individual. Put yourself in the shoes of a music store manager. What information about CDs would be important? Don't forget that a DBMS can work with pictures and sound. What information would you want to have about your customers? Your suppliers?

cal associations. This is also how hypertext software differs from DBMS software. DBMS software stores specific pieces of information (for example, PRICE for CDs). Hypertext, on the other hand, stores modules of information (cards) and allows you to define various logical relationships through key terms for each card.

Presentation Graphics Software. **Presentation graphics software** helps you to create high-quality presentations of information, including transparencies, handouts for presentations, on-screen presentations, and even 35mm slides. Using presentation graphics software, you can display numeric information in a visual form and textual information along with splashy titles, borders, pictures, sound, and even animation (see Figure 2-8). Presentation graphics software enhances

Figure 2-8

Presentation Graphics Software

Ⓟresentation graphics software can help you create great looking presentations that include graphs, color, photos, and 3D effects.

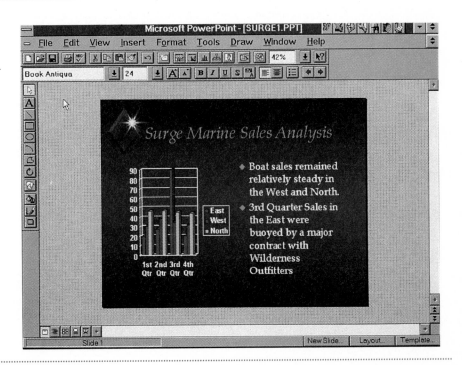

Table 2-5

**Popular Presentation
Graphics Packages**

Package	Manufacturer
Action!	Macromedia
Astound	Gold Disk
Bravo!	Alpha Software
Compel	Asymetrix
Corel Draw	Corel Corporation
FreeLance Graphics	Lotus Development Corporation
Harvard Graphics	Software Publishing Corporation
Micrografx Charisma	Micrografx
Persuasion	Aldus Corporation
PhotoPaint	Corel Corporation
PowerPoint	Microsoft Corporation
WordPerfect Presentation	Novell Corporation

visual presentation to include all types of visual imagery for creating high-quality, attractive, and appealing presentations.

Communication Software. Communication software helps you electronically send information to and receive it from another person. Communication software is often called *electronic mail,* or simply *e-mail.* Communication software is basically an automated version of the U.S. Postal Service, but don't expect a care package from home through communication software. Using communication software, you can connect to people within your organization (for example, your school or business) or external to your organization. Besides just sending and receiving information, communication software lets you identify groups of people to receive messages, reply to messages that you receive, attach documents (like spreadsheets) to messages, and save messages for later use.

Personal Information Management Software. At home, as well as in business, managing personal information can be difficult and time consuming. At some time

Table 2-6

**Popular Communication
Packages**

Package	Manufacturer
BeyondMail	BeyondMail Inc.
cc:Mail	Lotus Development Corporation
CrossTalk	Digital Communications Assoc.
DaVinci eMail	DaVinci Systems Corporation
Futurus Team Combo	Futurus Corporation
Microsoft Mail	Microsoft Corporation
Notebook Electronic Mail	On Technology
PerfectOffice	Novell Corporation
WinMail	Finansa Limited

or another, you have probably wished for a 24-hour-a-day personal assistant to manage information relating to what you have to do every day. **Personal information management software** helps you manage information relating to contacts, schedules, tasks, and finances.

Personal information management software can help you manage contact information through electronic address and phone books. For scheduling, personal information management software helps you record future events like meetings by year, month, week, day, and hour (see Figure 2-9). Good personal information management software will also tell you if you're scheduling a meeting that conflicts with another and helps you resolve the conflict. For task management, personal information management software helps you to create and monitor your "to-do" lists. To-do lists can be as simple as everything you want to get accomplished this week or as complicated as what you have to do to build your own house.

Finally, some personal information management software can help you work with your personal finances. Using Quicken, the most popular personal finance software, you can pay your bills electronically, download stock prices, fill out your tax forms, and even generate reports and graphs to show you exactly where your money goes and how much you have.

Box 2-3

E-Mail Me, Please

At the end of 1994, there were more than 41 million users of e-mail in the United States. Those 41 million users of e-mail sent over 18 billion messages. That's an average of over 430 e-mail messages per person.[1]

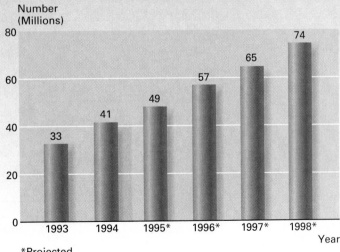

E-Mail Users in the United States

Number (Millions)

*Projected

Figure 2-9

Personal Information Management Software Calendar

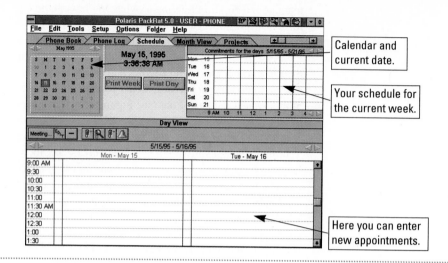

Calendar and current date.

Your schedule for the current week.

Here you can enter new appointments.

Groupware—Software for Working Together

Groupware is the most exciting and new type of application software that businesses are using today. **Groupware** is software that helps people communicate, share information, perform their work more efficiently and effectively, and work together to make decisions by using IT. You can use groupware to communicate and work with people both inside and outside your organization. Categories of groupware include:

▶ Electronic mail

▶ Group scheduling

Table 2-7

Popular Personal Information Management Packages

Package	Manufacturer
Arcadia Workplace Companion	Arcadia Technologies Inc.
Commence	Jensen-Jones Inc.
Computer Organizer	Impulse Software
DeskTop Set	OKNA Corporation
ECCO Professional	Arabesque Software Inc.
Instant Recall	Chronologic Corporation
Lotus Organizer	Lotus Development Corporation
Merlin	Merlin Software Development Co.
MS Money	Microsoft Corporation
On Schedule	Odyssey Computing Inc.
PackRat	Polaris Software Inc.
Quicken	Intuit
Sharkware	CogniTech Corporation
Time Planner Deluxe	H. M. Hinsch & Co., Inc.
Winfo Pro	Winware Inc.

- Electronic meeting support
- Whiteboard
- Videoconferencing
- Work flow automation

At the very foundation of groupware is electronic mail (e-mail). We discussed e-mail earlier when we looked at communication software. E-mail helps groups work together by handling basic electronic communications between individuals.

Group scheduling software helps you schedule meetings. It can take into account the schedules of all the group members (by evaluating their electronic calendars) and the availability of business resources such as conference rooms and equipment to help you determine the best possible meeting time and location. If you can't find a suitable time for everyone to meet or if the group members are spread across the country, you can use electronic meeting support software.

Electronic meeting support software lets your group have a "virtual" meeting on your computers. In a virtual meeting, everyone reads the agenda items for the meeting; provides input in the form of electronic messages that are stamped by day, time, and agenda item number and then sent to all group members; and reads and responds to messages left by other people. At the end of your virtual meeting, you can use the electronic meeting support software to consolidate the messages of the group, summarize the results, and provide everyone with the summary.

Whiteboard software lets people in a group interactively share and edit documents. For example, you and your co-workers could use whiteboard software to simultaneously work on a new campaign for a product. You could initially build a promotional flyer on your screen while the others watched on their screens. Remember, the others could be spread out all over the country. In turn, other people would modify the flyer while you watched.

Videoconferencing software is the category of groupware that includes interactive face-to-face meetings through computers. Great strides have been made in videoconferencing software to bring it to the desktop—so it's named *desktop videoconferencing* (see Figure 2-10). Today, you can purchase a desktop videoconferencing system for about $2,500, which includes all the necessary software, hardware, and even the camera unit. Of course, you can't have a videoconference by yourself, so other members of your group must also spend the same amount of money for their system.

The last category of groupware is work flow automation software (see Figure 2-11). **Work flow automation software** is designed to help you electronically create, distribute, and store standard business documents such as sales order forms. The use of work flow automation software supports the concept of electronic data interchange. **Electronic data interchange** (EDI) is the direct computer-to-computer transfer of information normally provided by the use of standard business paper documents (we'll look at some companies using EDI in Chapter 6). If you were working for a product distributor, work flow automation software would help you:

- create sales order forms
- distribute the forms electronically to customers
- receive forms electronically from customers
- move the forms within the company to the warehouse, shipping dock, and accounts receivable
- retransmit the order information and packing slip to the customers

Figure 2-10

Desktop Videoconferencing

Worldwide Desktop Videoconferencing[2]

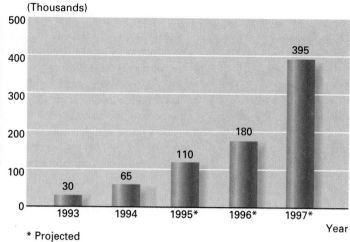

Units (Thousands)

Year	Units
1993	30
1994	65
1995*	110
1996*	180
1997*	395

* Projected

Figure 2-11

Work Flow Automation Software and the "Paperless Office"

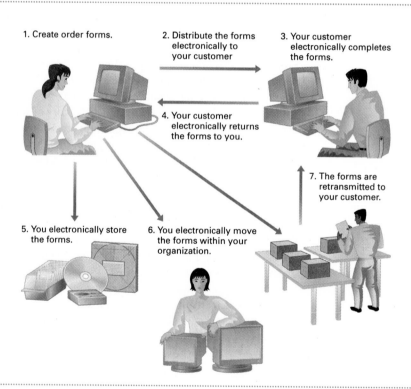

1. Create order forms.

2. Distribute the forms electronically to your customer

3. Your customer electronically completes the forms.

4. Your customer electronically returns the forms to you.

5. You electronically store the forms.

6. You electronically move the forms within your organization.

7. The forms are retransmitted to your customer.

Specialized Software Tools

The last category of application software includes tools that do not fit easily into one of the other six categories of application software. This category of application software is a kind of "catchall" category that includes software such as:

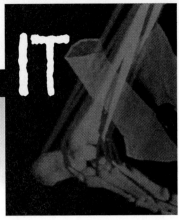

Schools all over the nation are using videoconferencing software to simultaneously teach classes on different campuses. Find out how your school or another is using videoconferencing software to achieve this. Are some types of classes more suited to videoconferencing? Which would they be and why? Would you like to take classes via videoconferencing?

- Multimedia
- Virtual reality
- Video capturing and editing

Multimedia and virtual reality are not just software—they are an intricate combination of software and hardware. **Multimedia** combines information of all forms (video, sound, text, and graphics) in a way that users (people to whom the information is being presented) can navigate through the information in any order they wish. Education, health care, and sciences are the fields currently making the greatest use of multimedia. Business, however, is moving forward quickly to use multimedia for applications such as marketing and training.

Virtual reality carries multimedia one step further to include the use of input and output devices that receive and transmit physical motion. Because of this, virtual reality encompasses the sense of touch. You can find virtual reality software being used in many different ways—for playing games (such as golf), viewing homes (three-dimensionally) before they are built, and teaching surgeons complicated medical procedures.

Caterpillar Corporation uses virtual reality in designing new construction machines. Operators wear a special helmet (called a headset) that puts them "inside" a machine (really a software simulation), and they wear gloves that link their hands to the software. In this way, Caterpillar can test the usability of a proposed design in a few weeks instead of taking many months to build a physical prototype.

Video capturing and editing software actually allows you to store and edit videos. Using video capturing and editing software, you can record a video with a camcorder or VCR, feed it into your system, and edit it (omit frames and add captions). Video capturing and editing, multimedia, and virtual reality software rely heavily on the use of input and output devices as well as software, so let's wait until we have covered Chapter 3 to more closely explore these types of software.

System Software

While you're using application software, the system software is in the background making sure that the hardware carries out the tasks you want to perform. System software, because it's the software closest to the hardware, must handle a number of difficult and tedious tasks. The major responsibilities and functions of system software include:

SOFTWARE THAT LEARNS
FROM ITS MISTAKES

Let's think for a moment about how you learned the alphabet many years ago. As the teacher showed you different characters, your brain actually began to develop a pattern for each one. As you saw the different letters over and over again, your brain continually refined the patterns until each one became completely unique. Now, when you see a letter, your brain compares it to the various patterns and determines which it is. If your brain can't find an exact match, it literally guesses what it should be—that's why you may have trouble at times reading someone else's handwriting.

Neural network software is a special type of software designed to mimic that learning process. That is why many people say that neural networks literally have the ability to learn. Neural networks have layers of neurons, just like your brain. Inputs are received by the first layer of neurons. These neurons in turn pass messages to the next layer of neurons based on the input they receive. This layer of neurons accepts the messages, evaluates their content, and passes messages to an output layer of neurons. The output layer of neurons also evaluates the messages and provides a decision. Let's look at how neural networks work.

To train a neural network for determining whether to accept or reject credit card applications, you would show (by providing inputs) the neural network hundreds of credit card applications and tell it whether they should be accepted or rejected. As you do this, the neural network adjusts the strength of the messages sent between the neurons. Inside each neuron is a mathematical formula that multiplies the inputs by weights to derive an output (or message). If the neural network determines in one level that an input is not important, it will lower the weight associated with that input, thus reducing the strength of the message sent to the next neuron when that input is received.

If you entered "high salary," "owns home," and "has a job for at least three years" and told the neural network this is a profitable customer, it would respond by increasing the weights for those inputs in the "GOOD CUSTOMER" neuron and decreasing the weights for those inputs in the "BAD CUSTOMER" neuron. Likewise, if you entered "has prior bankruptcy" and told the neural network this was a bad customer, it would increase the weight for that input in the "BAD CUSTOMER" neuron and decrease the weight for that input in the "GOOD CUSTOMER" neuron.

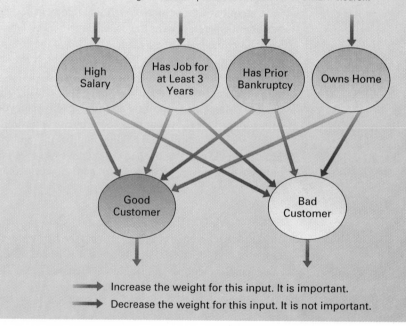

High Salary | Has Job for at Least 3 Years | Has Prior Bankruptcy | Owns Home

Good Customer | Bad Customer

→ Increase the weight for this input. It is important.
→ Decrease the weight for this input. It is not important.

Here are a few examples of how organizations are beginning to use neural networks.

▶ **Besides using neural networks to determine who should receive credit cards, companies like American Express are using neural networks to determine credit card fraud. Most people have a pattern for using their credit card—it may be that they always make small purchases, make purchases in only one geographic area, or make purchases only on the first or last of the month. These characteristics determine a person's buying pattern, and, by evaluating this purchase pattern, a neural network can help determine whether a new purchase was made by you or someone who may have stolen your credit card.**

▶ **The U.S. Postal Service uses neural networks to read handwritten addresses on envelopes. With a neural network, a digital picture of the envelope is taken and the neural network searches for five digits located below the rest of the address. When it finds them, it attempts to determine the zip code by looking at each number and comparing it to a number pattern.**

▶ **The Drug Enforcement Agency (DEA) even uses neural networks. In this instance, cocaine samples are evaluated to determine from which batch they originated. This helps the DEA determine the movement of cocaine within the United States by batch so that distribution channels can be determined and stopped.**

You must realize that neural networks have two limitations. First, they must be trained with literally thousands of examples before they become good at making a decision. This makes neural networks only good for a limited number of decision-making environments where numerous past decisions can be captured and used to train the neural network. Second, a different neural network—including the number of neurons and layers of neurons—must be developed for each problem. This precludes the widespread use of a general purpose neural network.

The first limitation cannot be overcome, but the second can. Many people are developing tools that make it easy for businesses to quickly build neural networks. In the future, you can expect to see businesses use more neural networks to their advantage.

▶ **System Initialization:** System initialization occurs when you first turn on your system. At this point, the system software stores your hardware device configuration (for example, type of monitor and the amount of internal memory available) and loads the operating system.

▶ **System Resource Management:** The **operating system** is the part of system software that controls application software execution and manages how the hardware works together. This is the part of the system software that we are most concerned with. We will devote the rest of the chapter to the operating system.

▶ **Utilities:** Operating system utilities spend most of their time managing the interface to storage devices (like hard disks and CD-ROMs). These utilities handle such tasks as file storage and retrieval, file copying, and disk format-

Box 2-4

Buying the Right Application Software

Buying the right application software can sometimes be like trying to find a needle in a haystack. Although no one really knows, there are probably over 50,000 different pieces of application software available today. But don't despair—follow some simple rules and you'll quickly be on your way to more productivity through application software.

▶ **Make sure it's the right type of application software: Different types of application software are designed to handle different tasks. First, clearly define what you want the software to do. This will tell you what type of application software to purchase.**

▶ **Test drive the software package: If possible, always "test drive" a piece of software before you buy it. Most computer stores will allow you to play with various packages before making a decision. If not, find a friend who uses the software you are considering buying.**

▶ **Consult other people: Perhaps the best source of software information is other people who use application software on a consistent basis. It's always a good idea to find several people who use a variety of packages. Ask them questions about various capabilities you are interested in.**

▶ **Make sure it's compatible with your operating system: If you already own an IT system, make sure your application software selection is compatible with your operating system. All software packages will clearly define under what operating software they will run.**

▶ **Make sure it's compatible with your hardware: Many application software packages require special hardware considerations (for example, a certain type of monitor or a minimum amount of internal memory). If you choose a package that your hardware will not support, you'll find yourself spending a considerable sum of money to upgrade your hardware.**

▶ **Purchase the most recent version: Finally, you should always purchase the most recent version of the software available. This is true because (1) the cost difference is probably minimal, (2) newer versions have more capabilities, and (3) as versions become older, you will receive less support when you have problems.**

ting. When you save a file in Lotus 1-2-3, for example, the system software utility for file saving actually takes over and completes the task.

▶ **Input/Output Management:** This part of the system software is responsible for input and output such as reading characters from the keyboard and displaying characters on the screen.

Characteristics of Operating Systems

A few short years ago, what operating system to buy was not a major consideration—you got the operating system designed for the hardware you bought. Today, however, there are many operating systems that provide different capabilities (for instance, password security access and built-in access to the Internet). All operating system software, like application software, is available off-the-shelf and has some common characteristics such as an installation process, registration, version number, support, and privileges. There are, however, some other characteristics that tend to differentiate them. These characteristics include:

Box 2-5

Is Your Computer Sick?

It may sound like a ridiculous question, but it's actually not. Computers, in a way, can get sick. That is, they can have a virus. A **virus** is a software program that causes your computer to malfunction. Computer viruses cause malfunctions as simple as making the screen go blank or as catastrophic as causing your hard disk to reformat itself.

What's really bad about computer viruses is that they migrate easily from computer to computer. For example, you could be working at school, copy a file that has a virus attached to it, then bring it home and infect your personal system. To protect against viruses, you can use antivirus software. **Antivirus software** is a type of utility software that protects against viruses. Once you install antivirus software on your system, it will monitor your storage devices by "scanning" any new files to make sure they are free of viruses. If the antivirus software detects a virus, it also has utilities for removing the virus.

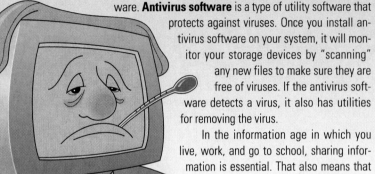

In the information age in which you live, work, and go to school, sharing information is essential. That also means that antivirus software is essential. Don't be caught without it, or expect your system to catch something you don't want—a virus. In Chapter 10, we'll discuss more about viruses and antivirus software.

- *Multitasking*—the ability to work with more than one application at a time.
- *Object linking and embedding (OLE)*—the ability to share information between applications. Once you've linked information (called an object) from one application to another, a change to the original information automatically causes a change to the object of information in the other application.
- *Networking*—the ability to connect several systems so that you can share hardware, software, and information and electronically communicate with other people.
- *Multiprocessing*—the ability to spread your work over several CPUs at the same time.
- *Security*—including requiring passwords.
- *Internal messaging*—built-in communications software.
- *Portability*—the ability of an operating system to work on different hardware—Apple, IBM, DEC, and others.
- *Compatibility*—the ability of an operating system to run application software designed for another operating system.
- *Plug and play*—gives you the ability to add input and output devices and storage devices to your system while it's actually running. Without plug and play, you would be forced to restart and reinitialize your system.
- *3D look*—the ability to generate three-dimensional images on screen.
- *Remote access*—the ability to access your IT system from another location. Remote access is an important component of the "virtual office."

TODAY'S BUSINESS ADVANTAGE

The "virtual office"—what's that? The virtual office is simply when people do their work at places other than the office. Organizations that have a large sales force often take advantage of the virtual office. Salespeople, equipped with portable systems, now spend all day in the offices of their customers. Let's look at two reasons why the virtual office is so successful.

First, the virtual office means that not everyone has to have physical office space. This cuts down greatly on the amount of building space needed by employees. At AT&T, for instance, account representatives who handle large national accounts don't have any office space. They report in periodically for meetings and discussions with their supervisor, but not to go to work. Can you imagine how much money a company would save if it didn't have to provide office space for 1,000 employees?

Second, the virtual office means that salespeople are out meeting their customers in person on a daily basis as opposed to waiting at their desk for an impersonal telephone call. Many organizations have raised their customer satisfaction levels because salespeople now spend more time with the customer instead of being in the office.

Now, let's see how IT is really the basis for the virtual office. To deal with customers, salespeople must have information—information relating to inventory levels, packaging information, and shipping dates. This information must also be accurate—if a salesperson wants to sell a customer 100 telephones, the salesperson must know exactly how many phones are in stock. Using their portable, the salespeople at AT&T quickly call up the home system and verify inventory levels. They can also instantly submit orders and tell their customers when to expect shipments.

Information technology has brought about the virtual office concept because IT has given salespeople the ability to be with a customer and, at the same time, have access to all of the information stored in other places.

Microsoft Family of Operating Systems

Microsoft is the primary supplier of operating system software for IBM-compatible workstations and portables. You can choose DOS, Windows, Windows NT, or Windows '95 from the Microsoft family of operating systems. **Disk Operating System** (DOS) is the oldest operating system—Microsoft developed it in 1981 and has released more than 10 different versions.

DOS enjoys great industry dominance, with over 20,000 pieces of application software designed to run under it. Using a character-based interface, DOS supports one person performing one task at a time. A character-based interface means that you must enter commands with a series of keystrokes. For example, to save a file in Lotus 1-2-3, you would enter a slash ("/"), an "F" (for File) and "S" (for Save), and then the file name. Although this may seem simple, the graphical user interface (GUI) provided by other operating systems is much easier to use.

Windows is a **graphical user interface** (GUI) shell that is laid on top of DOS. That is, to run Windows, you must also have DOS. Microsoft developed Windows primarily to compete with the graphical user interface of Apple's operating system on the Mac. In a GUI environment, you point and click on icons that represent functions you want to perform (see Figure 2-12). For example, if you want to delete text while using a word processing package, you simply highlight the text and point and click on the scissors icon.

Windows NT is Microsoft's most powerful operating system. For the individual, Windows NT is a great operating system for running advanced engineering applications (such as designing products), large financial applications, and any other tasks that involve intense number-crunching. In fact, you must have a minimum of 12 MB of internal memory just to run Windows NT, and that leaves very little room for your application software and information. Windows NT also supports object linking and embedding, multitasking, and the development of sophisticated 3D graphics.

The real reason, however, that Windows NT is becoming so popular is its ability to provide networking for a large number of computers, plus the fact that it has great networking features. Networking features of Windows NT include multiprocessing, built-in access to the Internet, remote access, protection against application software crashes, and security. With the Windows NT security system, you can even lock out a user account after a specified number of unsuccessful log-on attempts.

Windows '95 is the successor to Windows. Windows '95 is a great operating system for you if you primarily run general business management, personal productivity, personal information management, and education software. Windows '95 is designed to run on portables as well as workstations. Windows '95 offers many advantages over Windows, including multiprocessing, networking, video multimedia, and internal messaging.

Taligent

Taligent is a joint-venture operating system developed by IBM, Apple, and Hewlett-Packard. Taligent is designed to challenge Microsoft's dominance in the operating system area. Taligent is based on *objects.* An object is a self-contained agent that has all the necessary information and procedures for a given task. These objects are designed to make the Taligent environment more productive for application software developers and easier for you to use.

For application software developers, Taligent objects provide programming codes to handle a specific task. For example, if Lotus Development Corporation wanted to add video multimedia to Lotus 1-2-3, it would simply "call" the video object in Taligent. In doing so, Lotus would not have to write its own video multimedia code.

Figure 2-12

Graphical User Interface in Word for Windows

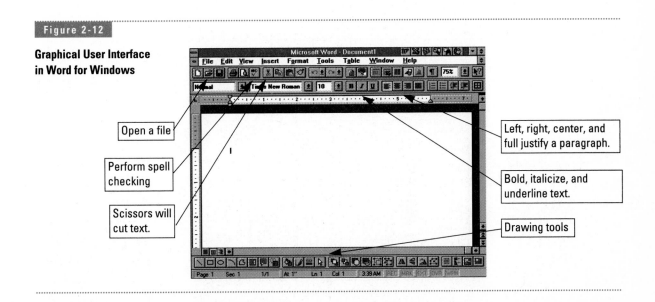

Open a file

Perform spell checking

Scissors will cut text.

Left, right, center, and full justify a paragraph.

Bold, italicize, and underline text.

Drawing tools

For you, Taligent uses interface objects made up of "*People, Places, and Things.*" This interface is intended to be easier to use and more intuitive. Suppose you wanted to call all your friends in New Mexico (see Figure 2-13). New Mexico would be the "Place," your friends would be the "People," and the telephone would be the "Thing." Using Taligent, you would:

▶ click on a picture icon of New Mexico

▶ be presented with a stack of cards for all your friends in New Mexico

▶ click on a card and move (or drag) it to the telephone icon

Taligent would then automatically call your friend.

OS/2

Operating System/2 (OS/2) is IBM's contribution to the operating system environment. It was actually started as a joint-venture product by both IBM and Microsoft. Microsoft, however, eventually dropped its work on OS/2 to focus on its Windows family of operating systems. OS/2 uses a GUI, supports multitasking and networking, and works well with applications that use micro-to-mainframe data sharing.

The latest release of OS/2 is called *OS2/Warp.* It is targeted to compete directly with Microsoft's Windows NT in both number-crunching intensive tasks by individuals and the networking of many computers. It has many of the same features as Windows NT, including networking, multiprocessing, full multimedia, and built-in access to the Internet. It does not, however, support remote access. Many experts view OS/2 Warp as by far the better technical design over its Windows rival.

Table 2-8

Microsoft Family of Operating Systems

Characteristic	DOS	Windows	Windows NT	Windows '95
Version	6.2	4.0	3.5	1.0
Character-based Interface	X			
Graphical User Interface		X	X	X
Single User	X			
Single Task	X			
Multitasking		X	X	X
Multiprocessing			X	
Networking			X	X
Object Linking and Embedding		X	X	X
Multimedia		Sound Video	Sound Video	Sound Video
Security			X	
Internal Messaging			X	X
Compatible with Other OSs		DOS	DOS, OS/2, Windows	DOS, Windows
Portability			X	
Plug and Play		X		X
3D Look			X	X
Remote Access		X	X	

Software: The Intellectual Interface

Figure 2-13

Taligent Interface "People, Places, and Things"

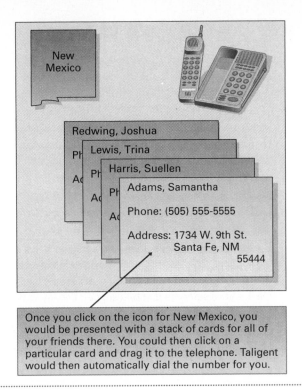

New Mexico

Redwing, Joshua

Lewis, Trina

Harris, Suellen

Adams, Samantha

Phone: (505) 555-5555

Address: 1734 W. 9th St.
Santa Fe, NM
55444

Once you click on the icon for New Mexico, you would be presented with a stack of cards for all of your friends there. You could then click on a particular card and drag it to the telephone. Taligent would then automatically dial the number for you.

UNIX

UNIX is an operating system first developed for use on minicomputers, the workhorse of business rather than personal computing. UNIX thus supported capabilities like networking and multitasking. Perhaps the greatest advantage to UNIX is its portability. UNIX can run on a variety of systems—workstations, minicomputers, and mainframes—and hardware (for example, IBM, DEC, and Apple). A wide variety of engineering application software has been written for UNIX, and it is gaining more business applications every day. UNIX is also a popular operating system in Europe.

System 7.5

Apple provides direct competition for IBM-compatible workstations and portables. Apple's use of a GUI approach in a way forced Microsoft to develop Windows for IBM-compatibles. Apple's most recent operating system is **System 7.5.** System 7.5 supports multitasking, object linking and embedding, high-quality graphics (better than IBM-compatibles), and great multimedia support.

When Apple first introduced its Macintosh machines, it set a new standard for ease of use. Macs are also superbly engineered to handle desktop publishing, graphics, and multimedia. Most photographers, many professors, and a large majority of people in the arts and publishing are Mac and Powerbook devotees (the Powerbook is Apple's portable machine).

Our brief discussion of operating system software is really a summary of a massive industry battle. Each of the leading operating systems offers particular strengths, and all of the leading vendors aggressively promote and improve their own products. Which is best for you? That's impossible to answer. Does it matter which you choose? Very much so. The operating system in many ways *is* the com-

Box 2-6

Buying the Right Operating System Software

Purchasing the right operating system is not quite like trying to find a needle in a haystack because there are fewer operating systems to choose from. But your choice of operating system software is just as important as your choice of application software. Let's consider some general guidelines for purchasing the right operating system.

▶ **Make sure your choice is compatible with current software:** If you currently have an IT system, you'll want to make sure your operating system selection is compatible with your current application software. Don't make the mistake of choosing the wrong operating system and then have to buy new application software.

▶ **Make sure it's compatible with current hardware:** Again, your operating system selection should be compatible with your current hardware configuration. Always remember—hardware is expensive to upgrade.

▶ **Let application software drive your decision:** If you're considering a new system, let the application software you choose determine what operating system you will use. Your application software selection is designed to meet your daily needs. Find operating system software that will support the application software you need.

▶ **Consider special characteristics:** Always consider the other characteristics of operating systems. If networking or full multimedia capabilities are important to you, make sure you choose an operating system that supports them.

Table 2-9

Taligent, OS/2, UNIX, and System 7.5

Operating System	Characteristics
Taligent	• Joint-venture product of IBM, Apple, and Hewlett-Packard • Uses interface based on "People, Places, and Things" • Will be Apple's primary operating system • Can be used with OS/2 and Windows NT
OS/2 and OS/2 Warp	• IBM development • Supports multitasking and networking • Runs DOS-based applications and Windows-based applications (OS/2 Warp only) • Comes with built-in access to the Internet through CompuServe (OS/2 Warp only)| • Supports full multimedia capabilities (OS/2 Warp only)
UNIX	• First developed for minicomputers • Portable • Many engineering applications • Gaining more business applications every day
System 7.5	• Operating System for Apple • Supports multitasking • Supports OLE • High-quality graphics • Great multimedia support

---

puter. It determines which application software will run best on your machine and determines many aspects of how you use it, just as your choice of a minivan with automatic drive versus a Suzuki with a manual transmission affects your driving style, options, and performance.

Purchasing and using the right application and system software will set you well on your way to greater productivity. It will not only help you in your personal life but also in your professional life. People today are using software to gain a personal advantage and help the organization gain a business advantage—there is no reason for you not to do so. As you approach the acquisition and use of software, try to keep some important things in mind.

Stay on Top of Changes

Software is changing every day; although you don't always have to change with it, you should stay informed of the changes taking place. Good sources of software changes include computer magazines like *PC Week, PC Magazine,* and *Macworld,* trade shows where software developers demonstrate their latest products, and television stations like the Public Broadcasting Station (PBS). Keep your eyes open.

Keep an Open Mind to Change

Most people find themselves in a rut. It's very easy to do; we get comfortable doing things a certain way and hesitate to change. New software is being developed today, and it's better than yesterday's software. Always keep an open mind and don't resist change if that change is for the better.

Help Your Organization Find the Right Software

Once employed, you may see that your organization could benefit greatly by using other application or system software. If so, prepare a good presentation that outlines the pros and cons of changing software. Present it to your immediate supervisor and ask him or her to review it with you. This may be a way to help your organization get ahead.

Acquaint Yourself with Software That You Don't Currently Use

Few people find it necessary to use all the different types of software available. This doesn't mean, however, that you shouldn't at least have some knowledge of what various types of software will do. Some day you may need to use desktop publishing software, but you won't be able to if you don't know what desktop publishing software can do.

Fully Utilize the Features of Software

You should attempt to fully exploit the features of the software you do use. Software today actually does more than its name might imply. Word processing is a good example. It does more than just process words for you; it gives you additional capabilities for working with tables and graphics. You will find great advantage in fully utilizing all the features your software provides.

Think Before You Buy

Finally, think before you buy. Your choice of application and system software will, in part, determine how productive you are. Don't sacrifice quality for a few dollars in savings. Think seriously about what you need, and then find the software that meets your exact needs. A little extra time and money up front will pay big dividends in the future. Boxes 2-4 and 2-6 provide some helpful guidelines.

Now You Can. . .

1 Describe the role of software in an IT system:

▶ *Software* is the set of instructions that the CPU executes to perform a particular intellectual task for you.

▶ Software is the intellectual interface because the software tells the CPU the necessary steps (instructions) that must be accomplished in performing a task.

▶ There are two types of software—application and system.

2 Describe the difference between application and system software:

▶ *Application software,* the software layer closest to you, helps you solve specific problems or perform specific tasks like writing a term paper and preparing a financial report.

▶ *System software,* the layer of software closest to the CPU , coordinates the interaction of all the hardware while you use the application software.

3 Describe the categories of application software:

▶ *General business management software* for automating functions that businesses perform every day such as payroll and accounts receivable.

▶ *Industry-specific software* for performing tasks particular to a given industry such as scheduling in a dentist's office.

▶ *Custom-developed software* that a business writes to perform tasks particular to the business.

▶ *Education software* for learning about a specific topic or area of interest.

▶ *Personal productivity software* for helping you do things that you could probably do manually.

▶ *Groupware* for helping people communicate, share information, perform their work, and work together to make decisions. Groupware includes electronic mail, group scheduling, electronic meeting support, whiteboard, videoconferencing, and work flow automation software.

▶ *Specialized software tools* including multimedia, virtual reality, and video capturing and editing.

4 Identify which types of personal productivity software can help you perform different tasks:

▶ *Word processing software* for helping you create, edit, save, and print documents that primarily consist of text.

▶ *Desktop publishing software* for creating documents that need more elaborate features than those created by word processing software.

▶ *Spreadsheet software* for defining how information relates mathematically to other information by physical location (cell address).

▶ *Information retrieval and management software* for defining how information is logically related. Database management system software and hypertext are examples of information retrieval and management software.

▶ *Presentation graphics software* for creating high-quality presentations of numbers and text along with splashy titles, borders, and pictures.

▶ *Communication software* for electronically sending and receiving information to and from another person.

▶ *Personal information management software* for managing information relating to contacts, schedules, tasks, and finances.

5 Explain the responsibilities of system software and identify different operating systems:

▶ Responsibilities of system software:

System initialization for determining your hardware configuration (for example, type of screen) and loading the operating system.

System resource management (the operating system) for controlling the application software execution and managing how the hardware works together.

Utilities for handling such tasks as file storage and retrieval, file copying, and disk formatting.

Input/output management for things like reading keyboard input and displaying characters on the screen.

▶ Different operating systems include:

▶ *Microsoft family:*

DOS—the oldest operating system; has a character-based interface and supports one person performing one task.

Windows—a GUI shell for DOS.

Windows NT—for running advanced engineering applications and large financial applications and connecting a large number of computers together.

Windows '95—for running general business management, personal productivity, personal information management, and education software.

▶ *Taligent*—an IBM, Apple, and Hewlett-Packard operating system that uses a "people, places, and things" interface.

▶ *OS/2 (Operating System/2)*—a joint-venture operating system by Microsoft and IBM to overcome the limitations of DOS.

▶ *UNIX*—first developed for minicomputers; very portable; more engineering applications than business applications.

▶ *System 7.5*—the operating system for Apple.

6 Understand the guidelines for purchasing application and system software:

▶ *For application software:*

Make sure it's the right type of application software.

Test drive the software package.

Consult other people.

Make sure it's compatible with your operating system.

Make sure it's compatible with your hardware.

Purchase the most recent version.

▶ *For system software:*

Make sure your choice is compatible with current software.

Make sure it's compatible with current hardware.

Let application software drive your decision.

Consider special characteristics.

Key Terms

Antivirus Software

Application Software

Communication Software

Custom-Developed Software

Database Management System (DBMS) Software

Desktop Publishing Software

Disk Operating System (DOS)

Education Software

Electronic Data Interchange (EDI)

Electronic Meeting Support Software

General Business Management Software

Graphical User Interface (GUI)

Group Scheduling Software

Groupware

Hypertext Software

Industry-Specific Software

Information Retrieval and Management Software

Multimedia

Operating System

Operating System/2 (OS/2)

Personal Information Management Software

Personal Productivity Software

Presentation Graphics Software

Software

Spreadsheet Software

System 7.5

System Software

Taligent

UNIX

Video Capturing and Editing Software

Videoconferencing Software

Virtual Reality

Virus

Whiteboard Software

Windows

Windows '95

Windows NT

Word Processing Software

Work Flow Automation Software

Self-Test

1. The two major types of software are
   _____ and _____.

2. _____ helps you to
   create, edit, save, and print documents that consist
   primarily of text.

3. The categories of application software include:

   A.

   B.

   C.

   D.

   E.

   F.

   G.

4. When a business creates its own software, the
   software is called _____.

5. The categories of personal productivity software
   include:

   A.

   B.

   C.

   D.

   E.

   F.

   G.

6. _____ helps you elec-
   tronically send information to and receive it from
   another person.

7. Categories of groupware include:

   A.

   B.

   C.

   D.

   E.

   F.

8. The software that automates specific functions businesses perform every day is:

   A. Industry-specific

   B. Office integration

   C. General business management

   D. Education

   E. Personal productivity

9. The type of software that helps you create high-
   quality presentations of information is:

   A. System 7.5

   B. Communication

   C. Presentation graphics

   D. Word processing

   E. Spreadsheet

10. The major responsibilities and functions of system
    software include:

    A.

    B.

    C.

    D.

11. The ability to work on more than one application
    at a time is called:

    A. Multitasking

    B. Security

    C. Remote access

    D. Portability

    E. Compatibility

12. _____ refers to your ability
    to access your IT system from another location.

13. The Microsoft family of operating systems
    includes:

    A.

    B.

    C.

    D.

14. The primary operating system for Apple is:

    A. UNIX

    B. DOS

    C. Windows

    D. Daytona

    E. System 7.5

15. What type of software includes the use of input and output devices that receive and transmit physical motion?

Short-Answer Questions

1. How does desktop publishing software differ from word processing software?

2. How does application software differ from system software?

3. How does hypertext differ from a database management system?

4. What is the role of whiteboard software?

5. What is object linking and embedding (OLE)?

6. What is the concept of plug and play?

7. What is the "people, places, and things" interface in Taligent?

Discussion Questions and Projects

1. The use of education software is gaining widespread acceptance. Interview a number of faculty members at your school and determine (a) what education software they are using (if any), (b) what education software is available in their areas of expertise, and (c) how they plan to use education software in the future.

2. A lot of people find that a good way for learning more about the software they use is to join a local users' group. Attend a users' group meeting in your town. Determine: the purpose of the meeting, the different types of people in attendance, and the major topics of discussion. Did you find the meeting helpful? Why or why not?

3. The "virtual office" is an interesting concept. You may get a job some day that allows you to work at home most of the time and just come in to the office occasionally. There are obviously a lot of advantages to this, but some people will attempt to abuse the concept. List some potential pitfalls to the virtual office concept and discuss how to avoid them.

4. Find a good example in a magazine about how a business is using work flow automation software to do electronic data interchange. Outline the benefits that business has realized. What do you think its competitive position would be today if it was not using work flow automation software?

Cruising the Net

1. On the Internet, you will find a lot of free software that you can easily download and use. Do some cruising to check out the free software and download some if you can. What kind did you find? Do you think it's any good?

2. There is a software called CUSeeMe on the Internet, developed by Cornell University, that allows online videoconferencing. Find out more about this tool and describe it. (Hint: Try the Web page at http://www.ind-state.edu/CU-SeeMe/index.html)

3. Access the Web page at http://www.yahoo.com/Computers/Software/ and describe what you found there.

4. Someone told you that you can find a large archive of Macintosh software on the FTP server at sumex-aim.stanford.edu. Describe how you would go about accessing this server and retrieving software.

Solutions to Self-Test (1) application, system—p. 36; (2) word processing software—p. 38; (3) general business management, industry-specific, custom-developed, education, personal productivity, groupware, specialized software tools—p. 37; (4) custom-developed—p. 37; (5) word processing, desktop publishing, spreadsheet, information retrieval and management, presentation graphics, communication, personal information management—p. 38; (6) communication software—p. 50; (7) electronic mail, group scheduling, electronic meeting support, whiteboard, videoconferencing, work flow automation—p. 52; (8) C—p. 37; (9) C—p. 49; (10) system initialization, system resource management, utilities, input/output management—p. 57; (11) A—p. 59; (12) remote access—p. 59; (13) DOS, Windows, Windows NT, Windows '95—p. 60; (14) E—p. 63; (15) virtual reality—p. 55.

Working in a Group

1. In this chapter, we've provided many tables that identify popular packages of application software. Pick a type of application software your group is interested in and prepare a report for the class that outlines the differences and similarities of the popular packages.

2. Visit some local printing shops in your town and discover how IT has changed the way they do business. Ask them how they determined what type of IT to buy. Finally, ask them if their IT met their expectations.

Input and Output Devices:

The Physical Interface

Your Objectives for This Chapter

1 Describe the role of input and output devices in an IT system. **2** Identify input devices by information versus command capture and method of capture. **3** Understand the guidelines for choosing the right input devices. **4** Identify output devices by their method of presentation. **5** Understand the guidelines for choosing the right monitor. **6** Understand the guidelines for choosing the right printer. **7** Describe IT systems that have converging hardware and software.

In the movie *Star Trek IV: The Voyage Home,* the crew of the Enterprise is faced with the seemingly insurmountable task of going back in time and bringing two humpbacked whales into the present to save your planet. While attempting to pull this off, Scotty and Dr. McCoy (Bones) try to finesse some materials out of a manager at a San Francisco distributor.

In return for the materials, Scotty promises to show the manager how to build transparent aluminum. The manager offers Scotty the use of his computer, and Scotty begins speaking to it and expecting a response—which he doesn't get. Scotty even goes so far as to "speak" into the mouse thinking it's a microphone. Finally, Scotty realizes where and in what century he is and says, "Oh, a keyboard. How quaint."

Scotty was expecting an input device that worked with speech; what he found were input devices in the form of a keyboard and a mouse. These types of input devices are different because they are designed to work with input in different forms. For example, a speech input device works with sound input, a keyboard works with direct or typed input, and a mouse works with input based on how you move it and to what you are pointing. But, no matter the form of the information, or if Scotty thinks keyboards are quaint in Stardate 3421.56, input devices are an integral part of an IT system because they begin the whole process of processing information by first capturing it.

Input devices—such as the keyboard—and output devices—such as a screen and a printer—make up the physical interface to an IT system (see Figure 3-1). Consider an ATM. You use the numeric keypad to enter your personal identification number and to indicate how much money you want to withdraw or deposit. Likewise, the screen (an example of an output device) displays various options and can show you your account balance, as does the printer.

Input and output devices, such as the numeric keypad and screen on an ATM and Scotty's non-existent speech recognition system, are the hardware devices that you use to enter information and commands and receive the results. Categories of input and output devices include:

Figure 3-1a

Your Focus in This Chapter: Input and Output Devices

Input devices capture information and commands that you enter. The information and commands are passed through the application and system software to the processing engine. The results pass back through the system and application software and are presented to you by an output device.

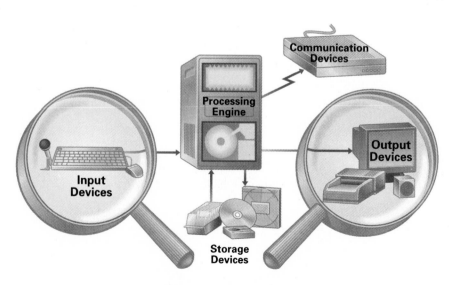

Figure 3-1b

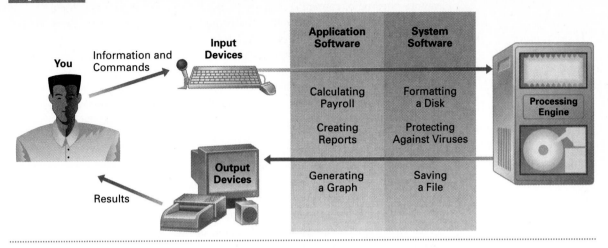

Input Devices	Output Devices
Keyboard	Audio
Audio	Soft Copy (monitors)
Pointing	Hard Copy (printers)
Scanning	
Specialized	

Input and output devices in many instances are your access tools to IT service, information, and power. When you phone an 800 number to order jeans from, say, Lands' End, you have no idea where the firm is located (it's in a small town in Wisconsin), nor do you need to know. Fax machines move documents across the world quickly and inexpensively, and bar code readers scan your groceries at the supermarket, ring up the price on the cash register, update the store's inventory, and even print out a discount coupon on the register's receipt.

When you key in your term paper or create the layout of a newsletter, the keyboard, function keys, mouse, and color monitor and printer strongly determine convenience, ease of use, and quality. A cellular phone is just the same as a phone with wires in terms of phone calls, but entirely different in terms of convenience. It's also, of course, much more expensive to use. That's the same with most input and output devices. A high-resolution color monitor that produces sharp images costs much more than a black-and-white one. A high-speed laser printer costs more than an ink jet printer. And so on.

Input and output devices vary greatly in features, cost, capabilities, and speed. Which ones you get to use in a given situation may lead you to say "how quaint," or they may be just what Dr. McCoy ordered.

Input Devices **Input devices** are the hardware components that let you enter information and commands into an IT system. As you learn about input devices, consider them from two points of view: information versus command capture and method of capture. *Information versus command capture* categorizes input devices according to whether you use them for entering information or commands—some input devices will let you do both. *Method of capture* breaks down input devices according to what form the information and commands are in that you are trying to capture. Method of capture is perhaps the most important way to view input devices because you can attain the greatest advantage from input devices by viewing them this way (see Figure 3-2).

Consider a simple example—a CEO at a major company has a letter that needs to be sent out. The CEO calls in an assistant who records the letter on paper while the CEO talks. The assistant then uses a system equipped with a keyboard to enter and edit the letter. Now, what's wrong with this way of writing letters? Very simply, the contents of the letter were expressed three times. First, the CEO spoke the contents of the letter; second, the assistant wrote the contents of the letter; and third, the assistant typed the contents of the letter.

In this example, the form of the information (the contents of the letter) originated as sound. So why not use a sound input device (specifically, automatic speech recognition) as the method of capture? Had the CEO done so, the contents of the letter would have been captured only once instead of three times. So as you consider which input device to use in a given situation, always ask yourself, "In what form does the information or commands that I want to capture originate?" The answer to that question will help you choose the best input device for your needs.

Keyboard

The **keyboard**, an input device that lets you enter both information and commands, is the most common input device used today, in both business and personal environments. In fact, the ATM numeric keypad that we mentioned earlier is actually a special form of keyboard. A standard keyboard looks similar to a typewriter, except that it contains many special keys not found on a typewriter (see Figure 3-3).

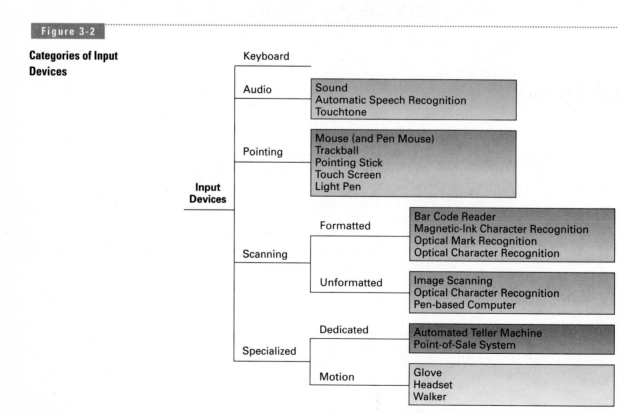

Figure 3-2

Categories of Input Devices

Audio Input Devices

If you're trying to capture information or commands that originate as sounds, you should use one of three types of audio input devices—sound, automatic speech recognition, or touchtone. Audio input devices are relatively recent additions to workstation and portable systems, but are becoming more widespread as each day passes. Automatic speech recognition is the newest, but you can expect it to become an integral component within the next two years. **Audio input devices** use two forms of hardware:

▶ A device that captures the sound (a microphone for sound and speech recognition and a signal acceptor for touchtone)

▶ A digital signal processor card that converts the sound into a digital signal

Sound input devices let you capture and record sounds so that you can change them if you wish and reproduce them at a later time. For example, you could use a sound input device to capture a favorite song, the sound of a doorbell, or even a dog barking. **Automatic speech recognition** *input devices* (called **ASR systems**), on the other hand, not only capture what you are saying but also have the ability to separate your speech into words and sentences (see Figure 3-4).

You've seen television shows or movies where people communicate with a computer by directly speaking to it. Some situations may seem a bit farfetched, but complete speech recognition (and production) is rapidly approaching through the use of ASR systems. In word processing, for example, you can use voice input for text (like the contents of a memo) and commands ("Save File as MEMO2").

Voice recognition has come a long way in the last 10 years and will soon be standard equipment on workstations. Most ASR systems today require discrete speech input as opposed to continuous speech input. Using *discrete speech input,* you must provide a complete break (or pause) between each word. Although this seems a bit cumbersome and slow, most people have been able to adapt quickly. *Continuous speech input,* on the other hand, lets you speak using a continuous word stream—the way you speak every day.

ASR systems are also either speaker-independent or speaker-dependent. *Speaker-independent* systems can be used by anyone, but these systems usually have a limited vocabulary that sometimes cannot be expanded. For example,

---

Figure 3-3

Keyboards

Ⓟhoto (a) shows a standard IBM-compatible keyboard; (b) and (c) show different styles of keyboards.

(a)

(b)

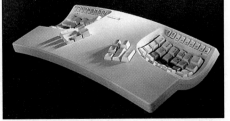
(c)

Input and Output Devices: The Physical Interface

Figure 3-4

How Automatic Speech Recognition Systems Work

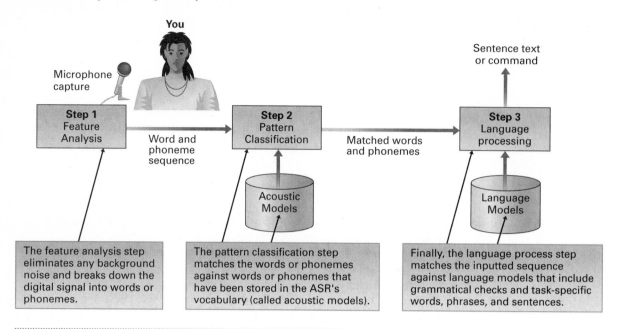

The feature analysis step eliminates any background noise and breaks down the digital signal into words or phonemes.

The pattern classification step matches the words or phonemes against words or phonemes that have been stored in the ASR's vocabulary (called acoustic models).

Finally, the language process step matches the inputted sequence against language models that include grammatical checks and task-specific words, phrases, and sentences.

Microsoft's Windows Sound System is a speaker-independent system that works with commands only. That is, you cannot enter information (such as the contents of a memo), only commands (save, print, and so on).

Speaker-dependent systems let you "train" the system so that it recognizes your voice. You train these systems by reading something similar to a Mark Twain novel. The system would begin to recognize your voice and build its vocabulary. However, speaker-dependent systems will only work for you—not anyone else.

The use of ASR systems has already become widespread in business. Sprint uses voice recognition to automate an individual's telephone book so that Sprint customers can say a person's name instead of dialing the telephone; AT&T and Northern Telecom use ASR systems for automated operator services when you call for a telephone number. For individuals who have lost the use of their hands, ASR systems also provide a way of interfacing with a system for entering information and commands.

Note that speech recognition is not the same as speech interpretation. Speech recognition just captures the words you say. The long-term goal of many IT research labs is natural language processing: computers *understanding* what you say. Today, computers can recognize sounds and words fairly easily. It will, however, be many years before people can talk to computers naturally. For example, how would you teach a computer that "fruit flies like a banana" means that fruit fly insects enjoy the taste of a banana and not that, when you throw any kind of fruit, it flies through the air like a banana?

The last type of sound input is using **touchtone** signals from a telephone to enter information and commands. For instance, in a telephone voice mailing system you use touchtone signals to input security passwords, off-site remote dialing (digital pagers would be an example), and speed dialing.

Many businesses let customers use the telephone to interact with an IT system, which reduces the number of customer service representatives needed. Credit card companies do this in two ways. First, as a cardholder, you can input touchtone signals representing your credit card number and obtain such information as your balance, available credit, and the date when your next payment is due. Second, retailers enter a credit card number to verify that the customer's balance is sufficient to cover a charge transaction.

Some universities are using telephones to allow students to register. Students use a touchtone phone to input their ID number and desired course selections. Using touchtone registration has helped many universities eliminate the long lines in which students typically have to wait and reduce the number of people needed to work registration.

Pointing Input Devices

Pointing input devices let you literally "point" to choose information and/or commands that you want to enter. Most of the time, you use pointing devices to enter commands rather than to enter information. Some popular pointing input devices include the mouse, trackball, pointing stick, touch screen, and light pen. The logic behind pointing devices as a preferred input device over keyboards is that it's easier and faster to point to what you want on a menu of options than to remember what to type in.

A **mouse** is the most popular pointing device. A mouse is a small handheld device that has a ball on the bottom. As you move the mouse across a flat surface, the movement of the ball is interpreted and the cursor moves on the screen accordingly. Once you move the cursor to the desired icon on the screen, you click on one of the mouse buttons to initiate the process. For this reason, mice are called "point-and-click" devices and used in graphical user interface (GUI) environments.

In recent years, mice—along with many other input and output devices—have become ergonomically correct. **Ergonomics** is a field of study that deals with human physical interaction with equipment. For example, there are many types of ergonomically correct chairs available that reduce back strain and ease shoulder strain. Today, various types of mice are available including left-handed mice, flat mice, and upright mice (see Figure 3-5). When purchasing a mouse, you should "test drive" different types to find the one most comfortable for you.

This may sound like a trivial issue, but the courts are full of litigation cases brought by unions and individual workers whose health has been shattered by cumulative trauma disorder (CTD). You should be careful to monitor your own ergonomics. Perhaps you often get aches in your neck or back after a few hours in front of the computer. If so, vary the height of your equipment on your desk, adjust your seating and posture, and take frequent breaks to walk around.

Discovering IT

How many television shows and movies such as *Aliens* and *Star Trek* can you name in which people carried on seemingly normal conversations with computers? Why were people talking to the computers and what functions did the computers perform? If you had to give a realistic guess, how long would you say it will be before you talk to computers in the same fashion?

There are also **pen mice**. A pen mouse looks like a fountain pen connected to the computer. The ball on a pen mouse is located at the tip end of the pen. With a pen mouse, you place the ball end on a flat surface and move it in a manner similar to a standard mouse. When the cursor is positioned correctly, you click on buttons provided on the pen mouse body.

A **trackball** is an upside-down, stationary mouse in which you move the ball instead of the device (see Figure 3-6). Trackball devices are especially useful when there is limited room for moving a mouse, as is often the case when people use portables on airplanes and trains. For that reason, you will find trackballs almost exclusively used on portable systems.

A pointing input device used exclusively on portables is called a pointing stick. A **pointing stick** is a small rubber-like device that causes the cursor to move on the screen as you apply directional movement. That is, if you wanted to move to the left side of the screen, you would push the pointing stick to the left. A pointing stick actually looks very similar to a pencil eraser that has been placed in the middle of the keyboard (see Figure 3-6). New, small portables such as IBM's ThinkPad, Gateway's HandBook, and TI's TravelMate include a pointing stick as standard equipment.

Touch screens are special screens that allow you to point at and touch a particular function (see Figure 3-6). Touch screens are similar to the point-and-click concept of a mouse except you use your finger to do the pointing. Visitor information centers and shopping malls use touch screens to allow people to locate places and get directions. Touch screens are also used for automated ticket sales for entertainment events, "make-your-own" greeting card systems, copier machines, and driver education exams.

Figure 3-5

Working with a Mouse

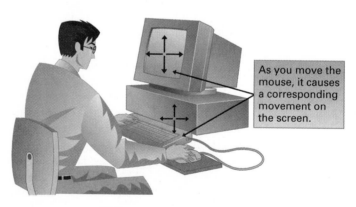

As you move the mouse, it causes a corresponding movement on the screen.

(a) How a mouse works

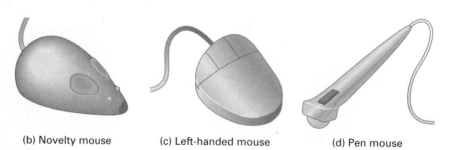

(b) Novelty mouse   (c) Left-handed mouse   (d) Pen mouse

A **light pen** is a special light-producing device used in conjunction with a light-sensitive (photoelectric) screen (see Figure 3-6). A light pen lets you point to the screen where you wish to add or change information or display more information. For example, federal air traffic controllers use light pen input for radar tracking. When several objects appear on radar, operators can use a light pen to point at a specific object and have more information appear, such as the type of aircraft it is and its altitude.

Scanning Input Devices

Scanning input devices provide a way for you to enter information already recorded on paper. For instance, you may wish to enter a handwritten note, capture a picture from a magazine, or even capture printed text—scanning input devices can help you do all of these. Scanning input devices are categorized by the structure of the information that you are trying to capture—formatted and unformatted.

Formatted Scanning Input Devices. **Formatted scanning input devices** let you enter information that exists on paper in a predetermined format. Formatted scanning devices include bar code readers, magnetic-ink character recognition devices, optical mark recognition devices, and optical character recognition devices (see Figure 3-7).

Many consumer products are now identified by bar codes—a series of vertical bars whose width and distance apart determine a number. A **bar code reader** interprets these bar codes and passes the number to the system for processing. Bar codes are particularly useful because they contain the manufacturer's identification number, the date the product was received, and the product number, which can be easily related to a price, tax status, and applicable discount.

Magnetic-ink character recognition (MICR) input devices electronically read a set of preprinted symbols. The best example of this is check processing in the banking industry, which handles as many as a billion checks per month. Your checks have printed magnetic symbols across the bottom left side. These represent

---

Figure 3-6

Other Pointing Input Devices

Pointing input devices such as (a) a trackball are useful when there is no room for using a mouse. Touch screens (b) are popularly used on copier machines. Light pens (c) let people point to places on the screen where they want more information to appear. Pointing sticks (d) are exclusively used on portable systems.

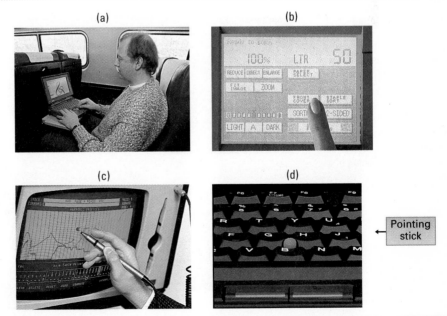

(a) (b) (c) (d)

Pointing stick

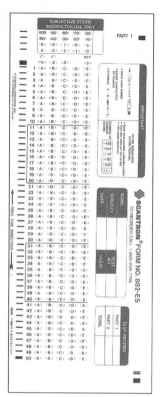

your bank's identification number, branch location, and your checking account number. When a bank processes one of your checks, the check is fed into a machine that reads those symbols and then a person types the amount of your check, which is magnetically recorded on the bottom right side. From there, your check can be processed, distributed to your bank, and eventually returned to you without any human intervention.

Optical mark recognition (OMR) input devices detect the presence or absence of a mark in a predetermined place. OMR devices are most commonly used for reading and scoring examination sheets. Professors commonly use OMR devices for grading multiple-choice and true-false exams, as do most college aptitude tests. OMR devices can also help you to record questionnaire information from a survey. A sample OMR form is shown here for your reference.

Optical character recognition (OCR) input devices work with both formatted and unformatted input (we'll look at unformatted OCR devices in a moment). With formatted input, OCR devices read preprinted information that has been standardized by the American National Standards Institute (ANSI). You will find this symbol set used commonly in clothing and department stores. Price tags on items in these places are printed using a special type style (called a *font*). Special OCR input devices (and OCR software) are able to read the price tag and record the price and other pieces of information.

Unformatted Scanning Input Devices.   **Unformatted scanning input devices** let you enter information that already exists on paper but not in a predetermined format such as pictures and handwriting. Unformatted scanning devices include image scanning devices and OCR devices.

Image scanning devices let you scan digital images of entire pictures and drawings as well as preprinted and handwritten text and include them in documents. Image scanning will help you include pictures and drawings in a document such as a term paper or advertising flyer.

If you're thinking about buying an image scanning device, keep two important considerations in mind—color versus gray-scale scanning and resolution. Gray-

---

Figure 3-7

Formatted Scanning Input Devices

Input devices that allow you to enter information that exists on paper in a predetermined format include:
(a) a bar code reader,
(b) MICR symbols on a check,
(c) optical mark recognition,
and (d) OCR scanning of a price tag.

(a)

(b)

(c)

(d)

scale scanners convert according to shades of gray—they will not scan in color. Color scanners will obviously scan in color but are more expensive. Scanner resolution is measured in dots per inch (dpi). The more dpi, the better (or higher) the resolution. Also, the more dpi, the more expensive the scanner.

Unformatted optical character recognition (OCR) input devices perform a function similar to image scanning devices except they convert a digital picture of text (preprinted and handwritten) into actual text that can be edited. For example, you can input handwritten notes into a word processing document and edit them as if you had typed in the text on a keyboard. A **pen-based computer** is a special IT system built around the use of unformatted OCR. Using a pen-based computer, you write on the screen with a special writing stylus; the system can then interpret your writing and put it in an editable format for a word processor or send it out as a fax. To date, pen-based computer systems are able to recognize handwriting fairly well—they correctly interpret about 96 percent of the letters written by different people. That still means they have a long way to go. For example, if you entered a 10-page term paper using a writing stylus, you would probably find about 500 to 600 errors (letters interpreted incorrectly).

Specialized Input Devices

As with application software, there are a number of special input devices that do not fit well into any of the above categories. We call these input devices *specialized input devices.* They include dedicated input devices and motion input devices (see Figure 3-8).

Dedicated input devices handle one specific functional task. ATMs and point-of-sale systems have dedicated input devices. ATMs use a numeric keypad as a dedicated input device that allows you to make only banking-related transactions. **Point-of-sale (POS) systems** are IT-based systems that capture information at the point of a sale and then transmit that information to another system that performs such tasks as inventory updating, inventory ordering, customer profile updating, and sales forecasting and analysis. All POS systems have dedicated input devices such as scanners, bar code readers, and/or terminals that do the initial capturing of information. Many POS terminals have keys dedicated for certain products or types of products.

Motion input devices record physical movement and are among the newest types of input devices. Motion input devices include gloves, headsets, and walkers. You use your hands every day for almost every task; the same is true when you work with an IT system. Most input devices, however, are not recording your hand motions like dexterity and strength of touch. **Glove input devices** capture and

Discovering IT

Visit a local shopping mall and see how stores are using scanning input devices. Did you notice that some stores are more efficient than others because they use certain types of scanning input devices? What types of scanning input devices did you see? Why do you think some were more efficient than others?

PERSONAL ADVANTAGE

Barb Goldman

"**I**f it weren't for computers, we'd probably be out of business!" exclaimed Barb Goldman. Barb and her husband Larry are part of a growing number of entrepreneurs who have built successful businesses based on IT. Barb and Larry own a mail-order taxidermy and woodcarving supply business that they operate out of their home.

"It actually just started as a hobby, but because of what we can do with information technology, our business now requires all of our energies as well as three part-time assistants," explains Larry. Larry is a professional taxidermist and woodcarver who cares to leave the management of the business to Barb. When it became apparent that they could potentially make the business go full time, Barb went back to school to learn about IT.

Today, Barb and Larry have a microcomputer system that includes a database management system for tracking customers and customer orders, various types of business management software, and two important input and output devices—an image scanning device and a color laser printer.

Barb and Larry used to prepare mail-order catalogs the old-fashioned way—creating text on the computer and leaving room for pictures they would later paste in. They would then make copies of the pages and send them out as mail-order catalogs. "Boy, did they look terrible," said Barb regretfully.

"We knew that people didn't take us seriously because of the quality of our catalogs. Our products were of the highest quality, but our presentation almost killed us!" That's when they decided to purchase an image scanning device, a desktop publishing package, and a color laser printer.

Barb went on to say, "Now we have a complete system. We use the image scanner to capture pictures, the desktop publisher to create text and manipulate the pictures, and our database management system even interfaces to print mailing labels right on the catalog. We would probably be out of business today if it weren't for information technology. Our small business is growing every day, and we are realizing our dream."

Barb and Larry are living a dream—they own their own business, and it's a business they love. IT has definitely played an important role in their success.

record the shape and movement of your hand and fingers and the strength of your movements. Significant research in glove input began in the late 1970s and today includes such applications as interpreting sign language, virtual reality, and computer-based puppetry. In fact, in the movie *Congo,* Amy the gorilla uses a glove input device and sign language to talk to humans.

Headsets act as both an input and an output device. As an output device, a headset has a screen in front of your eyes that covers your complete vision. As an input device, the headset captures the movement of your head—side to side and up and down. Headsets are almost exclusively used in virtual reality environments for changing the screen view according to the movement of your head.

Walkers are input devices that record the movement of your legs (including speed of travel). As with headsets, you will find walkers used most commonly in conjunction with virtual reality. At the end of this chapter, we'll discuss virtual reality as converging hardware and software and talk more about walkers.

Choosing the Right Input Device

Using the right input devices can increase your overall efficiency and your ability to capture information and commands in the most useful form. The main require-

Input and Output Devices: The Physical Interface

Figure 3-8

Specialized Input Devices

ATMs (a) help you perform banking-related transactions. POS systems (b) capture information concerning sales transactions. Gloves, head-sets, and walkers (c) capture physical motion in virtual reality.

(a)

(b)

(c)

ments you will have for input devices are (1) convenience, (2) ease of use, and (3) mobility. Also, keep these criteria in mind:

▶ **Personal versus business use:** Many input devices are used primarily in business environments; you might not gain much personal advantage from their use. For example, while bar code readers and OMR devices seem interesting and fun to use, you probably won't find much use for them in your home.

▶ **Information versus command capture:** Always keep in mind what you are trying to capture—information, commands, or both. While a mouse may be good for entering commands, it certainly won't work well for entering large amounts of text.

▶ **Method of capture:** Method of capture is often the most crucial characteristic to consider. To do this, you must first know the form of the information and commands that you are trying to capture; this will tell you what input device you should be using. You can expect more and more economical choices in the coming years—a keyboard and mouse are no longer your only practical options. For instance, consider the value of image scanning if you want to insert pictures and graphs into your term papers.

▶ **Standard input devices:** When you purchase a system, it will usually come with a mouse, a keyboard, and sometimes ASR. These may be just what you need—if they are, don't buy anything else.

▶ **Application software support:** Some types of application software will not support the use of certain input devices. After you've decided what application software you need (or have), check to make sure that it will interface with the input devices you are considering.

▶ **Operating system software support:** As with application software, some operating systems will not support certain types of input devices. Make sure

Avon Products is one of the world's largest cosmetics manufacturers and distributors; in 1992 alone, Avon processed more than 12 million orders. These orders not only came from department stores and drug stores but also from door-to-door salespeople. Like many cosmetics suppliers, Avon found that the concept of in-home cosmetics parties could generate a large volume of sales. These in-home cosmetics parties did, however, create several problems.

After the salespeople completed order forms from the parties, the forms were sent to the home office for processing. Order entry clerks then had to enter all the orders. Since the order forms were filled out by hand, the process was painstakingly slow and full of errors. Because of the long delivery time and the fact that many orders were wrong, Avon began to lose a lot of its customers—customers it counted on for a major portion of its revenue.

That's when someone decided to create a system that could read and process orders without any human intervention. If the system had problems with one of the orders, it would be kicked out for an order entry clerk to deal with. That way, the good orders would be processed much more quickly, leading to quicker turnaround times on order shipments.

That's exactly what Avon did. Avon created a system with digital image scanning and OCR to read and interpret the orders without any human intervention. The system worked great. Avon reported in 1993 that the system had improved accuracy by 76 percent, improved productivity by 75 percent, and cut order processing times by an amazing 67 percent. All these improvements led to a decrease in order entry costs of over 65 percent.

you have a good fit or you could be wasting your money. DOS, for instance, won't support writing stylus input.

▶ **Importance of consulting with others:** There are many brands of the different types of input devices. If you're considering some kind of ASR system, for example, talk to others who use these systems to find out their various capabilities.

Output Devices **Output devices** are the hardware components that let you see (or hear) the results of the commands you enter. You can categorize output devices by their *method of presentation*—audio, soft copy, and hard copy. Audio output devices are devices that present information in a sound form. Soft copy output devices present information in a displayed form on a screen, and hard copy output devices present information on paper.

Determining the correct type of output device to use is just the opposite of deciding on the right type of input device. With input devices you are concerned with the original form of the information you are trying to capture. With output devices you are concerned with the best final presentation of information.

Audio Output Devices

Audio output devices, which let you hear information, include sound output devices and speech synthesis. Audio output devices use two forms of hardware:

TODAY'S BUSINESS ADVANTAGE

POS systems are offering many advantages to all types of businesses today. These systems allow businesses to capture transactions at the point of sale and instantaneously update customer and inventory files. The captured information is then also used to order fast-selling products and perform an analysis of sales trends and develop forecasts. For businesses, this means reacting more quickly to purchases and keeping customers happy.

Here are just a few examples of businesses using POS systems to capture information immediately:

- **Britain's Woolworth's uses a POS system that links the company headquarters to its 800 retail stores.**
- **Perishable, deli, and bakery departments use POS information to forecast demand, which is then used by labor scheduling software to put employees and products in the right place at the right time.**
- **According to one survey, 80 percent of grocery chains, independents, and wholesalers said they would upgrade to POS systems as a way of ensuring pricing accuracy.**
- **Thiftway Food & Drug and H.E.B. Grocery recently installed graphics-based cash register systems to display products and cash register tapes.**
- **Grossman's Inc. uses pre-POS scanning devices to create a transaction list for customers waiting in line. The information is then transmitted to the store's computer network, and the cashier simply views the transaction list and collects money.**
- **Sutton Place Gourmet uses POS to give customers frequent-shopper discounts.**
- **Sue and John Sutter operate two HealthMart pharmacy franchises. They use a $30,000 POS system to improve inventory management, decrease labor costs, and look like a state-of-the-art operation.**
- **Blockbuster Entertainment Corp. uses retail kiosks (a type of POS system) that allows customers to order video games unavailable in the store. When customers request a video game, a copy of it is immediately downloaded from the corporate computer. This lets Blockbuster fill more orders without forecasting demand.**
- **Sea World of Texas uses a POS system to keep track of sales and stock to avoid losses.**
- **MGM Grand Hotels use POS systems to capture and transmit transactions to property management and for its complementary-item tracking systems.**

- A sound card that translates the digital recordings of the sounds
- A set of speakers (you can use any speakers that you have around the house—for example, you could hook up a set of Bose speakers to get really high-quality sound)

Sound output devices reproduce recorded sounds such as music and speech. Sound output devices are actually the flip side of sound input devices that capture sounds. Sound output devices reproduce recorded sound and speech, whereas **speech synthesis output devices** actually "create" speech output. Speech synthesis output is very similar to ASR, only in reverse (see Figure 3-9). A speech synthesis output system takes the text of a sentence and produces the equivalent speech sound for you to hear.

Soft Copy Output Devices

Soft copy output devices are screens or monitors; these are the most popular output device. There are two categories of soft copy output devices or monitors— **cathode ray tube** (CRT) and **flat panel displays**. These categories are based on the technology used to create the screen images (see Figure 3-10).

Flat panel displays are used on portable systems, while CRTs are used for workstations and larger IT systems. CRT technology is similar to that of a television picture tube, which is not possible on portables because of space limitations. While flat panel displays make excellent use of space, they do have their drawbacks.

Flat panel technologies still have a long way to go before their quality is as good as CRT technology. Most notably, flat panel displays still suffer from their relatively small size (for viewing), glare, and problems with "side-seeing" (looking at them from an angle).

Monitors, regardless of whether they are CRT or flat panel display, are often described by their use of color and resolution. Some screens basically use no color—these are called *monochrome*—while some produce up to 17 million colors. **Resolution** is determined by the number of pixels a screen contains. A **pixel** (short

---

Figure 3-9

How Speech Synthesis Systems Work

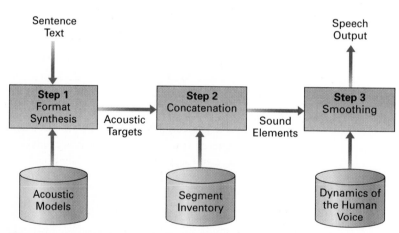

When your system determines what needs to be said, it passes a digital sound symbol set of the sentence text to a format synthesis process (step 1). During format synthesis, the digital sound symbol set is matched to a set of acoustic targets. These acoustic targets are similar to phonemes or symbols that you would see in a dictionary if you wanted to determine how to sound out a word. After the acoustic targets have been determined, they are passed to the concatenation process (step 2). During the concatenation process, the acoustic targets are matched to prerecorded sound elements of words. These sound elements of words are then passed to the smoothing process (step 3), which creates junctures between the words to mimic the human voice. After the smoothing process, the speech is actually output.

Input and Output Devices: The Physical Interface

for picture element) is the smallest display unit on a screen that can be turned on or off and made different shades of colors. Pixel resolution is measured in terms of the number of rows and columns that make up the matrix of pixels on a screen. For example, a 1024-by-768 resolution means that the screen has 1,024 rows and 768 columns of pixels (for a total of 786,432 pixels).

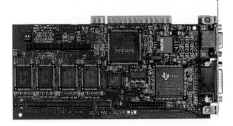

In reality, the type of monitor only partly determines the use of color and resolution. What really determines color and resolution is the graphics adapter card (sometimes called a *graphics card, graphics board,* or *graphic accelerator board*). A **graphics adapter card** is the interface board that connects the monitor to the rest of the hardware. The best soft copy output device for you then is a monitor connected to a graphics adapter card that will support the largest number of color shades and pixels. These monitors will create the sharpest and most colorful images. Cost, however, may be a consideration for you; monitors and graphics adapter cards that provide the highest-quality output are obviously the most expensive.

Choosing the Right Soft Copy Output Device. Using the right soft copy output device or monitor will help you see information in the best form possible. As you consider different types of monitors, always keep in mind:

▶ **Resolution:** The higher the resolution, the clearer and crisper your images will be.

▶ **Color:** Color today is very important; not only does it help differentiate information on the screen, it will also reduce the wear and tear on your eyes (remember ergonomics).

▶ **Size:** Monitors come in different sizes. Sometimes a standard 14-inch monitor is fine, but you may also find that a larger 16- or 17-inch monitor is more suitable to your tasks. This may be especially true if you are working with desktop publishing software or in an engineering or architectural environment.

▶ **The "Flicker" Question:** Monitors are either interlaced or noninterlaced. Interlaced monitors must make two passes per image; noninterlaced monitors only make one. So interlaced monitors seem to "flicker," while noninterlaced ones do not. This flickering can be hard on your eyes.

Hard Copy Output Devices

Hard copy output devices produce output on some tangible medium like paper. Hard copy output devices include printers and plotters. Printers are the most popu-

---

Figure 3-10

CRT and Flat Panel Display Technologies

Ⓢoft copy output devices include two types of monitors: (left) cathode ray tube displays are used for workstations and large IT systems, while flat panel displays (right) are used on portable systems.

---

lar hard copy output device. Plotters are special hard copy output devices capable of creating high-quality freehand drawings and pictures. Plotters are often used by architects and engineers to produce output such as product schematic drawings and home designs.

Printers. You can categorize **printers** in two ways—quality of output and process of output. *Quality of output* is the sharpness of the images and text produced. Quality of output can be draft, near letter quality, and letter quality. *Process of output* is how the printer records images and text on paper—impact and nonimpact. Impact printers actually strike the page to create an image or text (just like a typewriter), while nonimpact printers do not. Popular types of personal printers include dot matrix, ink jet, and laser (see Figure 3-11).

Dot matrix printers are impact printers that use a matrix of pins to strike a printer ribbon onto a page. With a dot matrix printer, the image of a character is configured on the matrix of pins and then those pins are impacted. The quality of output for a dot matrix printer is either draft or near letter quality, but not quite letter quality. **Ink jet printers** are letter quality nonimpact printers that spray ink onto the page. These ink droplets are formed by a special spray nozzle. Ink jet printers can also spray different colors onto the page. **Laser printers** use a laser beam source to create images on a drum. These images are magnetically charged to attract ink-like toner. The toner is then heated and a piece of paper passes over the drum and captures the images. Laser printers are nonimpact letter quality printers.

Dot matrix printers are the oldest of the three print technologies, the cheapest (less than a penny a page), and the noisiest (because they're impact); they also deliver the poorest image quality. Dot matrix printers, however, have found two market niches that they will undoubtedly serve for many years. First, because these printers are impact printers, they work extremely well for multipart forms. Second, you can purchase a dot matrix printer capable of printing 10 pages per minute for about $300. Speed at that price is not possible with ink jet and laser printers.

Ink jet printers are the most popular type of personal printer, accounting for almost 50 percent of the personal printer market (see Table 3-1). Ink jet printers provide high-quality output (letter quality as opposed to the near letter quality of dot matrix printers) at the lowest cost (at least $200 less than laser printers). Today you can buy an ink jet printer that prints four different colors for less than $500.

Laser printers are the choice of business printing. They are quiet, clean, cost effective, and produce black-and-white output that is the best quality of any of the three printer technologies. You can buy a laser printer that prints only black (called *monochrome*) for about $500 at a speed of six pages per minute. A color laser printer, however, will cost you $5,000 to $10,000.

Choosing the Right Printer. A printer may be the most important output device you will use. Paper is still widely used to pass information from person to person. High-quality, good-looking documents have much to say about the pride you take in your work. Here's a list of criteria to keep in mind when thinking about printers (see Table 3-2):

▶ **Color:** The cost of color printing is dropping daily. Color can greatly enhance the presentation quality of your material, even if it's only text.

▶ **Letter quality:** Although dot matrix printers are less expensive than other types, you will sacrifice some quality of the printed material.

▶ **Printing graphics:** The quality of graphics printing is the same as letter quality printing. Lasers do it best, followed by ink jets, then dot matrix.

Figure 3-11

Printers

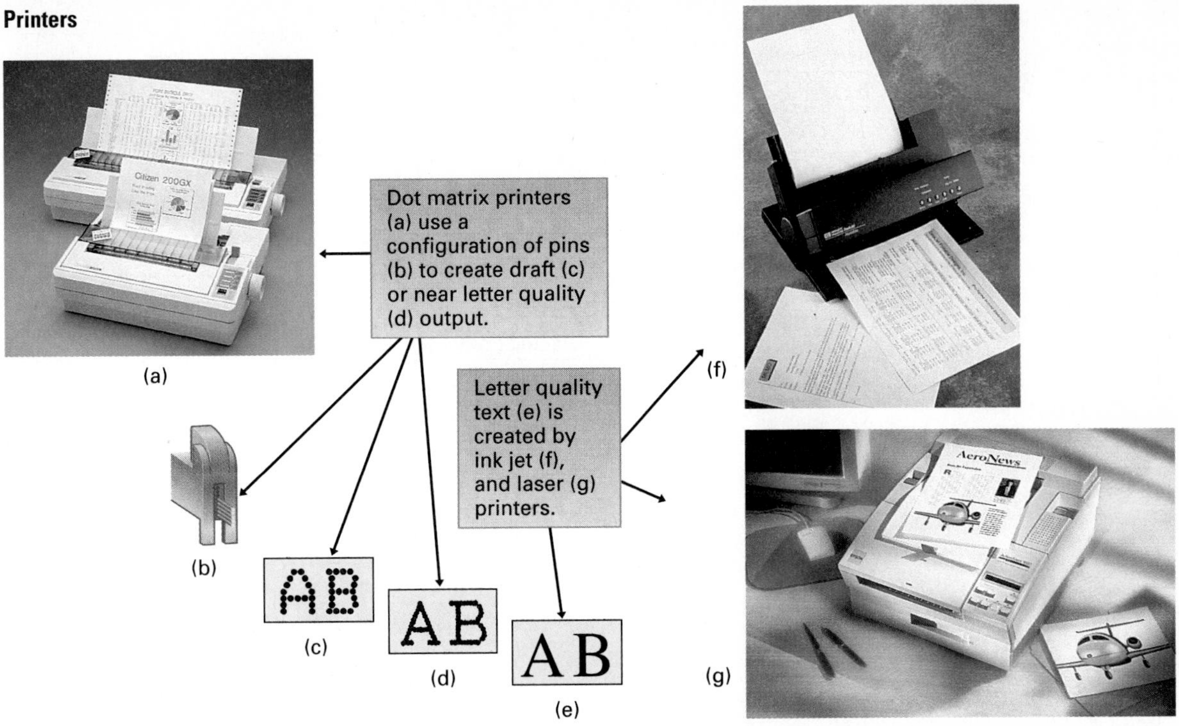

Dot matrix printers (a) use a configuration of pins (b) to create draft (c) or near letter quality (d) output.

Letter quality text (e) is created by ink jet (f), and laser (g) printers.

(a)

(b)

(c)

(d)

(e)

(f)

(g)

▶ **Speed:** Speed may or may not be important. Obviously, a faster laser printer will cost more than a slower laser printer, but the dividends may pay off for the time you save.

▶ **Manufacturer:** Many hardware manufacturers make printers. You should consult other owners as well as literature about printer quality and reliability and manufacturer reliability and support.

▶ **Special printing needs:** Some printers support special printing needs such as gum labels, envelopes, printing on both sides of the page, and using different paper sizes. If your needs extend beyond normal page printing, find a printer that will do everything you need.

Plotters. **Plotters** are special hard copy output devices for creating nontext images like architectural drawings, maps, diagrams, and charts. Plotters use a special writing instrument attached to an arm that moves over the page and writes or draws the output. Plotters are letter quality and impact hard copy output devices.

An interesting use of plotters is in automated greeting card systems. After you choose the style of card, picture, and what you want to say, a plotter takes over and actually draws your card. This way, you can have your own personalized greeting card. You can go to a Hallmark shop or a number of other stores and try this out for just a couple of dollars.

Table 3-1

Personal Printer Technologies in the United States[1]

U.S. Printer Sales

Units Shipped	1993	1994[a]	1995[a]
Dot Matrix	4,620,000	3,426,000	2,422,000
Ink Jet	3,290,000	4,613,000	5,857,000
Laser	3,031,000	3,397,000	3,661,000
Other	104,000	87,000	69,000
Total Sales	11,045,000	11,523,000	12,009,000

[a]Projected.

Leading Printer Manufacturers

	Dot Matrix	Ink Jet	Laser
1	Epson	Hewlett-Packard	Hewlett-Packard
2	Panasonic	Canon	Apple
3	Okidata	Apple	Okidata
4	Citizen	Epson	Epson
5	Star Micronics	Lexmark	Lexmark

Converging Hardware and Software

In Chapter 2, we briefly introduced three special software tools—video capturing and editing, multimedia, and virtual reality. Let's look at these in more depth now that we have addressed some closely related input and output devices.

Video Capturing and Editing

Video capturing and editing is the process of recording, storing, and editing video. This process requires a combination of software, input devices, and output devices. Let's see how it works (see Figure 3-12 on page 96). After you connect your video source—such as a camcorder, VCR, or cable line—to your IT system and begin "feeding in" the video, the video picture is separated from the audio signal. A sound board captures audio signals and translates them into digital form, while a video board converts the continuous video stream into a digital mapping of each frame. The digital

Discovering IT

Suppose you were going to buy a printer and your most important concern was to be able to print on paper that is 11 x 17 as opposed to typical paper that is 8 1/2 x 11. What type of personal printer would you buy—a dot matrix, ink jet, or laser printer?

Table 3-2

The Ins and Outs of Printer Technology

	Print Technologies		
	Dot Matrix	**Ink Jet**	**Laser**
Advantages	Inexpensive	Quiet	Exceptional quality
	Reliable	Compact	Color
	Prints multipart forms	Good quality	Graphics
	Can use wide paper	Speed	Most energy efficient
	Fastest	Color	
		Graphics	
Disadvantages	Poorest print quality	Potential smearing if ink doesn't dry	Prints graphics slowly
	Limited color	Cost per page is highest of the three	Size (larger than the other technologies)
	Noisy (impact)		Color is expensive
	Quality decreases as ribbon ages		
Cost	$100–$300 (personal models)	$200–$300 (no color)	$400–$1,000 (no color)
	$500+ (multipart printers)	$300–$400 (3-color) 500+ (4-color)	$5,000+ (color)
Cost per Page	Less than a penny	$0.02–$0.08 (no color)	$0.01–$0.04 (no color)
		$0.20–$1.20 (color)	

audio signals and the digital frames are then brought back together in the internal memory and passed on to a storage device such as your hard disk.

Now you can use your video editing software to alter the captured video and sound any way you wish and play the video. When playing a video, a similar reverse process takes place. First, the complete video (picture and audio) are sent to the internal memory where they are separated. The audio signals go to the sound board and then to an external set of speakers, while the video frames pass through a graphics adapter card on their way to a screen.

It sounds simple, and it actually is. With video capturing and editing you can remove video frames, repeat video frames, adjust speeds, overlay new audio sounds, and even add captions to video frames. If you want, you can even flip frames or turn them at 90-degree angles.

Multimedia

Video capturing and editing is actually a subset of multimedia. So the real question is, "What is multimedia?" **Multimedia** is a system that combines information of all forms (video, sound, text, and graphics) in such a way that users (people to whom the information is being presented) can navigate through the information in any order they wish. Most often, multimedia applications are stored on CD. So you could say:

▶ **Multimedia** is neither just hardware (input and output devices and a CD) nor software—it is a combination of both.

▶ **Multimedia** lets you combine information of all forms (video, sound, text, and graphics). You combine information by creating links between the information.

Box 3-1

Multimedia

Multimedia is exactly what the term implies—the presentation of information in many (*multi*) different ways (*media*). And the media can include video, sound, text, and graphics. If you would like to use existing multimedia applications, you're going to need some important hardware, including:

▶ **A mouse and keyboard—for navigating through the multimedia presentation**

▶ **A CD-ROM drive—because most multimedia applications today come on CD-ROM**

▶ **A graphics adapter card and monitor—for seeing**

▶ **A sound board and speakers for hearing**

If you're thinking about creating your own multimedia application, the hardware gets a little more complicated—and expensive. In addition to the hardware you'll need for just using a multimedia application, you'll also need these items:

▶ **Image scanner—for capturing pictures**

▶ **VCR—for capturing video on TV**

▶ **Camcorder—for capturing your own video**

▶ **Cassette deck and/or CD-player—to capture recorded sounds**

▶ **Microphone—to capture other sounds**

▶ **Any other special devices that can provide sound, such as a music keyboard**

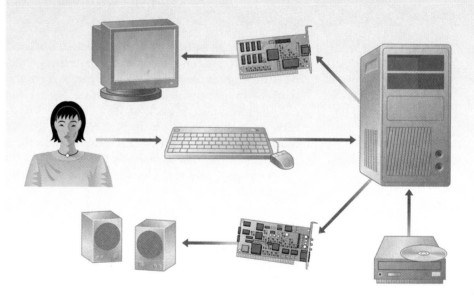

▶ **Multimedia** lets you present your information in such a way that users (people to whom the information is being presented) can navigate through the information in any order they wish.

Multimedia produces information for all the senses except touch and smell. The output of multimedia can be through such output devices as monitors (text, graphics, video), speakers (sound), and printers (text, graphics).

Multimedia software is actually very similar to hypertext. Using multimedia, however, you would create the equivalent of cards, except that the cards could con-

Box 3-1 cont

tain text, graphics, video, and sound. All of these cards relating to a particular subject would comprise a stack that could be linked and output at the same time. For
example, if you were doing a multimedia presentation on your favorite recording
group, you might link a picture of an album cover with the sound of the number-
one hit single from that album.

Finally, multimedia provides the person seeing (and hearing) the presentation
with tools for navigating through the presentation. In this way, you literally interact
with and control how the multimedia presentation will perform. Without these
important navigational tools, you don't have multimedia—you have a movie.

Multimedia is widely used in business today for creating powerful and exciting
presentations (see Figure 3-13). But businesses aren't the only ones enjoying the
advantages of multimedia—so is education. Today, students are learning by using
multimedia systems. Multimedia educational systems make books literally come to
life by presenting otherwise text-based information in the form of color video,
sound, and text. Multimedia is now being used for subjects ranging from music,
history, and literature, to sports medicine.

Virtual Reality

Virtual reality is perhaps one of the greatest technological advances that IT has
brought about. In a nutshell **virtual reality** is a three-dimensional computer simulation in which you actively participate. Virtual reality is a complex combination of

Figure 3-12

How Video Capturing and Editing Works

Incoming Video

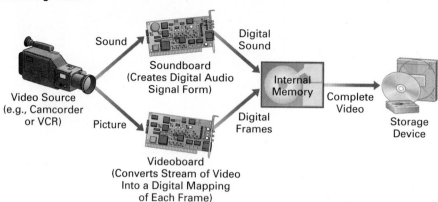

Outgoing Video

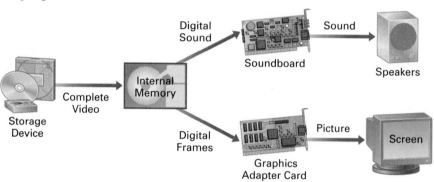

Discovering IT

Multimedia applications are available for almost any and every subject. What multimedia applications would you buy if you wanted to do the following:

▶ Find out who said "Veni, vidi, vici"—that is, "I came, I saw, I conquered."

▶ Find out anything and everything about sports.

▶ Get a glimpse into rock star Peter Gabriel's secret life.

▶ Put together the sounds of your own R&B band.

▶ Read the story "The Tortoise and the Hare."

▶ Learn about anatomy.

▶ Learn about astronomy.

hardware and software that makes you feel like "you are there." For example, home builders are using virtual reality to let home buyers experience a new home before it's built. The home buyers feel like they are walking inside the house. While walking through, they can literally change the style and color of the wallpaper, change the location of the electrical outlets, and move the cabinets for easier reach. This lets them request changes before the building process takes place.

Virtual reality differs from other IT systems in that special input and output devices are used to record and respond to physical movement. We discussed gloves and headset devices earlier, which are excellent examples of input devices used in virtual reality.

"Walkers" are also used in some virtual reality systems. Walkers are similar to treadmills. As you walk on the walker, the headset gives you the illusion that you are moving forward. When you come to a hill, the walker automatically adjusts its tension and angle to give you the illusion that you are walking uphill.

Virtual reality is popularly used for "real-life" video game playing and golfing, but it doesn't stop there. Car manufacturers create virtual car crashes to demonstrate safety features to potential customers. Aircraft manufacturers are also using virtual reality to teach mechanics how to assemble complex wiring on airplanes. Perhaps most important, virtual reality is being used in medicine to help physicians visualize internal organs, practice operations, and diagnose diseases.

Today, virtual reality is on the leading edge of IT, with limited applications. But it's rapidly growing in scope and quality. It opens up many opportunities that word-based and number-based systems can't.

Figure 3-13

Projected Business Uses of Multimedia

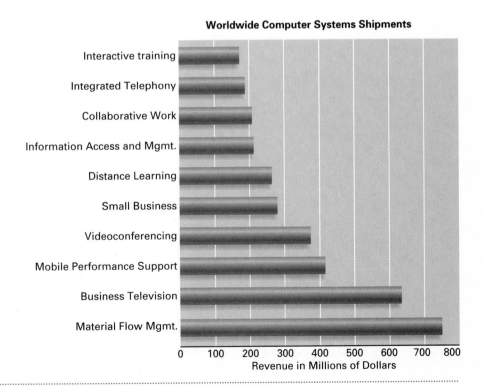

Worldwide Computer Systems Shipments

Input and Output Devices: The Physical Interface

9 7

VIRTUAL REALITY VACATIONS

Virtual reality is a combination of hardware and software that allows you to actively participate in an environment; it is a three-dimensional simulation that makes you feel like "you are actually there." Many different types of organizations are using virtual reality today to do business, and you can expect to see many more in the future. Today, organizations like Volvo are using virtual reality to demonstrate car safety features; others like Boeing are using virtual reality to teach complex airplane wiring. Let's speculate about using virtual reality to do something that we all like to do—vacationing!

One day, you and your significant other decide to take a vacation, but you haven't quite decided where to go. You can go to the library and read about various places or even obtain material from a travel agent, but why not "feel like you are actually there" by using virtual reality? The process would be simple—go to the travel agency and tell them what time of year you want to vacation and some proposed vacation spots.

The travel agent enters a few commands and hands you a headset and other motion devices. As you get connected, you step up on a walker and prepare to realize your vacation spots without actually being there. First, you see and feel what the Cayman Islands are like in March. Then you switch over to the Bahamas to see if the weather is any better during that time of the year.

The virtual reality system takes you on a tour of each place by showing you living quarters, food selection, and the nightlife, and even lets you experience snorkeling, parasailing, and scuba diving. What a concept! Don't think this example is too farfetched. Some travel agencies are already exploring the use of virtual reality to show customers their selected vacation spots.

Input and output devices are key IT components because they provide you with the physical interface to enter information and commands and receive results. In both your business and your personal life, you will find that using the right input and output devices will help you be more efficient, effective, and innovative. As you consider what types of input and output devices are best for you, keep these issues in mind.

Speed

Everyone is always worried about time; you wish you had more, and you constantly seek to save time. Certain types of input and output devices can help you do this. Always try to find input and output devices that will save you the most time. This will help you to be as efficient as possible.

Output Quality

The presentation quality of material goes a long way. Many business deals are won today based solely on the quality of a presentation and the presentation material. The quality of your work also says a lot about the pride you take in your work—whetaher it's for school or your job. Whenever possible, you should strive for high-quality, aesthetically appealing output that includes color and graphics combined with text. Don't sacrifice output quality for savings.

Stay Informed

Input and output device technologies are changing every day—some of these changes will allow you to interface with your system in ways that you never imagined. Keep informed of the changes taking place and take advantage of them fully.

Be Flexible

Don't be afraid to change as input and output device technology changes. The cost of new technologies is dropping dramatically, and the cost of a new investment in input and output technology can be regained quickly. You should not hesitate to evaluate new technologies and change when it makes good business sense.

Now You Can. . .

1 Describe the role of input and output devices in an IT system.

▶ Input and output devices are the physical interface to an IT system.

▶ They are the hardware devices that you use to enter information and commands and receive the results.

2 Identify input devices by information versus command capture and method of capture.

Input Device	Information or Command Capture?	Method of Capture
Keyboard	Both	Direct
Sound	Information	Audio
Automatic speech recognition (ASR)	Both	Audio
Touchtone	Both	Audio
Mouse	Command	Pointing
Trackball	Command	Pointing
Pointing stick	Command	Pointing
Touch screen	Command	Pointing
Light pen	Command	Pointing
Bar code reader	Information	Formatted scanning
Magnetic-ink character recognition (MICR)	Information	Formatted scanning
Optical mark recognition (OMR)	Information	Formatted scanning
Optical character recognition (OCR)	Both	Formatted and unformatted scanning
Image scanning	Information	Unformatted scanning
Automated teller machine (ATM)	Both	Dedicated
Point-of-sale (POS) system	Both	Dedicated
Glove	Both	Motion
Headset	Both	Motion
Walker	Both	Motion

3 Understand the guidelines for choosing the right input devices.

▶ *Personal versus business use*

▶ *Information versus command capture*

▶ *Method of capture*

▶ *Standard input devices*

▶ *Application software support*

▶ *Operating system software support*

▶ *Importance of consulting with others*

4 Identify output devices by their method of presentation.

▶ *Audio output devices:*

Sound output—devices that reproduce recorded sounds such as music and speech.

Speech synthesis—devices that actually create speech output.

▶ *Soft copy output devices:*

Cathode ray tube—for workstations and larger IT systems.

Flat panel display—for portable IT systems.

▶ *Hard copy output devices:*

Printers—most popular hard copy device.

Plotters—special device with a writing instrument attached to a movable arm.

5 Understand the guidelines for choosing the right monitor.

▶ *Resolution*

▶ *Color*

▶ *Size*

▶ *The "flicker" question*

6 Understand the guidelines for choosing the right printer.

▶ *Color*

▶ *Letter quality*

▶ *Printing graphics*

▶ *Speed*

▶ *Manufacturer*

▶ *Special printing needs*

7 Describe IT systems that have converging hardware and software.

▶ *Video capturing and editing*—lets you capture, record, and edit videos.

▶ *Multimedia*—combines all forms of output (except touch and smell) for exciting presentations that the user can control and interact with.

▶ *Virtual reality*—makes you feel like "you are actually there."

Key Terms

Audio Input Device

Audio Output Device

Automatic Speech Recognition (ASR System)

Bar Code Reader

Cathode Ray Tube (CRT)

Dedicated Input Device

Dot Matrix Printer

Ergonomics

Flat Panel Display

Formatted Scanning Input Device

Glove Input Device

Graphics Adapter Card

Hard Copy Output Device

Headset

Image Scanning

Ink Jet Printer

Input Device

Keyboard

Laser Printer

Light Pen

Magnetic-Ink Character Recognition (MICR)

Motion Input Device

Mouse

Multimedia

Optical Character Recognition (OCR)

Optical Mark Recognition (OMR)

Output Device

Pen-Based Computer

Pen Mice

Pixel

Plotter

Pointing Input Device

Pointing Stick

Point-of-Sale (POS) System

Printer

Resolution

Scanning Input Device

Soft Copy Output Device

Sound Input Device

Sound Output Device

Speech Synthesis Output Device

Touch Screen

Touchtone

Trackball

Unformatted Optical Character Recognition Device

Unformatted Scanning Input Device

Video Capturing and Editing

Virtual Reality

Walker

Self-Test

1. Input devices can be considered from the following different points of view:

    A.

    B.

2. Categories of input devices include:

    A.

    B.

    C.

    D.

    E.

3. The most common type of input device is the:

    A. Mouse

    B. Monitor

    C. Keyboard

    D. Pen-based computer

    E. Optical character recognition

4. _____ lets you speak into an ASR device using a continuous word stream.

5. Pointing input devices include:

    A. Mouse

    B. Touch screen

    C. Pen mice

    D. Light pen

    E. All of the above

6. _____ provide a way for you to enter information already recorded on paper.

7. The types of formatted scanning devices include:

   A.

   B.

   C.

   D.

8. What are three kinds of motion input devices?

9. Output devices by method of presentation include:

   A.

   B.

   C.

10. _____ let you hear the results of your commands.

11. What are the two types of monitors?

12. _____ is determined by the number of _____ a screen contains.

13. Printers can be categorized in what two ways?

14. Converging hardware and software include:

   A.

   B.

   C.

15. _____ uses a combination of text, graphics, video, and sound to produce information for all of the senses except touch and smell.

Short-Answer Questions

1. What is virtual reality?

2. What is the difference between impact and nonimpact printers?

3. How does speech synthesis work?

4. With what does the field of ergonomics deal?

5. Why are navigational tools important for multimedia presentations?

Discussion Questions and Projects

1. Many types of input and output devices will be used on the Information Superhighway. If you could build your dream Integrated Home Management (IHM) system, what input and output devices would you include? Why?

2. Many people think that because the keyboard is the oldest type of input device it will soon become obsolete. Do you think this will happen? Why or why not?

3. Formatted scanning devices like bar code readers and MICR have limited use in the home today. Can you see a time when we will use these types of input devices in our homes? Why or why not?

4. Virtual reality is an exciting new technology. Every day, new applications for virtual reality are surfacing. For what other types of environments could virtual reality be used?

5. Many people think that multimedia is already being abused in education. These people contend that learning through IT is not good because we will not learn how to do things (such as mathematics) on our own. Do you think that multimedia systems and learning through IT actually sacrifice the self-learning process? Why or why not?

Solutions to Self-Test (1) information versus command capture, method of capture—p. 75; (2) audio, pointing, scanning, specialized, keyboard—p. 75; (3) C—p. 76; (4) continuous speech input—p. 77; (5) E—p. 79; (6) scanning input devices—p. 81; (7) bar code readers, magnetic-ink character recognition, optical mark recognition, optical character recognition—p. 81; (8) gloves, headsets, walkers—p. 83; (9) audio, soft copy, hard copy—p. 86; (10) audio output devices—p. 86; (11) cathode ray tube (CRT), flat panel display—p. 88; (12) resolution, pixels—p. 88; (13) quality of output, process of output—p. 90; (14) video capturing and editing, multimedia, virtual reality—p. 92; (15) multimedia—p. 94.

Working in a Group

1. Multimedia is quickly transforming the video game industry. What types of multimedia-based video games are available for use on your computer at home? Visit a store that sells these types of games and try them out. Which ones did you like best? Least? Did you find a particular game that everyone liked? If someone wanted to play these games at home, what input and output devices would you recommend they have?

2. Pick out several people in class whom you talk to on a frequent basis. Now, find a desktop video-conferencing system that would allow all of you to talk and see each other at the same time. If you were to purchase such a system, what types of input and output devices would each of you have to have? What is the role of these input and output devices in desktop videoconferencing?

Cruising the Net

1. What tools exist today for doing multimedia on the Internet? Cruise the Internet and see what kinds of multimedia applications are available. What did you find? How does multimedia on the Internet compare to multimedia on your own system?

2. Search the Internet for different newsgroup bulletin boards that post information about new input and output devices. How many different newsgroups did you find? What were some of the specific topics posted on the bulletin boards?

3. When accessing the Net, are you able to display graphic images? Why or why not? What hardware devices affect this capability?

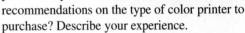

4. Perform a Net search using the key word *color printer*. Did you find any recommendations on the type of color printer to purchase? Describe your experience.

5. You often hear about ergonomics issues related to the use of various input and output devices. Perform a Net search using the key word *ergonomics* or connect to the Web page for Computer Related Repetition Strain Injuries at http://engr-www.unl.edu/ee/eeshop/rsi.html. Describe some of the issues.

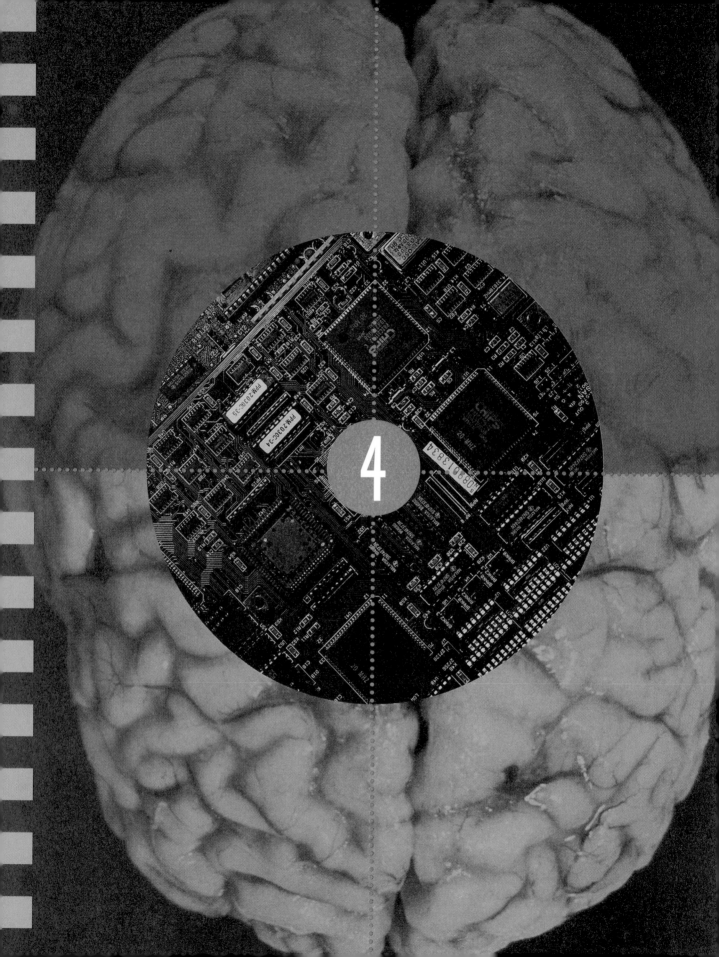

The CPU and Internal Memory:

Your Objectives for This Chapter

1 Describe the role of the central processing unit (CPU) and internal memory in an IT system.

2 Describe CPUs, including the components of a CPU, the speed and capacity of a CPU, and the features of superscalar CPUs. **3** Identify the different types of internal memory, describe their function, and indicate how their capacity is measured. **4** Understand the guidelines for purchasing the right CPU and amount of internal memory. **5** Compare different portable IT systems.

If you think about it for a moment, the hardware components of an IT system are actually very similar to you. You have input and output devices— your hands for touching, vocal cords for speech, nose for smelling, and eyes for seeing. You have the equivalent of communication devices—your central nervous system. You also have a brain—billions of tiny neurons that process information and store it temporarily (short-term memory) and permanently (long-term memory).

What's remarkable is that despite the advances in the power and speed of IT over the past decades (approximately 30 to 40 percent a year), its components are still primitive compared to you. Your brain has well over 100 billion neurons and around 100 trillion connections between them. Compared to you, the most powerful workstation today literally has the brain of a housefly.

The IT hardware equivalent to your brain for information processing and short-term memory is the central processing unit (CPU) and the internal memory— together these make up the processing engine (see Figure 4-1). The CPU is the hardware that actually processes information (based on software instructions) and directs the interaction of all the hardware components. The internal memory is the hardware that temporarily stores information and software instructions.

As you can guess, CPU performance (speed and size) and internal memory size determine the range and complexity of applications for which you can use

---

Figure 4-1

Your Focus in This Chapter: The Processing Engine

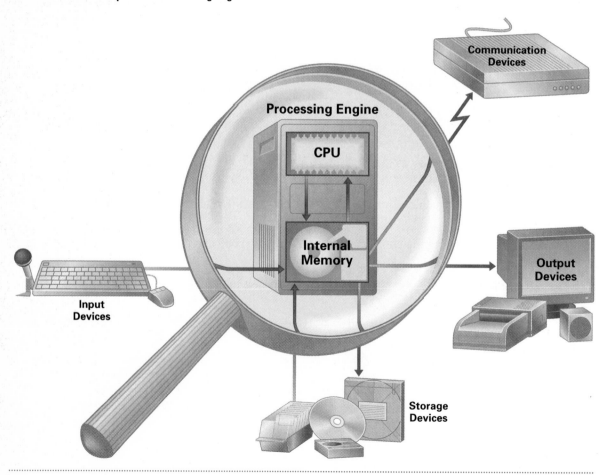

your system. The CPU is so important that most systems are described in terms of the generation of CPU chips they use. For example, a system with an Intel 80486 CPU is commonly referred to as a 486 machine. The speed that we have progressed from one generation to the next is astonishing, to say the least. Think of the Intel 8088 CPU chip used in the original IBM PC of the early 1980s as having a normal IQ of around 100 or an average SAT score. Each new Intel generation—the 80286, 80386, 80486, and the Pentium—is two to eight times smarter than its predecessor, not to mention exceedingly faster at processing your information. With the rapid advances in IT power, today's average CPU was yesterday's genius, and the Pentium has an IQ in the ten thousands and an SAT score in the millions!

Although the CPU and internal memory are probably the most technically complex of all the IT components, understanding some of their characteristics will pay off in a big way for you. Just consider the IQ and SAT analogy, and you can easily see that some CPUs are "smarter" than others and can therefore handle more complex tasks for you. As you consider the characteristics of CPUs and internal memory, common sense will help you determine what's best for you.

Typically, applications that involve complex calculations and manipulation of pictures and other nontext information generally require top-of-the-line CPU chips and extensive internal memory. If you glance at any computer magazine, you'll see adds for systems that look similar and handle much the same software but vary in cost by a factor of 2 to 5. Most of this variation in cost is due to the CPU. Which should *you* buy? The cheap one that runs too slow or the fast one that devastates your bank account and doesn't seem to be any quicker at turning out your (sometimes overdue) term papers? There's no simple answer, but in general the more intelligence your applications involve—doing calculations, manipulating lots of numbers, or creating and updating images—the more important the size and speed of your CPU and amount of internal memory.

The Central Processing Unit and the Internal Memory

The processing engine does the behind-the-scenes work in an IT system. No one ever sees the processing engine at work or hears what it is doing, but it really does a lot. It's just like your brain—other people don't see or hear your brain at work, but it's actually performing millions of tasks every second, including processing and temporarily storing information. And just as your brain is responsible for controlling how the rest of your body works, the CPU is responsible for directing how the hardware works. Let's take a closer look at the components of the processing engine—the CPU and internal memory.

The **central processing unit** (CPU) is the hardware that actually executes instructions, processes information, and directs how all the other hardware components work together. In fact, people commonly say the CPU is the "intelligence" of an IT system. You will also find that people use different names for the CPU—*chip, microchip,* and *microprocessor.* There are actually some differences (albeit subtle) among these terms, so let's be consistent and use the term *CPU* or *CPU chip.*

The CPU has two parts—the arithmetic/logic unit and the control unit (see Figure 4-2). The **arithmetic/logic unit** (A/L unit) executes application software instructions. Application software instructions include arithmetic operations—such as addition and multiplication—and logic operations, including comparisons (Is A<B?) and sorting. The **control unit** directs how all the hardware components work. It does so by interpreting software instructions and sending out control signals that tell the other devices (including the A/L unit and the internal memory) what to do.

The **internal memory** is a temporary storage area in an IT system that holds:

1 Information you are working with

2 Application software you are using

3 Operating system software (see Figure 4-2)

The internal memory, which is most often referred to as random access memory or RAM, is a lot like a scratch pad that you might use to figure out a math problem. On the scratch pad, you would temporarily write down equations, intermediate results, and values for variables. Once you figured out the solution, you would transfer the answer to your homework sheet and discard the scratch pad page. The internal memory serves the same function for the CPU; the CPU uses the internal memory

The CPU and Internal Memory

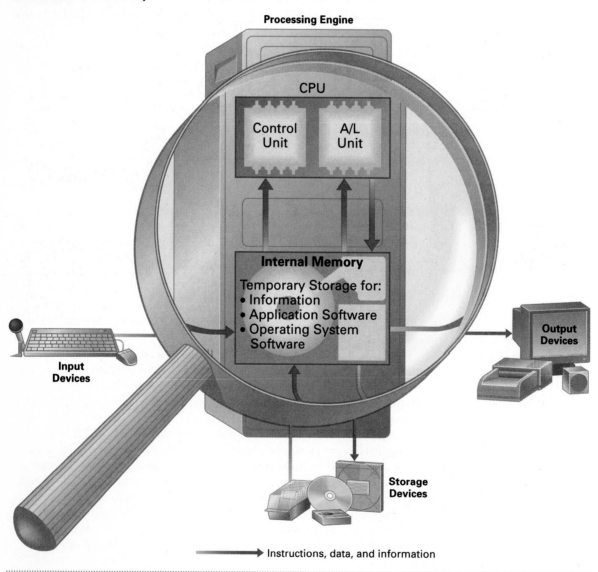

Instructions, data, and information

to temporarily store instructions and information while it is performing a particular task for you.

The most important characteristic of the internal memory is that it is only "temporary" or "volatile." That is, once you turn off your computer, all information is erased from the internal memory. In fact, you may have found yourself working on your system and lost information you were working with because of a power shortage or some other problem. Well, the reason you lost your information is that it was being held in the internal memory. As you work on your system, we would encourage you to save your information to a permanent storage device frequently to avoid losing it if your system (for whatever reason) loses power.

How the Central Processing Unit and Internal Memory Work

Let's take a brief look at how the CPU and internal memory work with the other hardware devices. Suppose you were working with a piece of application software and wanted to add two numbers and see the result. That part of the application software might look like:

1000 Print "Enter two numbers"

1010 Input A, B

1020 Let C = A + B

1030 Print "The result is"; C

Assuming that the operating system and application software were already in the internal memory, here is what would happen (see Figure 4-3):

Figure 4-3

What Really Happens Inside

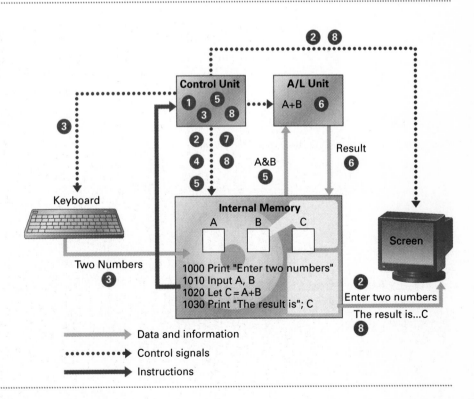

Data and information
Control signals
Instructions

1 The control unit begins the execution of the application software and interprets the first instruction.

2 The control unit tells the internal memory to send the message ("Enter two numbers") to the screen and tells the screen to display the message it receives.

3 The control unit interprets the next instruction (1010) and tells the keyboard to accept two numbers and send them to the internal memory.

4 The control unit tells the internal memory to accept the two numbers from the keyboard and store them in memory positions A and B.

5 The control unit interprets instruction 1020 and tells the internal memory to send the numbers stored in positions A and B to the A/L unit.

6 The control unit tells the A/L unit to accept the two numbers from the internal memory, add them, and return the result to the internal memory.

7 The control unit then tells the internal memory to accept the result from the A/L unit and store it in memory position C.

8 Finally, the control unit interprets the last instruction and tells the internal memory to send the message ("The result is") and the contents of memory position C to the screen. The control unit tells the screen to display the output.

Quite a complicated process to add two numbers, don't you think? Fortunately, you don't have to worry about such details. You are free to concentrate on solving the right problems with the right information. What you need to keep in mind, though, is that your CPU and internal memory determine the processing power and speed of your system. And the power and speed of your system will determine what applications you can perform.

Central Processing Unit and Internal Memory Representation of Data

In Chapter 3, we described the human physical interface to an IT system—input and output devices. You view these devices as the part of your system that allows you to enter information and commands, then to see (or hear) the results of your requests. While this is true from your point of view, input and output devices provide a different function for the internal memory and the CPU.

Figure 4-4

Passing Information to and from the Processing Engine

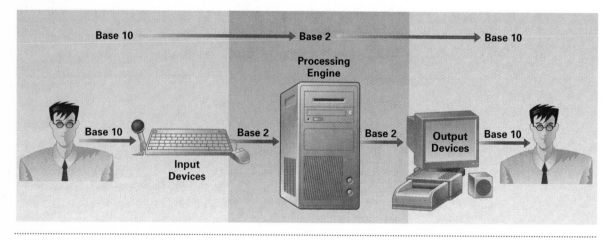

Input devices help change your information and requests into a form the internal memory and CPU can work with. In like fashion, output devices help change information stored in the internal memory into a form you can understand. This is necessary because the CPU and internal memory work solely with electronically coded signals. In reality, your CPU and internal memory cannot work with the letter "D" or the number 7.

When you work with information, you think in terms of characters ("A", "@", or "I") and a decimal numbering system, base-10. The internal memory and CPU, however, work with an information scheme called the **binary digit system**, or base-2 (see Figure 4-4). Base-2 has only two numbers, 0 and 1; the base-10 system has 10 numbers, 0 through 9. So when you enter the number 7 on a keyboard, the keyboard responds by changing the base-10 number 7 into a binary form and then passing it on to the internal memory.

In similar fashion, if you wanted to print the results of your requests, that information would be sent to the printer in a binary form; the printer, in turn, would convert it into its base-10 equivalent and print it out.

For example, the base-2 equivalent of the letter "D" is "01000100" in ASCII (see Figure 4-5). You can see that all the positions have only one of two possible digits—0 and 1. The digit positions in base-2 are called **bits** (standing for **bi**nary dig**it**). You can also see that 8 bits are grouped together to represent a character. This grouping of 8 bits is called a **byte**—which is exactly equal to one character. So when someone is talking to you about IT and uses the term *byte,* you should think of a byte as being one character (see Figure 4-6). Bytes are also grouped together to form words. Don't get confused here, though; an IT "word" is not the same as a word (*apple* or *workbench*) to you. In a moment, we'll explain the significance of words in IT.

The use of the binary system is not an arbitrary choice or one made because engineers wanted to create something "different." The entire IT field is built on an astonishingly simple concept—that *any* information can be coded in 0-1 format,

---

Figure 4-5

Representing Information in Binary (Base-2)

❶here are two methods for representing information in base-2: **A**merican **S**tandard **C**ode for **I**nformation **I**nterchange (**ASCII**) and **E**xtended **B**inary **C**oded **D**ecimal **I**nterchange **C**ode (**EBCDIC**). ASCII, originally developed as a 7-bit system, is used primarily on workstations and portables, while EBCDIC is generally used for mainframes and larger systems.

Character	EBCDIC	ASCII-8	Character	EBCDIC	ASCII-8
A	1100 0001	0100 0001	S	1110 0010	0101 0011
B	1100 0010	0100 0010	T	1110 0011	0101 0101
C	1100 0011	0100 0011	U	1110 0100	0101 0110
D	1100 0100	0100 0100	V	1110 0101	0101 0111
E	1100 0101	0100 0101	W	1110 0110	0101 1000
F	1100 0110	0100 0110	X	1110 0111	0101 1001
G	1100 0111	0100 0111	Y	1110 1000	0101 1010
H	1100 1000	0100 1000	Z	1110 1001	0101 1011
I	1100 1001	0100 1001	0	1111 0000	0011 0000
J	1101 0001	0100 1010	1	1111 0001	0011 0001
K	1101 0010	0100 1011	2	1111 0010	0011 0010
L	1101 0011	0100 1100	3	1111 0011	0011 0011
M	1101 0100	0100 1101	4	1111 0100	0011 0100
N	1101 0101	0100 1110	5	1111 0101	0011 0101
O	1101 0110	0100 1111	6	1111 0110	0011 0110
P	1101 0111	0101 0000	7	1111 0111	0011 0111
Q	1101 1000	0101 0001	8	1111 1000	0011 1000
R	1101 1001	0101 0010	9	1111 1001	0011 1001

Figure 4-6

People versus IT Representation of Information

❶he IT structure of information is according to bits, bytes, and words. You, on the other hand, structure information according to characters, fields, records, files, and databases. The common ground is between bytes and characters, which are the same.

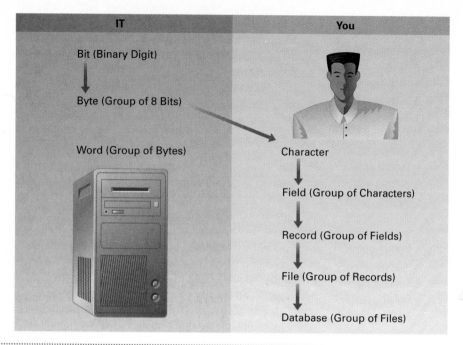

with 0 corresponding to the absence of an electrical pulse (off) and 1 to the presence of a pulse (on). The word *Jones,* the number 6805.75, a photo of the Mona Lisa, and a chord of music in a Brahms lullaby—all are simply digital bit streams. The CPU can process them all, and the internal memory can store them all.

Characteristics of the Central Processing Unit

The CPU is the most important hardware component of an IT system because it is responsible for coordinating the interaction of all the other hardware devices and for actually processing your information. More practically, the CPU is important because its size and speed determine how fast your system will perform tasks for you and often whether you'll even be able to use your system to perform some tasks.

Measuring Central Processing Unit Size

CPU size refers to the number of bytes that can be manipulated at one time by the A/L unit. Obviously, systems with larger CPUs will generally be faster than systems with smaller CPUs. You will also find that all operating systems require a minimum CPU size in order to run.

The term **word** that we introduced earlier is used to identify CPU size. For example, a 16-bit CPU has a word size of 2 bytes (2 bytes x 8 bits per byte). When people talk about CPU sizes, you will hear them refer to CPU size by the number of bits, not the word size. For instance, a 4-byte CPU would be termed a "32-bit" CPU. Whatever you do, don't confuse the "word" measure for CPU size with the way we use the term *word.* (Refer to Figure 4-6.)

The importance of CPU size is that the CPU can process only the number of bytes it can store at the same time. A 16-bit CPU can pick up and process 2 bytes,

Figure 4-7

4-Bit and 8-Bit Hands

By doubling the size of your processor (in this case, your hands) from 4 to 8, you have increased the range of numbers you can work with by a factor of 15. If going from a 16-bit to a 32-bit CPU increases the number range by a factor of over 65,000, what would be the factor increase if you went from a 32-bit processor to a 64-bit processor?

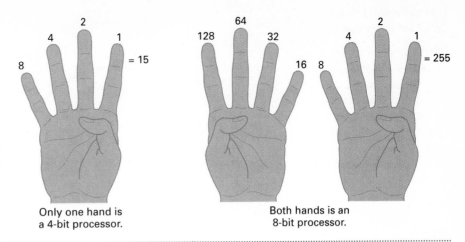

Only one hand is a 4-bit processor.

Both hands is an 8-bit processor.

but a 32-bit CPU can pick up and process twice that much. We can easily illustrate the impact of the difference: hold up the four fingers on your right hand (see Figure 4-7). Count your index finger as 1, your middle finger as 2, and your ring and little finger as 4 and 8. What you have done is create a binary digit system that can store 16 different numbers (1 through 15 and the number 0). It can't store the number 16, though.

Now hold up your left hand and code the bits (your individual fingers from little to index finger) as 16, 32, 64, and 128. Hold your hands side by side; your 8-bit double-hands can store the number 255 (256 numbers altogether when you include 0). Oddly enough, you have increased the number range by a factor of 16, though you have only doubled the "CPU" size. So the difference between a 16-bit and a 32-bit CPU may only appear to be a factor of 2 (doubling the size). In reality, the number range has increased by a factor of more than 65,000!

Measuring Central Processing Unit Speed

CPU speed refers to the number of instructions that can be executed by the CPU in a given amount of time—usually a second. Although it may be hard to believe, high-end workstations today are clocked at well over 100 million instructions per second. Let's see how the speed of a CPU is measured.

Your system has an internal clock that emits electrical pulses. These electrical pulses, besides keeping all the system operations on time, also determine how many instructions can be executed in a second. The time between the electrical pulses is called a **cycle**, and the number of clock cycles per second is measured in **megahertz**—millions of cycles per second. During each clock cycle, the CPU can execute *at most* one instruction (see Figure 4-8). So, for example, if a software instruction were to require 2.7 clock cycles to execute, the total time would be 3 clock cycles. Likewise, an instruction that only required 0.7 clock cycle to execute would take up exactly 1 clock cycle. So the more megahertz, the more instructions can be executed in a second.

If you look at any computer magazine, you'll see systems advertised according to MHz—the abbreviation for megahertz. For example, a 66-MHz system has an internal clock that makes 66 million cycles in a single second. That system, then, can execute at most 66 million instructions in a single second (remember, instructions per second ≤ cycles per second). Instructions per second are measured in **mil-**

Figure 4-8

The Relationship between Cycles and Instruction Speed

This instruction can be executed in less than one clock cycle. However, because a new instruction cannot be executed until the beginning of a new clock cycle, the time lapse between the end of the instruction execution and the beginning of the next is lost.

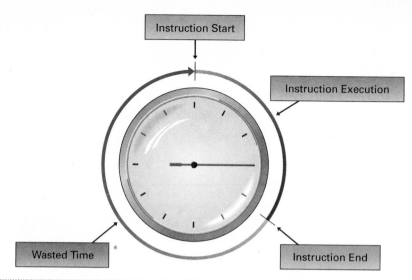

Instruction Start

Instruction Execution

Wasted Time

Instruction End

lions of instructions per second (MIPS) for workstation and portable systems; for larger systems, instruction speed is measured in terms of **billions of instructions per second** (BIPS).

Superscalar Central Processing Units

CPUs that can execute at most one instruction per cycle are called *traditional* or *scalar* CPUs. Scalar CPUs include Intel's x86 family (the chips used in IBM-compatible PCs) and Motorola's 68000 family (used in Apple computers). In the past few years, CPU manufacturers have been exploring ways to make CPUs that can execute more than one instruction per cycle. These CPUs are called **superscalar CPUs.** Superscalar CPUs include Intel's Pentium, the Apple-IBM-Motorola alliance's PowerPC, AMD's K5, Cyrix's M1, and NexGen's Nx586.

Most superscalar CPUs can execute more than one instruction per clock cycle because they have two or more A/L units that can process instructions simultaneously (see Figure 4-9). For superscalar CPUs such as Intel's **Pentium** that have two A/L units, software instructions are retrieved in pairs from the internal memory. The control unit evaluates the two instructions and determines if they can be processed simultaneously. If so, both instructions are sent to different A/L units for processing. If not, only one instruction is executed at a time to keep the A/L units in step.

What does all this mean for you? In a nutshell, it means more competition, which translates into lower prices and more processing power through innovation. Intel is already mass-producing its Pentium chip for the IBM-compatible market, as is Motorola with its PowerPC chip for the Mac market. AMD, Cyrix, and NexGen are aiming their CPUs at the IBM-compatible market, hoping that IBM-compatible manufacturers such as Compaq and Packard Bell are tired of being almost totally dependent on Intel for CPUs.

What makes all this very interesting is that Intel has already announced the next CPU in the x86 scalar family that will supposedly outperform any of today's most powerful Pentiums and the PowerPC. This CPU is code-named the P6. The IBM-compatible mainstream market merely sees the Pentium and P6 as natural steps along Intel's and Microsoft's evolutionary path. In fact, Microsoft's newer

Figure 4-9

Scalar versus Superscalar CPUs

Scalar CPU
1 Instruction + 1 A/L Unit = 1 Instruction per Clock Cycle

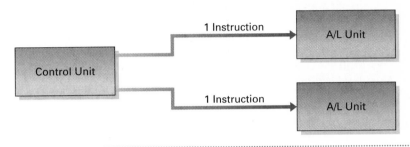

The Pentium: A Superscalar CPU
2 Instructions + 2 A/L Units = 2 Instructions per Clock Cycle

operating systems (Windows '95 and NT) are designed to fully exploit the capabilities of the Pentium.

Apple has decided to rest its entire future on the **PowerPC**. The PowerPC offers Apple one major advantage over the Pentium—the ability to run Windows and DOS applications. Historically, Apple has always been highly "proprietary," like IBM. It designed its machines to use only Apple peripherals or ones designed only for Apple machines and software written specifically for Apple machines. This radical departure from Apple's previous proprietary position may prove very important for its competitive position against IBM and the huge and growing market for IBM-compatible machines.

CISC and RISC Central Processing Unit Technologies

Another way to identify CPUs is by the instruction set they use—**complex instruction set computing** (CISC) and **reduced instruction set computing** (RISC). CISC technologies are most prevalent on business workstations and portable systems, while RISC technologies dominate engineering and scientific workstation environments. Let's see how the two came about and how they differ.

As CPUs and the internal memory became smaller yet more powerful, CPU manufacturers began to cram more built-in instructions in them (CISC technology). These instructions included things like logarithms and various interest rate calculations. The reason was simple: if the instructions were already present, the CPU would not have to execute a large series of individual instructions to perform a complex mathematical operation.

Although that may make sense, it does in fact slow down the CPU because it must sift through thousands of different instructions to get to the one it needs. In fact, a group of IBM scientists found that 80 percent of the processing of a typical application required only 20 percent of the available instructions. This led manufacturers to design RISC CPUs that had far fewer instructions than CISC CPUs.

Today, CISC is still the basis for the Intel family of x86 CPUs and the Pentium. RISC, on the other hand, is the basis for the PowerPC; other workstation CPUs developed for or by Apple, Data General, and DEC; and larger IT systems.

Buying the Right Central Processing Unit

After reading the preceding discussion of Intel, PowerPC, RISC, and the like, it's reasonable for you to ask, "What does this mean for me?" The answer is, "About as much as choosing a car." Both affect your everyday life, cost of living, convenience, and bank balance. Both also involve a huge range of options and prices. Just as you'd never go into a car dealer and say, "Give me a car," you can't think of saying, "Give me a computer." Buying too powerful a CPU can be a waste of money, and buying too small a CPU can limit you greatly. Here are some guidelines for choosing a CPU.

Application Software Interface

Many types of application software are not designed to take advantage of today's more powerful CPUs; still others will not run at peak performance if the right CPU is not present. When considering CPUs, think first about your application software and what it requires.

In general, leading software applications exploit every new generation of CPU and offer either new features or additional ease of use. Thus, for instance, the original version of Microsoft Word was a good word processing application on a 286 machine, if you were using it for straightforward text work. If you used it on a 386, it probably ran faster, but the 286 remained adequate. The Windows version of Word targeted at the 486 machines (Word 6.0) added such features as automatic correction of common spelling mistakes, file sharing, graphics, and rapid speed in indexing. All these features would be so slow on a 286 machine that using them would be frustrating and a waste of time. Thus, in general expect to upgrade your system in terms of CPU at least once every two years. Today, you may not need the latest Ferrari—the Pentium/PowerPC—but you can't afford to be stuck with a horse and buggy.

Choose a CPU that supports the operating system software you want to use.

Operating System Software Interface

As with application software, some operating systems require a CPU of a certain size, speed, or technology (RISC or CISC). A good rule of thumb is to determine what application software you need, what operating system will support your application software choice, and what CPU is best for that operating system.

In many instances, you will choose the operating system on the basis of the operating system your colleagues have or your company uses. It doesn't make much sense to adopt one that prevents you from sharing files, software, expertise, and communications facilities with other people.

Brand

If you've already decided on a brand (mainly, Apple versus IBM-compatible), you have in part already decided what kind of CPU you will have, but not necessarily the speed or size. For example, the IBM-compatible family of microcomputers uses the Intel x86 CPUs or the Pentium CPU, and Apple uses Motorola CPUs and the PowerPC.

PARALLEL PROCESSING AND FAULT-TOLERANT SYSTEMS

Believe it or not, many organizations would come to a grinding halt if their IT systems were only capable of performing millions of instructions per second. Many organizations need large systems that can perform billions of instructions per second. Many of these organizations would also come to a grinding halt if they lost the use of their systems. For these organizations, parallel processing and fault-tolerant systems are essential. Consider American Express—it processes thousands of credit card transactions every second and generates a substantial amount of revenue from providing credit card services.

So you ask, "How can thousands of transactions every second require billions of instructions per second?" Go back to our simple example of adding two numbers and displaying the result, and you'll get the idea. The processing of a single credit card transaction requires about 200 instructions, some of which translate into many more instructions that the control unit must process. The large number of instructions is necessary because of the steps that have to be completed in each transaction—accepting the credit card number, checking it for correctness (that is, making sure it's numeric and has the right number of digits), looking it up in a database, verifying that it wasn't stolen, confirming the expiration date, and so on. So you can easily see that companies like American Express need extremely powerful systems. That's where parallel processing comes in.

Parallel processing is the use of multiple CPUs in a single IT system to process many instructions in parallel, or simultaneously. Many parallel processing systems have hundreds of CPUs, making them extremely fast! Basically, a master control unit (using special operating system software) gathers a large number of instructions from the internal memory that can be processed simultaneously or in parallel. The master control unit then passes these instructions to the multiple CPUs, which handle the processing. Now, instead of a single instruction being executed every clock cycle, literally hundreds of instructions are executed in the same amount of time.

American Express, like other organizations, also cannot afford to lose the use of its IT system. American Express loses thousands of dollars in revenue for every second that its system cannot process transactions. Other types of organizations depend on their IT systems not for making money but for saving lives. Hospitals, nuclear power plants, and even the Space Shuttle program need their systems to work all the time because people's lives depend on them. That's where fault-tolerant systems come in.

Fault-tolerant systems are IT systems that have extra hardware (mainly the CPU, internal memory, and storage devices), software, and power supply components that can be used to keep a system running in case the primary hardware, software, or power supply components fail. Many organizations even use battery-powered backup power supply units in the event of the loss of electricity.

Fault-tolerant systems and systems that use parallel processing are extremely expensive but necessary because of the way businesses work today—especially because of their reliance on technology.

Speed and Size

As a general rule, the faster the CPU (in megahertz) and the larger the CPU (in word size), the more processing capabilities you'll have. But remember, don't always buy the fastest and biggest—you might not need it. For instance, Apple's PowerPC 604 (132 MHz) compared to the 601 (110 MHz) is a Ferrari for people who want to handle video, photographs, and music. But if you're doing 55-mph speed limit applications, do you really need that much horsepower? If you're in a 2,000-mph *business* speed operation, perhaps you do.

From our previous discussions, you know that the internal memory is a temporary storage area that holds the information you are working with, the application software you are using, and the operating system software. As you can guess, then, the amount of internal memory you have greatly affects how much information you can work with and how sophisticated your application and operating system software can be.

Measuring Internal Memory Size (Capacity)

You measure the capacity of internal memory in terms of bytes or characters (see Figure 4-10). Remember, an IT byte is the same as a character to you—"A" or "g" or "+." More practically, you will see terms such as kilobyte, megabyte, and giga-byte used. One **kilobyte** (KB) is equivalent to 1,024 characters (2^{10}). One **megabyte** (MB) is equivalent to 1,048,576 characters (2^{20}). One **gigabyte** (GB) is equivalent to 1,073,741,824 characters (roughly 1 billion or 2^{30}).

For example, WordPerfect 6.0 requires that you have at least 6 MB of internal memory capacity (8 MB is recommended), or roughly 6 million characters. If your system doesn't have that much internal memory, you'll have to add more internal memory or you'll not be able to run WordPerfect 6.0. Six million characters of temporary storage may seem like a lot, but many workstations today easily support more than 100 MB of internal memory; that's over 100 million characters.

You may ask, "Why would anyone, including myself, need so much internal memory?" It's simple—people today want to do more with different types of information. For example, CorelDRAW 5—a very popular presentation graphics software package that includes color, three-dimensional effects, sound, and some animation—requires that you have at least 16 MB of internal memory just for the software.

Figure 4-10

CPU and Internal Memory Measurements

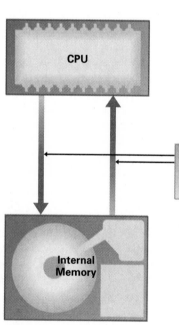

CPU

Size: In terms of words (the number of bytes that can be processed at one time). Usually given in bit measures (a 4-word CPU is called a 32-bit CPU).

Speed: In terms of MIPS (millions of instructions per second). MIPS are determined by megahertz (MHz). A megahertz, one million cycles per second, defines the cycle speed of the clock.

The electronic pathway over which information travels to and from the CPU and internal memory is called the **data bus**. Most processing engines use the same size data bus as CPU.

Internal Memory

Capacity: In terms of bytes (a single character). Powerful workstations support over 100 million bytes of internal memory capacity.

Types of Internal Memory

There are basically two types of internal memory—RAM (random access memory) and ROM (read-only memory). RAM is what we've been talking about so far—the temporary storage area for information and application and operating system software. ROM is a permanent storage area where certain system software instructions are located that help your system get going when you first turn it on. As an IT user, you are more concerned with the amount of RAM than with the amount of ROM.

Random Access Memory (RAM). **Random access memory**, or **RAM**, is the area of internal memory where your information and application and operating system software reside while you're using them. The amount of RAM internal memory in your system directly affects the sophistication and productivity of your efforts—the more internal memory you have, the more sophisticated your operating system and application software can be and the more information you can work with at one time (such as high-quality video). For example, Windows '95 requires that you have a minimum of 4 MB of RAM, while Windows NT requires at least 12 MB.

Cache memory is special ultrafast (hence more expensive) RAM that holds frequently used application software instructions and information. Cache memory is only used if the CPU notices that certain instructions are being processed over and over again or that the same information is being accessed on disk. For example, if you were using a DBMS application to access the same records on disk several hundred times a minute, the CPU would load those records into cache memory. This would eliminate the need to pass the records repetitively from the disk to the internal memory.

Likewise, some application software instructions may be placed in cache memory if they are being executed frequently. This helps because the software (or information) contained on cache memory chips can be accessed more quickly than software or information on standard RAM chips.

Virtual memory is permanent disk storage space used as "pseudo" RAM. With virtual memory, large applications and files that contain information can be split into segments, with portions residing on disk in virtual memory until they are needed. Virtual memory is especially useful if you do not have enough internal memory to work with a certain software application. For example, you can run an application in, say, 640 KB even if it needs, say, 6,400 KB.

It's like having to work with a catalog of 10 pages instead of 1. Just as you would spend time turning to page 8, then 5, and so on, the CPU spends time moving page 8 out of RAM and loading in page 5. As you can imagine, this greatly

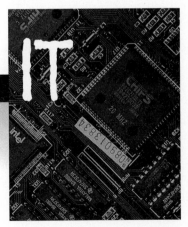

Discovering IT

Many IT systems today come with **1 MB of VRAM**, or video RAM. What is VRAM, and how does it differ from internal memory RAM? For what type of applications is VRAM important?

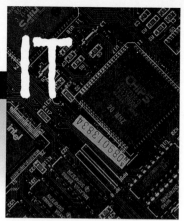

slows performance. A 20-MB desktop publishing application that had only 640 KB of internal memory, for instance, would spend almost all its time moving things in and out of the internal memory. More practically, a 20-MB desktop publishing application would probably not even run in 640 KB of RAM.

Read-Only Memory (ROM). **Read-only memory** (ROM) is the part of the internal memory that comes with certain system software instructions already built in. You do not have the ability to alter or erase the instructions in ROM. This software, located on the hardware, is sometimes called **firmware**. Instructions in ROM include input/output system management instructions and the necessary instructions to get your system working when you turn it on (system initialization).

There are some special ROM chips, however, that can be altered. These include **programmable read-only memory** (PROM), **erasable programmable read-only memory** (EPROM), and **electrically erasable programmable read-only memory** (EEPROM). PROM is internal memory specifically programmed by the manufacturer for a particular use. For example, your VCR contains PROM internal memory. This internal memory contains the instructions that allow you to program your VCR.

EPROM internal memory allows you, with a special ultraviolet light device, to change the instructions in a matter of minutes. You must first, however, remove the EPROM internal memory, make the changes, and then reinstall the memory—probably not something you would really like to do. EEPROM internal memory allows you to use special software to change the set of instructions. This eliminates the need to remove the internal memory before making changes.

How Much RAM Do You Need? Figuring out how much internal memory to buy is often the easiest task when purchasing an IT system. Let's look at some guidelines.

Find Out Your Application Software Requirements

When you determine which application software you'll be using, the internal memory requirements will be clearly stated. A safe rule of thumb is to make sure you have the *recommended* amount of RAM, not the *minimum*.

Determine Your Operating System Software Requirements

As with application software, the operating system software has a minimum and a recommended internal memory requirement. Add the recommended amount for the operating system software to the recommended application software requirement. If you choose a complex operating system—such as Windows NT or OS/2 Warp—never skimp on memory. In the language of the IT trade, these types of operating systems are "memory hogs." As we've said, always buy the recommended—not the minimum—amount of internal memory.

Upgrading Is Inexpensive

It costs about $40 per additional megabyte of internal memory. So you can double your internal memory (if you currently have 4 MB) for less than $200. You should, however, try to get the right amount of RAM when you initially purchase your system. You'll find that buying additional memory during your initial purchase is less expensive than buying it later.

Upgrading Is Easy

If you find that you didn't get enough internal memory initially, the process of upgrading is relatively easy. An experienced person can probably add more memory to your system in about 15 minutes.

PERSONAL ADVANTAGE

Internal Memory for Your Laser Printer

It seems strange to talk about internal memory for output devices such as laser printers, but it actually makes a lot of sense that these devices would have memory. Their memory is similar to internal RAM memory, but it only holds documents to be printed, not software instructions. Let's see how it works.

When you print a document to a laser printer, the entire document is immediately sent from RAM internal memory to the printer's internal memory. The document sits there while it is being printed. As each page is printed, it is also deleted from the printer's internal memory.

Sounds simple enough. So you ask, "Where's my personal advantage?" Your personal advantage is in having enough internal memory in your printer to hold the largest document that you need to print. Suppose you were printing a desktop publishing document that was 1.5 MB in size and your printer only had 1 MB of memory (standard size). Because there was not enough printer memory, part of your document would be left in RAM internal memory and sent to the printer as its memory was freed up. This would greatly decrease the speed with which your system could handle your other tasks because it would have to monitor the printer and take time to send information as the printer's memory became available.

It sounds like a pain, and it is. So get as much internal memory for your printer as you think you'll need. You can upgrade later if you need to, but it's much easier to get it right the first time.

Figure 4-11

Portable IT Systems

Ⓟortable IT systems come in three sizes—(a) notebook, (b) subnotebook, and (c) personal digital assistant (PDA). The notebook is the most powerful of the three, the PDA is the least powerful of the three but the most portable, and the subnotebook is the best of both worlds.

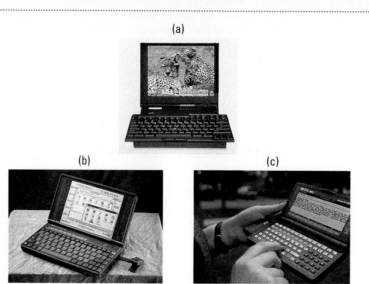

(a)

(b)

(c)

Portable Information Technology Systems

Have you ever noticed that more and more options are becoming available for how and when you use things? You can watch television at home, at a sports bar, in an airport, or while relaxing on the beach. You can pay your bills by sending them through the mail, going to the office of the business you owe money, having your payment immediately deducted from your checking account, or sending money electronically from home.

Working with information technology is no different. People have workstations they use at home or at work and also have smaller systems they can carry with them wherever they go. These smaller systems make up the category of portable IT systems (see Figure 4-11). Today some portable systems are so powerful that many people are choosing them for their work in the office or home as well as carrying them around. Types of portable IT systems include notebooks, subnotebooks, and personal digital assistants. Let's look first at notebooks and personal digital assistants, and then we'll explore the best of both worlds—the subnotebook.

Notebooks are the most common type of portable IT system. The term *notebook* was coined in the early 1990s when portable systems were designed so small that they resembled the size of a notebook (about 2 inches high, 11 inches wide, and 8.5 inches deep). Believe it or not, the first portables in the mid-1980s were

Table 4-1

Features of Portable IT Systems

Feature	Notebooks	Subnotebooks	PDAs
Weight (lbs.)	5–10	2–6	1–4
Dimensions (inches)	2 x 11 x 8.5	1.5 x 10 x 7.5	1 x 7 x 4
Active Color Screen	Yes	Yes	No
Maximum RAM	40 MB	32 MB	8 MB
Hard Disk Capacity	1 GB	800 MB	100 MB

Table 4-2

The Ins and Outs of Portable IT Systems	**Speed:** If you want to do things fast, choose a notebook first, a subnotebook second, and a PDA third.
ⓒhoosing between notebooks, subnotebooks, and personal digital assistants (PDAs) will depend on many things. Here are just a few for you to think about	**Size and Weight:** If "portability" is important, choose a PDA first, a subnotebook second, and a notebook third.
	Battery Life: Oddly enough, a subnotebook has the longest battery life (about 6 hours), followed by a notebook and then a PDA.
	Capabilities: Notebooks will run the greatest variety of application software. PDAs are dedicated for PIM software and some word processing, while subnotebooks are somewhere in between.
	Screen Resolution: Notebooks usually have the best screen resolution, followed by subnotebooks and then PDAs.

sometimes 6 inches high, 24 inches wide, and 15 inches deep! These systems also weighed in excess of 40 pounds. In fact, they were not even called portables—they were called "luggables."

Notebook systems are basically carry-around, battery-powered systems that offer you all the capabilities of a workstation, but to a lesser degree. Notebook systems today can process over 100 million instructions per second, and they offer other capabilities such as 1 billion bytes of disk storage, fax, color monitors, and multimedia. Notebook systems are excellent tools for you if you demand portability.

Personal digital assistants (PDAs) are portable IT systems designed mostly for personal information management. If you recall from Chapter 2, PIM software helps you manage information concerning contacts, schedules, tasks, and finances. PDAs typically weigh only about 2 pounds and can fit easily into a coat pocket or briefcase. Some PDAs today do offer you the ability to do limited note taking, document manipulation (word processing), and spreadsheet work, but don't expect to be able to do such memory-intensive tasks as presentation graphics.

Subnotebooks combine many of the rich capabilities of notebooks with the small size and portability of PDAs. Although you usually won't find all the capabilities of notebook systems on a subnotebook, subnotebooks do support color screens, fax transmission, and about 800 million characters of disk storage.

Subnotebooks are also smaller than notebooks but larger than PDAs. The average subnotebook is 1.5 inches high, 10 inches wide, and 7.5 inches deep.

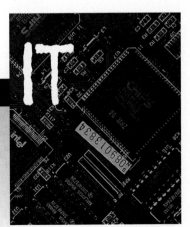

Discovering IT

Let's do a little fact-finding. Compare the cost of a notebook and a workstation that have the following characteristics. Which costs more? Why do you think this is true?

Characteristics

▶ **Pentium 75 MHz**

▶ **8 MB RAM**

▶ **520 MB Hard Drive**

▶ **Multimedia**

THE SMART CARD—A COMPUTER IN YOUR WALLET

Did you ever think we would have computers the size of a credit card that would fit into your wallet? Well, we do—they're called **smart cards**, and they're becoming increasingly popular. In Germany and Britain, for example, people carry smart cards that contain health information, including pictures of x-rays and MRI scans.

Smart cards are about the size of a standard credit card, but they contain a lot of high-tech extras. They contain a CPU, an operating system (on ROM), and a small amount of storage (about 64 KB). These cards are inserted into special slots in an IT system that helps update the information contained in the storage. You can already find smart cards being used for toll-road paying and in casinos.

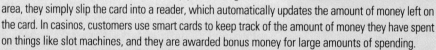

For toll-road paying, drivers purchase a card with a certain amount of money stored. Each time they pass through a toll area, they simply slip the card into a reader, which automatically updates the amount of money left on the card. In casinos, customers use smart cards to keep track of the amount of money they have spent on things like slot machines, and they are awarded bonus money for large amounts of spending.

We may all be carrying an IT system in our wallets some day. And you can expect business to take advantage of smart cards. Think about some of these possibilities:

▶ **Your school using smart cards to let you pay your tuition, buy books, pay for meals, and as a way of checking you into classes.**

▶ **Video rental stores using smart cards that allow you to check out videos without going to the front desk and then only requiring you to pay once at the end of every month.**

▶ **Automobiles in which you use your smart card to program the position of the seat and steering wheel, to program your maximum speed, and to track where you've been.**

▶ **Going to an interview with your résumé and letters of recommendation on a smart card instead of on printed paper.**

Just let your imagination run wild and see how many different uses of a smart card you can think of.

Subnotebooks also weigh only about 4 pounds. If you're thinking about using a portable IT system, Tables 4-1 and 4-2 may help you decide which is best for you.

Notebooks and subnotebooks are a lot like the word processing and desktop publishing software we discussed in Chapter 2. That is, much the same way the differences between word processing and desktop publishing software are becoming less obvious, so are the differences between notebooks and subnotebooks. Notebooks are becoming increasingly smaller while subnotebooks are gaining every day in power and function.

Three years from now, you may not even be able to find these two distinct categories of portable systems. And, who knows, five years from now, PDAs may not be a specific category of portable technologies.

The CPU and the internal memory are critical hardware components of your IT system. These two components handle complex behind-the-scenes tasks and greatly affect your productivity. Here are a few things to keep in mind to get the most out of your processing engine.

Buy for the Future

Many people today will undoubtedly purchase systems only to find that their needs quickly outgrow their system. It pays to consider the processing power and internal storage capacity you'll need in the future when buying today.

Let Software Requirements Drive Your Needs

Choosing the right system involves a series of related and simple steps:

1. **Determine your information processing needs.**
2. **Find the application software that will meet your needs.**
3. **Find an operating system to support your application software.**
4. **Choose the processing speed and internal memory capacity that will support your operating system and application software.**

In short, let your needs drive your application software selection, let your application software drive your operating system selection, and let your operating system and application software drive your CPU and internal memory selection.

Be Mobile in Your Work

You don't have to be at work to actually do work. Many people are finding that they can remain productive while working on the run using portable systems. If this is true for you, make sure you choose the right type of portable—a notebook, a subnotebook, or a PDA.

Personal Productivity

A leading multinational company once researched the following question: "What's it worth to gain an additional hour of effective work a day?" The answer may surprise you—60 percent of your salary. For you personally, an additional hour of effective work a day may mean the difference between an A and a B in a certain class.

Your advantage comes from working smart and making smart decisions about the technology you use. Many people don't make the right choice. Some of these people say IT is too expensive—oddly enough, so is a car. Sure, you can use a typewriter for your term papers and walk to work. But . . .

Now You Can . . .

1 Describe the role of the central processing unit (CPU) and internal memory in an IT system.

▶ *CPU:*

A part of the hardware in an IT system.

Processes information (based on software instructions).

Directs how all the hardware components work together.

▶ *Internal memory:*

A part of the hardware in an IT system.

Temporary storage area for information, application software, and operating system software that you are working with.

2 Describe CPUs, including the components of a CPU, the speed and capacity of a CPU, and the features of superscalar CPUs.

▶ *Components of a CPU:*

The *arithmetic/logic (A/L) unit,* which executes application software instructions.

The *control unit,* which interprets software instructions and tells the other hardware devices what to do.

▶ *Measurements:*

CPU size is measured in terms of the number of bytes that can be processed at one time. This measure is usually expressed in its bit equivalent.

CPU speed is measured in terms of the number of instructions that can be processed in a single second. Instructions per second are determined by the clock cycle speed expressed in megahertz (millions of clock cycles per second).

Superscalar CPUs (like the Pentium and PowerPC) can execute more than one instruction per clock cycle.

3 Identify the different types of internal memory, describe their function, and indicate how their capacity is measured.

▶ *Random access memory (RAM)* is the temporary storage area for information as well as for application and operating system software.

Cache memory is an area where frequently used software instructions and information are stored.

Virtual memory is permanent disk storage space used as "pseudo" RAM if large applications and files need to be split.

▶ *Read-only memory (ROM)* is the part of the internal memory that comes with certain system software instructions already built in. These are the instructions necessary to get your system working when you turn it on.

Programmable read-only memory (PROM) is special ROM that comes programmed specifically for you from the manufacturer.

Erasable programmable read-only memory (EPROM) can be changed by using a special ultraviolet light device. First, however, you must remove the internal EPROM chips.

Electrically erasable programmable read-only memory (EEPROM) can be quickly changed by using special software.

▶ *Measures of the internal memory* are by size or capacity expressed in bytes.

4 Understand the guidelines for purchasing the right CPU and amount of internal memory.

▶ *Buying the right CPU:*

Application software interface

Operating system software interface

Brand

Speed and size

▶ *Buying the right amount of internal memory:*

Find out your application software requirements.

Determine your operating system software requirements.

Internal memory is cheap

Upgrading is easy

5 Compare different portable IT systems.

▶ *Notebook* IT systems are carry-around, battery-powered systems that offer you all the capabilities of a workstation, but to a lesser degree. Notebooks can process over 100 million instructions per second and offer other capabilities such as 1 GB of disk storage, fax, color monitors, and multimedia.

▶ *Subnotebooks* combine many of the rich capabilities of notebooks with the small size of PDAs.

Subnotebooks support color monitors, fax, and about 800 million characters of disk storage.

▸ *PDAs* work best with personal information management software and let you do limited note taking, document manipulation (word processing), and spreadsheet work.

Key Terms

Arithmetic/Logic Unit (A/L Unit)

Billions of Instructions per Second (BIPS)

Binary Digit System

Bit

Byte

Cache Memory

Central Processing Unit (CPU)

Complex Instruction Set Computing (CISC)

Control Unit

Cycle

Data Bus

Electrically Erasable Programmable Read-Only Memory (EEPROM)

Erasable Programmable Read-Only Memory (EPROM)

Fault-Tolerant System

Firmware

Gigabyte (GB)

Internal Memory

Kilobyte (KB)

Megabyte (MB)

Megahertz (MHz)

Millions of Instructions per Second (MIPS)

Notebook

Parallel Processing

Pentium

Personal Digital Assistant (PDA)

PowerPC

Programmable Read-Only Memory (PROM)

Random Access Memory (RAM)

Read-Only Memory (ROM)

Reduced Instruction Set Computing (RISC)

Smart Card

Subnotebook

Superscalar CPU

Virtual Memory

Word

Self-Test

1. The processing engine has two parts—the _____ and the _____.

2. The _____ is the hardware that actually executes instructions, processes information, and directs how all the other hardware components work together.

3. The part of the CPU that interprets software instructions and sends out signals to tell the other devices what to do is called the:

   A. Arithmetic/logic unit

   B. Internal memory

   C. Read-only memory

   D. Control unit

   E. Random access memory

4. The internal memory is a temporary storage area that holds:

   A.

   B.

   C.

5. A group of _____ make up a _____, which is the same as a character to you.

6. CPU size is measured in terms of:

   A. Speed

   B. Instructions per second

   C. Clock cycle time

   D. Words

   E. None of the above

7. Clock cycle time is expressed in _____, which is millions of cycles per second.

8. _____ technologies are most prevalent on business workstations and portable systems, while _____ technologies dominate engineering and scientific workstation environments.

9. Internal memory capacity is measured in terms of _____.

10. 1,024 characters is equivalent to a:

    A. Kilobyte

    B. Megabyte

    C. Gigabyte

    D. Terabyte

11. The permanent internal memory storage area that contains certain system software instructions used when you turn on your system is called:

    A. Virtual memory

    B. Cache memory

    C. RAM

    D. ROM

    E. Control unit

12. Read-only memory (ROM) is also called _____.

13. What are three types of ROM memory?

    A.

    B.

    C.

14. _____ are portable IT systems whose capabilities most closely resemble those of a workstation IT system.

15. Which type of portable IT system is the smallest?

    A. Notebook

    B. Subnotebook

    C. Personal digital assistant (PDA)

    D. They are all the same size

Short-Answer Questions

1. How is your brain equivalent to an IT system processing engine?

2. How do arithmetic and logic operations differ?

3. How do superscalar CPUs differ from other CPUs?

4. Why is ROM called firmware?

5. How does your application software determine how much internal memory you need?

6. What are the three types of portable IT systems? How do they differ in size and capability?

Discussion Questions and Projects

1. People say that the "intelligence" of an IT system is the CPU. Do you think the CPU is really intelligent? If you don't, can you foresee a time when IT systems might actually be intelligent? Why or why not?

2. Superscalar CPUs offer a great speed advantage over traditional CPU technologies. Do you think superscalar CPUs will eventually replace traditional CPUs altogether? Why or why not?

3. A 60-MHz Pentium CPU can execute up to 112 million instructions in a single second. Doesn't that seem like a lot? Do you think technology has progressed to the point that we cannot take full advantage of it? If we don't need that much speed, why are manufacturers continuing to build faster CPUs?

Solutions to Self-Test: (1) central processing unit (CPU), internal memory—p. 107; (2) central processing unit (CPU)—p. 107; (3) D—p. 107; (4) information you are working with, application software you are using, operating system software—p. 108; (5) bits, byte—p. 111; (6) D—p. 112; (7) megahertz—p. 113; (8) complex instruction set computing (CISC), reduced instruction set computing (RISC)—p. 115; (9) bytes—p. 118; (10) A—p. 118; (11) D—p. 119; (12) firmware—p. 120; (13) programmable read-only memory (PROM), erasable programmable read-only memory (EPROM), electrically erasable programmable read-only memory (EEPROM)— p. 120; (14) notebooks—p. 122; (15) C—p. 123.

Working in a Group

1. Have each member in your group browse through a different computer magazine to answer the questions below. Then, as a group, compile your answers for a short presentation to the class.

   A. What are currently the most popular CPUs?

   B. What are their clock speeds?

   C. What are their sizes?

   D. How do they compare in cost?

2. Below, we've listed many popular application software packages for IBM and compatible computers. Find out how much internal memory is required to run these packages. Also list the version associated with each package, and refer to Chapter 2 to determine the application software type for each.

Application Software	Application Software Type	Version	Internal Memory
Adobe PageMaker			
Borland dBASE			
Borland Paradox			
CorelDRAW			
Intuit Quicken			
Lotus 1-2-3			
Lotus AmiPro			
Microsoft Access			
Microsoft Excel			
Microsoft FoxPro			
Microsoft Word			
Quattro Pro			
WordPerfect			
Harvard Graphics			

Cruising the Net

1 Search the Web using the key word *pentium*. Describe what types of information you found.

2 Connect to the Web page for the Apple Power Macintosh/PowerPC information at http://apple.com/ppc/ppchome.html or Gopher to Apple Computer Higher Education gopher server. What are the processing speeds (MHz) of various Power Macintosh models?

3 Conduct a Net search to see if you can find the memory requirements for new operating system software. (Hint: Connect to the Web page for Microsoft at http://www.microsoft.com/).

4 How good are portables for cruising the Net while on the road? Do some research to see how notebooks, sub-notebooks, and PDAs differ in offering you access to the Internet. Also, do portables offer as much accessibility as workstations?

Storage Devices and Databases:

Organizing Your World

Your Objectives for This Chapter

1 Compare the types of permanent storage devices, including magnetic, optical, and magneto-optical.

2 Describe tape storage devices and their role in an IT system.   **3** Understand the guidelines for purchasing storage devices.   **4** Explain the advantages of databases and DBMSs over file management systems.   **5** Describe the subsystems of a database management system and their function.

Have you ever found yourself searching around your home or office for a piece of paper or file that contains important information? Well, we all have, and it's frustrating. In fact, according to the International Institute of Speakers and Speechwriters, one survey revealed that the average executive wastes four weeks a year looking for items that have been misfiled, mislabeled, or misplaced. Four weeks—that's more time than the average executive spends on vacation.

Misplacing information is only one problem—arranging it in the most logical fashion is yet another. Think about writing a term paper. Basically, you do some research in the library, copy several magazine articles, check out a few books, and make note cards concerning information you found in reference material. Now you've got the information you need, but the problem is how to organize it.

You see, having the right information is not enough—you must also have it logically and physically organized so that you can easily access it and make the most sense of it. In the information age in which you live, time, as well as information, is money. Having the right information and being able to put your hands on it quickly will increase your productivity and add to the bottom-line performance of your organization.

Figure 5-1

**Your Focus in This Chapter:
Storage Devices and
Databases**

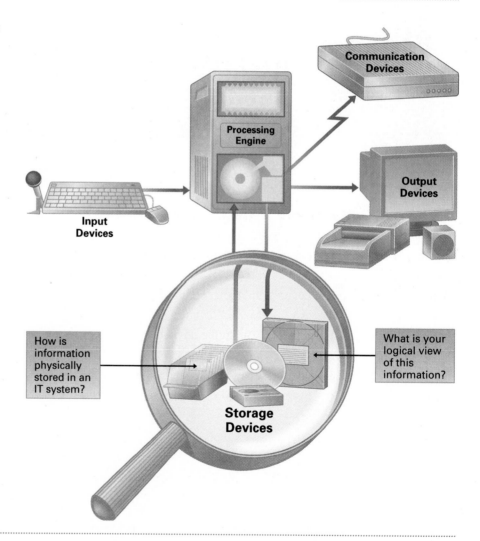

In this chapter, we're going to focus on the logical and physical organization of information (see Figure 5-1). Once you've got the right information, you must physically store it so that you can get to it easily and make changes as needed. You must also logically organize your information so that it makes sense to you. For example, while writing your term paper, do you want to organize your research material by topic? Date? Author? How do you catalog it all?

You should notice here that we are interested in both the physical and logical views of information. The physical view deals with how information is stored on storage devices within an IT system, while the logical view deals with how you arrange information while you're working with it. Let's first look at the physical view of information and the types of storage devices that you'll find on IT systems. Then we'll turn to databases and database management systems—tools for logically organizing information.

Storage Devices

In Chapter 4 we discussed RAM internal memory and described it as being temporary or volatile. That is, whenever you turn off your system, the contents (information and software) of RAM are erased. Your system must have a way of more permanently storing information and software so that you can retrieve and use them at a later time—that is the role of storage devices. **Storage devices** are hardware devices that more permanently store information and software on IT systems. You will commonly see terms like *permanent, nonvolatile, secondary,* and *auxiliary* used to describe these types of hardware devices—we'll simply call them storage devices.

Storage devices actually consist of two physical parts: (1) the storage medium on which information and software are stored, and (2) the device that reads and writes to and from the storage medium. It's no different than taking notes in class or listening to a CD. For note taking, (1) your paper or notebook is the storage medium on which you record your notes, and (2) your pen or pencil is the device that you use for recording and changing your notes. When listening to a CD, (1) the CD is the storage medium for the music, and (2) the CD player is the device that reads from the CD.

Storage devices can be categorized in two ways: by their method of storage and by their method of access (see Table 5-1). *Method of storage* refers to the technology used to write information onto a storage medium. The most popular types of technology include magnetic, optical, and magneto-optical. Method of storage is similar to the method you use to record information on paper: typing, writing with a pen, or writing with a pencil.

Method of access refers to the order in which information is written to and read from the storage medium—direct and sequential. To understand access methods, consider the difference between cassette tapes and CDs. Cassettes are sequential because you cannot listen to a certain song without first listening to or passing over (using fast forward) all songs preceding it. CDs, on the other hand, use a direct method of access because you can, for instance, listen to the third song by going directly to it and bypassing the first two songs.

Like cassettes and CDs, most storage devices are either disk or tape. Disk storage devices use a direct method of access and magnetic, optical, and magneto-optical methods of storage. Tape storage devices use a sequential method of access and magnetic method of storage. Let's consider disk storage devices first, and then we'll look at tape storage devices and their role in an IT system.

Table 5-1

Categorizing Storage Devices

Storage Device	Method of Storage			Method of Access	
	Magnetic	**Optical**	**Magneto-Optical**	**Sequential**	**Direct**
Floppy Disk	X			X	X
Internal Hard Disk	X			X	X
Hard Disk Cartridge	X			X	X
Hardcard	X			X	X
CD-ROM		X		X	X
Erasable Optical Disk (EOD)			X	X	X
Tape	X			X	
Flash Memory	X			X	X
Holographic	?	?	?	X	X

Disk Storage Devices

Disk storage devices are the most common type of storage device used in today's IT systems. These storage devices are so named because of the shape of their storage medium. The storage medium is called a **disk**—a round platter on which information is written on tracks in the form of concentric circles (something very similar to CDs, as Figure 5-2 shows). Information is stored and retrieved by a device called a **disk drive**. The disk drive rotates the disk and moves a read-write mechanism over the tracks.

The storage capacity of disk storage devices is measured in the same way as the internal memory—in kilobytes, megabytes, gigabytes, but also terabytes (roughly 1 trillion characters). Disk storage devices can use magnetic, optical, or magneto-optical methods of storage. These methods determine the storage capacity of disk storage devices.

Magnetic Disk Storage Devices. **Magnetic disk storage devices** represent information on a disk by creating electromagnetic charges on a metallic oxide film covering the surface of the disk storage medium. The presence of a magnetic charge represents an on bit (1), and the absence of a magnetic charge represents an off bit (0). The greatest advantage of magnetic disk storage devices is that the disk drive can easily change information on a magnetic disk by altering the electromagnetic charges that have been previously stored.

The storage capacity of magnetic disks ranges from a few hundred kilobytes to several gigabytes (billions of characters). Types of magnetic disks include floppy disks, internal hard disks, hard disk cartridges or packs, and hardcards.

Floppy disks (sometimes called *diskettes*) are circular, flexible plastic platters protected by a jacket—the plastic platter is rotated within the jacket while inside the disk drive. The most popular floppy disks come in 5.25" and 3.5" sizes. The 5.25" disks come in a flexible jacket, while the 3.5" disks are stored in a hard plastic jacket (see Figure 5-3).

The smaller, 3.5" disks are quickly replacing the 5.25" disks as the primary floppy disk on workstations and portables for many reasons. First, since they are smaller, they are easier to carry. Second, because they are contained within a hard plastic jacket, 3.5" disks are less susceptible to physical damage. And third, even

Figure 5-2

The Physical Characteristics of Magnetic Disks

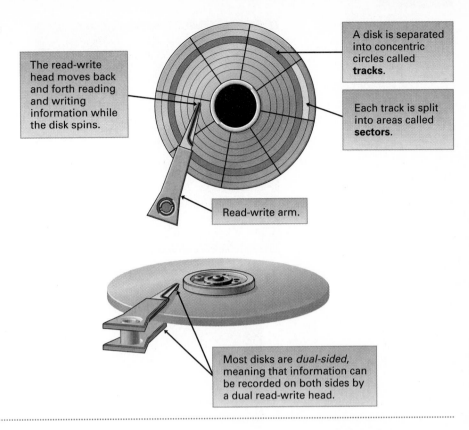

The read-write head moves back and forth reading and writing information while the disk spins.

A disk is separated into concentric circles called **tracks**.

Each track is split into areas called **sectors**.

Read-write arm.

Most disks are *dual-sided*, meaning that information can be recorded on both sides by a dual read-write head.

though 3.5" disks are physically smaller, they can store as much information as a 5.25" disk.

Hard disks are composed of many rigid platters, unlike floppy disks, which have one flexible plastic platter. Because hard disks have multiple platters, they can hold much more information than floppy disks. Hard disks include internal hard disks, hard disk cartridges or packs, and hardcards (see Figure 5-4).

An **internal hard disk** is a single unit that contains both the disk drive and the storage medium (multiple platters). An internal hard disk looks like part of the front panel of your system. Hard disk capacities range from 20 MB to over 2 GB. Nearly all workstations and portables come equipped with an internal hard disk.

A **hard disk cartridge** is a disk storage device in which the disk drive is separate from the hard disk storage medium. Hard disk cartridges provide you with the increased storage capacity of hard disks and the ability to change disk media, as with floppy disks. Although a single hard disk cartridge cannot hold the same amount of information as an internal hard disk (of the same size), hard disk cartridge systems can, in fact, store more information than an internal hard disk because you can use multiple disk cartridges. Hard disk cartridges for larger systems (minicomputers, mainframe computers, and supercomputers) are called **hard disk packs**.

Hardcards are a type of hard disk that can be added to your system by inserting it into an expansion slot. Hardcards are especially useful if you have a limited amount of physical room for your system or already have another hard disk. Hardcards, however, do not hold as much information as other types of hard disks.

Figure 5-3

Floppy Disk Characteristics

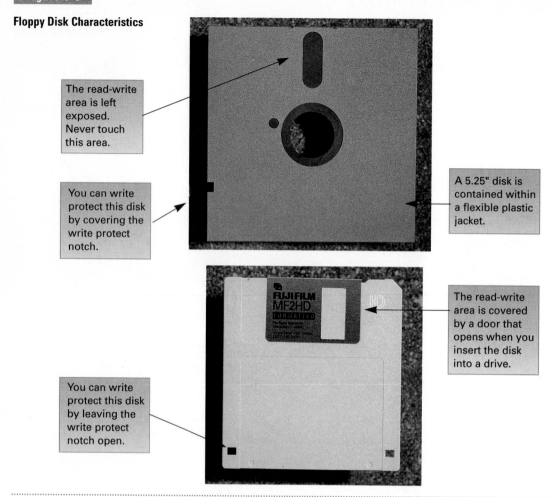

The read-write area is left exposed. Never touch this area.

You can write protect this disk by covering the write protect notch.

A 5.25" disk is contained within a flexible plastic jacket.

The read-write area is covered by a door that opens when you insert the disk into a drive.

You can write protect this disk by leaving the write protect notch open.

Optical Disk Storage Devices. Optical disk storage devices are one of the most promising types of storage devices today. **Optical disk storage devices** use a laser beam device to read and write information to an optical disk medium. The greatest advantage to optical disks is that more information can be stored as a result of the precision of laser technology. The typical CD-ROM, a type of optical disk, today holds 650 MB of information. Recently, however, a number of manufacturers have developed CDs that can hold as much as 6 GB of information—that's 6 billion

Table 5-2

Caring for Floppy Disks

Beware—floppy disks aren't tough. Keep these rules in mind:

Avoid Extreme Temperatures: Floppy disks are sensitive to extreme temperatures. Heat can cause them to melt, and the cold can cause them to become brittle and break.

Never Touch the Read-Write Area: Touching the read-write area (with anything—your finger, a pen, moisture, and so on) can ruin the oxide coating. If it's ruined, say good-bye to your information.

Avoid Putting Weight on Disks: Don't place objects on floppy disks—this may cause damage to the read-write area as well. Remember, floppy disks are supposed to be used for information storage, not beverage coasters!

Avoid Strong Magnetic Fields: Information is stored on disks through a process of magnetization. It only makes sense that if your disk comes close to a strong magnetic field, the information will be altered or lost.

Avoid Bending Disks: Magnetic disks are called "floppy" because the disk itself is made of a flexible plastic. They are not floppy because you can bend them or fold them in half.

Figure 5-4

Hard Disk Storage Devices

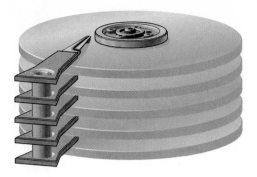

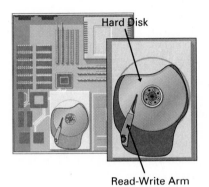

Hard Disk

Read-Write Arm

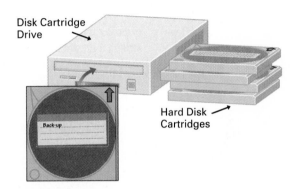

Disk Cartridge
Drive

Back-up

Hard Disk
Cartridges

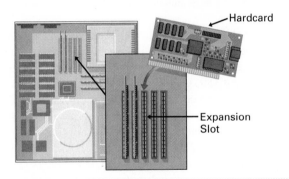

Hardcard

Expansion
Slot

characters of information. The most notable drawback to most types of optical disks is that information cannot be changed once it has been written to the optical disk medium. Let's see how it works.

The structure of an optical disk resembles that of a sandwich (see Figure 5-5). An optical disk has four layers—the two outer layers are protective plastic, and the two middle layers are a plastic read-write surface and a layer of reflective aluminum. When an optical disk is created, a laser burns pits into the bottom of the plastic read-write surface. These **pits** and the area between them called **lands** represent bits; a pit is bit 0 (off), and a land is bit 1 (on). A layer of reflective aluminum is then pressed onto the bottom of the plastic read-write surface, and the two protective layers of plastic are sandwiched around (one on the top and one on the bottom) the plastic read-write surface.

Suppose you had a notebook computer with a 340 MB hard drive and needed a total of 500 MB for storing information and hardware. Many people actually have this problem. Explore various ways to add more storage capacity. What did you find?

When reading information from an optical disk, the laser penetrates the layer of protective plastic and emits a light against the reflective aluminum. If the light strikes a pit, the light is scattered and not reflected back. If the light strikes a land, the light is reflected back and interpreted as an on bit (1).

The most popular type of optical disk is **compact disk read-only memory** or **CD-ROM.** Large databases of information are stored and distributed on CD-ROM disks. For example, many libraries have card catalogs on CD-ROM. You can even purchase Digital Directory Assistance's PhoneDisc PowerFinder CD-ROM and have over 91 million residential and business addresses and phone numbers at your fingertips. Financial service companies such as Standard & Poor's and Value Line store and distribute financial information on CD-ROM so investors and financial analysts can have fast and easy access to whatever information they need. CD-ROM is also the primary storage medium for multimedia applications and virtual reality.

CD-Recording. As we've already stated, the greatest drawback to optical disk storage is that you can't change the information once it's been recorded on disk. But that doesn't mean you can't create your own CD (see Table 5-4). You can—using **CD-recording** (CD-R) technology. To do this, though, you need special software and a special recording device for storing information on a CD.

Software for CD-R is called **premastering software**. Premastering software allows you to simulate a recorded CD on your magnetic hard disk before actually writing it to the CD. After using the premastering software to create your simulated CD, you use a special hardware CD writing device to create the lands and pits on a blank CD. Once you've created your own CD-ROM, you can only read from it; writing over existing information is still not possible.

Magneto-Optical Storage Devices. Magneto-optical storage devices combine the best of both magnetic and optical storage devices. **Magneto-optical (MO) storage**

Table 5-3

Caring for Hard Disk Storage Devices	
Caring for hard disks is not quite as tedious as caring for floppy disks, but don't forget to . . .	**Avoid Head Crashes:** A "head crash" occurs when the read-write mechanism comes into contact with the disk surface. If this happens, that part of the disk is usually destroyed. You can avoid head crashes by keeping your system relatively free from dust and avoiding quick, jerky motions when moving it.
	Avoid Strong Magnetic Fields: As with floppy disks, information is stored on a hard disk using a process of magnetization. Exposing the disk to a strong magnetic field may result in information alteration or, most likely, loss.
	Avoid Extreme Temperatures: Like floppy disks, hard disks are also sensitive to extreme temperatures (both heat and cold).

Figure 5-5

Information Storage on Optical Disks

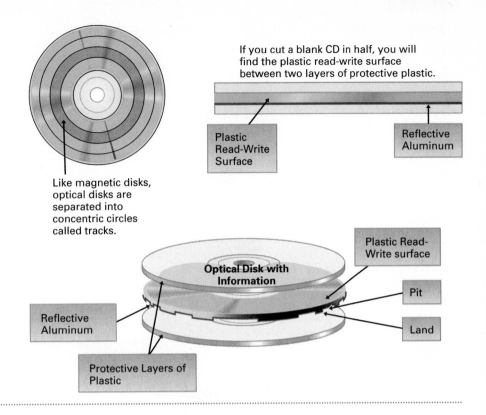

If you cut a blank CD in half, you will find the plastic read-write surface between two layers of protective plastic.

Plastic Read-Write Surface

Reflective Aluminum

Like magnetic disks, optical disks are separated into concentric circles called tracks.

Optical Disk with Information

Plastic Read-Write surface

Pit

Reflective Aluminum

Land

Protective Layers of Plastic

devices use a laser that allows information to be packed more densely, but they also use a form of magnetization that lets you change the stored information. The storage media used by magneto-optical storage devices are called **erasable optical disks** (EOD). Many IT analysts predict that a single EOD will soon be able to hold over 10 gigabytes of information.

EODs use a layer of crystalline metal alloy and a layer of reflective aluminum between two protective layers of plastic (see Figure 5-6). For writing, a laser heats the metal alloy, allowing the crystals to move. A writing mechanism (similar to a magnetic writing device) magnetically adjusts the alignment of the crystals. For reading, a laser pierces the protective plastic and emits a light toward the reflective

Table 5-4

Creating Your Own CD-ROM

Ⓨou might find it exciting to create you own CDs. If so, here are some guidelines to help you select the best CD-recording system for yourself.

Cost: CD-R technology is still relatively expensive. Complete CD-R systems (including premastering software and the CD-recording drive) cost anywhere from $1,500 to $5,000. That's expensive for just a toy. If you have time, wait a while — prices will drop.

Once Written to, Never Again: When you write to a CD, you'd better do it right the first time. Once you've written to a CD, you can't change it. Spend all the time you need during the premastering process to get the CD just the way you want it.

Consider a Dedicated Machine: Once you begin the writing process from the hard disk to the CD, the slightest interruption can ruin a CD. For example, if you happen to be in the process of writing to a CD and your system accepts an incoming fax, there is a good chance that the CD writing process will not be successful. Also, you must have enough available hard disk space (for premastering) to store the information you want to put on a CD. You might want to purchase a system just for creating CDs.

Premastering Software Flexibility: The premastering process is crucial for successful and professional CD development. Some premastering software packages are powerful and flexible, while others offer only a few capabilities. Buy the best, or be prepared to create only simple CDs.

Figure 5-6

Magneto-Optical Storage Devices

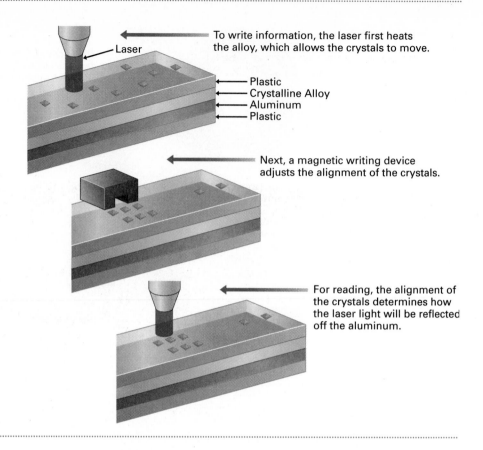

To write information, the laser first heats the alloy, which allows the crystals to move.

Laser

Plastic
Crystalline Alloy
Aluminum
Plastic

Next, a magnetic writing device adjusts the alignment of the crystals.

For reading, the alignment of the crystals determines how the laser light will be reflected off the aluminum.

aluminum. The reflected light passes back through the crystals, whose alignment determines the representation of an on bit (1) or an off bit (0).

Tape Storage Devices

Tape storage devices (simply called *tape drives*) use a magnetic method of storage and a sequential method of access to read and write information to and from a magnetic tape. These magnetic tapes are similar to cassette tapes. A magnetic tape for storage is split into columns that run up and down and tracks that run the length of the tape (see Figure 5-7). A read-write device stores in or reads a character or byte from each column. Each track for a given column stores one bit; a magnetized position is bit 1 (on), and a nonmagnetized position is bit 0 (off).

The amount of information that can be stored on a magnetic tape (called **tape density**) is measured in terms of **bytes per inch** (BPI). For example, a 9,600-BPI tape can store 9,600 bytes or characters per inch. If the tape were 3,600 feet long, it would be capable of storing roughly 400 million characters of information.

Tape drives use a sequential method of access because the read-write head must pass over all preceding information to get to the information you want. For instance, to obtain the information that begins in the 23rd inch, the read-write head must pass over the first 22 inches. Again, this is similar to a cassette tape—if you want to hear the fourth song, the read-write head must pass over (using fast forward) the first three songs.

Magneto-optical disks that are small enough to be used on portables are called *floptical disks* or *flopticals*. How much information can a floptical store? How does the cost of a floptical drive and disk compare to magnetic drives and disks? When would you choose to use a floptical disk as opposed to a regular magnetic disk?

Throughout this book, we have stressed the importance of information and IT systems to an organization and to you. Whether it's part of a strategic business plan, a payroll report, or your personal address list, information that is lost costs money. Actually, lost information costs *double*—it costs because you can no longer use it, and it costs money to get it back (see Table 5-5). Sometimes a price cannot be put on lost information because there is absolutely no way of *ever* it getting it back.

That's where tape drives come in (see Figure 5-8). Tape drives are used primarily for backing up information contained on other types of storage devices (for instance, your hard disk). That way, you'll have a copy of your information and software in case the original is lost or damaged. Let's look at some general guidelines for purchasing the right tape drive.

▶ **Don't consider cost:** Today's tape drives (the devices that read and write information to and from a tape) cost between $150 and $500. The more expensive ones obviously provide more flexibility and capabilities. Don't hesitate to spend the extra money—it's a small price to pay for exactly what you need and for peace of mind. Also, the tapes themselves only cost about $20.

Figure 5-7

Information on Magnetic Tape

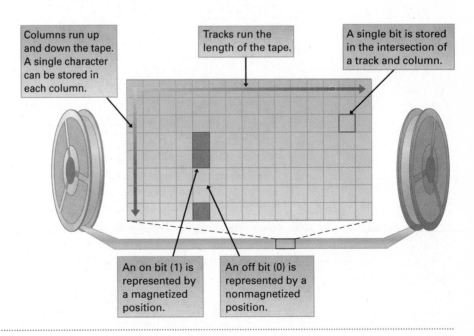

Columns run up and down the tape. A single character can be stored in each column.

Tracks run the length of the tape.

A single bit is stored in the intersection of a track and column.

An on bit (1) is represented by a magnetized position.

An off bit (0) is represented by a nonmagnetized position.

Storage Devices and Databases: Organizing Your World

Figure 5-8

Tape Drives

Storage tapes for workstations looks similar to VCR tapes, except they are about half the size. These small tapes can hold up to 2 billion characters of information and can back up a full hard disk in as little as 30 minutes. If you're considering buying a tape drive, here are some of the more popular ones.

	Colorado Jumbo 250	Colorado Jumbo Trakker 250	Exabyte FS1G	Iomega Tape250 Internal Plus	Iomega Tape250 Parallel Port	Tecmar TapePort 250
Type	Internal	External	Internal	Internal	External	External
Price	$159	$350	$715	$189	$325	$350
Capacity (MB)	250	250	1500	250	250	250
Tape Price	$23	$23	$25	3 for $65	3 for $65	5 for $145

Table 5-5

The Price of Not Having Information[1]

Information is big business today. When businesses lose access to their information, they lose money.

Industry	Revenues Lost (in Millions) Due to System Downtime
Manufacturing	$2,422
Banking	$230
Securities	$226
Telecommunications	$189
Travel/Transportation	$182
Retail	$99
Insurance	$25
Total	$3,373

▶ **Portability:** Some tape drives are built into your system (internal), while others may be easily moved from one system to another (external). External tape drives are slower than internal ones, but they offer the advantage of portability.

▶ **Tape capacity:** It would be ideal if you could back up all your information and software on only one tape—that will depend on the tape capacity of the tape drive you choose. Tape capacities range from 200 MB to 2 GB.

▶ **Backup speed:** The time it takes to perform a full system backup varies greatly among tape drives. Some tape drives can back up a 250-MB hard drive in as little as 5 minutes, while others will take as long as 75 minutes.

Table 5-6

Tips for Backing Up with Tape Drives	**Tapes Don't Last Forever:** Your tapes will eventually wear out. Change tapes every 50 backups or about every year. Remember, tapes don't cost much.
	Back Up Consistently: Develop a backup schedule and stay with it. Once it becomes a habit, you'll think nothing of the small amount of time it takes.
	Back Up on Autopilot: Many tape drives come with software that will automatically perform the backup for you. If so, take advantage of it.
	Back Up Frequently Changing Information: If you have some information that changes frequently, back it up more often than you would other information.
	Back Up Information and Software: Although your information may be the most important thing to you, don't forget the tools you use—operating system and application software.
	Back Up Twice: We recommend that you keep two backups of your most important software and information. The possibility does exist, however remote, that both your current system and backup could be lost or damaged.
	Tape Storing: The whole idea of backing up is to create a copy of your information and software in case the original is lost or damaged—possibly by fire, flooding, and even theft. It doesn't make much sense to have your backup destroyed along with your original because of a fire. Always store your tapes in a safe place other than in the same location as your IT system.

Alternative Storage Devices

Storage devices (both the storage media and the devices) are changing as rapidly as all other types of IT are; it was just a few years ago that CD-ROM became available. Let's take a brief look at two types of storage technologies that may play an important role in the future—flash memory and holographic storage.

Flash Memory. Flash memory has actually been around several years but has suffered from certain physical limitations and costs. **Flash memory** is a special permanent memory chip. It resembles RAM internal memory in look and size, but it doesn't lose its contents when you turn off your system. Flash memory, however, still takes up more room than a hard disk and costs about five times as much.

In spite of its drawbacks, many people believe that flash memory will continue to drop in size and price, making it a viable replacement for disk storage devices on portable systems. Today, flash memory is being used in smart cards and personal digital assistants (PDAs).

Holographic Storage. Everyone knows what holograms are—those interesting images that can be turned at different angles to show different pictures. Holograms use a three-dimensional surface to store different pictures on different faces of crystal-like objects. **Holographic storage** in an IT system is a radical departure from traditional disk or tape storage methods. With disk and tape, information is stored and retrieved one character at a time. With holographic storage devices, however, a "picture" of all the information would be stored and retrieved with a single read or write.

Disk and tape use a two-dimensional approach for storage—length and width. Holographic storage devices, on the other hand, also incorporate depth for additional storage capacity, so that they are three dimensional. Some initial experiments with holographic storage have proven that an entire set of encyclopedias can be stored holographically on one square inch that has the thickness (depth) of a credit card!

Suppose you own a marketing research firm that specializes in gathering and distributing mailing lists for businesses in your state. What type of information would be important? Which storage technology would be best for storing and distributing this type of information? What factors did you consider in making your decision?

Which Storage Technology Is Best for You?

Like many other people, you may be pondering the question, "So which storage technology is best for me?" To answer simply, you need three storage technologies for sure, and possibly a fourth and fifth. At a very minimum you need CD-ROM, an internal hard disk, and a floppy disk. These are storage technologies that no system would be complete without. And, quite possibly, depending on what you want to do, you should carefully evaluate CD-R and a tape drive.

CD-ROM, a hard disk, and a floppy disk drive are standard storage hardware today. On CD-ROM you'll find an enormous amount of information relating to every conceivable topic such as biology, dinosaurs, geography, ancient African civilizations, and new customs laws that will affect how export businesses work. Don't cut yourself short by neglecting to get CD-ROM—it's much easier to research these topics in the comfort of your own home than in a library with thousands of books. You'll also find that a great deal of software is being distributed through CD-ROM as opposed to floppy disks. The cost of CD-ROM drives is now just a few hundred dollars. The CDs themselves are getting so cheap that when you buy a system, it will typically include up to a dozen CD games, encyclopedias, and atlases free.

A hard disk is simply the "standard" of storage technologies today. Although magneto-optical disk quality and viability are increasing, a good hard disk will serve you well for many years. When you're figuring out the size of hard disk you need, remember one simple rule—buy absolutely as much capacity as you can afford. It's kind of like the old adage, "Your expenses will always rise to meet your income." No matter how much extra storage space you have on a hard disk, you'll always find new information and software to use it up.

The last minimum requirement is to always have a floppy disk drive—probably a 3.5" drive. Floppy disks make it easy for you to share information with your friends and colleagues, and most software still comes on floppy disk as opposed to CD-ROM. 5.25" disk drives are on their way out—even if it costs an extra $100, make sure that you get a 3.5" drive built into your system.

A hard disk is simply the "standard" of storage technologies today.

Whether you get CD-R or a tape drive will be a question of cost, capability, and necessity. CD-R technology is still relatively expensive, but costs are dropping every day. If you want the capability of creating your own CDs, you have to be prepared to spend the extra money for premastering software and the special hardware device that creates CDs. If you can't decide whether to get CD-R, you probably don't really need it. Wait a while as CD-R prices drop and as their function and ease of use increase.

Tape drives give you the ability to back up your information and software quicker and easier than doing so with floppy disks. The question is, "Is the savings in time worth the cost?" The answer to that question is absolutely, "Yes!" Whether your system is for personal or business use, always have a tape drive, and, more importantly, use it frequently.

The physical storage of information in an IT system is certainly important because you want to be able to store all the information and software you need, to access that information and software quickly, and to maintain backups. However, your logical view of information is perhaps even more important than the physical storage of information. In the next section, we cover how you logically view information and why your logical view will affect your ability to access physically stored information.

Your Logical View of Information

Let's suppose that you and four of your friends have decided to go into the mail-order CD business. Everyone has decided that you will be president of the company and that the other four will manage the functions of sales, billing, shipping, and inventory, respectively. Basically, your company works like this:

1 The inventory manager will order the most popular CDs and provide a list of those CDs to the sales and billing managers.

2 The sales manager is responsible for finding customers, sending out advertising flyers, and making sales. All sales information will be forwarded to the shipping manager so that the CDs can be sent out. If sales are made on credit, the sales manager will notify the billing manager.

3 The shipping manager is responsible for sending out shipments of CDs and letting the inventory manager know which CDs have been removed from inventory.

4 The billing manager is responsible for sending out bills and collecting the money from credit sales. If certain customers are delinquent in their payments, the sales manager will be notified so that credit sales to those customers can be stopped.

As it turns out, you have a great plan and find that sales are booming. Soon, though, you begin getting complaints from your managers that there is not enough time to handle all the paperwork. The solution seems simple: you authorize the purchase of an IT system for each of your managers (see Figure 5-9). Now they have their own system with all the information they need right at their fingertips. That way, the sales manager can automatically generate flyers for all customers, the billing manager can easily keep track of billing addresses and delinquent customers, and so on.

Everything seems to be working smoothly again, and you're beginning to think that retirement is just around the corner. One morning, though, you get two disturbing phone calls—one from a customer and one from the billing manager. It seems that one of your customers placed an order and then moved before receiving the order. However, he or she contacted the sales manager, who in turn made the address change but failed to notify the shipping manager. In the meantime, the shipping manager filled the order and sent it out to the wrong address. Needless to say, your customer is unhappy and wants the money back immediately and is also considering turning you over to the Better Business Bureau.

If that wasn't enough, the phone call from the billing manager may even be worse. It seems that one of your customers has not paid a bill in some time. The

Figure 5-9

**Getting Technology in the
Hands of Your Managers**

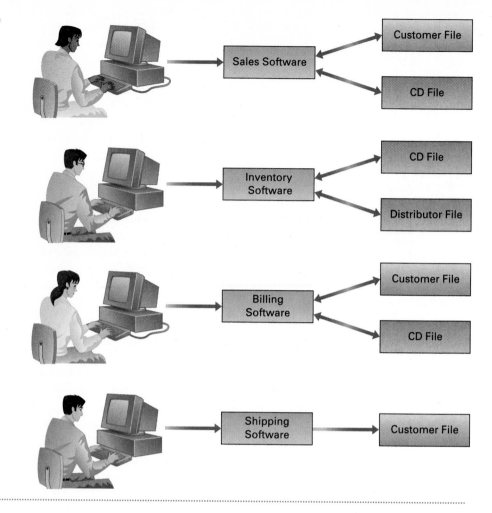

billing manager sent a notice to the sales manager to stop credit sales to that customer. The sales manager, however, didn't receive the notice in time and made a $2,500 sale on credit to that customer. Obviously, you'll never see that money!

All of a sudden, your brilliant business plan doesn't sound so brilliant. You might be surprised, but there are actually thousands of businesses that operate this way, and it's a wonder that some of them are still in business (many aren't). It's not that their business plans are bad—it's a matter of simply not having the right information in the right place at the right time. Let's go back and evaluate the structure and location of the information in your CD mail-order business.

In Figure 5-10, you can see the information used by each of your managers. Consider the information used by the sales manager to understand how we logically view information. To the sales manager, as to everyone else, the smallest unit with which information can logically be represented is a character (such as the "R" in R&B). A logical grouping of characters is called a **field** (for instance, the CD_CATEGORY field for CDs). A **record** is a logical grouping of related fields. For example, all the fields in row 3 describe the record for the CD titled *Hard Rock*.

Finally, a **file** is a logical grouping of records that describe similar things (CDs in this case). As you can see, everyone has his or her own files of informa-

Figure 5-10

**Your CD Mail-Order
Business Information**

Sales Manager Information
CD File

CD_NUM	CD_NAME	CD_GROUP	CD_CATEGORY	CD_PRICE
12345	Easy Sea	Var. Artists	Easy Listening	$11.99
32456	In the Heart	49th St. Gang	R&B	$12.99
65789	Hard Rock	The Bees	Rock	$17.95
43567	Soul Rap	49th St. Gang	R&B	$14.75
76543	Down & Out	Billy Jim	Country	$11.99
•	•	•	•	•
•	•	•	•	•
•	•	•	•	•

Customer File

CUST_NUM	CUST_NAME	CUST_ADDR	CUST_PHONE
4356	Pamela Kertuck	P.O. Box 342	478-8876
8799	Bill Williams	1277 W. 12th St.	478-4532
4590	Benjamin Travers	5467 Magnolia	481-5432
•	•	•	•
•	•	•	•
•	•	•	•

Inventory Information

CD_NUM	CD_COST	CD_QOH	CD_DIST_NUM

DIST_NUM	DIST_NAME	DIST_ADDR	DIST_PHONE

Billing Information

CUST_NUM	CUST_NAME	CUST_ADDR	CUST_PHONE

CD_NUM	CD_NAME	CD_PRICE

Shipping Information

CUST_NUM	CUST_NAME	CUST_ADDR

tion, which seems to make sense. And last, the software that each person uses to maintain the information in the files is called a **file management system** (Refer to Figure 5-9). So your company has an inventory file management system, a billing file management system, a sales file management system, and a shipping file management system.

There are three basic problems with using files and file management systems. First, the same information may be stored in many different places. This problem is known as **data redundancy**. For example, Bill Williams's phone number appears in three different places. Second, because the same information exists in several places, there is the issue of data integrity. **Data integrity** deals with the correctness of the information as it appears in an IT system. The integrity of the information was lost for your unhappy customer because, although the person's address was correct in the sales file, it was not correct in the shipping file; this is the loss of data integrity.

Finally, file management systems create a great dependency between the structure of the information and the software that maintains it. This problem is called **program-to-data dependency**. You see, the structure of the information contained in the files must be stored with the software. So, for example, it you wanted to store new information about a customer, such as a four-digit zip code extension, not only would the three customer files have to be changed but the three file management systems as well. When the federal government proposed changing the zip codes to eight numbers and to use characters, one IT industry association estimated it would cost companies over $12 billion to change all their file management systems.

Databases and Database Management Systems

Because of the problems associated with file management systems, many people began to toy with the idea of storing all the organization's information in one place and providing software that anyone could use to access any of the information. Today, these concepts are known as a database and a database management system. A **database** is a group of related files, and a **database management system** (DBMS) is the software designed to create, store, and manipulate a database (see Figure 5-11).

The concept of a DBMS is directly analogous to a library's card catalogs. The author catalog uniquely identifies a title, edition, date, and physical location. The title index uniquely identifies, author, edition, and so on. If a book is deleted, its author card is removed. Where a DBMS goes further is in automatically deleting the title card as well.

Figure 5-11

Database Management Systems and a Database

❶n a database environment, all information is stored in one place—the database. The data dictionary is also stored with the information. The data dictionary provides the structural description of the information. The database management system provides software that everyone can use to submit information requests, changes to the information, and changes to the structure of the information.

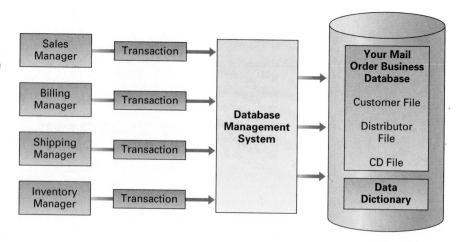

A DBMS also goes beyond just cross-referencing author, title, and subject categories. A DBMS can reference information in incredibly complex ways, even down to the level of the equivalent of individual words. So you could ask, "What books contain any sentences with the word *France* and also *agriculture?*" Some DBMSs even take into account synonyms and will locate *French agriculture* as well as *agriculture in France.*

A Data Dictionary

In addition to being composed of a group of related files, a database contains a data dictionary. A **data dictionary** contains the description of the structure of the information found in the files of a database. Consider CD_NUM in the CD file in Figure 5-12, which shows a partial database for your CD mail-order business. The data dictionary for this field would indicate that it is numeric with five digits, that it must be present, and that it must be unique among all CDs. Because CD_NUM is unique, it is a primary key. A **primary key** is a field in a given file that uniquely describes each record. By defining CD_NUM as the primary key, you would be saying that a given CD number describes only one CD. In the student records at your school, your ID number is the likely primary key. Your birthday can't be, nor can your name; neither is unique.

Let's also take a look at the CD_DIST_NUM in the CD file. Its data dictionary would identify it as a numeric field with three digits. The data dictionary would also contain the fact that CD_DIST_NUM in the CD file must exist in DIST_NUM in the Distributor file. In specifying these details, you have defined the logical rela-

Figure 5-12

The Data Dictionary

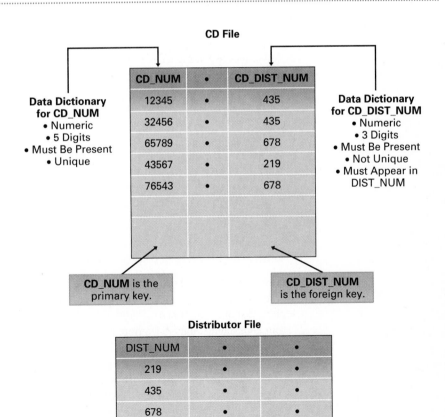

SAVING LIVES WITH INFORMATION

Kaiser Permanente is the largest and oldest HMO in the United States. It has remained the largest HMO for many years by providing the best possible health care services at an affordable price. Recently, Kaiser took a bold step toward a new method of improving and prolonging the lives of diabetics. No, it's not a new medical procedure or drug. It's called an information warehouse—a large computer database.

In 1994, Kaiser set up a database of the 84,000 diabetics among its 2.4 million Northern California members. The database includes information from billing, admitting, various lab departments, doctors' records, and surveys. What Kaiser found was alarming, to say the least.

Although diabetes is the leading cause of blindness, Kaiser discovered that only 15 percent to 20 percent of diabetic patients were getting their eyes checked routinely. Kaiser also discovered that medical practitioners in routine office visits were not making strong enough recommendations for combating obesity and stress, two factors that make diabetes even worse. As a result, Kaiser is enforcing more rigorous eye-screening programs and setting up patient support groups for obesity and stress.

Now, you may be wondering how this helps Kaiser—it certainly helps diabetics, but what does it do for Kaiser? Simply put, money spent on preventive programs now means less money spent on expensive diabetic treatments in the future.

The key to the success of the Kaiser program is IT—tools such as databases and DBMSs that support the concept of the information warehouse. And Kaiser isn't the only health care organization realizing the advantage of good IT. The industry as a whole is expected to spend more than $6 billion in 1996 on information technology.[2]

tionship between the CD file and the Distributor file. That is, each CD must be distributed by a distributor that appears in the Distributor file.

As you can see, the data dictionary is just as important as the database itself. Most notably, the data dictionary can help enforce integrity constraints. **Integrity constraints** are restrictions placed on the information so that it will always be correct. For example, after specifying that CD_NUM must be unique, you could not enter two CDs with the same CD number. Likewise, because CD_DIST_NUM in the CD file must match a distributor number in the Distributor file, you would not be able to assign a distributor number that did not exist to a CD. Being able to use the data dictionary to enforce integrity constraints is a major advantage of databases.

Subsystems of a Database Management System

Now that we've looked at some of the characteristics of a database, let's turn to the software that creates, stores, and manipulates a database—the database management system, sometimes called the *database manager*. A DBMS is composed of four subsystems: data definition, data manipulation, data administration, and application generation (see Figure 5-13).

The **data definition subsystem** of a DBMS helps you create and maintain the data dictionary and define the structure of the files in a database (see Figure 5-14). Because the data definition subsystem stores the data dictionary with the information in a database, program-to-data dependency is eliminated. The **data manipulation subsystem** of a DBMS lets you add and delete records, change field contents, and

Storage Devices and Databases: Organizing Your World

Figure 5-13

**Software Subsystems
of a Database Management
System**

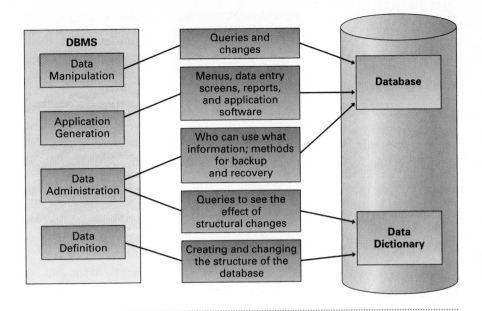

view the database. You can view the information in a database by using queries (such as DISPLAY ALL CD_NAME FOR CD_DIST_NUM = 456) or simple, easy-to-use commands such as BROWSE, LIST, and SELECT.

The **data administration subsystem** of a DBMS lets you perform such tasks as establish users of a database, specify who can update which information, and develop methods for backing up the database and recovering the database in the event of a failure. The data administration subsystem also lets you query the data dictionary so that you can determine the impact of proposed changes to the structure of the stored information. Finally, the **application generation subsystem** contains tools that help you create and update other features such as menus, data entry screen forms, reports, and application software. The application generation subsystem may also contain **code generators**. Code generators let you specify the desired results of information processing requests. The code generator then produces the application software to meet those needs. This lets you be more concerned with what information you need and less about how to obtain that information.

Database Models

There are four different ways to logically represent and store information in the form of a database—hierarchical, network, relational, and object-oriented. We refer to these different ways as *models*. The hierarchical and network models were the first models used to develop databases. Today, however, most organizations are using the relational and object-oriented models to design databases (see Figure 5-15). Let's see how these two work.

The Relational Database Model. The **relational database model** uses a series of tables or files called **relations** to store information (see Figure 5-16). Each relation contains information about a class of similar entities. An **entity** is something about which you wish to store information and that can be uniquely described with a primary key (such as a student, a car, a class, and so on). A grouping of similar

Figure 5-14

Data Definition Subsystem

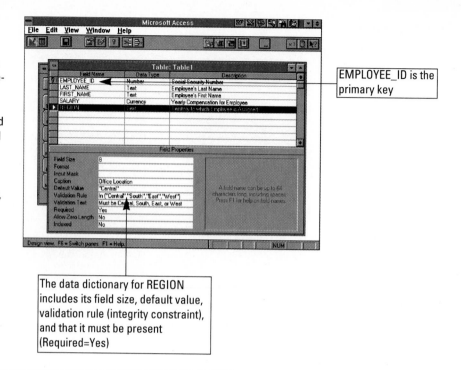

This is an example of the data definition subsystem in Access, a database management system made by Microsoft. Notice that EMPLOYEE_ID has been defined as the primary key. The Field Properties box shows the characteristics of the highlighted field (REGION). The field size is eight characters, and the caption for the data entry screen is "Office Location." The default value is "Central," and the only valid entries are "Central," "South," "East," or "West." The error message that will appear on the screen if the wrong office location is entered is contained in the "Validation Text" sub-box.

EMPLOYEE_ID is the primary key

The data dictionary for REGION includes its field size, default value, validation rule (integrity constraint), and that it must be present (Required=Yes)

entities is called an **entity class**. In your mail-order CD business, for example, CD is an entity class, and CD 12345 is a specific entity that can be uniquely described by its CD number (12345). The columns of information (called **attributes**) in each relation relate only to the primary key for each row.

The relationships between the relations are kept in the form of foreign keys (defined by the data dictionary). A **foreign key** is a primary key of one relation that appears as an attribute in another relation. For instance, the DIST_NUM attribute is

Figure 5-15

The Increasing Use of DBMSs

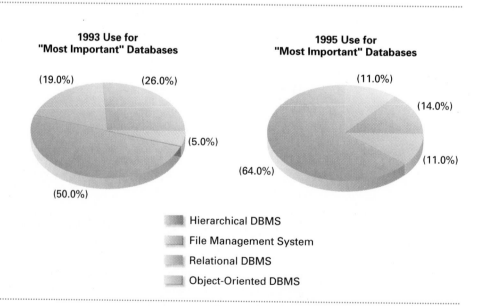

1993 Use for "Most Important" Databases

(19.0%) (26.0%)

(5.0%)

(50.0%)

1995 Use for "Most Important" Databases

(11.0%)

(14.0%)

(11.0%)

(64.0%)

■ Hierarchical DBMS
■ File Management System
■ Relational DBMS
■ Object-Oriented DBMS

Figure 5-16

The Relational Database Model

CD Relation

CD_NUM	CD_NAME	CD_GROUP	CD_CATEGORY	CD_DIST_NUM	QOH	CD_COST	CD_PRICE
12345	Easy Sea	Var. Artists	Easy Listening	435	11	$7.50	$11.99
32456	In the Heart	49th St. Gang	R&B	435	13	$6.25	$12.99
65789	Hard Rock	The Bees	Rock	678	2	$9.75	$17.95
43567	Soul Rap	49th St. Gang	R&B	219	0	$8.00	$14.75
76543	Down & Out	Billy Jim	Country	678	4	$8.00	$11.99
•	•	•	•	•	•	•	•

Distributor # is the primary key in the Distributor relation and the foreign key in the CD relation. Distributor # defines the relationship between CDs and distributors. What other attributes help define relationships?

Distributor Relation

DIST_NUM	DIST_NAME	DIST_ADDR	DIST_PHONE
219	Cinema Albums	1734 East. 2nd	871-2838
435	Pearl Records	P. O. Box 3456A	871-2000
505	Xanadu Music	P. O. Box 6533-T	478-5555
678	Vision Outlet	1297 Main St.	481-1912
•	•	•	•

Customer Relation

CUST_NUM	CUST_NAME	CUST_ADDR	CUST_PHONE
4356	Pamela Kertuck	P.O. Box 342	478-8876
8799	Bill Williams	1277 W. 12th St.	478-4532
4590	Benjamin Travers	5467 Magnolia	481-5432
•	•	•	•

Purchases Relation

PUR_NUM	PUR_DATE	PUR_CUST_NUM	PUR_CD_NUM	PUR_QUAN
2478	11/02/95	8799	32456	2
2479	11/02/95	4590	65789	1
2480	11/03/95	4356	65789	3
2481	11/04/95	8799	76543	1
•	•	•	•	•

the primary key in the Distributor relation. It is also the foreign key in the CD relation. This helps you keep track of which CDs come from which distributors.

FINDING A GOLD MINE IN A DATABASE

Finding a *what* in a database? That's right — a gold mine! Today, businesses are using powerful DBMS software to mine their databases for information, information that is as valuable as gold. It's called *data mining.* Let's consider the case of AT&T and the AT&T Universal Card. Let's face it — there are a lot of credit cards out there, and most offer similar interest rates, use capabilities, and repayment options. So it's difficult for a company to offer a new credit card and hope to attract a large customer base.

In 1990, that's just what AT&T did. By using its large database of long-distance calling customers, AT&T was able to identify customers with good credit ratings, with active purchase histories, and who would most likely use another credit card. The end result was more than a million credit card customers in the first three months and over $1 billion worth of charges per month at the end of the first year. There is gold in a database, and it's called information.

AT&T is just one example of literally hundreds of companies that are fine-tuning their marketing efforts by keeping detailed records on their customers and using that information to target groups of customers for new products or services. Not only that, companies are also purchasing lists of information to generate potential customers. When you graduate, for example, you'll probably receive numerous credit card applications in the mail. You see, credit card companies know that people with an education make good credit customers (for the most part).

Data mining is only possible because of databases that store vast amounts of information and DBMS that provides an easy to use interface to accessing that information. The next time you receive mail that's obviously been generated by a computer (junk mail to some people), ask yourself "How did they get my information, and how did they decide that I would be a good target for this kind of mail?[3]

Primary keys and foreign keys help enforce certain integrity constraints. For example, you would not be able to delete Pearl Records (distributor 435) in the Distributor relation if Pearl Records appeared as a foreign key in the CD relation. Also, you would not be able to enter a new distributor record with 435 as the primary key because 435 is already being used as the primary key for Pearl Records.

The Object-Oriented Database Model. The **object-oriented database model** uses a series of objects similar to relations in the relational database model. Objects,

Discovering IT

Put yourself in the shoes of a teacher; suppose you wanted to build a relational database for tracking students and grades. What are the important entity classes (Hint: Class is one)? What would be the attributes and primary key for each entity class? If you wanted to let students access your database to see their grades, what type of processing restrictions would you place on them? Which subsystem of your DBMS would you use to place the restrictions?

however, differ from relations in one important way. **Objects** contain fields that describe each record, but they also contain a list of services or actions that can be used to add, change, or delete records and fields. These services or actions are called **methods**.

Therefore, objects encapsulate both information and methods in one place. For your CD mail-order business, one object would be Purchases (see Figure 5-17). The Purchases object would contain information such as purchase number, purchase date, customer number, CD number, and quantity purchased. Along with those pieces of information, such methods as ADD_NEW_PURCHASE, UPDATE_ EXISTING_ PURCHASE, and DELETE_PURCHASE would be stored. The steps to be taken to carry out these methods would be stored in a **method dictionary**, something similar to a data dictionary.

For instance, if you wanted to record a sale to Pamela Kertuck for two Easy Sea CDs, you would submit a message. That message would be "Add new purchase to CUST_NUM 4356 for 2 of CD_NUM 12345." When the DBMS receives the message, it executes the steps contained in the method dictionary for that message.

Another feature of the object-oriented database model is inheritance. **Inheritance** can be used to pass information from one object to another; inherited information, however, is not stored in the inheriting object. For example, when the sale was made to Pamela Kertuck, the Purchases object for that transaction inherited information from other objects such as CD_PRICE from the CD object.

The object-oriented database model is also better equipped to handle complex data types such as graphics, drawings, and images than the relational database model. Many businesses involved in computer-aided design and computer-aided

---

Figure 5-17

The Object-Oriented Database Model

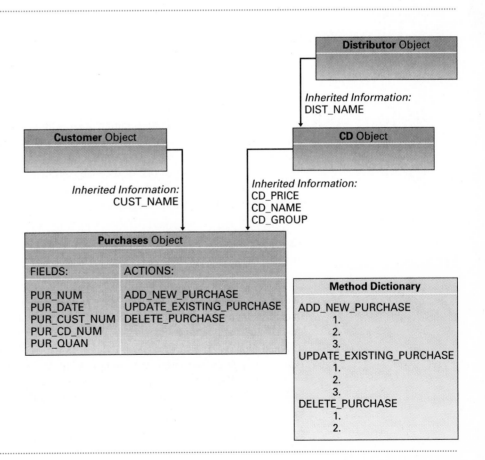

A Relational Database That Stretches

Diane Henderson owns a small business in Denver, Colorado, that specializes in developing exercise programs for people who have discomfort in some part of their body (tightness in the neck, lower back pain, tired eyes, sore hands, and so on). She has developed a relational database that helps her keep track of customers, stretching exercises, the tools used while stretching (for example, rope or bar), and the areas of discomfort.

When Diane first started thinking about building a database, she decided to create fields in her customer file that would list the areas of discomfort. Then she found out that today's DBMSs will store pictures. So she simply created a picture of a body and allowed the customer to shade the areas of discomfort. Then Diane created a field in her database that was a picture of a body. She could then shade the picture of the body on the computer just as her customer did on paper.

Now, when Diane displays the information for a particular customer, she immediately sees a body map on the screen. This type of visualization helps her recommend stretching exercises and tools. Her latest project is to create pictures of the stretching exercises instead of just instructions. Then she'll be able to quickly print them and give them to her customers. We guess Diane really has figured out how to make a database stretch.

---

manufacturing (CAD/CAM) are increasingly turning to the object-oriented database model as a way to store both part schematics and instructions for manufacturing and assembling those parts in an object. In a manufacturing environment, CAD information (the design of part schematics) and CAM instructions (how to manufacture and assemble parts into an eventual product) are not easily separated and therefore need to be stored together.

CAD/CAM is actually quite similar to the process that you would go through if you purchased a mountain bike and then had to assemble it. When you open the packaging, you won't find two separate documents—one that describes the parts and one that describes the instructions. Instead, you would find one document that includes a description of the parts combined with the instructions to put them together. CAD/CAM is just one of the many applications that lend themselves to an object-oriented model. In the future, you can expect to see more applications developed using the object-oriented database model.

Defining the Correct Structure of a Database

Creating a database with the correct structure is a key issue, not only in business but for you as well. A database with the correct structure will not only help you overcome many of the limitations of file management systems, it will also help you quickly and easily change information and find the right information in the most efficient manner. The most common approach to defining the structure of a database is through the use of an entity-relationship (E-R) diagram.

An **E-R diagram** is a graphical method of representing entity classes, attributes, and relationships. An E-R diagram uses six basic symbols:

1 A rectangle to denote an entity class

2 A diamond to denote a relationship between two entity classes

3 An oval to denote attributes

4 A line to connect symbols

5 A "1" to denote a single occurrence

6 An "M" to denote multiple occurrences

In Figure 5-18, you can see the E-R diagram for your CD mail-order business.

When you build an E-R diagram, the first step is to define the entity classes. For your CD mail-order business, the entity classes are CD, DISTRIBUTOR, CUSTOMER, and PURCHASE. The second step is to define and model the relationships between the entity classes—this is the step in which you make use of diamonds, 1s, and Ms. For example, the relationship between CD and DISTRIBUTOR would be read as follows:

1 A DISTRIBUTOR can distribute many CDs, and

2 A CD can be distributed by only one DISTRIBUTOR.

The final step is to identify which attributes belong to which entity classes. Again, in Figure 5-18, you can see that the CUSTOMER entity class has the following

Figure 5-18

An Entity-Relationship Diagram

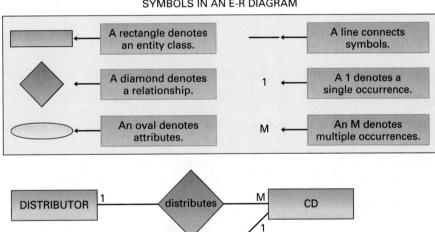

SYMBOLS IN AN E-R DIAGRAM

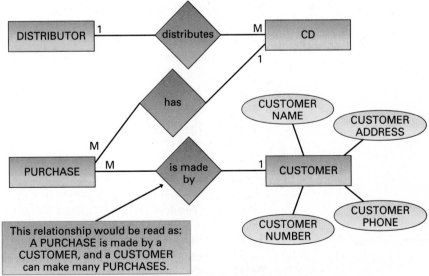

attributes: CUSTOMER NUMBER, CUSTOMER NAME, CUSTOMER ADDRESS, and CUSTOMER PHONE.

Once you have completed your E-R diagram, the entity classes become files (relations in the relational database model), and you would then go through a process called normalization. Normalization is used to verify that the attributes are in the appropriate files and that you have all of the files you need. How normalization works is outside the coverage of this book. If you're interested in databases and how normalization works, we encourage you to pick up almost any modern database management system book and read more about normalization.

Advantages of Databases and Database Management Systems

Databases and DBMSs are designed to overcome the limitations of file management systems and enhance your effectiveness. Advantages of databases and DBMSs include:

▶ **Eliminating program-to-data dependency:** Using a DBMS, the organization of the information (the data dictionary) is stored with the information, not the application software. As a result, the application software does not have to be changed if there is a change in the organization of the information itself (for example, adding the four-digit zip code extension).

▶ **Reducing data redundancy:** Because all information is stored in one place (the database), data redundancy is greatly reduced, if not eliminated altogether.

▶ **Supporting data sharing:** Having all of the information in one place means that all people, regardless of the department they are in or what their jobs are, can gain access to the information they need.

▶ **Ensuring data integrity:** The integrity of information in a database is much higher than in file management systems. This is true because only one copy of the information is stored, which requires only one change if necessary.

▶ **Ensuring data security:** DBMS software can allow information access to only those people who actually need it. Although all the information is stored in one place, this helps ensure that only the right people see the right information. For example, using the data administration subsystem, you could specify that the shipping manager could look at, but not change, information relating to the cost and price of CDs.

▶ **Viewing information as a resource:** Storing all information in a database has helped organizations recognize that information and IT are valuable resources. Organizations need to realize that information—like materials, inventory, and personnel—is a resource that can be used to make money. We'll address the importance of information to organizations in detail in Chapter 8.

▶ **Database and DBMS concepts are consistent:** In the class you're taking, you may learn how to use a personal DBMS such as Access, dBase, FoxPro, or Paradox. In business, you'll find these same packages as well as ones (for example, DB/2 and Oracle) designed to work specifically on larger systems and handle organizational databases. Your advantage is that the same concepts that apply to personal DBMSs and databases also apply to these larger systems. No matter what type of database and DBMS environment you work in, the concepts of primary keys, integrity constraints, foreign keys, and so on are exactly the same.

Storing all the organization's information in one place (a database) has created the need for managing the database. **Data administration** (or database administration) is the function within the organization that is responsible for ensuring that the correct information is available to users and applications when needed. The data administration function falls into three categories: communicating with people, planning and development, and establishing policies and procedures.

Communicating with People

The purpose of using databases and DBMSs is to support the information and information processing needs of people. People's needs should be the driving force behind the development and use of the organization's database. Communicating with these people involves: (1) accepting new information and information processing requests, (2) assessing the viability of those requests, (3) notifying people of any changes that are being or have been made to the database and the way the DBMS works, and (4) training.

Planning and Development

Careful planning must go into the development of databases and database applications to ensure that everyone's needs are being met. Planning and development considerations include:

▶ Determining what new databases and database applications need to be developed

▶ Monitoring the development process

▶ Monitoring the creation of the data dictionary

▶ Approving new application development

TOMORROW'S BUSINESS ADVANTAGE

DBMSs THAT TALK ANY LANGUAGE

In Chapter 9, we're going to explore today's global economy and how global businesses are operating all over the world. It's a substantial opportunity for everyone, including you, because new markets are opening up and new jobs are becoming available in other countries every day. The only question is, how does a business unit in Taiwan share its information with the head office that's located in Milan, Italy? Somewhere along the line, someone has to translate the information.

But what if DBMSs were designed in such a way that you could choose the language—English, Cantonese, Italian, whatever—that you wanted to work in. When someone else in a foreign country electronically received your information, he would simply choose his language and be able to immediately see what you had done in a different language.

There is actually some software available today that will let you type a letter in one language and then translate it into another, but with a database that contains people names and product names, the translation process is much more difficult. In fact, right now you could say it's impossible.

When DBMSs that can understand and translate into any language become available, you can expect to see global businesses take advantage of them in a big way.

Online Databases

Imagine having vast amounts of different information at your fingertips. This possibility exists through online databases. Online databases are information repositories supported by the government, private institutions, and private interest groups. These sources are available to you for a small setup fee and either a monthly charge or a charge per information request. Can you imagine gathering all your material for a research paper in the comfort of your own home? Well, you can, and it will definitely increase your productivity and probably your grade.

We have included a brief list of online databases. When you have the chance, you should learn what these and other online databases have to offer.

CLAIMS: Three separate databases that list more than 2.3 million U.S. patents that have been issued.

MEDIS: Complete text of various journals, textbooks, and other databases dealing with all areas of medicine.

Dow Jones QuickSearch: Company information, current stock quotes, financial overviews, income statements, and company versus industry performance.

Magazine Index: References for more than 500 well-known magazines on current events, the arts, sports, business, technology, and other topics.

Business Dateline: Articles appearing in more than 350 regional business publications from the United States and Canada.

Peterson's College Database: A directory of colleges and universities in the United States and Canada.

Federal News Service: Transcripts of all federal and government press conferences, speeches, and interviews.

Ei Compendex Plus: Information on various disciplines of engineering, from marine to chemical to electrical to nuclear.

CENDATA: Statistical data from the U.S. Census Bureau, including demographic data from the 1990 census.

LEXIS: Legal information.

INSPEC: More than 4 million records covering international literature on physics, electronics, and computer technology.

SEC Online: Coverage of annual reports, 10Ks, and proxy filings for more than 5,600 companies, all listed on the NYSE, Amex, or NASDAQ exchange.

PAIS International: A bibliographic index of public policy publications in business, economics, law, finance, government, political science, and related fields.

Investext: Financial and market reports written by industry analysts from investment banks and financial research organizations.

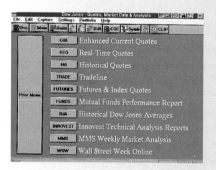

▶ Ensuring that testing is successful and complete

▶ Making sure that there is adequate hardware to support new databases and database applications

Table 5-7

IT Jobs in the Database Area

IT specialists who deal with databases and DBMSs are among the highest-paid IT professionals. In the table, we've listed three different IT jobs in the database area, along with their overall average salary and average salary in 17 industries.[4]

Salary	Database Manager	Database Analyst	Database Security Administrator/Analyst
Overall Average[a]	$58,453	$52,844	$73,279
By Industry:			
Banking	$72,583	$52,928	$52,583
Distribution	$73,500	$63,000	$53,500
Insurance	$64,875	$57,187	$49,200
Transportation	$54,000	$48,750	$54,000
Utilities	$51,750	$50,678	$44,000
Government	$58,205	$52,821	$48,256
Education	$63,066	$50,146	$44,678
Retail	$63,000	$39,875	$51,149
Hardware/Software	$57,000	$50,125	NA
Chemical	$67,000	$58,500	$59,127
Food/Beverage	$53,000	$48,000	NA
Agriculture	$59,000	$56,000	$49,000
Metal/Plastics	$62,750	$49,275	$51,000

[a]Includes year-end bonuses.

Establishing Policies and Procedures

Policies and procedures for interacting with databases and database applications are one of the most often overlooked functions. These policies and procedures, however, are crucial for successful database and database application development and use. Policies and procedures must be developed for:

- Ensuring the integrity of the information
- Determining error control and recovery operations
- Evaluating database performance
- Developing databases and database applications
- Backing up and storing databases and database applications
- Ensuring security and privacy

The distinction between logical and physical information is a key one in the IT field. The entire history of information management deals with the provision of tools (such as DBMSs) that extend your ability to work at the logical level of information organization and not to have to know anything at all about the physical level.

Viewing Information Logically

DBMSs are by far the most complex software in the IT toolkit. They also involve substantial overhead during use—in terms of both processing and storage. Managing IT information for you, then, is a delicate balancing act between efficiency and effectiveness. Consider major airlines such as United and American Airlines, whose reservations systems process close to 2,000 transactions a second.

If you added just one-tenth of a second of overhead to each of these, it would be like having cars on the New Jersey turnpike in rush hour sit for an extra minute at a toll booth; traffic would gridlock. Information storage for IT systems is crucial—this includes both the physical and logical aspects of information storage. Your ability to retrieve information quickly and store it for extended periods will increase your effectiveness in whatever you do.

At the personal level, your use of a DBMS will probably not be like gridlocking the traffic on the New Jersey turnpike. From a business point of view, however, the wrong choice of a DBMS or database model might start a processing-inefficient avalanche that cannot be stopped, short of literally pulling the plug on the whole system.

Being Able to Get What You Need

Your ability to obtain the exact information you need will help you in whatever you do. This includes not only having the right information stored, but also, and perhaps more important, having the information stored in such a way that you can easily and quickly access it with the appropriate software. Whether you use a file management system or a DBMS, make sure that your information is stored in the most logical and accessible fashion.

Making Changes When They Occur

You store information to reflect a real-world environment. Those environments are changing every day, which means that your information must also change; if it does not, it will be of little use. Make sure that the way you logically store information will support quick and easy updating.

Physical Information Storage

Knowing, in detail, about the physical storage of information is becoming less and less of an issue. Sure, you still need a general knowledge of how different types of devices work and how different storage media physically store information. Of greatest importance, however, are simply cost, capacity, and keeping backups.

Now You Can. . .

1 Compare the types of permanent storage devices, including magnetic, optical, and magneto-optical.

▶ *Magnetic:*

Floppy disks are circular, flexible plastic platters protected by a jacket.

An *internal hard disk* is a single unit that contains both the disk drive and the storage medium.

A *hard disk cartridge* is a unit in which the disk drive is separate from the hard disk storage medium.

Hard disk packs are hard disk cartridges for large systems.

Hardcards are a special type of hard disk that can be inserted into an expansion slot.

▶ *Optical:*

CD-ROM uses a laser beam to read and write information. It is read-only.

▶ *Magneto-optical:*

Erasable optical disks use both magnetization and optical storage technologies so that you can create and change whatever information you want.

2 Describe tape storage devices and their role in an IT system.

▶ *Tape storage devices* use a magnetic method of storage and a sequential method of access to read and write information to and from a magnetic tape. They are similar to cassette tapes.

▶ Magnetic tape storage is used primarily as a means of *backing up* information and software contained on other types of storage devices.

3 Understand the guidelines for purchasing storage devices.

▶ *Have at least three:*

CD-ROM

A *hard disk*

A *floppy disk*

▶ *And perhaps:*

CD-recording

A *tape storage device*

4 Explain the advantages of databases and DBMSs over file management systems.

▶ *Eliminating program-to-data dependency:* By creating and maintaining a data dictionary stored with the database and not the software.

▶ *Reducing data redundancy:* By storing only one copy of information in the database.

▶ *Supporting data sharing:* By allowing people, regardless of their position or location, to access the database by using the DBMS software.

▶ *Ensuring data integrity:* By storing only one copy of the information, which requires only one change.

▶ *Ensuring data security:* By using the data administration subsystem to specify who can access what information.

▶ *Viewing information as a resource:* By helping the organization see that information is a resource that can be used to make money.

▶ *Database and DBMS concepts are consistent:* No matter what type of database and DBMS environment you work in, the concepts of primary keys, integrity constraints, foreign keys, and so on are exactly the same.

5 Describe the subsystems of a database management system and their function.

▶ *Data definition subsystem* helps you define the structure of the files in a database. This information is kept in the data dictionary, which is a part of the database itself.

▶ *Data manipulation subsystem* lets you add and delete records, change field contents, and view the database.

▶ *Data administration subsystem* supports such things as establishing new users, deciding who can update which information, and developing utilities for backup and error control and recovery.

▶ *Application generation subsystem* lets you specify what information you want to see without specifying how to get the information.

Key Terms

Application Generation Subsystem

Attribute

Bytes Per Inch (BPI)

CD-Recording (CD-R)

Code Generator

Compact Disk Read-Only Memory (CD-ROM)

Data Administration

Data Administration Subsystem

Data Definition Subsystem

Data Dictionary

Data Integrity

Data Manipulation Subsystem

Data Redundancy

Database

Database Management System (DBMS)

Disk

Disk Drive

Disk Storage Device

Entity

Entity-Relationship Diagram

Entity Class

Erasable Optical Disk (EOD)

Field

File

File Management System

Flash Memory

Floppy Disk

Foreign Key

Hardcard

Hard Disk

Hard Disk Cartridge

Hard Disk Pack

Holographic Storage

Inheritance

Integrity Constraint

Internal Hard Disk

Land

Magnetic Disk Storage Device

Magneto-Optical (MO) Storage Device

Method

Method Dictionary

Object

Object-Oriented Database Model

Optical Disk Storage Device

Pit

Premastering Software

Primary Key

Program-to-Data Dependency

Record

Relation

Relational Database Model

Sector

Storage Device

Tape Density

Tape Storage Device

Track

Self-Test

1. The three types of technology (methods of storage) used to write information onto a storage medium include:

   A.

   B.

   C.

2. Circular, flexible plastic platters protected by a jacket are called:

   A. Floppy disks

   B. Hardcards

   C. Internal hard disks

   D. Disk packs

   E. Flash memory

3. A _____ is a disk storage device in which the disk drive is separate from the hard disk storage medium, whereas an _____ is a single unit that contains both the disk drive and the storage medium.

4. The most popular type of optical disk is:

   A. Erasable optical disk

   B. Hard disk

   C. CD-ROM

   D. WORM

   E. Hologram

5. A type of storage device that uses only a sequential method of access is:

A. CD-ROM

B. Tape

C. Erasable optical disk

D. Erasable optical tape

E. Hologram

6. The amount of information that can be stored on a magnetic tape is measured in terms of _____.

7. A logical grouping of records is called a:

A. Field

B. Record

C. File

D. Database

E. Byte

8. A logical grouping of f̶ ̶ ̶ ̶alled a:

A. Field

B. Record

C. File

D. Database

E. Byte

9. _____ is software designed to create, store, and manipulate a _____.

10. The description of the structure of the information in a database is contained in the:

A. Data definition subsystem

B. Data dictionary

C. Structure dictionary

D. Method dictionary

11. _____ are restrictions placed on the information so that it will always be correct.

12. Objects encapsulate both _____ and _____ in one place.

13. The four subsystems of a DBMS include:

A.

B.

C.

D.

Cruising the Net

1 The Internet has many online databases. Pick one to explore that interests you and prepare a short report for the class that includes:

A. The name of the database

B. What type of information it has

C. ⌐ ⌐ service provider that offers the database

   ⌐ost (monthly charge and per-access fee, if any)

E. How to navigate to the database

2 Using the Internet, find an electronic library card catalog system. Query the card catalog system for all information relating to France's agricultural exports. How much information did you find? What steps did you have to go through? Were they easy or difficult?

3 Search the Internet for different newsgroup bulletin boards that post information about personal DBMSs such as dBASE and Paradox. How many different newsgroups did you find? What were some of the specific topics posted on the bulletin boards?

4 Access the Library of Congress Catalog (Telnet to locis.loc.gov) or access the Web page (telnet://locis.loc.gov). Do an author search on "Pitter, Keiko." How many entries did you find? What kind of books did this author write?

5 Perform a Net search on "floptical." Describe the resources you found. (Hint: For example, the Web page for Iomega Corporation is http://www.iomega.com/)

Solutions to Self-Test (1) magnetic, optical, magneto-optical—p. 133; (2) A—p. 134; (3) hard disk cartridge, internal hard disk—p. 135; (4) C—p. 136; (5) B—p. 140; (6) bytes per inch—p. 140; (7) C—p. 146; (8) D—p. 148; (9) database management system, database—p. 148; (10) B—p. 149; (11) integrity constraints—p. 150; (12) information, methods—p. 155; (13) data definition, data manipulation, data administration, application generation—p. 150; (14) data administration—p. 159.

14. _____ is the function within an organization that is responsible for ensuring that the correct information is available to users and applications when needed.

Short-Answer Questions

1. How does the physical organization of information differ from the logical organization of information?

2. How does the physical method of storage differ from the method of access?

3. Why are magnetic disks called "dual-sided"?

4. What is the difference between a pit and a land on an optical disk? Which represents an on bit and which represents an off bit?

5. How does tape differ from disk?

6. Why are CD-ROM, a floppy disk drive, and a hard disk considered the minimum storage technologies for you?

7. Why does lost information cost double?

8. What are the problems with file management systems?

Discussion Questions and Projects

1. Optical disk storage devices, such as CD-ROM, physically alter the platter when storing information—this is why they are considered "read only." How do you think optical disk manufacturers can change the way information is stored so that it can be easily changed? Do you think your ideas will ever come about?

2. Integrity constraints are restrictions placed on information so that it will always be correct. What integrity constraints would you suggest for the four files—CD, DISTRIBUTOR, CUSTOMER, and PURCHASES—for your CD mail-order business in Figure 5-16? If you could add additional processing constraints, who (of your managers) would you allow to create, change, and delete fields and records in each file?

3. In the table, we've listed many different sizes of magnetic disk storage devices. Complete the table to show the cost of each and the manufacturer. Did you obtain your information from a computer store or a mail-order business?

Size	Cost	Manufacturer
150 MB		
210 MB		
260 MB		
340 MB		
428 MB		
528 MB		
730 MB		
1050 MB		
1700 MB		
2100 MB		
2900 MB		

4. Suppose you were working at home and your hard disk "crashed." Investigate the various ways you might be able to restore your hard disk and retrieve your lost information. Did anyone you talked to ask if you had backed up your information and software?

Working in a Group

1. Interview a local business and determine whether it uses a file management system or a DBMS to keep track of information. Prepare a short report for the class that describes what you found. If the business uses a DBMS, find out which specific product it uses and the reasons why.

2. Put together a group of your friends and come up with your own business. What information would be important for you to keep track of? Now do some research and find a DBMS that will fit your needs. How are you going to divide the duties among you and your friends, and how does that affect what processing with the DBMS that each of you should be able to do?

6

Communications and Connectivity:

Living in a Networked World

Your Objectives for This Chapter:

1 Describe the different types of IT networks according to span of control, ownership, and geographic span. **2** Describe local area networks (LANs), including configurations, application software considerations, and communications protocols. **3** Describe the role of communication devices in an IT network. **4** Explain the responsibilities of the network administration team and identify the most appropriate participants. **5** Explain the "hot topics" in communications and connectivity that will shape the future of business and your life.

Introduction Bass Brewery is one of England's largest beer manufacturers. It produces more than 50 types of beer in more than 150 different packages. These include beer for domestic consumption, beer for international exporting, cask-conditioned beers, beer in pint packages, and the more U.S.-traditional six-packs, twelve-packs, and cases of beer. All these types of beer and packaging are necessary to maintain high levels of sales in a market that demands widely varying products and batch sizes.

Obviously, the type of ingredients, the timing of throwing the yeast, and the length of time the beer is allowed to ferment give Bass beers their distinctive, world-acclaimed flavor. Behind all this, however, is an automated state-of-the-art networked computer system that manages two facilities—the brewhouse and the packaging hall. The brewhouse is where the beer is manufactured, and the packaging hall is where the beer is placed in the appropriate containers with various labels attached. Using this networked computer system, Bass has reduced transition times to a different type of beer from hours to just a few minutes.

With a simple touch of a computer screen in the network, the production manager can switch all the production facilities to a new type of beer. This includes starting cleaning fluid throughout the brewhouse so there is no risk of contamination. Recipes are then electronically sent to the brewhouse vats, and information about bottling sizes and labels is electronically sent to the packaging hall. Throughout the process, both the automated brewhouse vats and the packaging hall electronically send production information back to the production manager.

The type of computer system employed by Bass is called an *IT network,* and IT networks are what we want to explore in this chapter (see Figure 6-1). The Bass network supports what is called *computer-integrated manufacturing (CIM)*—the complete design, testing, and manufacturing of products through the use of IT. If the work in the brewhouse and the packaging hall was not coordinated by a network, Bass would spend a great deal of time manually coordinating the effort between the two. This would ultimately lead to losses in productivity and to downtime.

Figure 6-1

Your Focus in This Chapter: Networks

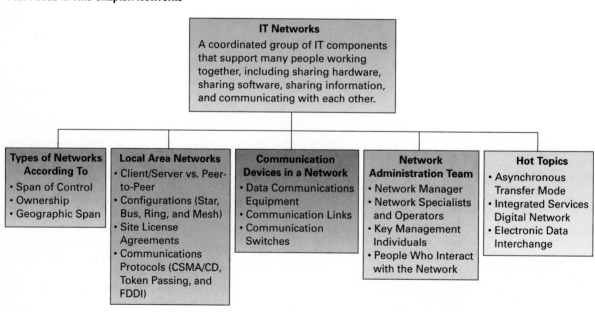

Networks are the most exciting and rapidly changing aspect of IT. Just as Bass has used IT networks to change the way it does business and produce beer, businesses and individuals all over the world are using IT networks to change the way they do business and communicate with other people. It's no exaggeration to say that telecommunications—the technologies and services on which IT networks are based—is the single most revolutionary force in business and society today. Of course, the very concepts of the Internet and the Information Superhighway rest on IT networks.

Indeed, you live in a networked society. Just as society would be in chaos if it lost the use of telephones (a type of communication network) or the highway system (a type of transportation network), it would also be in chaos if it lost the use of IT networks. Think about it for a moment—your school uses a network to coordinate the work of the registration office, the departments scheduling classes, the payroll office, and so on. Banks and other financial institutions use a worldwide computer network to transfer billions of dollars around the world every day and give you access to your money any time, day or night. The railroad industry uses a network to schedule freight shipments and assign rail tracks to incoming and outgoing trains at stations. The list of the uses of IT networks in the world today is endless.

Because networks are so prevalent, it's important that you understand the fundamentals of networks—what they can do, how they basically work, what types of networks are best for a given situation, and what the future of networking holds. You know how to make a long-distance phone call, dial 911 in an emergency, and obtain directory assistance because telephones are an integral part of your life. IT networks are also an integral part of your life; this means that you need to know their characteristics as well.

What Is an IT Network?

An **IT network** (which we'll refer to simply as a *network)* is a coordinated group of IT components that support many people working together. Networks allow people to:

1. Share hardware
2. Share software
3. Share information
4. Communicate with each other

Let's consider a network for your CD business from the previous chapter (see Figure 6-2). Having a network would mean needing to have only one laser printer that everyone could use (hardware sharing), providing only one copy of the DBMS (software sharing), having only one database that contains all the information (information sharing), and supporting electronic communication among everyone. As you can easily see, networks help businesses run more smoothly and efficiently, not to mention economically.

Networks are also increasingly central to providing convenience and service. An ATM in effect puts your bank branch at your fingertips. With 800 numbers you can make airline reservations, buy from catalogs, get credit card balances, and so on. The customer service agents who handle your purchase or reservation are able to do so because they are linked by networks to the systems that have the needed information and software to process your transactions. Let's look at some examples of how networks are being used.

Telecom—the Dutch telephone company—recently installed a network that brings together four separate systems for making new telephone connections for its

Figure 6-2

Your CD Business Network

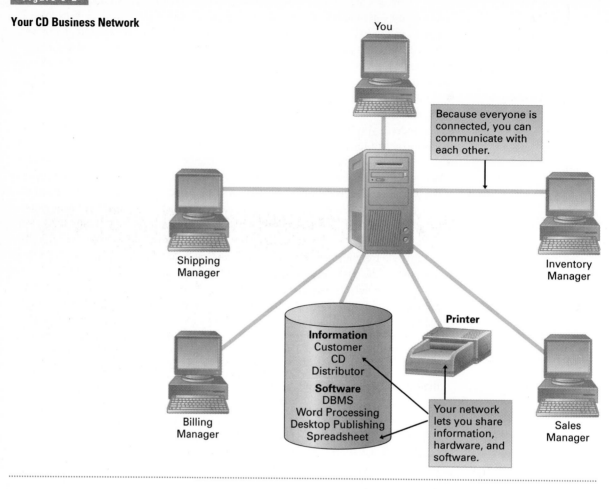

You

Because everyone is connected, you can communicate with each other.

Shipping Manager

Inventory Manager

Printer

Information
Customer
CD
Distributor

Software
DBMS
Word Processing
Desktop Publishing
Spreadsheet

Billing Manager

Your network lets you share information, hardware, and software.

Sales Manager

customers. These four separate systems include customer information, local connection information, credit checking, and a database of installed equipment. Without a network, customer service agents would be forced to look at and use four separate screens of information. Simply put, no work would ever get done, resulting in unhappy customers. Because of the new network, customer service agents look at only one screen, fill out only a single form, and can provide a telephone connection in one to two days.

The Nationwide Banking Society (NBS) has created a network of multimedia kiosks that essentially become virtual bank branches. Using these multimedia kiosks (located in such diverse areas as bus terminals, airports, and shopping malls), customers can explore NBS's financial products, such as mortgages and insurance. Customers "walk through" the virtual door to the institution by touching the screen. Once inside the "virtual branch," they explore services by touching parts of the screen. At any time, a customer can get help by touching a picture of a member of NBS's staff.

Many businesses are exploring the use of intelligent networks. An **intelligent network** is a special network that converts POTS (plain old telephone services) to PANS (pretty awesome new stuff). Intelligent networks basically know where you are, who you are, and who you want to get in touch with and why. For example, if you wanted to dine Chinese, an intelligent network would tell you where the closest

Chinese restaurant was—sometimes using a computer-generated voice. If you were working at home, you would simply tell an intelligent network what services you have access to while at work and it would provide the same services to you at home.

Banks are beginning to use ATMs as a personal messaging service for you. The worldwide ATM system is a network that lets you process banking-related transactions anywhere at any time. But what if your bank needed to verify a signature on a check? Instead of trying to reach you at your home or office, banks can print personal messages on your ATM transaction receipt. Banks can even notify you via ATM that your bank loan was approved or tell you that it's time to renew your certificates of deposit.

What we've just told you is only a small part of how businesses are using IT networks. Networks are fundamental for business success today. The most important challenge facing businesses as they use networks is deciding which type of network to use. That's where your knowledge of networks—how they work, their characteristics, and their advantages and disadvantages—gives you a definite advantage. If you can make informed choices regarding networks and know best how to exploit the advantages of networks, you will become invaluable.

Types of Networks

Countless networks exist today all over the world. These networks range from complex systems composed of thousands of people, millions of dollars of equipment, and endless miles of cabling all the way down to simple systems where two people share the same printer.

When an organization decides to implement a network, it must decide on the specific operating characteristics of the network that will best fit its needs and then build the network accordingly. No two organizations work in exactly the same way, so why should they have identical networks? If you think about it, that means the chances are good that each network is unique, because no two organizations will have identical operating requirements. That's why we say that networking is helping to build the *new organization* (as well as your new life). Networks can be distinguished in three different ways: span of control, ownership, and geographic span.

According to Span of Control

Span of control describes the number of CPUs in a network that help manage how the network functions and how people communicate with each other and process information. Span of control is also called *functional control* or *location of control*. Span of control can be centralized, distributed, or hybrid (see Figure 6-3). Centralized, distributed, and hybrid networks are also referred to as *network architectures*.

A **centralized network** has one main CPU that processes all information requests and handles communication. The main CPU in a centralized network is usually a mainframe or minicomputer capable of handling the processing workload of many people simultaneously. People interface with the CPU (called the *host computer)* by using any of the input and output devices we discussed in Chapter 3 as well as by using a terminal.

A **terminal** is a hardware device combining a keyboard and monitor. Terminals that have no storage or processing capabilities are called *dumb terminals.* Because dumb terminals do not have any processing capabilities, they must be connected to a host computer that can perform any processing functions necessary. Some terminals, however, do have limited processing capabilities—these are called *intelligent terminals.*

Figure 6-3

Centralized, Distributed, and Hybrid Networks

Centralized Network

The **host computer** (usually a mainframe or minicomputer) handles all information processing, manages communication, and stores all software and information.

Terminals are connected to the host computer. These terminals rely on the host computer to handle all information processing.

Distributed Network

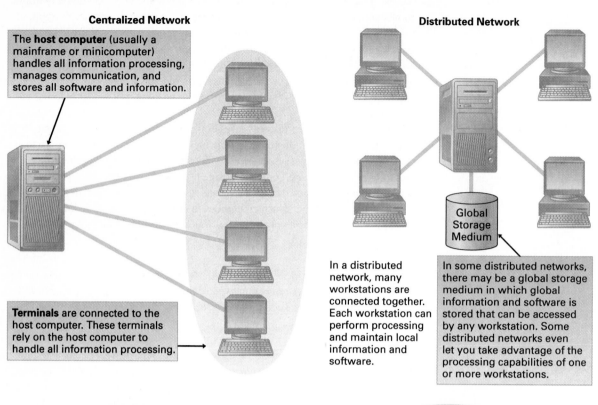

In a distributed network, many workstations are connected together. Each workstation can perform processing and maintain local information and software.

In some distributed networks, there may be a global storage medium in which global information and software is stored that can be accessed by any workstation. Some distributed networks even let you take advantage of the processing capabilities of one or more workstations.

Global Storage Medium

Hybrid Network

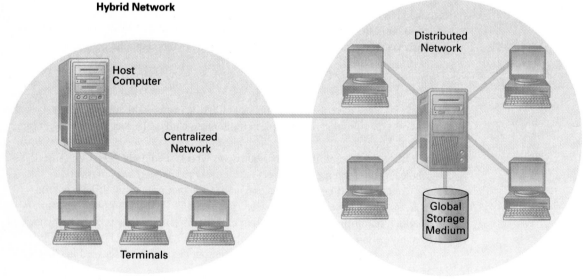

Host Computer

Centralized Network

Terminals

Distributed Network

Global Storage Medium

A **distributed network**, on the other hand, is a collection of workstations connected to each other, along with various shared storage devices and input and output devices (for example, scanners and printers). In a distributed network each workstation can handle some, if not all, of its own processing. Workstations in a distributed network also maintain local information and software. The term *local* refers to information, software, and processing capabilities (the CPU) that are accessed and used only by the workstation in which they reside.

In some distributed networks, global information and software may be stored on a global storage medium. In addition, some distributed networks allow you to take advantage of processing capabilities of other workstations. This type of global processing is often called *cooperative processing* or *distributed processing.*

A **hybrid network** is a network that combines the central processing of a host computer, as in the centralized network, but with the distributed processing capabilities of a distributed network. Many large organizations use hybrid networks because they provide organizationwide processing via a centralized host CPU and local control and processing through the use of connected workstations.

The characteristic that can be used to distinguish among centralized, distributed, and hybrid networks is location—this includes processing, software, information, and control. As you can see in Table 6-1, the processing, software, information, and control are located and maintained within the host computer in a centralized network. For a distributed network, these four elements are spread among the workstations and any global storage mediums. Finally, a hybrid network combines the location characteristics of both the centralized and distributed networks.

Until a few years ago, the centralized solution was the only practical option. Until low-cost CPUs generated a flood of ever-more-powerful workstations and personal computers, almost every element of transaction processing had to be handled by a large computer. But now the local systems can share in the processing. Today and well into the future, the distributed and hybrid approaches are the emerging blueprints for corporate IT resources.

According to Ownership

Network ownership determines who has the right to utilize the communication facilities (such as telephone lines or satellites) used to connect a network. Network ownership can either be public or private. **Public networks** are communication facilities owned and operated by a common carrier such as AT&T and MCI that serves a large number of subscribers, usually on a pay-as-you-go basis. The most obvious example of a public network is standard telephone service. Other examples of public networks include CompuServe, America Online, and Prodigy; because these types

Table 6-1

Distinguishing Characteristics of Centralized, Distributed, and Hybrid Networks

Location	Centralized	Distributed	Hybrid
Processing	• Completely handled by the host-computer CPU.	• Distributed among the workstations.	• Host computer provides organization-wide processing combined with distributed among the workstations.
Software	• Always resides with the host computer.	• Can be global and local.	• Organizationwide software resides with the host computer, while software for personal and work-group computing is contained within the distributed network.
Information	• All within the host computer.	• Some global and some local.	• Organizationwide information resides with the host computer, while personal and work-group information is contained within the workstations.
Control	• Centralized to the host computer	• Some or all may be distributed to the workstations.	• Centralized to the host computer combined with distributed among the workstations.

of public networks provide information and software in addition to communication facilities, they are sometimes called **value-added networks** (VAN). Not all public networks, however, are value-added networks.

Roadway Package System (RPS) grew from a 36-terminal pickup and delivery service to a $1 billion international carrier in 1994 because of its use of IT. RPS uses bar code technology and a VAN communication system to transmit information to a central computer system. Services on the VAN include RPS COLLECT, which automatically bills consignees for incoming packages. It also includes RPS ACCESS, which connects a customer's workstation to RPS's central system for instant information updates, automated package pickup requests, and package tracking.

Private networks are networks in which an organization has the exclusive rights to use the communication facility. For example, if an organization needs to communicate between Boston and San Francisco, it can lease a communication facility (from a common carrier) for its exclusive use. This is an example of a private network, because the leasing organization has the only exclusive rights to use the communication facility. Private networks of this type usually operate on a fixed-price, lease basis.

Another type of private network is one in which the communication facility is owned and operated by the organization with the network. Consider your school as an example. It probably has a network that connects all the administrative offices so that they can share information about class schedules, financial aid, and students. Your school may also have a network of computers that you can use to complete your homework assignments. In this instance, the distance covered by the network is relatively small (your whole campus), so your school has decided to own, operate, and maintain the communication facility for your network(s).

According to Geographic Span

Geographic span is the distance covered by a network. Geographic spans can be as small as an office or as large as the entire world. Networks that cover a limited geographic area such as an office or office building are called **local area networks** (LANs). A LAN is also an example of a private network because the distance span is so small and because the organization would own the communication facility used to connect the LAN (as is probably the case with your school).

Networks that cover a larger area such as a city are called **metropolitan area networks** (MANs). MANs typically cover distances no greater than 10 to 20 miles and rely on the communication facilities provided by a common carrier. In fact,

A TRAVEL AGENT WITH A WAN

Rosenbluth International Alliance (RIA) is a global strategic business alliance for "mom and pop" travel agencies all over the world. In fact, member travel agencies of RIA operate in over 35 countries with more than 1,000 offices and have total sales in excess of $5 billion.

RIA is actually the brainchild of Rosenbluth Travel, headquartered in Philadelphia. Rosenbluth has created a "virtual" global organization by creating a wide area network (WAN) that electronically links travel agents all over the world. This alliance lets these smaller travel agencies share in a technology base that none of them—including Rosenbluth—could afford alone. Besides the technology advantage, the members of the alliance get advantages of scale in purchasing and discounts from major airlines and hotels. Again, this would not be available to any of the travel agencies individually.

The WAN that serves RIA is an electronic collection of local area networks that operate 24 hours a day all over the world. The WAN links the travel agencies' LANs to airline and hotel reservation systems and processes thousands of transactions every second so fast that an individual travel agent would think he or she was the only one on the system.[1]

How important is IT to RIA? Well, you know about the advantages of scale each travel agency enjoys, but consider this—when the WAN is down, business stops. Think about it—for every minute the system is down, RIA members lose $10,000! Now, how important is IT to RIA?

the term *MAN* was originally coined to describe networks that used communication facilities provided by a city or metropolitan area. If your school has campuses spread throughout your town or city, it may have several LANs located on separate campuses that are connected to form a complete network called a MAN.

Finally, networks designed to cover large geographic areas are called **wide area networks** (WANs). WANs are used by businesses today that have operations in different states and possibly in different countries. For example, large retailers such as Wal-Mart use a WAN to connect all the retail stores to each other and to the home office. Wal-Mart leases communication facilities from a number of different common carriers all over the country to get every store and the home office connected. Using a WAN means that inventory information for all retail stores can be analyzed at the home office, resulting in quicker and larger-scale reordering of products selling quickly.

Ryder Systems, Inc. also uses a nationwide WAN. The WAN gives Ryder the ability to track maintenance information on its thousands of trucks. Ryder's management personnel then use this information to identify recurring maintenance problems and equipment obsolescence.

These three terms—LAN, MAN, and WAN—are most often used to describe distributed and hybrid networks; you would rarely hear someone refer to a centralized network as being a local or metropolitan area network. Although centralized networks can cover very small or very large areas as well, there is no generally accepted way of describing centralized networks in terms of geographic span.

A Closer Look at Local Area Networks

Local area networks are the most common type of IT network, the fastest growing, and the most technically varied. Recall that a LAN is a private network designed to work in a limited geographic area, such as a room or a building. There are two types of LANs—client/server and peer-to-peer (see Figure 6-4). A **client/server network** is a distributed network in which many workstations (called clients) are connected to a central workstation (called the server). The **clients** are the workstations in a client/server network that maintain local software and information and do as much of the processing as possible.

A **server** in a client/server network is a workstation that is responsible for any of the following four functions: file control, printer control, communications control, and network control. These functions are often referred to as the intelligence of the network, or simply as *network intelligence. File control* (handled by the file server) manages information and software access on the network global storage devices (for instance, hard disk). *Printer control* (handled by the printer server) manages the use of the network printers by multiple people.

Communications control (handled by the communications server) manages the ability of the network (or of an individual on the network) to communicate externally with other people or other systems. Finally, *network control* (handled by the network server) manages the communication within the network. Most often you will find that all four of these functions are contained within a single workstation.

A **peer-to-peer network** is a distributed network in which many workstations are connected to each other and do not rely on a server for global software and information, information processing tasks, or communication within the network. Basically, a peer-to-peer network consists of many workstations connected together that can share input and output devices and communicate with each other. Peer-to-peer networks are less expensive than client/server networks and work well in small-business environments (typically 50 workstations or less). Peer-to-peer networks do not support such network characteristics as multiprocessing and the pres-

Figure 6-4

Client/Server and Peer-to-Peer Networks

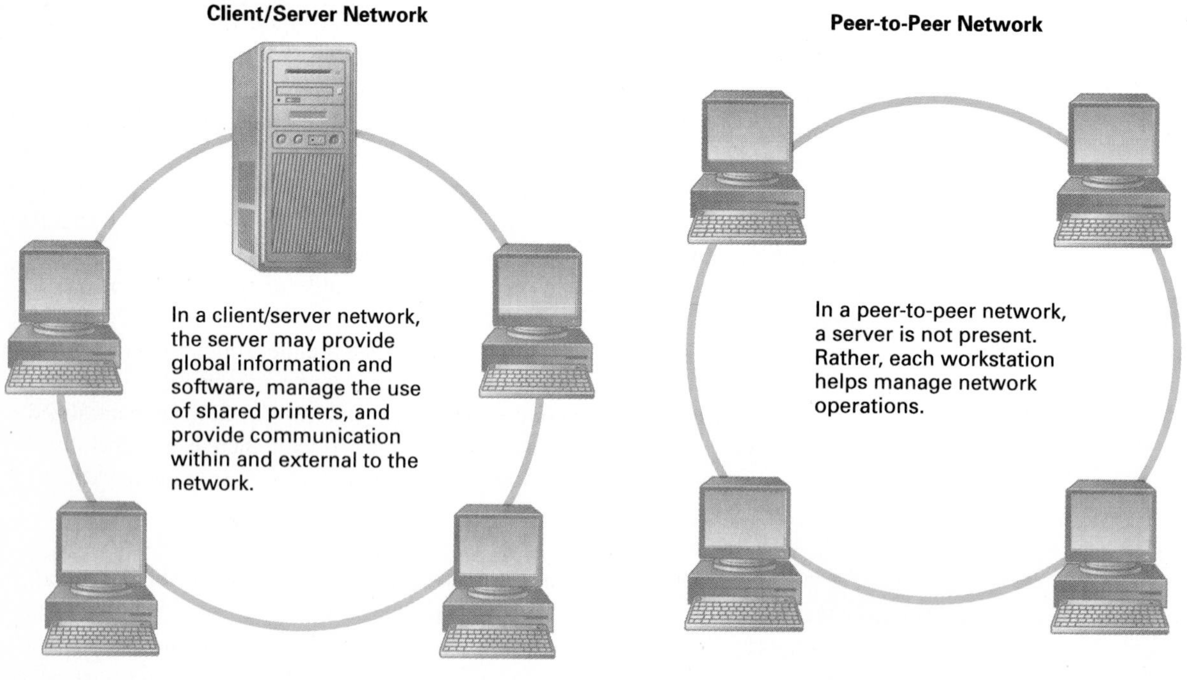

Client/Server Network

In a client/server network, the server may provide global information and software, manage the use of shared printers, and provide communication within and external to the network.

Peer-to-Peer Network

In a peer-to-peer network, a server is not present. Rather, each workstation helps manage network operations.

ence of a global storage medium on which information and software are stored. These are common characteristics of most client/server networks.

Local Area Network Configurations

LANs—either client/server or peer-to-peer—can be built in a variety of shapes or forms. These shapes are called *configurations* or *topologies*. A **LAN configuration** defines the manner in which the various nodes in a network are connected. A **node** is any IT device in a network, including a terminal, workstation, scanner, printer, modem, disk drive, and so on. The common LAN configurations are star, bus, ring, and mesh.

A **star configuration** has a central workstation from which all other nodes radiate (see Figure 6-5). A star configuration is usually associated with a client/server network, so the central workstation acts as a network and file server. This means that the central workstation is responsible for handling all information and software requests and communication among the other nodes.

A **bus configuration** is a network in which the nodes are connected to a single communication medium over which all information, software, and messages must travel (see Figure 6-6). The communication medium is called the *bus*. Each workstation in a bus configuration listens to the bus and determines if a traveling message is intended for it. Each workstation does so by looking at a unique address attached to the message. The intended workstation is the only one that actually accepts the message and provides an acknowledgment—the other workstations simply disregard the message. A bus LAN configuration is commonly used for both client/server and peer-to-peer networks.

A **ring configuration** is a network in which the connections of the nodes (usually through a common communication medium) form a closed loop (see Figure 6-7). Transmissions are passed in a circle around the network. Each workstation must receive each message and determine if it is the intended recipient. If it is not, it must regenerate the transmission and pass it on around the network. A ring configuration treats a message like an envelope making the rounds of your office. "Is

Figure 6-5

Star LAN Configuration

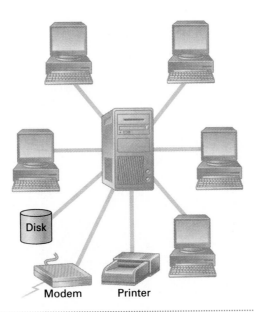

this addressed to you?" If so, open it up. If not, pass it on. As with a bus LAN configuration, a ring LAN configuration is commonly used for both client/server and peer-to-peer networks.

A **mesh configuration** is a network in which node connections are made according to transmission traffic. Transmission traffic describes the volume of information that travels between different nodes in a network. In its pure form, a mesh configuration has all nodes connected to all other nodes (see Figure 6-8). Mesh configurations are particularly useful if the physical structure of the other networks does not match the logical flow of information among the workstations.

Mesh configurations provide extremely fast transmissions between workstations because the transmission path contains only one link. There is, however, a

Figure 6-6

Bus LAN Configuration

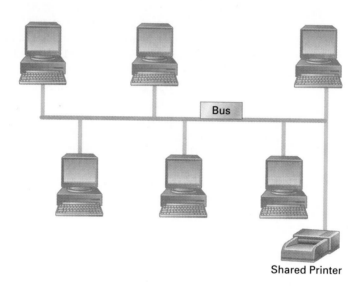

Shared Printer

Figure 6-7

Ring LAN Configuration

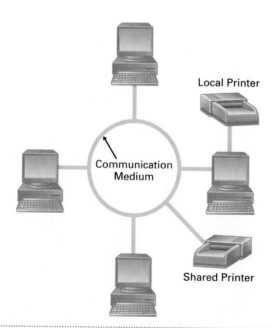

Local Printer

Communication Medium

Shared Printer

great cost associated with mesh configurations. The cost of a communication medium from each workstation to all other workstations as well as the cost of the physical connections themselves at a workstation for all other workstations make a mesh configuration more expensive than the other configurations.

The decision of a network configuration is crucial, because it strongly affects the efficiency of communication across the LAN (see Table 6-2). Like other traffic systems, LANs generate congestion, depending on the configuration, speed, volume of traffic, use of servers, and functions. While you're unlikely to be directly involved in technical decisions about LAN design unless you become an IT specialist, you will be affected in your work by these decisions. Why? Because LANs will be your primary interface between your own workstation and other people, information, network hardware, and network software.

Software in a Local Area Network

As you might guess, software in any network—including LANs—is much different from that for a personal, single-user environment. In a network, many people share and simultaneously use application software and information. More important, the operating system for a network must be capable of managing how all the devices and workstations work together and communicate. Network operating system management is no small task, and you will find even more types of operating systems for networks than you will for IT systems that support a single individual.

Application Software. Let's go back to your CD mail-order business. Your basic software needs would include word processing, desktop publishing, spreadsheet, and a DBMS. Because you have chosen to create and use a network in the form of

Figure 6-8

Mesh LAN Configuration

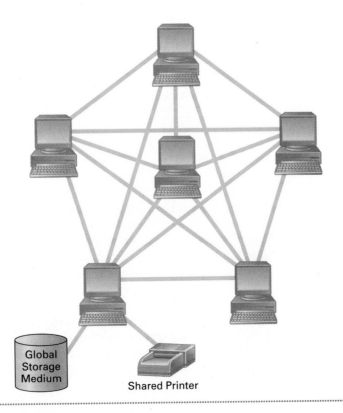

Global Storage Medium

Shared Printer

Table 6-2

The Business Choice of a LAN Configuration

Configuration	Why Businesses Choose Them	Why Businesses Don't Choose Them
Star	• Network control is centralized at one point. • Network intelligence is limited to the central workstation. • Radiating workstations can use the CPU processing capabilities of the central workstation.	• Congestion at central workstation can slow transmissions. • Failure of the central workstation renders the network useless. • Workstations can only communicate with each other by going through the central workstation. • All workstations have their own communication media, which can become expensive. • The central workstation has a physical limitation for the number of workstations that can be connected.
Bus	• Workstations can communicate directly with each other. • Workstations only receive messages intended for them. • High transmission speed for communication is possible. • Adding another workstation amounts to making another connection to the bus. • A single shared communication medium is inexpensive. • The loss of one workstation does not affect the functionality of the network.	• This approach is only appropriate for a limited geographic area. • Causes of faults and failures are difficult to determine. • Failure of the single communication medium renders the network useless. • Network intelligence may be distributed to each workstation.
Ring	• All workstations share the same communication medium. • The loss of one workstation does not affect the functionality of the network. • Adding another workstation amounts to making a new connection to the communication medium. • The cost of a single shared communication medium is low.	• Each workstation must pass on unintended messages to the next workstation. • Response speed degrades as the network increases in size. • Network intelligence must be distributed to each workstation.
Mesh	• This approach allows a fast response time for transmission. • A single workstation failure does not affect the functionality of the network. • Network connections are defined by the movement of information.	• Network intelligence must be distributed to each workstation. • Adding a new workstation can become expensive. • Making many connections between workstations is costly.

a LAN, you would purchase only one package of each application software (called the *master copy* or *network copy*) and place it on the network so everyone could use it—this alone saves a great deal of money because everyone shares the software. When necessary, each person would retrieve a copy of the application software, with the network copy remaining with the file server.

To do this, you must obtain a site license agreement from the software manufacturer. A **site license agreement** is a contract between an organization and a software manufacturer that grants your organization the right to let many people access and use the one network software copy. The site license agreement states how many people may simultaneously use a copy of the software.

If you find that more people need to use that package than stated in the site license agreement, additional fees must be paid for each person. These fees, however, are much less than the price of the individual software package. Site license agreements are an excellent way for people in an organization to use the same application software without having to pay the full price for each person.

System Software. The **network operating system** (NOS) **software** is responsible for managing (1) the communication within a network, (2) any multiprocessing that takes place, (3) the sharing of hardware devices, and (4) any communication external to another network. As with workstations and personal computers, a variety of NOSs are available from many vendors (see Table 6-3). Your choice of NOS software will depend on the network configuration you use (although many NOSs will run on different configurations), whether you have a client/server or peer-to-peer network, what capabilities you want the network to have, and what communications protocol will be used.

A **communications protocol** is the set of procedures that defines how two devices communicate with each other in a network. The communications protocol in a network is defined by the NOS you choose. Communications protocols are necessary because networks have multiple devices that must communicate with others, sometimes at the same time. Although many communications protocols exist, three are increasingly dominating the network industry—carrier sense multiple access with collision detection, token passing, and fiber distributed data interface.

The **carrier sense multiple access with collision detection** (CSMA/CD) protocol manages communication by having each node "listen" to the network for communications. CSMA/CD works like a telephone party line. If you want to make a phone call, you pick up the line to see if it's busy, in which case you hang up and try again later. If the line is not busy, you are free to make your call. Likewise, you recognize that an incoming phone call is for you by the number of rings. The number of rings assigned to you essentially becomes your telephone address. In a network, sometimes two nodes attempt to send messages simultaneously. When this happens, a collision occurs. In CSMA/CD, however, each node listens to the network to see if its message created a collision. If so, both sending nodes wait a random amount of time and retransmit their messages.

A **token passing** communications protocol literally "passes" around an electronic token or message board that each node gets to use in turn (see Figure 6-9). When a node receives the token and notices that it is not being used, it can place a message on the token and pass it around. When a node receives the token and sees that there is a message, it accepts the message if it is the intended recipient or passes it around the network if it is not. Because only one token is being passed

Discovering **IT**

Does your school use a **local area network** (LAN) in the computer labs? If so, what kind of topology does it have? What can you do on the LAN that you would not have been able to do if the workstations weren't connected? If your computer lab doesn't have a LAN, can you identify any problems a LAN could solve? Which configuration do you think would be best?

Table 6-3

**Popular LAN Network
Operating System (NOS) Software**

	Power LAN[b]	LANtastic[b]	Windows for Workgroups[b]	Personal NetWare[b]	MosesALL![b]	VINES[c]	OS/2 LAN Server[c]	Windows NT[c]	NetWare 4.X[c]	NetWare 3.X[c]
No. of Nodes Supported	Un[a]	Un	Un	Un	8	Un	100	Un	Un	Un
Twisted-Pair Cable	Yes	Yes	Yes	Yes	No	Yes	Yes	Yes	Yes	Yes
Coaxial Cable	Yes	Yes	Yes	Yes	No	Yes	Yes	Yes	Yes	Yes
Bus	Yes	Yes	Yes	Yes	No	Yes	Yes	Yes	Yes	Yes
Ring	Yes	Yes	Yes	Yes	No	No	Yes	Yes	Yes	Yes
Global Disk Space-Supported	N/A	N/A	N/A	N/A	N/A	20 GB	1.5 TB	1700 TB	32 TB	32 TB
Multi-processing	No	No	No	No	No	Yes	Yes	Yes	No	No
Remote Access	No	No	Yes	Yes	No	Yes	Yes	Yes	Yes	Yes
Configure Groups of Users to Security	Yes	Yes	Yes	Yes	No	Yes	Yes	Yes	Yes	Yes
Price for 5 Nodes (Includes Server for Client/Server NOSs)	$395	$499	$1,095	$395	$495	$3,892	$3,328	$1,799	$1,359	$1,359

[a]Unlimited.
[b]Peer-to-peer network operating systems.
[c]Client/server network operating systems.

**Network Nodes Installed in 1994[2]
(Percentage of licenses sold)**

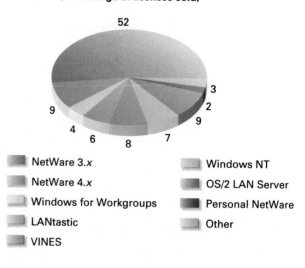

- NetWare 3.x
- NetWare 4.x
- Windows for Workgroups
- LANtastic
- VINES
- Windows NT
- OS/2 LAN Server
- Personal NetWare
- Other

Figure 6-9

**Token Passing
Communications Protocol**

❶n this figure Node 1 sends
a message to Node 4, which
in turn provides an acknowledgment.

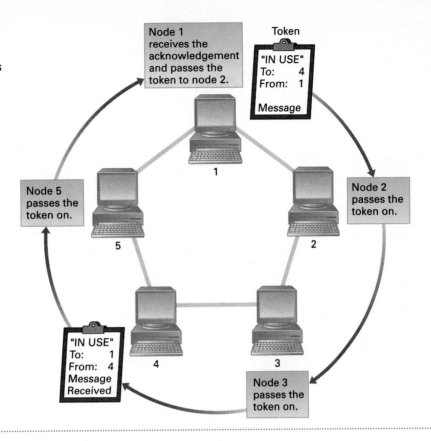

around (always in the same direction), collisions do not occur as in a CSMA/CD
communications protocol.

A **fiber distributed data interface** (FDDI) communications protocol uses
token passing with high-speed optical fiber as the communication medium. In reality, FDDI uses two rings transmitting in different directions. One ring is the primary
ring, while the other is a backup in case the primary ring fails.

FDDI is used in networks that have a large number of people who need to transmit large sets of information quickly. FDDI is also used as a "backbone" structure for
connecting many networks (see Figure 6-10). As organizations begin to incorporate
more multimedia applications (sound, video, and text) on networks, FDDI promises
to become the communications protocol of the future.

Network Communications Devices

In Chapters 3 through 5, we focused on three of the four hardware IT building blocks—input and output devices, the processing engine (CPU and internal memory), and storage devices. Now we want to focus
on communication devices—the hardware building block that makes IT networks
possible. **Communication devices** are the hardware devices that provide the connections between all the other hardware devices in a network. Network communication devices include data communications equipment, communication links, and
communication switches.

Figure 6-10

Using FDDI to Connect Networks

Ⓐ fiber distributed data interface (FDDI) is often used to connect multiple networks. FDDI uses a token ring communications protocol on an optical fiber medium. This makes communication among the networks extremely fast.

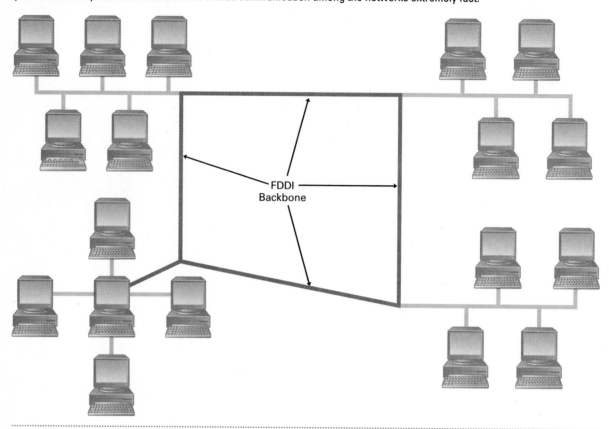

FDDI
Backbone

Data Communications Equipment

Data communications equipment (DCE) includes the hardware that makes the physical connection between the nodes and the actual network. For example, DCE connects a workstation to the bus communication medium in a bus configuration.

The most familiar piece of DCE is a modem. A **modem** *(mod*ulator-*dem*odulator) is a device that converts the digital signals of your IT system into an analog form that can be transmitted over a telephone network and then converts the analog signals back to digital signals at the other end of the transmission (see Figure 6-11). Many communication media, like the standard telephone system, pass signals in analog mode; IT systems, however, work in digital mode (a stream of 0s and 1s). A modem, therefore, converts digital signals into analog signals for the sender and then converts analog signals to digital signals for the receiver.

Communication Links

Communication links are the electronic pathways over which information travels from sender to receiver. Figure 6-12 shows a configuration of nodes with communication links connecting them. A **path** consists of all the communication links that the information travels over. For example, from node A to node C there are

Figure 6-11

Making the Network Connection

❶f the communication medium used to connect the network is analog, data communications equipment such as a modem must be used. In IT networks that exclusively use digital signal processing, a modem is not needed. However, a device must still be present that provides the node connection to the network. One such device is a **network interface card**—a special network card that fits into one of the expansion slots in the back of your workstation.

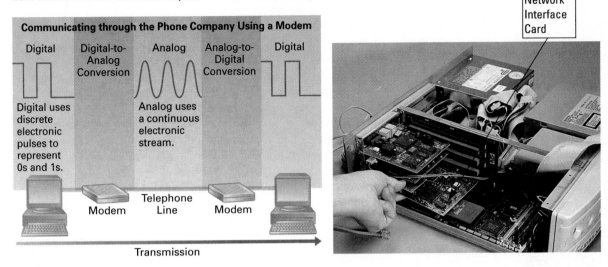

Communicating through the Phone Company Using a Modem

| Digital | Digital-to-Analog Conversion | Analog | Analog-to-Digital Conversion | Digital |

Digital uses discrete electronic pulses to represent 0s and 1s.

Analog uses a continuous electronic stream.

Modem   Telephone Line   Modem

Transmission

Network Interface Card

Figure 6-12

The Electronic Pathway of Information

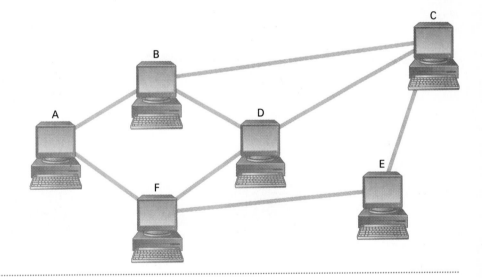

many paths with many links: A ➔ B ➔ C, A ➔ F ➔ D ➔ C, and so on. Setting up communication links amounts to much more than just providing connections between nodes. Communication links have many different characteristics, including transmission speed and the communication medium itself. These characteristics affect the movement of information and the quality of the transmission.

Transmission speed is a measure of how much information—usually in bits—can be passed across a communication link in a single second. Transmission speed is measured in **bits per second** or **bps**. For example, 4 mbps is 4 million bits per second or roughly 500,000 characters. Today's fastest communication links are measured in terms of billions of bits per second (gbps).

Transmission speed not only determines how fast information travels but also what kind of information can be transmitted. Consider the fact that one second of digital voice requires 56,000 bits and that one second of television-quality full-motion video requires 10,000,000 bits. As you can easily tell, fast and reliable transmission speeds will greatly affect the use of technology-related presentations such as multimedia and virtual reality.

Communication Media. A communication link implies that there is something over which information travels. Whether it's a telephone line, cable, or airwaves, information must travel over something. We call this the **communication medium**. Popular communication media today include twisted-pair cable, coaxial cable, optical fiber, microwave, satellite, and broadcast radio.

Twisted-pair cable, which consists of two insulated copper wires twisted in a spiral, is the most popular communication medium in use today (see Figure 6-13). Twisted-pair cable makes up the bulk of the world's public telephone network. A single twisted-pair cable commonly provides speeds up to 16 mbps for short distances (typically not more than 1 to 2 miles). More typically and realistically for network communication, though, twisted-pair cable can handle between 2,400 to 28,800 bps. Distance, noise on the line, and interference limit its reliability.

Figure 6-13

Guided Communication Media

Twisted-pair cables

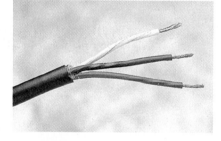

Coaxial cables

Optical fibers

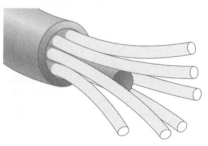

Communications and Connectivity: Living in a Networked World

For human speech transmission, this is not much of a problem; if there's a crackle on the line, you can still understand what your friend is saying. Data communications requires much more accuracy. For example, a crackle that changes a credit card number from "5244 0811 2643 741" to "5244 0810 2643 741" is more than just a nuisance. The many DCE devices in a network, such as a modem, are responsible for transmitting information at the speed that ensures accurate reception.

A recent innovation has made it practical to send 1.5 mbps through twisted-pair cable, an astonishing increase in speed that promises to shake up the cable TV and phone industries. *ADSL* (another acronym in the telecommunications alphabet soup of terms, this stands for asynchronous distributed subscriber link) uses a computer chip to code digital information and send it over existing phone networks.

"So what?" is a reasonable reaction when you read that bland statement. What's not bland is that this has allowed Bell Atlantic to launch *soft video dial tone*—that is, to transmit movies on demand through twisted-pair cable. All of a sudden, the small California firm that created the ADSL chip and technique has taken away the cable TV industry's strong card—the perceived need for coaxial cable and optical fiber to provide the transmission speed required for movies—and brought phone companies into the home entertainment business.

Coaxial cable consists of one or more central wires (usually copper) surrounded by thick insulation capable of carrying 500 mbps, or about 15,000 voice calls at once (see Figure 6-13). In fact, the cable used to connect your television set to a cable service is coaxial cable. Besides being faster than twisted-pair cable, coaxial cable is also much less susceptible to outside interference and information damage because of its construction.

Optical fiber uses a very thin glass or plastic fiber through which pulses of light are passed (see Figure 6-13). Unlike twisted-pair and coaxial cable, which transmit information in an electromagnetic form, optical fiber transmission converts bit signals into pulses of light. A pulse of light represents an on bit (1), while no light pulse represents an off bit (0).

Optical fiber is gaining widespread use for connecting IT systems, especially across great distances. Optical fiber offers advantages in size (a single fiber has the diameter of a strand of human hair), speed (up to 1,400 mbps or 1.4 gbps), and quality (much greater transmission reliability). The greatest drawback to the use of optical fiber in some instances is cost.

Twisted-pair, coaxial, and optical fiber are called **guided communication media** because information travels over an enclosed path (for example, the cable or fiber). Other types are called **unguided communication media** because they

Discovering IT

Digital pagers and cellular phone systems are quickly becoming part of your everyday life. Interview someone at a business that provides services for these types of wireless technologies. Ask what type of communication medium is used and what the potential types of interference might be. Also, find out what measures have been undertaken to avoid such interference.

broadcast (radiate) information in many directions. Unguided communication media include microwave, satellite, and broadcast radio.

Microwave media use a high-frequency band of radio broadcast transmission. Microwaves are "line-of-sight" media that use dish-shaped antennae for sending and receiving information (see Figure 6-14). That is, the microwave signal is not capable of bending around the surface of the earth, so the sending and receiving antennae must be within sight of each other.

Satellite media are basically microwave systems in space. A satellite is an amplifier or repeater, which receives information from a node on earth, repeats the information, and sends it to one or more receiving nodes on earth (see Figure 6-15). The satellite itself is in geosynchronous orbit 22,300 miles above the earth's sur-

Figure 6-14

Unguided Microwave Communication Media

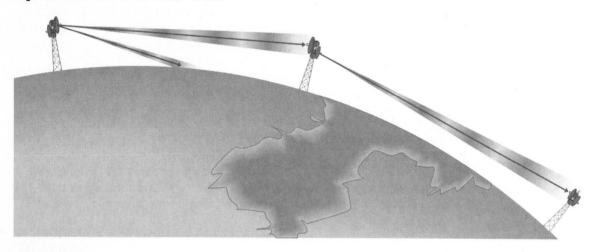

Figure 6-15

Unguided Satellite Communication Media

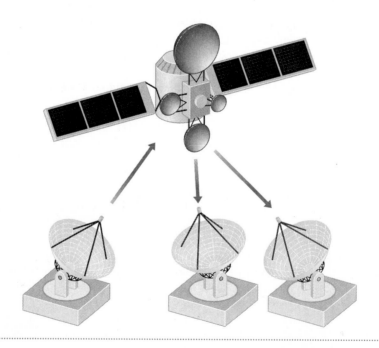

Communications and Connectivity: Living in a Networked World

GOING WIRELESS

For the Travelers Corporation, LANs that use physical cables—twisted-pair, coaxial, or optical fiber—to connect workstations are more of a headache and expense than they are a benefit. You see, Travelers recognized that its employees needed to be networked to be more efficient and effective, but that using physical cables for networking—even in the same building—took too long to set up and cost too much.

When you think about it, installing a LAN can be an enormous construction project involving drilling holes in walls, pulling wiring, and paying electrical contractors a lot of money. Then, of course, adding a new workstation or moving around offices or office furniture requires that much of the same work be done again.

So Travelers decided to go wireless with its LANs. Not satellite, microwave, or broadcast radio, but rather Infralan—an infrared spectrum transmission product that is compatible with IBM's token ring local area network. With Infralan, the Travelers Corporation has cut the time to install a LAN from between 30 and 150 days to just a few hours and has slashed cabling costs from $100 per workstation to just $10.

Travelers is just one of many businesses exploring wireless technologies for networking, and you can expect to see more LANs connected via wireless technologies in the coming years (see the accompanying graph). But wireless technologies affect more than just the business world—they affect your life as well. Simple examples include cellular phones and digital pagers. The same technologies that are the basis for these products will probably someday be the basis for the way you connect to the Information Superhighway.[3]

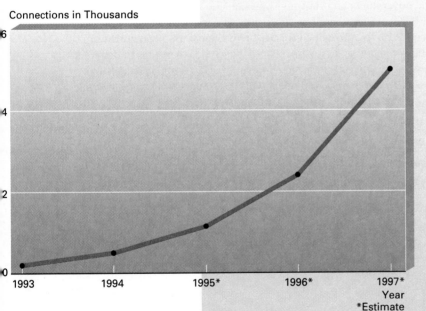

Worldwide Total Wireless LANs

Connections in Thousands

1993 1994 1995* 1996* 1997*
Year
*Estimate

face. *Geosynchronous* means that the satellite rotates as the earth rotates so that it appears to be stationary overhead. The signal takes an eighth of a second to go from earth to the satellite and an eighth of a second in the opposite direction.

Many automobile rental organizations such as Hertz and Avis and most automobile manufacturers are beginning to use satellite technology to put intelligent vehicle highways (IVH) systems in cars. IVH systems use a special in-car computer connected to a satellite management system. The satellites can pinpoint the exact location of the car and transmit that information to the in-car computer. The in-car computer can then tell the driver the directions to a specific destination. So if you were lost or wanted to find the nearest video rental store, you could use your in-car computer to get immediate directions based on your location.

Satellite media are very cost effective for moving large amounts of information, especially when there are many receiving nodes. Again, satellite media are unguided, meaning that many nodes can simultaneously be receiving the same transmission. Large multinational corporations have found that satellite communi cation is very advantageous when a particular country does not have a supporting communications infrastructure for guided media.

Retailers like Kmart generally have a *very small aperture terminal* (VSAT) satellite dish on the roof of every store. These VSATs cost under $10,000. They link the store to a central "hub" satellite to access information or update sales records. The hub can broadcast price and promotion information to all of the nodes (store VSATs). The overall cost of this type of network is not influenced by the number of VSAT nodes, just as CBS's cost for broadcasting programs is not affected by the number of TV sets receiving its signal.

Broadcast radio media are similar to microwave, except that the receiving node does not have to have a dish-shaped antenna or be in the line of sight. Broadcast radio wave media are popularly used for digital paging, cellular phone systems, and wireless personal communication networks within a building or in a limited geographic area. Broadcast radio waves, however, are much more susceptible to reflections from buildings and other physical structures and interference from other signaling devices.

The federal government and state highway agencies are developing *electronic toll collection* (ETC) systems based on broadcast radio media. Using ETC systems, electronic tags on vehicles transmit a broadcast radio signal to tollgate receivers, which automatically debit the driver's account. This obviously means that drivers do not have to stop at each tollgate, which ultimately reduces traffic congestion. Some states are using information provided by ETC systems to raise or lower tolls depending on traffic congestion or the time of day.

Communication Switches

Communication switches are the hardware devices that bring together the communication media and route communications throughout a network (see Figure 6-16). A

Communication Switching

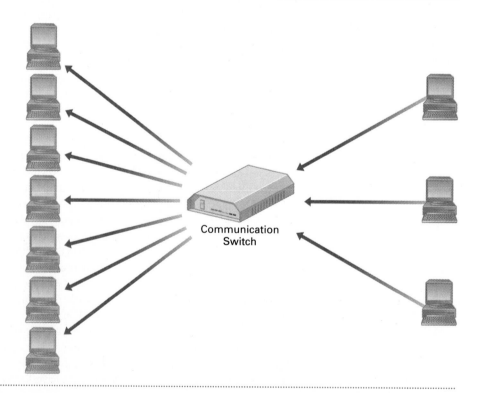

Communication
Switch

VIRTUAL REALITY ON THE INFORMATION SUPERHIGHWAY

Business and the Information Superhighway go hand in hand. The Information Superhighway will offer businesses instant access to people all over the world for product advertising and selling. Club Med, Chrysler, American Express, Reebok International, Miller Brewing, and Jim Beam—just to name a few—are already advertising on the Internet. In fact, Reebok lets you electronically chat with professional athletes who endorse its products.

Currently, the most effective advertising on the Internet is done through multimedia presentations. These presentations include sound, video, color, text, and tools that let you browse through the advertisement in any order you wish. So advertising with multimedia on the Internet is much more effective than advertising on television.

You can already advertise products interactively, with color, sound, and full-motion video—so what's next? The answer is virtual reality. Virtual reality is the next best thing to being there. Virtual reality applications make you feel like you are actually participating in a presentation. Consider Chrysler—advertising on the Internet amounts to showing new vehicles (through video) and piping in music and a sales pitch from a salesperson. But who's going to buy a new car without test driving it first? Exactly—no one.

That's where virtual reality comes in. Can you imagine putting on your virtual reality outfit (gloves, headset, and so on) at home, cruising the Information Superhighway, and virtually "trying out" products? Who knows—you may be able to try on clothes, experience theme park rides, go white-water rafting, and lie on the beaches of Maui without ever leaving the comfort of your living room.

Back to real reality now. Virtual reality is one of the latest innovations in IT, but it has a long way to go. Good virtual reality applications are expensive and take years to develop. Virtual reality equipment—that is, gloves, walkers, and headsets—is also in its primitive stages, not to mention the fact that the senses of taste and smell have yet to be incorporated.

Once virtual reality gets good, the next obstacle to overcome is piping it through the Information Superhighway to your home fast enough so that you don't think everything is happening in slow motion. Remember, a virtual reality presentation includes video, sound, and response motions. All of these require vast information spaces that must be transmitted quickly to your home.

If you were sitting at home right now and could have virtual reality piped into your living room, how would you want to spend the rest of your day?

communication switch is like an airport. Airplanes stop at airports, drop off and pick up passengers, and then proceed to another destination. Communication switches perform a similar function; communications arrive at a communication switch in a network and are then routed to their destination. Communication switches include multiplexers, cluster controllers, front-end processors, and interconnecting units.

Multiplexers aggregate several communication media and allow them to share a single communication medium that usually operates at a much higher capacity and greater speed (see Figure 6-17). Multiplexers are used in pairs; one multiplexer aggregates communications at a remote site, and the other disaggregates the communications at the host computer site. Multiplexers are extremely cost effective if there are many devices in one geographic area that need to communicate with a host computer in another geographic area.

Cluster controllers also manage a group of devices that share a single high-speed communication medium connected to another location (see Figure 6-18). Cluster controllers, however, differ from multiplexers because they do not aggregate and disaggregate the communications of the devices. They merely handle the

Figure 6-17

Multiplexing Communications

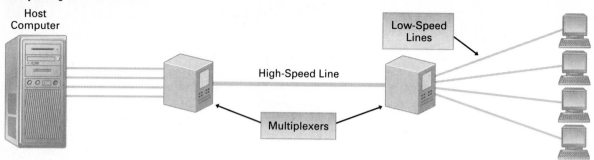

Figure 6-18

Cluster Controllers

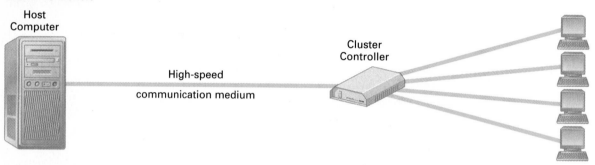

Figure 6-19

Separating the Processing and Communication Workload

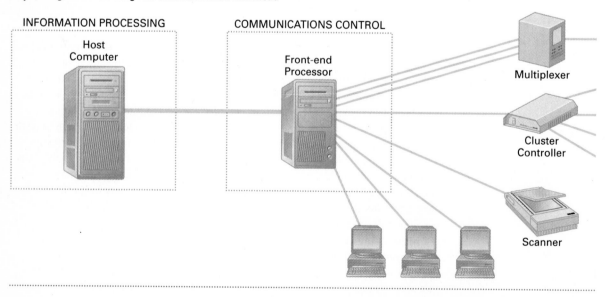

communication congestion and competition for the single communication medium the devices share.

Front-end processors are special computers that handle the communications function for the host computer (see Figure 6-19). In an IT network without a front-end processor, the host computer is responsible for handling information processing requests as well as communicating with all the devices. This communication responsibility can lead to greatly decreased processing performance. If this is the case, a front-end processor is used to relieve the host computer of its communication responsibilities.

Internetworking units are special hardware devices that connect two or more networks. For example, if an accounting firm has two local area networks that need to communicate with each other—one in Los Angeles and one in Cincinnati—the two networks would be connected using an internetworking unit.

The three types of internetworking units are bridges, routers, and gateways (see Figure 6-20). The choice of which internetworking device to use depends on the communications protocols and configurations of the networks to be connected.

A **bridge** connects two networks of the same kind, such as two IBM ring configurations. Because the networks are the same, the bridge acts only to pass messages and communications between the networks. A **router** connects networks that are dissimilar with respect to some operations like node addressing and message size. A router, for instance, would be used to connect a bus and star LAN. **Gateways** are used to connect networks that are totally dissimilar. For example, a gateway would be used to connect an IBM LAN and an Apple LAN. Gateway internetworking units are also used to connect distributed and centralized networks to create a hybrid network. Internetworking devices constitute the fastest-growing area of telecommunications, as

Figure 6-20

Connecting Networks

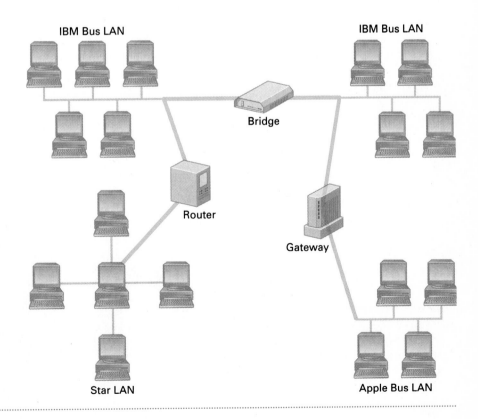

IBM Bus LAN

IBM Bus LAN

Bridge

Router

Gateway

Star LAN

Apple Bus LAN

many organizations are turning to internetworking devices to tie together individual networks to create efficient communication across their locations.

People are the most important component of an IT system. The people component of an IT network includes more than just users like you, though. Just as the appropriate use of an organizational database requires a data administration person (Chapter 5), networks must also be administered and managed by designated individuals.

The **network administration team** is responsible for ensuring that the network matches the structural and operational characteristics of the organization and meets people's day-to-day processing and communication needs. Because of this, the network administration function should be a team effort. The network administration team should include a network manager, network specialists and operators, key management individuals from various functional areas such as the director of accounting or the warehouse supervisor, and people who interact with the network on a daily basis (see Figure 6-21). Key management individuals and people who interact with the network on a daily basis participate on the network administration team to provide input for new networking requests and changes in existing network functions.

Network Manager

The **network manager** coordinates the overall efforts of the network administration team and acts as a liaison to the strategic task force of the organization. In many organizations the network manager will take on the title of director of networks, network administrator, or LAN manager. The network manager must understand how the organization works and must be aware of future plans for organizational change. The network manager's functions include:

▶ Providing a mechanism for new networking requests

▶ Overseeing the evaluation of those requests

▶ Monitoring the development process of new networks or network changes

▶ Ensuring that the network satisfies all requirements

Discovering IT

Interview one or two people, either at school or at a place of business, who participate in the network administration function. Into which group do they fall? What are their primary responsibilities? Ask them what adverse effects there would be if they lost the use of their network.

Figure 6-21

The Network Administration Team

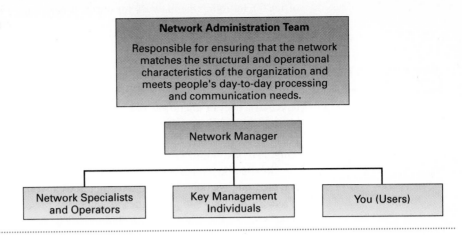

Network Administration Team

Responsible for ensuring that the network matches the structural and operational characteristics of the organization and meets people's day-to-day processing and communication needs.

Network Manager

Network Specialists and Operators | Key Management Individuals | You (Users)

Network Specialists and Operators

Network specialists and operators are responsible for designing, implementing, and testing the network and monitoring it during use. These responsibilities include solving technical problems, determining why problems occur and implementing controls to avoid them, installing equipment, and fine-tuning the network during use to ensure that maximum performance is achieved.

Network operators are also responsible for many day-to-day activities. These activities include maintaining hardware and software, providing periodic backups,

Table 6-4

Salaries for Network Specialists[4]

Salary	Director, Networks	Telecommuni- cations Manager	Telecommuni- cations Specialists	Network Administrator	LAN Manager
Overall Average[a]	$69,374	$55,811	$43,253	$44,492	$45,757
By Industry					
Insurance	$115,536	$86,500	$49,000	$55,340	$61,755
Banking	$97,864	$66,701	$50,200	$43,952	$42,377
Distribution	$90,000	$73,333	$54,000	$54,333	$52,166
Retail	$85,233	$60,750	$49,666	$50,357	$55,333
Health	$67,938	$44,938	$32,666	$39,892	$60,181
Transportation	$66,001	$59,500	$48,750	$55,666	$45,250
Education	$60,141	$52,480	$39,464	$44,937	$44,075
Utilities	$59,357	$47,833	$38,250	$51,400	$54,000
Nonprofit	$51,333	$53,166	$51,500	$52,000	$52,750
Agriculture	$110,000	$57,500	$41,500	$46,000	$45,500
Chemical	$104,025	$63,309	$56,523	$48,083	$50,937
Metal/Plastic	$84,000	$57,250	$52,583	$43,138	$43,441
Food/Beverage	$62,417	$45,166	$36,000	$36,000	$42,125

[a]"Including year-end bonuses."

responding to questions (for example, "How do I send a file to someone in another office?"), initiating the network for normal operations, and restarting the network after failure.

Hot Topics in Communications and Connectivity

Telecommunications is the most rapidly changing and most exciting area of IT. Almost every day, you can pick up a newspaper or magazine and read about a new technological development or business application of IT telecommunications. In this chapter, we've given you just a brief overview of basic concepts of IT telecommunications; to tell you everything there is to know would be impossible.

So you ask, "What does tomorrow's IT telecommunications look like?" To tell you the truth, we don't know and neither does anyone else. You can, however, look at today's hot topics to get an idea of where we're headed. We've already told you about some of these hot topics, including ADSL and WANs. Here are a few others that are causing change not only in the IT field but also in your life.

Asynchronous Transfer Mode

Asynchronous transfer mode (ATM) is a transmission method for sending information that divides a long message into smaller units (called *packets*). These packets are sent out over a network and then reassembled at the destination. The advantage is that your packets move through the network on something similar to a conveyor belt, with packets from other people that are going to other destinations mixed in. This lets a large number of people share very-high-speed communication links.

Consider a simple example of using multimedia on a network (see Figure 6-22). At the point of origin, the multimedia presentation is split into several different packets, perhaps with one packet containing sound, one packet containing text, and another packet containing the video. The packets then move through the network to

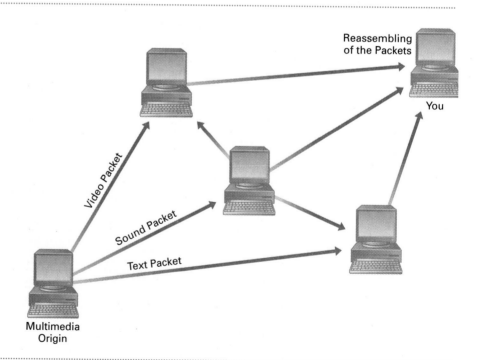

Figure 6-22

Multimedia via Asynchronous Transfer Mode

Getting in Touch

Ⓢo how does all this affect you? Well, for some of the material on topics such as multiplexers, controllers, and FDDI—not much right now. In fact, a lot of the topics we've discussed in this chapter have little effect on your personal life. Why do you have to learn about them? Because they will greatly affect your life in business. With what you now know, you still can't go out and install a LAN, but you can make an informed decision regarding the type of configuration that's best for a given situation.

Your own personal advantage is getting connected to the Internet and getting everything out of it that you possibly can. Consider this—about 35 million people currently use the Internet. If you're in a class with, say, 30 other students, chances are good that at least 7 use the Internet. If you're not among those 7 or so people, you're at a disadvantage. Let's look at a brief list of what those 7 people might be doing on the Internet when they go home tonight.

1. **Electronically (and instantly) communicating with their family and friends all over the world.**

2. **Electronically ordering products such as pizzas, CDs, and concert tickets.**

3. **Doing library searches for term papers at any time, day or night—even when the library's closed.**

4. **Sending questions to your instructor and getting an answer before the next class.**

5. **Doing virtual garage sale shopping.**

6. **Getting free software—personal productivity and game software.**

7. **Reading up-to-the-minute news, sports, and weather information.**

8. **Viewing the Smithsonian collection of photographs.**

9. **Finding great cooking recipes for tonight's meal.**

10. **Reading today's issue of the *New York Times* and other newspapers and magazines electronically.**

11. **Chatting on newsgroups about their favorite topics—the Indy 500, the latest fashions, and who's picked to win next year's Super Bowl (obviously, someone from the NFC).**

12. **Getting mail in different languages and using Internet help facilities to translate it.**

13. **Sending electronic letters to senators and congresspeople about an upcoming vote.**

14. **Accessing a nationwide phone book of names and addresses (including all the orthodontists in Tupelo, Mississippi).**

15. **Accessing any census data—including the number of bathtubs per person in the United States.**

The list is endless. If it involves communicating with other people or obtaining information, you can probably do it on the Internet. It's really up to you—is the Internet your personal advantage or your personal disadvantage?

you, where they are reassembled. The packets don't necessarily have to travel the same path. This way, the NOS can optimize the transmission by choosing the links with appropriate speed and a minimal level of congestion.

For you, ATM is the wave of the future—it's not completely here yet, but it's coming. To take advantage of ATM, you will have to carefully consider the types, volumes, and locations of information to be transmitted across the business network. The success of such IT applications as videoconferencing, interactive television, document imaging, multimedia, and virtual reality will depend on ATM and on your ability to use ATM effectively.

Integrated Services Digital Network

Integrated services digital network (ISDN) is the plan and international communications standard for the transition of the world's public telephone system from analog to digital for the purpose of transmitting all types of information simultaneously over twisted-pair telephone lines. Current telephone systems are limited in the amount of information they can transmit, the speed of the transmission, and the services they can provide. ISDN is the blueprint for how a telephone system can transmit all forms of information 10 to 30 times faster than today's speeds and handle two different applications simultaneously on the same line.

ISDN originated in the 1970s in Europe. Today, it is more a concern of the telecommunications service providers than of specific businesses or individuals. It is up to these telecommunications service providers to determine how quickly ISDN will come about, what price businesses and individuals will have to pay, and its advantages and disadvantages compared to other communication alternatives.

Electronic Data Interchange

Electronic data interchange (EDI) is the direct computer-to-computer transfer of information normally provided by the use of standard business paper documents, such as invoices and purchase orders. EDI is quickly becoming the norm for intercompany transactions, especially in ordering, distribution, payables, and receivables. EDI is a concept that relies on (1) telecommunications—what you have studied in this chapter, (2) software such as groupware (discussed in Chapter 2), and (3) teamwork between the businesses doing EDI. Teamwork is the key—if the businesses can't work together, EDI will be a failure. Here are just a few examples of how EDI is being used in business today.

▶ Levi Strauss has created an EDI system called *LeviLink* for its customers. By using LeviLink, one customer with a chain of 60 stores was able to reduce its replenishment cycle from 14 to 3 days, reduce order delivery time from 9 to 3 days, and completely eliminate its regional warehouses.

▶ R. J. Reynolds offers a 5 percent discount to all its customers who pay through EDI. The reason is simple—EDI has saved R. J. Reynolds between $5 and $10 million in labor costs, inventory, and lead time.

▶ Westinghouse has used EDI to streamline the procurement process for many of its larger customers. One such customer is Portland General Electric (PGE). Because PGE uses EDI with Westinghouse, elapsed time from order to delivery has been cut from 15 days to one-half day, and processing costs have been slashed from $90 to $10.

▶ Finally, the Port of Rotterdam uses a cargo-clearing EDI system called INTIS. With INTIS, goods are cleared in an average of 15 minutes, compared with 2 days for the United States, and the return of export order documents because of errors has been reduced by 50 percent.

The most successful people in society, business, and school have many common characteristics—dedication, a willingness to work hard, a commitment to excellence, and so on. Most of these successful people also have something else in common—they take advantage of today's IT networks. Whether it's using a fax machine, tapping into the valuable resources of the Internet, or making a recommendation to implement a peer-to-peer LAN in a small office, success in part is defined by the extent to which networks and their capabilities are exploited.

That same advantage can be yours. You don't hesitate to get in your car and go across town to a library or pick up the phone to ask someone a question, so why should you hesitate to use networks to your advantage? The real question is, "How can you join the parade?" Well, here's a list that might help.

Get Networked!

It's as simple as that. No matter where you are—school, work, or home—find out how to tap into the valuable resources that networking provides. If you work for a company that doesn't have any networking capabilities, you might prepare a preliminary report that details how networks work, what they can do for the organization, and how much it will cost.

Explore on Your Own

Once you're networked, explore the networking capabilities on your own. You can do this in a number of ways—taking classes, reading literature, and just simply plugging away at your workstation. If you know the capabilities of your network, you'll be better prepared to make use of the network for your own personal benefit (personal advantage) and the company's benefit (business advantage).

Keep Your Eyes Open for Opportunities

We've stated many times that IT is changing every day, and nowhere is it truer than in the area of IT networking. If you stay well informed of the changes taking place, you can make the most of your networking opportunities.

What is EDI to you? EDI is the way companies are and will be doing business. More important, EDI is becoming a business requirement. Companies such as Sears and General Motors will not do business with suppliers who are not linked to them through EDI. In fact, according to a 1995 *Computerworld* survey, 92 percent of the companies said they had EDI capabilities with their customers and 81 percent said they had the same links with their suppliers.[5] If your business can't do EDI, you may not be in business.

Now You Can . . .

1 Describe the different types of IT networks according to span of control, ownership, and geographic span.

▶ *Span of control:*

Centralized network:

One CPU (host computer) processes all information requests and handles communication.

All software resides with the host computer.

All information resides with the host computer.

The host computer maintains complete control.

Distributed network:

Processing is distributed among connected workstations.

Software can be local and global.

Information can be global and local.

Control is distributed among the workstations.

Hybrid network:

The host computer provides organizationwide processing combined with distributed processing among the workstations.

Organizationwide software resides with the host computer, while the distributed network contains software for personal and work-group computing.

Organizationwide information resides with the host computer, while the workstations contain personal and work-group information.

Control is centralized to the host computer, and distributed control exists among the workstations.

▶ *Ownership:*

Public networks are communication facilities owned and operated by a common carrier that serves a large number of subscribers, usually on a pay-as-you-go basis.

Value-added networks are public networks that provide information and software in addition to communication services.

A *private network* is one in which an organization has exclusive rights to use the communication facility.

▶ *Geographic span:*

Local area networks cover a limited geographic area such as an office or office building.

Metropolitan area networks cover a larger area such as a city.

Wide area networks cover large geographic areas.

2 Describe local area networks (LANs), including configurations, application software considerations, and communications protocols.

▶ A *client/server LAN* is a distributed network in which many workstations (called clients) are connected to a central workstation (called the server).

▶ A *peer-to-peer LAN* is a distributed network in which many workstations are connected to each other and do not rely on a server for global software and information, information processing tasks, or communication within the network.

▶ A *star configuration* has a central workstation from which all other nodes radiate.

▶ A *bus configuration* is a network in which the nodes are connected to a single communication medium over which all information, software, and messages must travel.

▶ A *ring configuration* is a network in which the connections of the nodes (usually through a common communication medium) form a closed loop.

▶ A *mesh configuration* is a network in which node connections are made according to transmission traffic.

▶ With *application software,* you must obtain a site license agreement to allow multiple people to use the same software package.

▶ *Communications protocols* define how two devices communicate with each other in a network.

Carrier sense multiple access with collision detection (CSMA/CD) manages communication by having each node "listen" to the network for communications.

Token passing literally "passes" around an electronic token or message board that each node gets to use in turn.

Fiber distributed data interface (FDDI) uses token passing with high-speed optical fiber as the communication medium.

3 Describe the role of communication devices in an IT network.

▶ *IT communication devices* are the hardware devices that provide the connections between all the other hardware devices in a network.

Data communications equipment (DCE)—for example, modems and network interface cards—includes the hardware that makes the physical connection between the nodes and the actual network.

Communication links are the electronic pathways over which information travels from sender to receiver.

Transmission speed is a measure of how much information—usually in bits—can be passed across a communication link in a single second.

▶ *Guided communication media:*

Twisted-pair cable

Coaxial cable

Optical fiber

▶ *Unguided communication media:*

Microwave media

Satellites

Broadcast radio

▶ *Communication switches* are the hardware devices that bring together the communication media and route communications throughout a network.

Multiplexers aggregate several communication media and allow them to share a single communication medium that usually operates at a much higher capacity and greater speed.

Cluster controllers manage a group of devices that share a single high-speed communication medium connected to another location.

Front-end processors are special computers that handle the communications function for the host computer.

Internetworking units connect networks to each other. *Bridges* connect networks of the same kind. *Routers* connect networks that are dissimilar with respect to some operations like node

addressing and message size. *Gateways* connect networks that are totally dissimilar.

4 Explain the responsibilities of the network administration team and identify the most appropriate participants.

▶ *The network administration team* is responsible for ensuring that the network matches the structural and operational characteristics of the organization and meets people's day-to-day processing and communications needs.

Participants should include:

The network manager

Network specialists and operators

Key management individuals

You (users)

5 Explain the "hot topics" in communications and connectivity that will shape the future of business and your life.

▶ *Asynchronous transfer mode (ATM)* is a transmission method for sending information that divides a long message into smaller units (called packets).

▶ *Integrated services digital network (ISDN)* is the plan and international communications standard for the transition of the world's public telephone system from analog to digital for the purpose of transmitting all types of information simultaneously over twisted-pair telephone lines.

▶ *Electronic data interchange (EDI)* is the direct computer-to-computer transfer of information normally provided by the use of standard business paper documents, such as invoices and purchase orders.

Key Terms

Asynchronous Transfer Mode (ATM)

Bits Per Second (bps)

Bridge

Broadcast Radio

Bus Configuration

Carrier Sense Multiple Access with Collision Detection (CSMA/CD)

Centralized Network

Client

Client/Server Network

Cluster Controller

Coaxial Cable

Communication Device

Communication Link

Communication Medium

Communication Switch

Communications Protocol

Data Communications Equipment (DCE)

Distributed Network

Electronic Data Interchange (EDI)

Fiber Distributed Data Interface (FDDI)

Front-End Processor

Gateway

Guided Communication Media

Hybrid Network

Integrated Services Digital Network (ISDN)

Intelligent Network

Internetworking Unit

IT Network

LAN Configuration

Local Area Network (LAN)

Mesh Configuration

Metropolitan Area Network (MAN)

Microwave

Modem

Multiplexer

Network Administration Team

Network Interface Card

Network Manager

Network Operating System (NOS) Software

Network Specialists and Operators

Node

Optical Fiber

Path

Peer-to-Peer Network

Private Network

Public Network

Ring Configuration

Router

Satellite

Server

Site License Agreement

Star Configuration

Terminal

Token Passing

Transmission Speed

Twisted-Pair Cable

Unguided Communication Media

Value-Added Network (VAN)

Wide Area Network (WAN)

Self-Test

1. What are the three ways in which IT networks can be distinguished?

   A.

   B

   C

2. _____ describes the number of CPUs in a network that help manage how the network functions and how people communicate with each other and process information.

3. The characteristic that can be used to distinguish among centralized, distributed, and hybrid networks is one of _____, which includes:

   A.

   B.

   C.

   D.

4. _____ cover a limited geographic area such as an office, while _____ cover large geographic areas that can include countries all over the world.

5. A network that serves a large number of subscribers usually on a pay-as-you-go basis is called a:

   A. Private network

   B. Subscriber network

   C. Value-added network

   D. Public network

   E. Bus network

6. Complete the accompanying table by identifying the advantages and disadvantages of the four types of local area networks.

Advantage or Disadvantage	Star	Bus	Ring	Mesh
Network control is centralized at one point.				
The nodes communicate directly with each other.				
The loss of one node does not affect the functionality of the network.				
All nodes share the same communication medium.				
The movement of information defines network connections.				
The failure of one node renders the network useless.				
All nodes have their own communication media.				
The failure of the single communication medium renders the network useless.				

7. _____ includes the hardware that makes the physical connection between the nodes and the actual network.

8. The most familiar piece of data communications equipment is a(n):

   A. FDDI

   B. Satellite

   C. Twisted-pair cable

   D. Network interface card

   E. Modem

9. The most popular communication medium in use today is:

   A. Microwave

   B. Optical fiber

   C. Coaxial cable

   D. Twisted-pair cable

   E. Satellite

Cruising the Net

1. If you don't have access to the Internet, find out what options you have for gaining access. Ask someone at school or work and inquire about local Internet service providers. List your options.

2. Access the Web site at http://www.intr.net, which provides access to the Internet for people in the Washington, D.C., area. What options do users have in accessing the Internet through this service? Explore the Internet to see if a familiar Web page exists for an Internet service provider in your area.

3. Suppose you have an IT system and want to be able to communicate with other people outside your home. Do a little research at a local computer store and find out what communications hardware and software you would need and how much it would cost.

4. There are services on the Internet that will help you translate a letter into a different language. Find those services on the Internet. How do they work? For which languages will they work?

5. Find the electronic address for one of your state senators or congresspeople and write the person a letter about an important political issue. Do you think you'll get a response? Do you think the response will be a personal one or will look like a standard mass mail letter?

10. Unguided communication media include:

    A.

    B.

    C.

11. _____ are the hardware devices that bring together the communication media and route communications throughout a network.

12. What must you obtain in order to allow many people to share and use the same application software package?

13. A _____ is the set of procedures that defines how two devices communicate with each other in a network.

14. The network administration team is composed of:

A.

B.

C.

D.

15. Three hot topics in communications and connectivity that will shape the future of business and your life include:

A.

B.

C.

Solutions to Self-Test (1) span of control, ownership, geographic span—p. 173; (2) span of control—p. 173; (3) location, processing, software, information, control—p. 175; (4) local area networks, wide area networks—p. 176; (5) D—p. 175; (6) See Table 6-2—p. 182; (7) data communications equipment—p. 186; (8) E—p. 186; (9) D—p. 188; (10) microwave, satellite, broadcast radio—p. 190; (11) transmission switches—p. 192; (12) site license agreement—p. 182; (13) communications protocol—p. 183; (14) network manager, network specialists and operators, key management individuals, you (users)—p. 196; (15) asynchronous transfer mode (ATM), integrated services digital network (ISDN), electronic data interchange (EDI)—p. 198.

Short-Answer Questions

1. Why are some networks called value-added networks?

2. How does optical fiber differ from other types of guided communication media?

3. Why are microwaves termed *line-of-sight* communication media?

4. How are multiplexers and cluster controllers the same? How are they different?

5. What is the difference between bridges, routers, and gateways?

6. How do token passing and CSMA/CD work?

7. What is asynchronous transfer mode (ATM)? Why is it becoming important?

Discussion Questions and Projects

1. We discussed four LAN configurations—star, bus, ring, and mesh. Do you think that a standards organization should attempt to develop guidelines that would combine the best of these configurations into a single configuration? If so, what do you think would be the characteristics of that configuration? If you don't think we should attempt to create a common configuration, why not?

2. Many colleges and universities throughout the country are using networks and videoconferencing to teach classes at remote campuses. In fact, your school may be doing this. If so, prepare a short report that details some of the hardware and software used and the classes being taught.

3. Keep track of all the ways you communicate for the next week. How could your communication have been handled via IT? What types of hardware devices would be required?

4. In Figure 6-2, we depicted the LAN for your CD mail-order business as a star configuration. Do you think the star configuration is best, or would a bus, ring, or mesh configuration be better? What was your rationale for choosing a particular configuration?

Working in a Group

1. Interview someone at a local business that has an IT network. Find out what kind of network the business has. If that business communicates externally to other people or businesses, ask how it works. Also, ask how its operations would work if it couldn't use a network. Report your findings to the class.

2. Distributed and hybrid networks are quickly replacing centralized networks as the primary architectures for IT networks. Address the following questions:

   A. What business environments are most suitable for a distributed network?

   B. What business environments are most suitable for a centralized network?

   C. What business environments are most suitable for a hybrid network?

   D. Do you think distributed and hybrid networks will ever totally replace centralized networks? Why or why not?

Building IT Systems:

Your Objectives for This Chapter

1 Understand why organizations want your involvement when they develop IT systems and why they develop IT systems. **2** Describe the stages of the in-house system development life cycle (SDLC).

3 Describe how outsourcing affects the SDLC. **4** Understand helpful SDLC tools, including prototyping, data flow diagramming, and computer-assisted software engineering (CASE).

Introduction

Consider building a home. What steps would you go through? First, you would ask yourself, "Why do I want to build a new home?" Perhaps your current home is too small or it's so old that the cost of repairs and maintenance leaves you strapped for cash each month. Next, you would begin writing down the characteristics of your new home—how many rooms, placement of the doors and electrical outlets, size of the backyard and garage, and location. You'd address future issues as well—designing your home to make it easy to add rooms or change the layout. If you're recently married, you'd plan ahead for children; do you add extra rooms now?

After determining what you wanted, you could actually design and build your home yourself or hire other people such as architects, plumbers, and carpenters to do it for you. When it's finished, you would move in, handle maintenance, and make additions as necessary. Some maintenance, such as repainting, would be routine, but some would involve a special project—extending the deck, for instance, or adding a swimming pool.

When an organization develops a new IT system (which we'll simply refer to sometimes as a *system)*, it goes through much the same process as building a home; this process is called the **system development life cycle** (SDLC). After determining that a problem or opportunity exists and gathering the necessary requirements or characteristics of the new system, an organization may choose to let its own IT specialists design and build the new system or hire another organization or independent consultants to do it.

Recall that an IT system contains software (both application and system), hardware (input and output devices, a processing engine, communication devices, and storage devices), information, and people. IT systems don't just magically appear, and building a new system is no small task, just as building a new home is no "weekend project." Each component of a new system must be carefully considered, both individually and in terms of how it will work with the other components so that the organization will receive the greatest benefit from the new system.

In this chapter, we introduce you to the SDLC for IT systems (see Figure 7-1). Our discussions include how organizations use their own IT specialists to develop systems—called *in-house development*—and how organizations hire someone else to do the work—called *outsourcing*. We also take a brief look at the process of developing software—an important function within the SDLC—and at some tools that businesses are using to help them develop software more efficiently.

Figure 7-1

Your Focus in This Chapter: Building IT Systems

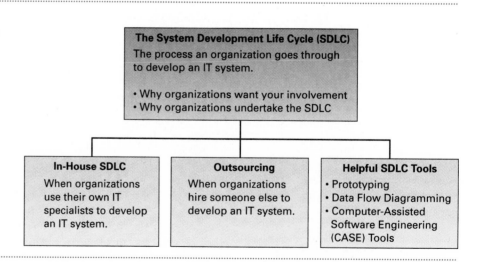

Why Organizations Want Your Involvement

The success of the system development process—which will have an impact on the success of the organization—depends on the active participation of many people. People who participate during the system development process include IT specialists, users (the people who will interact directly with the new system), and customers (people who will benefit from the new system). It may seem odd that customers participate in the development of a new system, but not really. Many organizations today are asking their customers what they would like to see in a system. As we explore the system development process, we'll use an example in which you—as a student—participate in helping your school develop a new registration system.

As an employee of an organization, you are a user of its IT systems. It is therefore important that you help develop new systems, because they will directly affect your ability to do your job efficiently and effectively. Of course, you won't be responsible for the design of many of the technical or physical aspects of a system such as LAN configuration, database layout, and so on, but you will know the logical system requirements. That is, you'll know what the system, regardless of its technical and physical structure, must be able to do.

As an employee of an organization, you will potentially wear many hats (perform different tasks) during the system development process. These may include being:

1. A business process expert
2. A manager of other people
3. A liaison to the customer
4. A quality control analyst

No matter which of these hats you wear or roles you take on, organizations need your participation to develop the best possible system.

As a Business Process Expert

First and foremost, you need to understand that systems are developed for people—to help them be more efficient and effective and to help them better position the organization to get ahead of the competition. For this reason and this reason alone, you are the most important person in the SDLC—you are the business process expert because you know what has to happen. Think about it for a moment—if you were an accountant for an organization that was developing a new accounting system, who would best be able to specify what the new system must do? That's right—you. You must share your knowledge with the people developing the new system. If you don't, expect a system that does *not* meet your needs.

As a Manager of Other People

Managers not only deal with personnel issues such as hiring employees and determining who gets raises, but they also make sure that certain operations run smoothly, efficiently, and effectively. During the SDLC, managers are responsible for seeing to it that a proposed system will meet the overall needs of their workers, that workers have a way of communicating their needs, and that changes are communicated back. As a manager, you are responsible for the productivity of your work force—this means you must watch out for your own good as well as that of other people.

As a manager, you are also responsible for making sure that money is well spent. That means that you are responsible for justifying a proposed system from a business standpoint and monitoring the process of the SDLC. Your goal is to ensure that the project meets its budget and schedule and develops a quality system.

As a Liaison to the Customer

In an organization, most people tend to think that IT systems are developed for their use. While this is true, you must also realize that your function in an organization is to meet the needs of other people—the customers. For example, people who work in the registration office need to keep you (the students) in mind when a new registration system is being built. As you specify the requirements of a new system, always keep the ultimate customer in mind. Make sure that systems are developed to keep existing customers happy and entice the competition's customers to join your organization.

It's very easy for, say, the registration office to focus on operational priorities such as accuracy of data, fast processing, and error checking. They may not realize that the new form you have to fill out is hard to understand, that the system makes it hard for you to add and drop classes, or that it requires extra work for you. In your career, whether as a technical developer, a manager, or a user of a proposed system, *never* exclude the customers from providing input and feedback.

As a Quality Control Analyst

Finally, during the SDLC, you must act as a quality control analyst. As a quality control analyst, you must make sure, at each stage of the SDLC, that the system is being developed according to your desires. Your active participation and review during the SDLC is the only way of ensuring that the final system is the best system. Take time to carefully review documents and attend all meetings—remember, your time investment will pay off in a big way in the future. Project management and quality assurance are among the most valued skills in organizations that rely on IT for their business efficiency and effectiveness.

A major reason for this is "runaway" projects. These are ones that get out of control or that only appear to be in control. Here's a fairly recent example from the airline industry.

American Airlines developed a new reservation system called CONFIRM to provide major hotel chains, including Marriott and Hilton, and car rental companies with the capability American already had through its SABRE system. SABRE is among the five most successful IT innovations in terms of competitive value, and American is among the best ever in exploiting IT. So Marriott and the others saw it as the best option.

The project fell two years behind schedule. Its budget doubled. Finally, it was scheduled to go "live" in mid-1992. However, with under three months to go, it was found to contain "bugs"—errors that would take 18 months to fix. It was finally abandoned and $300 million written off, with court cases everywhere about who was liable for the loss. Each party accused the others of poor communication, constant design changes, inadequate testing, and weak project management.

When the best of the best have such problems, think of what can happen in the average firm. The damage was huge—to Marriott's competitive position and American Airlines' reputation. Its chairman stated that this was the worst experience in his 20 years of leadership of the company.

It's simple enough to say that organizations today develop systems to take advantage of IT. These advantages include performing tasks more efficiently and effectively and providing new products or services (innovation). More specifically, though, organizations undertake the SDLC to (1) convert a manual system to an automated system, (2) totally overhaul an existing system, (3) make changes to an existing system, (4) make minor revisions to an existing system, or (5) invent a new system.

In your personal life, converting a manual system to an automated system includes doing your personal tax returns on the computer and electronically submitting them to the IRS instead of doing them with pen, calculator, and paper and using the postal service for delivery. In business, it includes maintaining hiring, performance appraisal, and promotion records, and preparing human resource reports electronically.

Totally overhauling an existing system involves throwing away the old inefficient way of handling tasks and building a system to do them the right way. For you, this may mean throwing away word processing files that keep track of names and addresses and using personal information management software instead to maintain your contact lists. For a bank, it may mean replacing a cumbersome loan application system that requires filling out forms that take weeks to be processed while being passed from one department to the next, with one where you apply by phone. The application is processed online in minutes.

BayBank in New England did this in 1994 by copying the mail-order system of L. L. Bean. BayBank sends customers a colorful 53-page catalog offering 160 different financial products. Customers in turn order these by phone and fax, replacing

AMERICAN AIRLINES' SABRE SYSTEM

In 1987, the president of American Airlines was asked about the possibility of selling the airline and the SABRE system. If he had to sell one or the other, which would it be? His answer may surprise you. He very bluntly and without hesitation stated that he'd sell the airline and keep the SABRE system. He went on to explain that it would probably be easier to build another airline than to go through the process of developing the SABRE system.

Why? Because one of the most difficult tasks people undertake is the development of an IT system—sometimes even more difficult than building an airline. Many systems—like American Airlines' SABRE system—take years to develop and millions of dollars. Just as important as the cost and time it takes to develop a complex and huge system is the fact that American Airlines has an unbelievable advantage over its competitors because of the SABRE system. Have you ever wondered why other airlines don't develop their own versions of SABRE? The answer is simple— it would take too long, cost too much, be no better than the SABRE system, and American has already captured the entire market.

If you still don't believe that the SABRE system is vitally important to American Airlines, consider the fact that it's physically stored in a mountain (like NORAD, the nation's defense system) with six levels of security. Some things can never be replaced, nor can their development ever be duplicated. Businesses are finding that out today, they're taking their systems development seriously, and they're gaining an advantage over their competitors.

forms, visits to the bank, and interviews with loan officers. The mail-order processing center of BayBank now does the business equivalent to 30 brick-and-mortar branches.

The First Bank system in Minneapolis lets customers interact directly with an IT system that processes their application for a car loan, automatically checking credit files on other companies' computers. They can obtain a loan in 15 minutes. It cost First Bank $41 to process a loan manually. The IT replacement, which does nothing "new," costs $7 per loan. That's a reduction of almost 80 percent. The bank gains efficiency and cuts costs while the customers gain convenience—that's a win-win situation for everyone (except the competition).

Making changes involves just that—making changes to one or more processes that a system handles. For you, this may mean modifying your calendar management system so you can download information from the university's online calendar and class schedule systems. Businesses go through the process of making changes on a payroll system when they choose a new insurance carrier.

Making minor revisions involves really just fine-tuning the way an existing system works. For example, you may add a spreadsheet printout to your calendar management system that shows your air travel expenses for each month. In a business, minor changes include changing the percentage deduction for social security in a payroll system and creating a graph that shows report information in a more visual form. Making minor revisions and changes to an existing system may not require that the complete SDLC be followed.

Inventing a new system involves using IT to do something you've never done before. So, for example, you could build a system to help you get a job when you graduate: creating and providing status reports concerning application letters, replies, interviews, references, follow-up letters, company names, addresses and contacts, and so on.

In business, using IT to invent a new system is *big* business. Consider Dell Computers—Dell literally invented ordering PCs by phone through catalogs, with customized assembly and delivery by UPS or FedEx. This new automated system has completely eliminated the need for retail stores and storage warehouses by Dell. Dell grew from a start-up company to one with $2 billion in sales in under 10 years, a level it achieved before its founder's 30th birthday.

The In-House System Development Life Cycle

You now know why organizations undertake the SDLC and why your participation is vital, regardless of your

Discovering IT

Suppose you wanted to build a system that would help you get a job when you graduate. What types of software would you use to (1) create status reports concerning application letters, (2) maintain a list of companies that you would like to work for, and (3) build your resume? How effective do you think your job search would be if you didn't use these technology tools?

career direction, so let's look at what goes on during the SDLC. First, we'll discuss the SDLC for in-house development and then how outsourcing affects the SDLC. The **in-house system development life cycle** (in-house SDLC) is a set of six stages that an organization goes through to develop an IT system. During these six stages, the organization relies on its own IT staff to carry out the necessary tasks. The six stages of the in-house SDLC include:

1. Define the problem/opportunity
2. Gather requirements for the new system
3. Design the new system
4. Develop the new system
5. Implement the new system
6. Maintain the new system

In Figure 7-2, you can see that a decision concerning whether to continue follows each of the first three stages. During these times, the organization must carefully assess the worth of the proposed system and decide whether to continue.

Figure 7-2

The In-House System Development Life Cycle (SDLC)

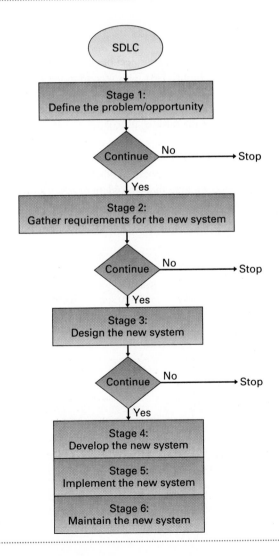

These decisions are not to be made lightly; many system development projects require years and millions of dollars to complete stages 3 and 4. It's better to spend extra time in the early stages and cancel or modify the project than find later that its conception is flawed.

In Figure 7-2, the SDLC is shown as a series of sequential stages. In reality, there is much iteration among the stages. For example, an organization could be in stage 3 (design the new system) and find that some requirements of the new system had not been captured. In this case, the organization would return to stage 2 (gather requirements for the new system), gather the necessary requirements, and then proceed again to stage 3. Iteration among the SDLC stages for the purpose of refining the design of a new system is crucial. When you become involved in the process of developing a new system, you'll find that this type of iteration occurs to a great extent.

To help illustrate what goes on in each of these stages, let's consider an example. Suppose that your school wanted to develop a new system that would automate such tasks as scheduling classes and registering students. Your school has asked you as a student to participate in the process of developing this new system—after all, you are a "customer" who will be directly affected by the new system. After we discuss what is involved in each stage, we'll return to this example and see how everything works with respect to a real problem.

Stage 1: Define the Problem/Opportunity

Every system development project begins with recognizing that a problem or opportunity exists (see Figure 7-3). This recognition may come in the form of a management mandate ("We want to begin advertising on the Internet"), a user request or complaint ("I work in the customer service department and the system always goes down when we're the busiest; it really makes the customers mad, and some of them swear to never shop here again"), a customer suggestion ("When I receive my electric bill, it would be nice to know how this month's charges compare to last month's and last year's"), or in a variety of other ways. Whatever the case, this is what begins the SDLC—recognizing that a problem or opportunity exists.

Now the organization can begin laying the groundwork for solving the problem or taking advantage of the opportunity. "Laying the groundwork" includes

Table 7-1

Salaries for Programmers and Analysts[1]

Salary	Systems Analyst	Senior Systems Programmer	Systems Programmer	Senior Programmer/ Analyst	Programmer/ Analyst
Overall Average	$48,314	$53,730	$44,666	$46,235	$40,537
By Industry					
Banking	$56,785	$58,852	$51,750	$53,290	$45,369
Nonprofit	$51,000	$45,000	NA	$48,642	$34,285
Insurance	$45,054	$70,122	$49,525	$56,442	$42,591
Transportation	$46,444	$50,000	$47,750	$47,071	$40,500
Utilities	$44,000	$58,125	$31,000	$46,050	$41,571
Education	$43,676	$49,942	$43,290	$45,261	$35,396
Health	$38,208	$52,500	$42,800	$56,307	$36,127
Agriculture	$49,666	$51,333	$56,500	$47,333	$38,678

Figure 7-3

**Stage 1: Define the
Problem/Opportunity**

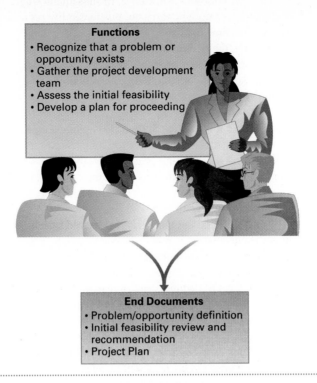

Functions
- Recognize that a problem or opportunity exists
- Gather the project development team
- Assess the initial feasibility
- Develop a plan for proceeding

End Documents
- Problem/opportunity definition
- Initial feasibility review and recommendation
- Project Plan

defining exactly what the problem or opportunity is, gathering the project development team, performing an initial feasibility review, and developing a project plan for proceeding.

The most important document to come out of this stage is a statement that explicitly identifies what the problem or opportunity is. This document varies in length, but it generally should not exceed two pages. Be careful here—this definition should be as quantifiable as possible, outline the scope of the proposed project, and focus on the problem or opportunity and not symptoms. So, for instance, it's far more useful to state the problem as "average time to register is 27 minutes with 47 minutes being the longest" than as "registration takes too long."

The **project development team** should generally include a project manager, several IT specialists, management individuals from the area in which the new system will be located, and several users and customers—people who will work directly with and be affected by the new system. Among the IT specialists is one or more systems analysts and one or more programmers. A **systems analyst** is an IT specialist who works with users to define how the current system works, what changes need to be made, and how the new system will work. On many project development teams, the project leader will be a systems analyst. A **programmer** is an IT specialist responsible for writing the software code. These responsibilities primarily fall into stage 4 when the technical system design is converted into a working system.

The project development team then completes an initial feasibility review and makes a recommendation. The **initial feasibility review** quickly determines if the benefits of the proposed system outweigh the expected costs of its development. This review can be based on time (How quickly is the new system needed?), cost (Is there even any money in the budget?), personnel requirements (Is staffing available to undertake a new project?), and technical requirements (Does hardware exist that will do what we want?). In subsequent stages of the SDLC, the project development team will carry out this feasibility review again as more concrete numbers become available.

Finally, the project development team develops a plan for proceeding. The **project plan** includes proposed dates for completing major tasks. For example, you may set dates for completing the remaining five stages and develop general budget guidelines.

Your School's Registration System. Complaints have consistently been coming in from the students—the lines are too long, classes are always closed, the right classes aren't offered, and so on. Basically, there's a problem, but the problem hasn't been stated yet. In fact, if you took the first complaint—the lines are too long—the obvious (but wrong) solution is to increase the number of people working during registration.

What you find out though is that the old system—built 10 years ago—is not fast enough to handle the number of students today. You also note that the current automated registration system is in no way linked to the manual class scheduling system, which means that classes are scheduled without respect to registration trends.

Your school's administration responds by putting together a project team that includes a project manager, two systems analysts, a software programmer, two hardware specialists, the director of the registration office, and two office workers in the registration office. The administration has posted a notice asking for three students to participate on the project development team. You gladly volunteer, hoping that your efforts now will mean shorter lines in the future.

The project team then tackles the initial feasibility review. While the project manager and a few others inquire about budgetary constraints, you and the systems analysts visit a nearby college with approximately the same number of students. When you find out how much their system cost and how long it took to develop, you return with the information. In a meeting one afternoon, the IT specialists agree that the new system is not too difficult to develop, the project manager says there is ample money to cover the development costs, and you all agree that a new system can be up and running within a year—about the same time the old system will reach overload. Your recommendation: proceed forward.

At the end of the meeting, the project development team generates a project plan. Some initial dates are set for completing the remaining stages, and the team decides to initially target $1 million as a budget. Now you're off and running to stage 2—gathering requirements for the new system.

Stage 2: Gather Requirements for the New System

During the requirements gathering stage, the project team documents how the current system works, the changes that need to be made, and how the proposed system will work (see Figure 7-4). At this point, the project development team focuses on the logical requirements of the proposed system, not necessarily on the physical requirements. For example, how much student information (name, social security number, classes completed, and so on) must be stored is determined but not whether magnetic or optical disk will be used. The logical requirements that must be gathered include input requirements (what information comes into the system), output requirements (what information must be generated by the system), and processing requirements (the necessary steps to convert the input to output). As these are specified, the project development team must include projected requirements

(How many students will we have in the year 2000?) as well as current requirements (How many students do we have today?).

Requirements can be gathered in a number of ways. The more important approaches include observing the current system as it works; collecting sample forms, reports, and copies of screens; conducting interviews with users and customers; and reviewing policies and procedures for the current system.

The end documents of this stage include a description of how the current system works, what changes need to be made, how the new system will work, and input requirements, output requirements, and processing requirements. Once this is complete, the project development team further refines its feasibility review and determines whether or not to proceed.

Your School's Registration System. In your next meeting, the project manager begins by explaining that the next step is to document how the registration system currently works, what changes need to be made, and how the proposed system will work. The project development team decides that the "divide and conquer" strategy will work best, so responsibilities are assigned as follows:

▶ Project manager: Document how faculty and administrators go about scheduling classes. Obtain copies of all forms and reports used during the class scheduling process. Ask the faculty to specify any additional information they would like to see on the reports.

▶ Two systems analysts: Document how much information is currently stored by the system, including student information, registration information, and class scheduling information. Also, obtain copies of all forms and reports currently used. Ask the registration office to specify any additional information it would like to see on the reports.

Figure 7-4

Stage 2: Gather Requirements for the New System

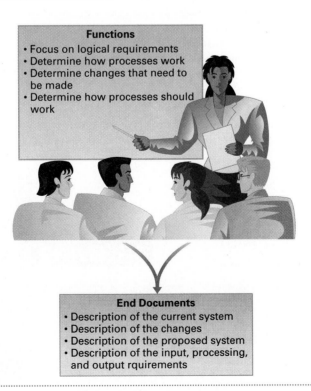

Functions
- Focus on logical requirements
- Determine how processes work
- Determine changes that need to be made
- Determine how processes should work

End Documents
- Description of the current system
- Description of the changes
- Description of the proposed system
- Description of the input, processing, and output rquirements

---

- ▶ Software programmer: Work with the office of external affairs to develop projections for future student enrollments.

- ▶ Two hardware specialists: Document the current hardware system.

- ▶ Director of registration: Interview at least five students and get their view of how the registration system should work.

- ▶ Two office workers: Interview at least five faculty members and get their view of how the class scheduling system should work.

- ▶ You and the other two students: Document the process a student goes through to register, from discussing class selections with an advisor to paying the bill.

In your next meeting, everyone provides documentation concerning what they've found and a heated discussion ensues. It seems that you forgot to put any faculty members on the project development team, and they are an important part of the class scheduling system. As you take a step back and look at things, the project development team decides that you're working with two problems instead of one—registration and class scheduling.

The faculty don't really mind the way they go about scheduling classes, and it seems to work fairly well. So you decide to focus only on the registration system and save the class scheduling system for the next project development team. You quickly revise your statement of the problem and proceed from there.

At this point, you split into two groups to define how the current system should work. Group 1 is responsible for combining the current information requirements with future student enrollments and defining forms and reports, and group 2 will review the current method of registration (see Figure 7-5) and the way students want it to work and will propose a new method of registration.

The following week, you gather again and share your findings (see Figure 7-6). Basically, you've decided that the system should present the students with a list of classes for which they can register before they complete the enrollment form. This way, they cannot request a class that is either closed or for which they have not had the prerequisites. Things seem to look good, and the proposed method of registration appears to excite everyone. The project still looks feasible from a cost, technical, and schedule point of view, so the project development proceeds to stage 3.

Stage 3: Design the New System

In the design stage, the project development team converts the logical system requirements from stage 2 into a technical system design (see Figure 7-7 on page

Discovering IT

Graphically lay out the steps you go through for registration at your school. Now, lay out the way you would like registration to work. Can IT be used in your proposed registration system? Do you think your proposed method would be better for students? Teachers? Administrators? The registration office?

Building IT Systems: The Tools You Use and Your Role

Figure 7-5

What You Found: How Registration Works for the Students

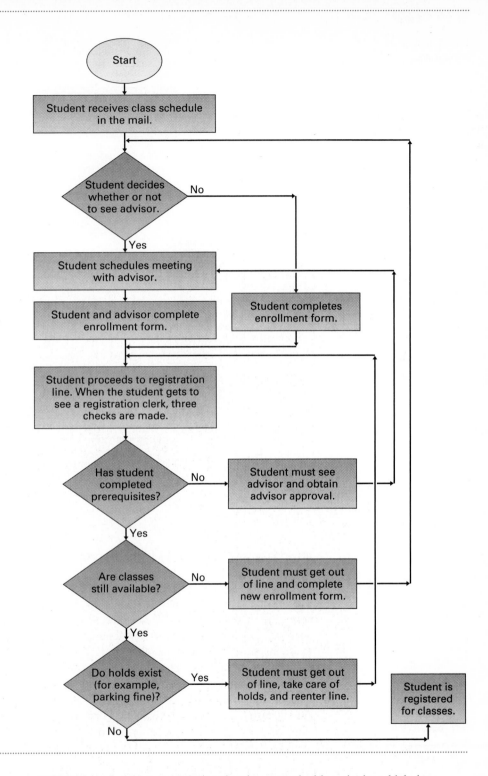

223). This technical system design then becomes the blueprint by which the system is built in stage 4—similar to the blueprints for your new home. This technical system design includes descriptions of screen and report formats, file and database layouts, processing requirements (software), the necessary hardware, any

Figure 7-6

**How Registration
Should Work**

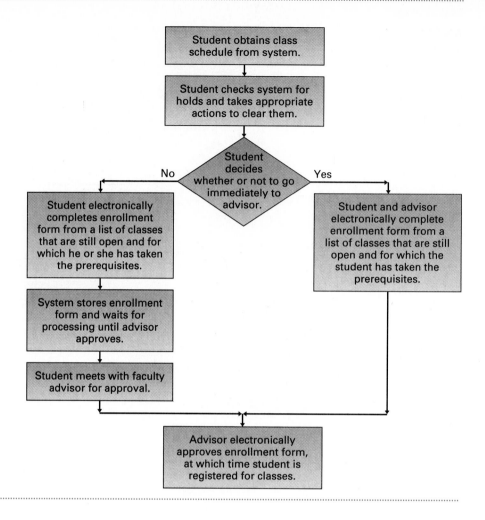

networking capabilities, and a list of the people who will develop the new system in stage 4.

During this stage, the project development team may generate several alternatives for the design of the new system. If so, the project development team must assess the feasibility of each and determine which is best. Consider storage hardware as an example; the project development team will have to determine whether to use magnetic, optical, or magneto-optical storage devices.

During the first two stages, users and customers have a very active role in the system development process. Beginning with stage 3, however, they begin to provide less direct input and act more as quality control analysts. That is, the technical system design is completed mostly by IT specialists; users and customers are responsible for reviewing the proposed alternatives and the recommended solution to ensure that they meet the requirements specified in stage 2.

Your School's Registration System. At your next meeting, the project manager begins by telling you that it's now time for the IT specialists to use their expertise and create a technical design for the new system. The project manager also tells you that your role—as well as that of the other students, the director of registration, and

Figure 7-7

**Stage 3: Design the
New System**

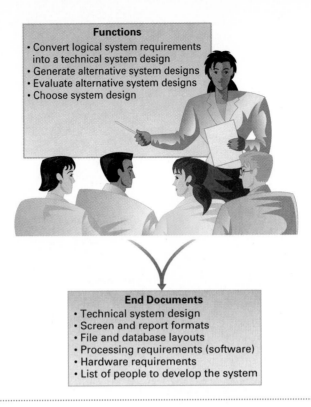

Functions
- Convert logical system requirements into a technical system design
- Generate alternative system designs
- Evaluate alternative system designs
- Choose system design

End Documents
- Technical system design
- Screen and report formats
- File and database layouts
- Processing requirements (software)
- Hardware requirements
- List of people to develop the system

the two office workers—is now to review the final design to make sure that it meets the logical requirements. The next meeting is scheduled for the first of the month.

At the first of the month, you show up early for the meeting, excited about seeing the new system design. The IT specialists have done a great job—they've considered every possible technical design, from registration by telephone to totally eliminating faculty advisors. Figure 7-8 shows the network, which is a combination of a star configuration and a bus configuration for handling registration. You should also notice that the IT specialists are recommending the use of a central database that includes the student, class, faculty, and registration files.

The network is a great solution, because it allows the registration office to maintain control over the registration process while giving students and faculty the flexibility to do their own work. For instance, the proposed system includes workstations where students can build individual class schedules. These individual schedules will be stored on the global storage device and accessed by the faculty advisor during the advising period. The proposed system will also let the faculty use DBMS software to query the registration system and obtain such information as a list of classes that have already reached capacity.

The IT specialists have also done a feasibility study and found that the proposed system will come in well under budget. The budget includes adding three software programmers to help with the development in stage 4. Everyone shares in your enthusiasm and proceeds to the next stage.

Stage 4: Develop the New System

During the development stage, the IT specialists convert the technical system design into an actual IT system (see Figure 7-9). Converting the design into an

Figure 7-8

**Partial Technical Design for
the New Registration System**

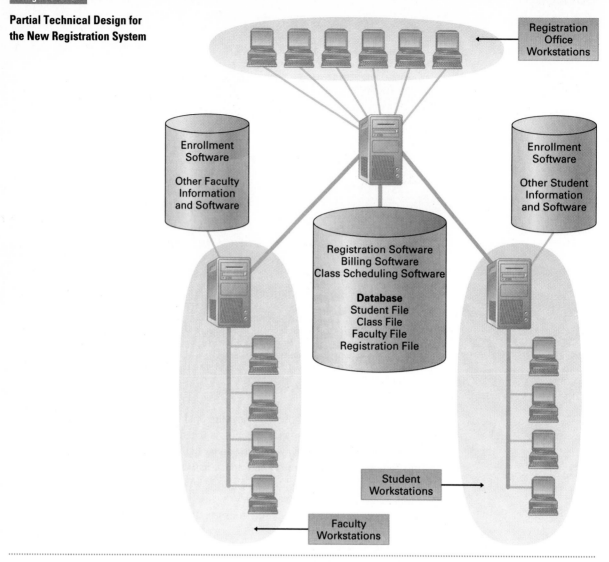

actual system includes writing the necessary software and making sure that it
works (sometimes called *programming* and *testing*), building the files and databases, and generating the screens and reports. As in stage 3, most of this work is done
by the IT specialists, while the users and customers participate as quality control
analysts.

The end documents of this stage include the software and software documentation, file and database documentation, and a detailed description of the hardware.
The project development team may also have to develop a plan for installing the
hardware if new facilities (like buildings or rooms) have to be used or existing
facilities have to be modified.

Your School's Registration System. The project manager explains to you that the IT
specialists will also handle most of the work in the development stage. Your role
again will be to review screens and reports to make sure that they are complete and
provide all the necessary information.

Stage 5: Implement the New System

The implementation stage involves actually installing the hardware and software, training users, and using the new system. Most important, the implementation stage involves converting from the old to the new way. Converting from the old to the new way can be achieved in many ways—parallel, plunge, piecemeal, and pilot.

Parallel conversion involves using both the old and new systems until the project development team determines that the new system works correctly. Parallel conversion is probably the most expensive (it may require some people to perform the same task two different ways), but it's also the safest. **Plunge conversion** amounts to totally discarding the old system and immediately begin using the new system. Although this method is fast and inexpensive, it's the riskiest if the new system doesn't work.

Piecemeal conversion occurs when one portion of the new system is implemented and verified before other portions are implemented. For example, if an organization were implementing a new accounting system, it may choose to implement the payroll portion before implementing the inventory, accounts receivable, and accounts payable portions. Finally, conversion can be achieved by **piloting** the system. In this instance, only a portion of the users start using the new system until it is verified. After that, the remaining users convert to the new system.

Your School's Registration System. Finally, it's time to begin using the new system. The project development team has chosen to implement the new system using both parallel and piloting methods of conversion. One hundred students will register for classes using both the old and new systems. This provides two benefits for the project development team. First, by using the old and new systems the team can verify that the outputs of the new registration system match the outputs of the old

Figure 7-9

Stage 4: Develop the New System

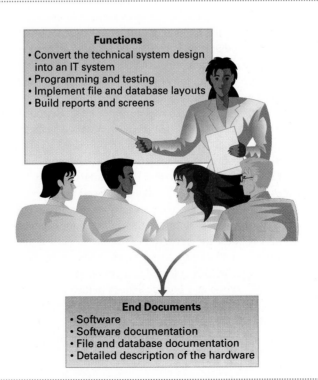

Functions
- Convert the technical system design into an IT system
- Programming and testing
- Implement file and database layouts
- Build reports and screens

End Documents
- Software
- Software documentation
- File and database documentation
- Detailed description of the hardware

system. Second, by using only a portion of the students, the team can iron out any problems before the next semester, when all students will use the new system.

As it turns out, the new system is a huge success. Everyone applauds your efforts, and you have the satisfaction of knowing that you've done a good job.

Stage 6: Maintain the New System

The last stage of the SDLC is maintaining the new system. At the beginning of this stage, the project development team is scaled back to include only a few IT specialists and a project manager. These people act as contacts if problems or questions arise with the new system.

During this stage, members of the project team monitor the system to make sure it continues to work correctly and makes changes as the need arises. Today, businesses and how they work are changing—IT systems must do the same. For example, your school's registration system may change next year if someone decides that it would be nice if the system provided students with the option of seeing screen prompts in different languages.

Outsourcing—The Request for Proposal Process

Outsourcing occurs when an organization decides to let someone else take over and develop, operate, and/or maintain part of its operations. For example, many organizations today outsource activities such as maintenance and repair, distribution, food service, and the SDLC of IT systems. For the SDLC of IT systems, many organizations hire consultants to assist during requirements gathering and design, contract programmers for the development (programming and testing) of software, and individuals or organizations to implement a new system, train users, and maintain the hardware and software.

Besides being a cost-effective mechanism, the real logic behind outsourcing is to focus management effort and resources on the firm's priority areas of business. For example, your school may outsource food services, security operations, and perhaps even the managing of the bookstore. Why? Well, obviously someone has determined that it makes financial sense to let someone else take over these areas, but, more important, this lets your school administrators focus internal efforts on providing you with the best possible education. Education, after all, is your school's priority mission.

Let's return to your registration SDLC. Suppose that your project development team determined that the new system was needed by next summer and there was not enough time to develop it in-house. So you decide to let someone else design and develop the system for you (outsourcing). Figure 7-10 shows the SDLC for developing a new system through outsourcing. Notice that design and development (stages 3 and 4) have been replaced by generate request for proposal (RFP), evaluate RFP returns, and choose a vendor. In developing an IT system, the key to finding the right system and the right vendor is generating a good RFP.

A **request for proposal** (RFP) is a document that outlines the necessary requirements for a new system and solicits bids from other organizations or individuals (generically referred to as *vendors*). A good RFP provides a description of the organization and future changes in the organization (for example, the number of students in the year 2000). The RFP then defines the problem/opportunity and provides a complete description of how the current system works and the logical requirements for the new system. Characteristics of a good RFP include:

Figure 7-10

Letting Someone Else Do the Work—The New SDLC

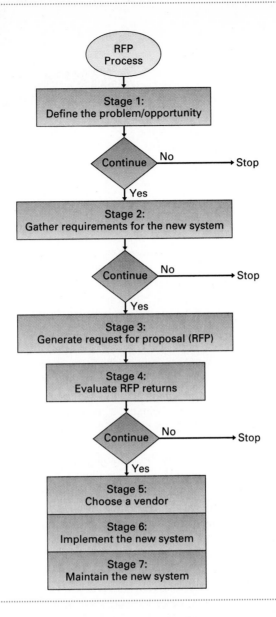

- Organizational background described
- Future projections outlined
- Complete problem/opportunity defined
- Requirements listed and ranked
- Evaluation criteria completely detailed
- Contact person specified
- Deadline for RFP returns stated
- Timetable for project completion included
- Concise
- Thorough

Notice that an organization considering outsourcing specifies only logical requirements—not physical requirements. The vendors responding to the RFP will propose the physical requirements (that is, technical system design). Rankings of importance (for instance, necessary, nice, optional, bad) may also be included with the list of logical requirements, which help the vendors generate a solution that better matches the needs of the organization.

A good RFP will also outline how the RFP returns will be evaluated. For example, a simple scoring mechanism can be used: (2) necessary, (1) nice, (0) optional, and (- 1) bad. The organization can then order the RFP returns by the sum of the scores; the highest score would meet the most needs, while the lowest score would meet the least. Finally, a good RFP identifies a contact person within the organization, the deadline for RFP returns, and a timetable in which the system must be completed.

Once a vendor is chosen, both organizations enter into a contract agreement that includes information concerning the total costs, how and when payments will be made, an exact deadline for the completion of the system, testing criteria by which the system will be evaluated and accepted, how training will take place, and post-implementation maintenance and support (if necessary). This contract is a legally binding document that specifies your organization's responsibilities as well as the vendor's.

Every day, more and more organizations are choosing to do outsourcing in the area of IT. The reasons are simple. First, outsourcing eliminates the need to keep a complete staff of trained IT specialists within the organization. Some IT specialists will always be needed, though, to handle the day-to-day operations and solve problems as they arrive. Second, there are many organizations today that just specialize in developing IT systems for other organizations. These types of organizations can make better use of the most up-to-date technology and provide a great deal of expertise.

Finally, outsourcing the development of an IT system is usually much faster than in-house development. Consider the hospital industry—there are about 15 organizations in the United States today that provide outsourcing IT system support to the hospital community. These organizations already have systems developed for areas that include patient care, patient admission and billing, radiology, and physician support. In less than a year, any of these organizations can provide a working IT system in any of these areas—something that would probably take years to develop in-house.

Don Tyson of Tyson Farms once said, "There is no such thing as second place in business. Either a business stays ahead of its competitors, or it falls behind." Don should probably know—his company sells more than half the chickens in the United States because it refuses to fall behind. Businesses today are getting ahead and staying ahead by deploying innovative, state-of-the-art technologies and computer networks. No longer can technology just be used to track assets and liabilities and perform payroll.

Most restaurant chains, however, have lagged behind in the use of technology because they do not understand the effects of high-powered technology on their internal operations. More important, technology is changing so fast that new hardware and software must be purchased every year or so, which is an intolerable expense for most restaurant chains.

The solution to this problem is outsourcing. Other industries have readily embraced outsourcing. In fact, two-thirds of the U.S. construction firms rely on outsourcing to handle most corporate financial functions. Of those, 70 percent say that outsourcing plays a key role in their ability to generate growth.

For a restaurant chain, outsourcing is appropriate for all computer functions, including accounting, payroll processing, managing telecommunications among divisions and departments, and integrating all systems so that data have to be entered only once.

Outsourcing frees restaurant chain management to focus on the primary business operations. Those operations include overall restaurant management, franchise development, personnel scheduling, food ordering, food quality, and service quality. After all, it's kind of hard for a restaurant manager to monitor the quality of food preparation if he or she is tied up with generating payroll information or wondering how to get a report that includes graphs as well as numeric information.

Helpful System Development Life Cycle Tools

You were probably able to read through the previous registration system example in less than an hour. In real life, though, it would probably take a school a minimum of one year to go from realizing that a problem with registration existed to implementing a new system. That's if the system were outsourced; to do in-house development would require well over two years.

You see, the requirements gathering, design, and development (stages 2, 3, and 4) of a new IT system is a complicated and lengthy process. During these stages, most of the time is spent on specifying, designing, writing, and testing the software—we call this process **software development**. Why is software development so difficult, and why does it take so long to do? The reasons include the following:

▶ **Incomplete or ambiguous requirements specifications during requirements gathering:** People attach different terms to different things. For example, at your school what is the difference between a class, a course, a course offering, a class section, and a course section? Or does your school use terms that differ from these? If the exact definitions of terms such as these are not determined early in the SDLC, developing software to perform certain tasks is almost impossible.

▶ **Lack of user and customer involvement throughout the SDLC:** Users and customers have the expertise to define how a current system works, what changes need to be made, and which characteristics will make the new system the best system. If the project development team doesn't include the users and customers during early stages, the software will reflect what the project development team thinks needs to happen—not what should happen.

▶ **Requirement changes over the course of time:** Because the SDLC often takes many years to complete, it only makes sense that some requirements will change during that time. For example, in two years your registration system may need to take into account the fact that class overflows can be handled by videoconferencing; today, that may not be a consideration.

▶ **Computers are simpleminded:** Software is the set of instructions that a computer follows to perform a task, and software must be defined in excruciating detail. For example, Word—the word processing package offered by Microsoft—contains over 1 million instructions. This vast number of instructions is necessary because computers are simpleminded; you must provide exact instruction sets that a computer needs to execute.

▶ **One error means big failure:** One error in software means, no matter how large or small or for what reason, the system will be a big failure. What if a friend gave you a list of 10 steps to get somewhere and told you to turn right in step 3 when you should have turned left. Well, eventually, you would find your way, but not a computer. Once it encounters an error, it stops—period. Think about the weekend in 1993 when the ATMs operated by a bank in Washington "ate" 2,000 customer cards, confiscating them all because of one error in a simple line of code.

In reality, there is no *foolproof* way of developing IT systems that will guarantee a fully working system that completely meets all requirements each and every time. There are, however, some tools that project development teams can use to create the best system possible, and most of these tools focus on software development. We certainly don't have the time or space to explain all of them to you, so let's focus on three that have been very successful—prototyping, data flow diagramming, and computer-assisted software engineering tools.

Prototyping

A **prototype** is a simulation or experimental model of a proposed system or product. **Prototyping** is the process of developing a simulation or experimental model. Prototyping is widely used in manufacturing products such as automobiles, airplanes, and motorcycles. It would be foolish for an automobile manufacturer to roll an automobile off the assembly line without first building a prototype to test characteristics such as aerodynamics, fuel consumption, and comfort. Prototyping is also used to develop simulations of software for proposed IT systems—we call these *software prototypes.*

Box 7-1

Programming Languages

Ⓓeveloping or writing software consumes the most time during the SDLC. Software can be written in one of many programming languages. A **programming language** is a set of rules that define the syntax for how software must be written. In Chapter 4, we used the following software as an example:

1000 Print "Enter two numbers"

1010 Input A, B

1020 Let C = A + B

1030 Print "The Result is"; C

This piece of software was written in a programming language called BASIC (for **B**eginner's **A**ll-Purpose **S**ymbolic **I**nstruction **C**ode).

About 50 different programming languages are used today. Programming languages are defined not only by the syntax used, but also by orientation (for example, mathematical versus business oriented) and generation. Just as all other components of IT have progressed through stages or generations, so have programming languages.

First- and second-generation programming languages are called *low-level* languages, because their syntax does not require a great deal of conversion to binary form. Most operating system software is written using a second-generation programming language. Third- through fifth-generation programming languages are called *high-level* languages because their syntax requires a great deal of conversion to binary. In fact, the BASIC program above is an example of a third-generation programming language. Other third-generation programming languages include COBOL (a business-oriented language), FORTRAN (a mathematical and scientific language), PL/1, C, and RPG (a report generator). All third-generation languages are called *procedural* languages because the exact set of steps to complete a task must be specified.

Fourth- and fifth-generation programming languages are called *nonprocedural* or *natural* languages. If you use one of these, you only have to specify what you want the end result to be without specifying all the necessary steps. For example, you could enter a request similar to "WHO WORKS IN THE NORTHERN TERRITORY" using a fourth- or fifth-generation language. To achieve the same result using a third-generation programming language, you might have to write as many as 100 lines of code! Examples of fourth- and fifth-generation programming languages include MUMPS, FOCUS, SQL, and ORACLE.

If you're considering a career in the IT field, it is likely that your first job will be as a programmer, creating software in one of many programming languages. If so, you should do some research to find out which programming languages are used by businesses for which you are interested in working and learn as many of them as possible.

Prototyping can be used as a tool within the SDLC or it can be used as a replacement for the SDLC. In fact, prototyping is a popular alternative to the SDLC when the system is relatively small and can be developed in a relatively short time.

Whether prototyping is to be used as a tool within it or as a replacement of the SDLC will depend on the characteristics and nature of the system to be developed. For example, when American Airlines developed the SABRE system, prototyping was used as a tool within the SDLC. Prototyping helped the developers of the SABRE system define user requirements, test certain operational aspects of the system, and develop many of the user interfaces (for example, screen and report layouts). On the other hand, if you're using a spreadsheet package to develop a report for your finance class, you would probably not follow the stages of the SDLC; rather you would develop an initial prototype of your report and continually refine it until you were happy with the results.

The Prototyping Process. Prototyping is a continual refinement development tool. It requires that users and the project development team continually refine a prototype until everyone agrees that the prototype is correct. As Figure 7-11 shows, the four steps in the prototyping process include:

1. Identifying basic requirements
2. Developing the initial prototype
3. User reviewing
4. Revising and enhancing the prototype

The prototyping process begins with identifying the basic known requirements of an IT system. These basic requirements include, at a minimum, what information will be input and output. If possible, an outline of the processes that must take place to convert the inputs to outputs would also be prepared. Basic requirements, however, usually do not include data editing rules and end-of-period processing requirements (for example, end-of-the-month or end-of-the-year reports and information archiving).

The most important thing to remember during this step is that not all requirements have to be gathered. If you recall, the prototyping process allows the users to dynamically determine requirements while working with the prototype. So don't

The Prototyping Process

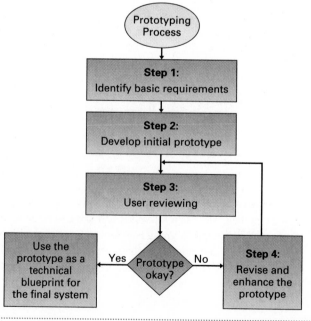

Figure 7-12

User Interface Prototyping

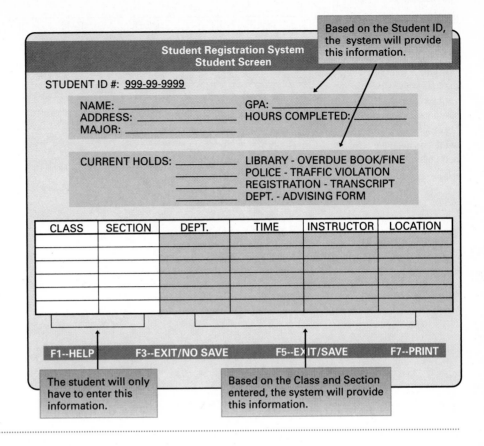

spend too much time quizzing users about every single detail—the details will work themselves out later in the prototyping process.

Once the basic requirements have been gathered, you build the initial prototype. Building the initial prototype is kind of a rough process. Most often, the initial prototype shows only user interfaces and does not include many of the processing requirements. Your college registration project team might choose to prototype the system by building input forms that the students would fill out to make sure the forms are easy and understandable (see Figure 7-12).

Step 3 begins the truly repetitive process of prototyping. When first entering this step, the users evaluate the initial prototype and suggest changes or make additions. In subsequent returns to step 3 (after step 4), the users evaluate new versions of the prototype. You should make sure that members of the project development team and several users review the prototype together. Don't let users evaluate the prototype by themselves, and don't limit the evaluation of the prototype to one user. Prototype reviewing should be done by many users while someone on the development team is taking notes—this is part of the dynamics of prototyping. It's also important that many users participate to make sure that any discrepancies among them are settled. In Figure 7-13, you can see how the project development team has revised your initial student registration screen.

The final sequential step in the prototyping process is to revise and enhance the prototype according to suggestions made by the users. In this step, changes are made to the current prototype, and new processing requirements are added. Once

Figure 7-13

Revising the Prototype

On your registration system, the project team has decided to create a pull-down menu that will show students the various classes. That way the students can browse the class selections and see what classes have already been filled.

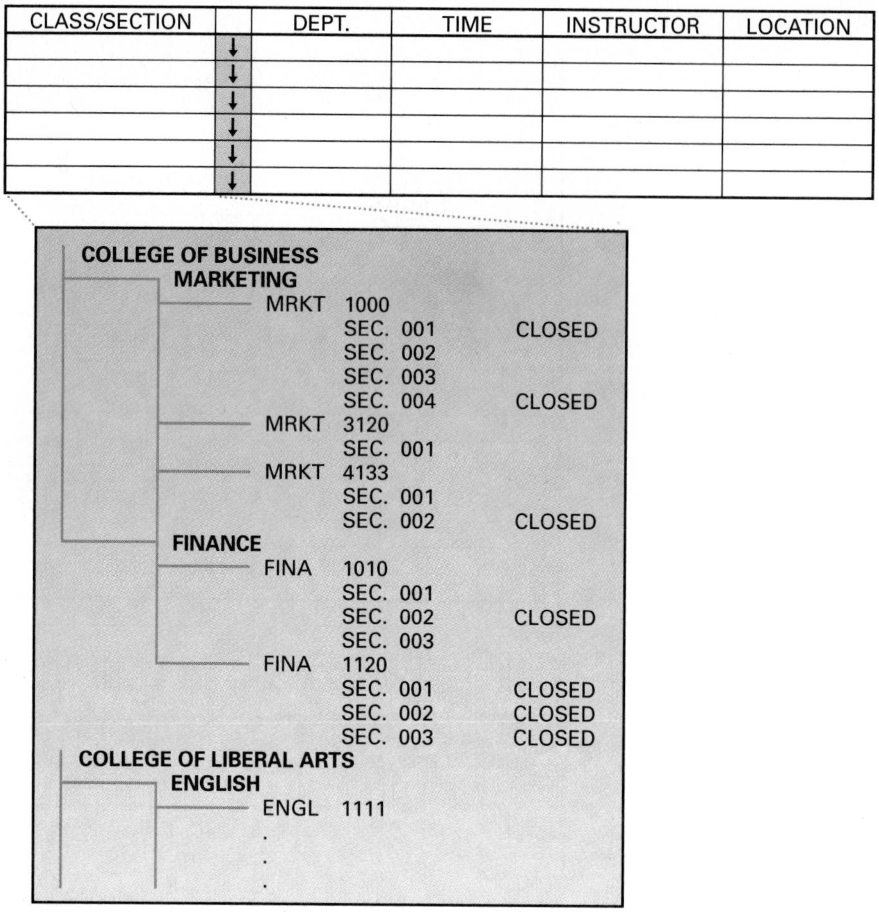

CLASS/SECTION		DEPT.	TIME	INSTRUCTOR	LOCATION
	↓				
	↓				
	↓				
	↓				
	↓				
	↓				

```
COLLEGE OF BUSINESS
    MARKETING
            MRKT  1000
                  SEC. 001        CLOSED
                  SEC. 002
                  SEC. 003
                  SEC. 004        CLOSED
            MRKT  3120
                  SEC. 001
            MRKT  4133
                  SEC. 001
                  SEC. 002        CLOSED
    FINANCE
            FINA  1010
                  SEC. 001
                  SEC. 002        CLOSED
                  SEC. 003
            FINA  1120
                  SEC. 001        CLOSED
                  SEC. 002        CLOSED
                  SEC. 003        CLOSED
COLLEGE OF LIBERAL ARTS
    ENGLISH
            ENGL  1111
                  .
                  .
                  .
```

the prototype has been revised, step 3 is repeated. The cycle between steps 3 and 4 is repeated until the prototype satisfies the requirements of the users.

The Advantages and Disadvantages of Prototyping. As a development tool for IT systems, prototyping has both advantages and disadvantages. They include:

Advantages

1. Encourages active user participation
2. Gives users a feel for the new system
3. Becomes a blueprint for the final system
4. Helps resolve discrepancies among users
5. Aids in determining technical feasibility
6. Helps sell the idea of a proposed system

Disadvantages

1. Leads users to believe the final system will follow shortly
2. Leads to a gloss-over effect
3. Gives no indication of likely performance under operational conditions

In our discussion of the four steps of prototyping, we have already addressed the first four advantages. Let's look at two other advantages of prototyping, and then we'll look at the disadvantages.

Prototypes can aid in determining the technical feasibility of a proposed system and in selling the idea of a proposed system. Whether or not an IT system can actually solve a problem or perform a specific task is often unknown. In this instance, a prototype can help in determining the technical feasibility of a system. Prototypes that prove that something can be done are called **proof-of-concept prototypes**. Prototypes can also help sell the idea of a proposed system—these are called **selling prototypes**. Selling prototypes help convince the project development team and users that the new IT system will be better than doing things the old way.

Prototyping basically has three disadvantages. First, it often gives users the idea that the final system will come shortly after the approval of the prototype— this is not necessarily true. A prototype, although it contains many of the features of the final system, is usually very processing inefficient (slow), not developed for the proposed hardware and software, and doesn't contain many of the administrative functions of the software such as backup and recovery mechanisms and end-of-month or end-of-year processing. The users should understand that the prototype is only a blueprint—not the final system.

Second, prototyping sometimes leads to a *gloss-over effect*. The gloss-over effect occurs when important characteristics of the software system are omitted because the focus of the development is on other issues or when users assume the operational or processing characteristics of the prototype are accurate because they see the desired inputs and outputs. They tend to see these operations and processes as *black boxes* (you know what goes in and comes out but not what happens inside). The project development team must carefully detail these characteristics before the final system can be developed.

PERSONAL ADVANTAGE

Prototyping

"Prototyping is the way I do my business," says Paul Romano, a systems consultant near Phoenix, Arizona. "I own my own computer consulting business. When someone wants a system developed, I always prototype it first."

Paul went into business for himself about eight years ago developing IT systems for organizations and individuals. Before he tells his clients what he will charge, he prototypes the input screens, forms, output screens, and reports. This helps give Paul an idea of what the system entails.

"It's actually quite simple when you think about it. I get together with my clients and develop a prototype of the inputs and outputs. From there, I ask them what processes are necessary to convert the inputs to outputs. From that, I can determine how long it will take me to develop the system.

The first couple of projects I did I didn't use prototyping. That was a mistake—both systems took a lot longer than I expected because the users kept adding new requirements. Prototyping not only helps me, but it also helps the users figure out exactly what they need."

Paul, like many others, has found that prototyping helps from both the development and the user side. Prototyping helps the users to better define their requirements, and it helps Paul figure out how long it will take to develop the system.

"Prototyping is the way to go," says Paul. "Without it, my hours would be long and my pocketbook would be shallow."

Finally, prototypes give no indication of how the system will perform (in terms of speed and convenience) during actual use. During the prototyping process only a few people use the proposed system; during actual use, though, hundreds of people may use a system simultaneously. This problem surfaced for the Department of Motor Vehicles in a state on the East Coast. During the prototyping process, the system seemed to work fine for 20 workstations in two locations. When the system was finally installed for all locations (which included over 1,200 workstations), the system spent all of its time just managing communication traffic to the various locations —it had absolutely no time to complete any transactions.

Data Flow Diagramming

A **data flow diagram** (DFD) is a graphical tool that shows the processes that act on data and information as they flow through a system. To help illustrate a data flow diagram, let's return to your CD mail-order business.

In a DFD, you find will four symbols (see Table 7-2). The first symbol is a rectangle that represents a **source** (a person or organization from which data originates) and a **sink** (a person or organization that receives information from the system). The second symbol is a circle that represents a process. A **process** transforms inputs into outputs within your system.

The third symbol is two parallel lines that represent a data store. A **data store** is a file, which can be paper or computer stored, that contains information. The final symbol is a directed line that represents a flow of data or information within the system.

Data flow diagramming incorporates a top-down decomposition approach to modeling the processes within a system. In the first step of data flow diagramming, you build what is called a context-level diagram. A **context-level diagram** shows how your system interacts with the sources and sinks by identifying the flows of data from the sources and the flows of information to the sinks. A context-level dia-

Table 7-2

Symbols in a Data Flow Diagram

SYMBOL	DESCRIPTION	EXAMPLES IN YOUR CD MAIL-ORDER BUSINESS
	Represents a source or sink.	Sources: Customers Distributors Sinks: Customers Distributors
	Represents a process that transforms inputs to outputs.	• Process Customer Order • Pay Distributor for Order
	Represents a data store.	• Customer • Inventory • Distributor • Purchase
	Represents a flow of data or information.	• Customer Order • Inventory Reduction • Credit Status

Building IT Systems: The Tools You Use and Your Role

Figure 7-14

**Context-Level Diagram for
Your CD Mail-Order Business**

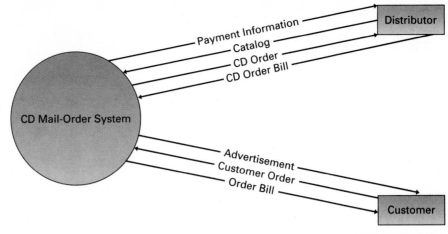

gram, however, does not show any of the processes within your system—that will occur at a later time.

In Figure 7-14, you can see the context-level diagram for your CD mail-order business. It identifies that Customer and Distributor are both sources and sinks. It also identifies the flows of data and information from and to Customer and Distributor. Some of these include Advertisement to Customer, Customer Order from Customer, Catalog from Distributor, and CD Order to Distributor.

The second step in data flow diagramming involves exploding the context-level diagram to show the major processes within your system and the flow of data and information to and from the processes. The exploded context-level diagram is called a *second-level diagram*. In Figure 7-15, you can see that the second-level diagram includes the following processes: Process Customer Order, Ship Order to Customer, Produce Advertisement, Process Incoming Catalog, Order CD from Distributor, and Pay Distributor for Order.

To read the second-level diagram, simply start at any process and evaluate the flows of data and information to and from it. For example, the Ship Order to Customer process takes in Customer Order from the Process Customer Order process. The Ship Order to Customer process then reduces the inventory quantity on hand by sending Inventory Reduction to the Inventory data store, indicates that a purchase has been made by sending Customer Purchase to the Purchase data store, and produces Order Bill that is sent to Customer along with the CDs ordered.

The third step in data flow diagramming is to continually explode each process within the second-level diagram and subsequent levels until each detail of a process is completely modeled. For example, if you further exploded the Ship Order to Customer process, you would build a DFD that shows how the inventory reduction, storing a purchase, and producing an Order Bill processes interact with each other and the appropriate data stores.

Entire books have been written on how to perform the process of data flow diagramming. Our example here is only partially complete, but you get the idea of what happens. Data flow diagramming is a very useful tool within the SDLC because:

1 It graphically displays what happens within a system.

2 It helps you understand how a system interacts with sources and sinks.

Figure 7-15

**Second-Level Diagram for
Your CD Mail-Order Business**

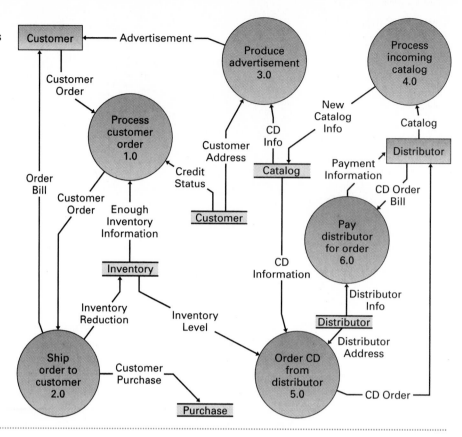

3 It helps you define what data stores are necessary.

4 It helps you understand the nature of the processes within a system that act on data and information.

5 It helps you understand the flow of data and information within a system.

Discovering IT

In our school registration system example in this chapter, what or who are the sources and sinks? Can you draw the context-level diagram? The second-level diagram? If you were to use a software drawing tool to help you draw the DFDs, which one would you choose? Why?

Figure 7-16

CASE Tool Use in the SDLC

Ⓓuring the SDLC, CASE tools are most often used during the software development process. The software development process includes gathering requirements for the new system, designing the new system, and developing the new system

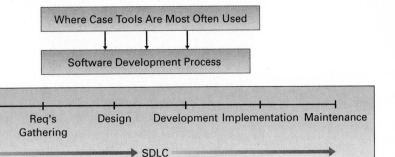

Computer-Assisted Software Engineering Tools

Software is actually nothing more than an automated set of steps that perform some process; if you were executing the steps yourself, you would call it a manual process. If you think about it, the SDLC is also a set of steps that perform some process—the process of developing an IT system. When you and other individuals undertake the SDLC, it is a manual process. But what if software were available that automated the process of developing IT systems? There is—and it's called **computer-assisted software engineering tools** or **CASE tools**.

CASE tools are software tools that automate some portion of the SDLC. CASE tools can help perform tasks within the SDLC such as identifying the problem or opportunity, gathering requirements, generating sample screens and reports, generating a technical blueprint from the requirements, and providing documentation (see Figure 7-16). CASE tools can also be used to develop software—which is a very interesting concept of using software to generate software. That is, CASE tools can be used to automate the process of specifying logical requirements and converting those logical requirements into software.

In our previous example of data flow diagramming, it might have occurred to you that building a data flow diagram is a somewhat difficult task just from the point of view of drawing all the processes, making sure that all information flows have been identified, and so on. Well, you're right. While DFDs are excellent graphical tools for understanding the nature of a system, most people find them tedious to draw and lay out. Many CASE tools support the drawing of DFDs. These CASE tools can help you lay out a DFD and make sure that all information flows have been correctly identified and defined.

CASE tools can significantly affect the time it takes to complete the SDLC and the quality of a new IT system. Organizations today are beginning to use CASE tools for many reasons, which include:

▶ **Documentation production:** CASE tools generate a lot of documentation, such as descriptions of how processes work, data dictionaries for databases, data flow diagrams, and software documentation. Software documentation becomes important if changes have to be made in the future. The documentation that CASE tools produce becomes a "knowledge repository" that will be very beneficial in the future.

▶ **Changing the design, not the software:** If changes do occur, you use the CASE tool to change the technical design and then simply regenerate the software. This greatly reduces the amount of time it takes to do maintenance.

A successful career in an organization means that you will be involved, probably many times, in the SDLC of a new IT system. You will be directly involved in contributing your knowledge of a business area to the technical design of, say, a new customer service system, a system to meet a federal government reporting regulation, or a system that provides information on product sales.

A painful lesson from 40 years of experience with large-scale systems development has been that it's even harder in many instances to make systems work organizationally, and the single most scarce resource in doing so is people—people who can bridge business, organizational, and technical issues.

That person can be you. Obviously, this immense career advantage takes time to build, and it may be several years before you work on a system development project. What we have done in this chapter is to alert you to the career opportunity by giving you an overview of how systems can be effectively designed and delivered. Here's our three-step process for being a success in the development of IT systems.

Learn Your Business
Before you can participate in the development of a new IT system, you must understand how business works. It doesn't matter if you choose human resource management, physical therapy, or nuclear physics as a field of study—learn it well. It's hard to tell an IT specialist what function a computer must perform if you don't know how to perform that function yourself.

Understand the IT Business
As we've said many times before, IT is everywhere and it always will be. You're not going to read in the next issue of *BusinessWeek* that corporate America has decided IT is a farce and won't be around next year. Stay on top of IT. That is, understand what IT can do for you and your business—that's the most important part.

Be the Translator Between the Two
During the system development process, people who can speak both languages—business and IT—will be the real winners. If you understand the translation process both ways—how your logical needs map into IT developments and how IT developments can be used in your area of expertise—you will succeed. It's as simple as that.

▶ **Reverse engineering:** Reverse engineering is the process of building design documents (the system technical blueprint) from software. Many CASE tools will allow you to use existing software and reverse the process to automatically build design documents.

▶ **Producing correct software:** CASE tools use the technical blueprint to produce software. Not only do they produce software fast (sometimes 1,500 lines per minute), they also produce correct software. Correct software doesn't have to be tested to see if it works; it only has to be tested to see if it meets the processing requirements.

Now You Can . . .

1 Understand why organizations want your involvement when they develop IT systems and why they develop IT systems.

> *Why organizations want your involvement:*
> You are a business process expert.
> You are a manager of other people.
> You are a liaison to the customer.
> You are a quality control analyst.

> *Why organizations undertake the SDLC:*
> Convert a manual system to an automated system.
> Totally overhaul an existing system.
> Make changes to an existing system.
> Make minor revisions to an existing system.
> Invent a new system.

2 Describe the stages of the in-house system development life cycle (SDLC).

> *Define the problem/opportunity:* Recognizing that a problem or opportunity exists and laying the groundwork for solving the problem or taking advantage of the opportunity.
> *Functions:*
> Recognize that a problem or opportunity exists.
> Gather the project development team.
> Assess the initial feasibility.
> Develop a plan for proceeding.
> *End documents:*
> Problem/opportunity definition.
> Initial feasibility review and recommendation.
> Project plan.

> *Gather requirements for the new system:* Determining how the system currently works, what changes need to be made, and how the proposed system will work, focusing on logical requirements only.
> *End documents:*
> Description of the current system.
> Description of the changes.
> Description of the proposed system.

Description of the input, processing, and output requirements.

> *Design the new system:* Converting the logical system requirements into a technical system design.
> *Functions:*
> Generate alternative system designs.
> Evaluate alternative system designs.
> Choose a system design.
> *End documents:*
> Technical system design.
> Screen and report formats.
> File and database layouts.
> Processing requirements (software).
> Hardware requirements.
> List of people to develop the system.

> *Develop the new system:* Converting the technical system design into an actual IT system.
> *Functions:*
> Convert the technical system design into an IT system.
> Programming and testing.
> Implement files and database layouts.
> Build reports and screens.
> *End documents:*
> Software.
> Software documentation.
> File and database documentation.
> Detailed description of the hardware.

> *Implement the new system:* Installing the hardware and software and using the new system.
> *Functions:*
> Train users.
> Convert from the old to the new way.
> *Conversion methods:*
> *Parallel:* Using both the old and new systems.
> *Plunge:* Totally discarding the old system.
> *Piecemeal:* Installing only a portion of the new system.
> *Piloting:* Installing the new system for only a portion of the users.

- *Maintain the new system:* Monitoring the new system to make sure it continues to work correctly and making changes as the need arises.

3 Describe how outsourcing affects the SDLC.

- *Outsourcing* is when an organization decides to let someone else take over and develop, operate, and/or maintain part of its operations.

- For the SDLC of IT systems, organizations outsource by:

  Hiring consultants to assist during requirements gathering and design.

  Hiring contract programmers for the development of software.

  Hiring individuals or organizations to implement a new system, train users, and maintain the hardware and software.

- During the SDLC, the design and development stages (3 and 4) are replaced by: generate request for proposal (RFP), evaluate RFP returns, and choose a vendor.

- A *request for proposal* (RFP) is a document that outlines the necessary requirements for a new system and solicits bids from other organizations or individuals.

4 Understand helpful SDLC tools, including prototyping, data flow diagramming, and computer-assisted software engineering (CASE).

- *Prototyping* is the process of developing a prototype—a simulation or experimental model.

  The prototyping process:

  Identifying basic requirements.

  Developing the initial prototype.

  User reviewing.

  Revising and enhancing the prototype.

- *Data flow diagramming* is a graphical tool that shows the processes that act on data and information as they flow through a system.

  A context-level diagram shows how your system interacts with the sources and sinks by identifying the flows of data from the sources and the flows of information to the sinks.

  Second- and subsequent-level DFDs explode prior-level DFDs to show the processes at a more detailed level.

- *Computer-assisted software engineering (CASE) tools* are software tools that automate some portion of the SDLC.

Key Terms

Computer-Assisted Software Engineering (CASE) Tools

Context-Level Diagram

Data Flow Diagram (DFD)

Data Store

In-House System Development Life Cycle (In-House SDLC)

Initial Feasibility Review

Outsourcing

Parallel Conversion

Piecemeal Conversion

Piloting Conversion

Plunge Conversion

Process

Programmer

Programming Language

Project Development Team

Project Plan

Proof-of-Concept Prototype

Prototype

Prototyping

Request for Proposal (RFP)

Selling Prototype

Sink

Software Development

Source

System Development Life Cycle (SDLC)

Systems Analyst

Self-Test

1. The _____ is the process an organization goes through to develop an IT system. It can be undertaken to:

   A.

   B.

C.

D.

E.

2. Methods of converting from the old to the new way include:

A.

B.

C.

D.

3. A _____ is a document that outlines the necessary requirements for a new system and solicits bids from other organizations or individuals.

Matching: Match the six stages in the in-house SDLC to their functions and end documents.

    A. Define the problem/opportunity

    B. Gather requirements

    C. Design

    D. Develop

    E. Implement

    F. Maintain

Functions

____ 4. Programming and testing

____ 5. Focus on logical requirements

____ 6. Evaluate alternative system designs

____ 7. Train users

____ 8. Gather the project development team

End Documents

____ 9. Description of the current system

____ 10. Initial feasibility review and recommendation

____ 11. List of people to develop and use the system

____ 12. Software and software documentation

13. A _____ is a simulation or experimental model of a proposed system or product.

14. A _____ is a graphical tool that shows the processes that act on data and information as they flow through a system.

15. _____ are software tools that automate some portion of the SDLC.

Cruising the Net

1 Connect to the Web page for Yahoo directory at http://www.yahoo.com/. Follow the link to Business, then to Management Information Systems. Did you find any topics that may be pertinent in building an IT system?

2 Connect to the Web page at http://ibd.ar.com/Catalogs/Catalog.HomePages.html, which lists various software vendors. Locate a listing for a CASE tool. Describe what you found.

3 Connect to the Web site for Dell Computers, http://www.dell.com/. Describe how you can obtain its product catalog.

4 Access the Web page for *Management Information Systems Quarterly* at http://www.cox.smu.edu/mis/misq/central.html. Browse through the Web page and describe what type of resource this is. Did you find anything pertaining to systems development?

Short-Answer Questions

1. What things should you consider when doing an initial feasibility review?

2. Why is your participation important during the SDLC?

3. What are the advantages and disadvantages of prototyping?

4. What are the benefits of CASE tools?

5. How does the in-house development of an IT system differ from outsourcing?

Solutions to Self-Test (1) system development life cycle, convert a manual system to an automated system, totally overhaul an existing system, make changes to an existing system, make minor revisions to an existing system, invent a new system—p. 210; (2) parallel, plunge, piecemeal, pilot—p. 225; (3) request for proposal—p. 226; (4) D—p. 224; (5) B—p. 218; (6) C—p. 222; (7) E—p. 225; (8) A—p. 216; (9) B—p. 219; (10) A—p. 217; (11) C—p. 222; (12) D—p. 224; (13) prototype—p. 230; (14) data flow diagram—p. 236; (15) CASE tools—p. 239.

Discussion Questions and Projects

1. The in-house system development life cycle (SDLC) is a set of six stages for developing an IT system. What do you see as the advantages and disadvantages of this process? How do you think the disadvantages can be overcome?

2. On which stage of the in-house SDLC do you think organizations spend the most time? On which stage do you think they should spend the least time? Justify each of your answers. If your answers to the two questions differ, explain why.

3. When people build spreadsheets, they most often use the process of prototyping. Explain why this statement is true.

4. Outsourcing is becoming very popular. Make a list of the possible functions in an organization that can be outsourced. Also, identify the advantages and disadvantages of outsourcing these functions. Next, make a list of outsourcing opportunities in your home.

Working in a Group

1. Suppose your group was in charge of developing a prototype for a new registration process at your school. What would the input forms (or screens) and registration printouts look like for the students? What about the drop/add forms? How different are the ones you developed from those currently being used?

2. As a group, interview an IT specialist who uses a CASE tool. Prepare a short report to the class that includes:

   A. The name of the CASE tool

   B. What part of the SDLC it automates

   C. The advantages of that CASE tool

   D. The disadvantages of that CASE tool

8

LEFT MULTI-PURPOSE DISPLAY   RIGHT MULTI-PURPOSE DISPLAY

Information Technology in Business:

Your Objectives for This Chapter

1 Understand the structure of a business organization, how management functions, and the characteristics of information within an organization.   **2** Describe the five types of IT systems that support an organization.   **3** Describe how decision support systems help you make decisions.   **4** Define artificial intelligence and describe how expert systems can be used in decision making.

Organizational success depends on how well organizations use their resources. If you ask people what the most important of these resources are, they will most likely cite capital funding, people, materials, and facilities. Many of them don't think of IT as a business resource; instead, they see it as something different from what they do—a technical tool, not a business tool. In reality, IT is both a key business resource and an exciting opportunity for business innovation. Here are just a few examples of innovations made possible by IT. All of them are part of your everyday life, but 10 to 20 years ago they were impractical or even unimaginable.

1 Pay-per-view cable television movies

2 Convenient product ordering (using 800 numbers) from Lands' End, L. L. Bean, Dell Computers, or other firms, with delivery within two days

3 Instant loan approvals in under 10 minutes

4 State tax refunds that can be authorized in Virginia in 15 minutes, with the check mailed the next morning

5 Films like *Forrest Gump,* in which a scene shows a huge crowd of around 100,000 people outside the White House; it's actually a multimedia computer-generated image that used only 20 real actors

6 *USA Today* providing the scores of West Coast late-night sports events for East Coast readers, even when the morning edition of the *Washington Post* and *New York Times* don't have the East Coast scores

We could easily turn this list of 6 examples into a list of 6,000.

Some people, however, don't really think of IT as an important organizational resource even when it's central to their business. For example, 85 percent of financial service firms in New York, according to a 1992 survey, did not view IT as important enough to have backup facilities in case their primary IT systems failed. These types of firms depend *totally* on IT (see Figure 8-1).

You, however, are part of a new tradition. You recognize that IT is not only an integral part of how you live your life but also how businesses operate and manage their operations. When you think about it, everything that happens in an organization serves one of two purposes—the execution of day-to-day operations and managing those operations. Whether it's for building automobiles on an assembly line, processing and delivering customer orders, or deciding where to build the next

---

Figure 8-1

Revenue Loss without IT (percentage of normal revenue)

According to a 1993 survey in Dallas, Texas, 162 businesses estimated that they would lose over 50 percent of their revenue if they lost use of their IT systems for only 15 days.[1]

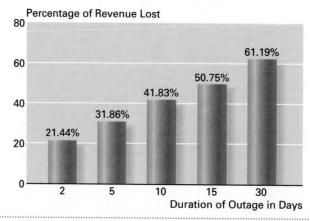

Average Revenue Loss as Percentage of Normal Revenue

Percentage of Revenue Lost

- 2: 21.44%
- 5: 31.86%
- 10: 41.83%
- 15: 50.75%
- 30: 61.19%

Duration of Outage in Days

Figure 8-2

**Your Focus in This Chapter:
How Organizations Use IT**

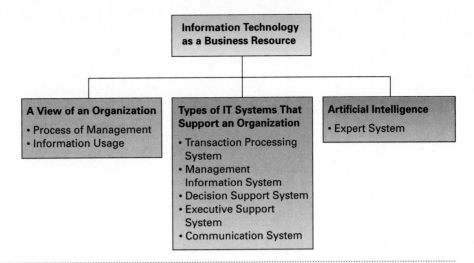

product distribution center, IT is a valuable resource. When, as in the six examples at the beginning of this chapter, IT is the base of execution of operations, it obviously has to be at the base of the management of those operations. IT is not merely "technology," IT is business.

A View of an Organization   An organization is often viewed as a pyramid structure (see Figure 8-3). The pyramid is split into four strata or levels. The people who carry out the day-to-day operations of the organization exist at the lowest level. Sometimes these people are called line workers or simply employees; we'll use the term *nonmanagement employees*. People at this level have responsibilities that include processing customer orders, making products, providing services, and distributing products. They generally work closest to the customers, and leading firms are increasingly realizing that they are the ones who need IT tools to provide top-quality service.

The remaining three levels—operational management, tactical management, and strategic management—represent the management personnel of the organization. People at these three levels are responsible for determining the direction of the organization (setting goals and objectives), monitoring the activities of the organization, and making necessary changes in the way the organization works so that the goals and objectives can be met. Let's concentrate on these three levels of management for a moment so that you can understand the function of management within an organization.

The Process of Management

Every day, you undertake the process of management—you manage your money, your time, and maybe even other people. But what does the term *management* really mean? Let's adopt the following definition:

Management is the process of planning activities, providing the necessary staffing to accomplish activities, organizing the activities and staffing in a meaningful way, directing the accomplishment of activities, and controlling the accomplishment of activities.

Figure 8-3

The Structure of an Organization

From our definition, you can see that management involves five functions: planning, staffing, organizing, directing, and controlling. Now the question becomes, "What are planning, staffing, organizing, directing, and controlling?" The old answer to that question rarely included IT. That was largely left to the computer or data processing department. Even today, few business managers are fully comfortable handling IT as an integral part of their sphere of responsibility. Indeed, if you look at any of the IT trade publications like *CIO, Information Week,* or *Datamation,* you'll find articles in almost every issue about how to align business operations and IT, bridge the understanding and culture gap, and help business managers lead the deployment of IT.

Functions of Management. Planning is the process of establishing goals and objectives and developing the required activities to meet those goals and objectives. Venture Stores Inc. recently used IT to help it plan, implement, and achieve its global retailing operations. After using IT to determine the best places for global retailing, Venture Stores created a system that tracks information regarding transactions and shipment costs, international letters of credit, and various auditing functions worldwide. Venture Stores claims that its use of IT helped it establish global retailing and has significantly reduced paperwork and maintenance costs.

Staffing is the process of selecting the appropriate people to meet the goals and objectives of the organization by accomplishing required activities. Staffing, however, does not stop with hiring (selecting) people—it also includes training, assigning duties, and determining pay scales. To help managers learn how to better plan for staffing levels, Holiday Inn Inc. uses an interactive multimedia learning system. Holiday Inn spent $66 million on this learning system and anticipates full participation by all of its 1,700 hotels. Why? Because Holiday Inn believes that learning through this system will help managers maintain high-quality service in the face of staff turnover ranging from 60 to 100 percent a year. Holiday Inn is also paying to have the system modified for different languages for use in its international operations.

Organizing is the development of an organizational structure that will allow people to carry out their activities in the best way possible. The organizational structure defines the layout of the organization (for example, the number of divisions), identifies who reports to whom, and outlines the policies and procedures that establish how the organization will work.

Directing is the process of leading the organization through communication, inspiration, and motivation. Directing may also include providing counseling programs and recognizing good work.

Finally, **controlling** is the process of monitoring people's efforts to accomplish activities to make sure that they move the business toward its objectives. Controlling includes comparing accomplishments with objectives, identifying problems and opportunities, resolving problems, establishing procedures for avoiding problems, and modifying plans when necessary.

Many food retail chains are turning to IT to help them control the costs of buying meat from packing plants. The system called Computer Assisted Retail Decision Support (CARDS) helps retailers determine the savings they will accrue by buying already-trimmed meat from packing plants. This type of system will help ensure uniformity among meat packers, which is a difficult point of control for most food retail chains.

Levels of Management. The process of management can be viewed by function (planning, staffing, organizing, directing, and controlling) and by level. When we say level, we refer to the position of management within the structure of an organization. In general terms, management has three levels—strategic, tactical, and operational (see Figure 8-4).

Strategic management rests at the top of an organization and consists of senior or executive managers such as the chief executive officer (CEO), president, and board of directors. This level of management is responsible for developing the overall goals, objectives, strategies, and policies of an organization. Strategic management is often called *long-range management,* because it deals with the long-range future of the organization, typically over a period of two to five years.

The Limited Inc. uses a merchandise selection system to help strategic management determine which lines of merchandise will sell best during the holiday season. The strategic management of The Limited claims that the utilization of such a system translates into higher gross margins and fewer markdowns. In the turbulent environment of fashion retailing coupled with holiday-season buying (or lack of it), a merchandise selection system greatly increases strategic management's ability to develop goals, objectives, and strategies.

Tactical management is the level of management immediately below strategic management. **Tactical management** deals with the development of medium-range objectives, procedures, and policies that will ensure that strategic management goals and objectives are met. The term *medium-range* typically refers to a one- to two-year period.

Tactical management at King Soopers is using IT to schedule truck deliveries, route trucks efficiently, and manage its transportation information. King Soopers has been able to reduce its number of trucks from 25 to 20 because of the increased efficiency realized from such a system. Tactical management is now using the stored transportation information to project transportation needs into the next several years and identify the best locations for distribution centers.

Operational management is the lowest level of management in an organization. **Operational management** develops short-range goals and objectives that will meet the medium-range goals and objectives of tactical management. Operational management also focuses on monitoring and controlling the day-to-day operations of the organization.

Controlling the day-to-day operations at River Hills West Healthcare Center used to be a nightmare—now it's easy because of IT. Every time a doctor wrote a new prescription order for a patient, a secretary had to transcribe the order to a phone order, a pharmacy sheet, and several other patient forms. All of these then had to be checked by nurses.

Figure 8-4

Levels of Management

Strategic Management
- CEO, president, board of directors
- Overall, long range goals, objectives, strategies, and policies
- 2 to 5 years

Tactical Management
- Middle management
- Medium-range objectives, procedures, and policies
- 1 to 2 years

Operational Management
- Supervisory management
- Short-range goals and objectives
- Monitor and control day-to-day operations

All that has now changed. Instead of all of the various transcribing and checking of prescription log sheets, the nurses simply write the first three letters of the name of a drug on an electronic notepad. The handheld system immediately responds with a list of patient choices and check-off boxes for doses and the time of day the drug was administered. The system then uses a wireless link to a central DBMS that instantly updates patient records and drug inventory levels. Operational management estimates that this system has eliminated at least five stages of paperwork. In the health care industry where rising costs are driving many people away from the appropriate care, River Hills has found a way to use technology to make health care more affordable by being able to maximize its operations.

Information in an Organization

You already know that we are in the information age—so what an organization knows (information) will determine, in part, how successful it is. Therefore, IT systems are an important set of tools (organizational resources) to capture, maintain, and move information within the organization. As you explore the way information is used within an organization, there are some important things to keep in mind— the flow of information, the characteristics of information, and the types of decision making that information supports.

Flow of Information. Within an organization, information moves in all directions—up, down, and side to side. The **side-to-side flow of information** defines the communications between the various functional units. For example, the sales division may need to know the status of work in progress from the production division. IT tools such as groupware and videoconferencing help people bridge not only time zones and locations, but also departments.

Without IT, most communication between departments was either face-to-face exchanges in sporadic meetings or massive paper flows. This meant that side-to-side communication was extraordinarily difficult and most interactions were with people in the same location. This often led to an "us" versus "them" view among departments. IT helps change that by often making it easier to communicate with people than to avoid doing so.

The **upward flow of information** consists of information that describes how the organization is operating. For example, information about specific sales orders originates at the lowest level and moves through the levels of management to people who decide whether to increase or decrease inventory. It then continues upward to people who decide on product development, marketing, and investment in manufacturing plants.

Historically, IT has played a major role in facilitating upward flows. Information gathered as part of everyday operations is consolidated and passed up to decision makers who monitor and respond to problems and opportunities. For example, when you buy a pair of in-line skates at Sears, the clerk uses a POS system to process your purchase. The POS system immediately sends information to that store's computer databases, which track sales and inventory. If you purchase those skates with an American Express card, communication devices take over and transmit your credit card number and amount of purchase to American Express' computer, which in turn provides a confirmation number or refuses to accept the charges.

Other communication devices such as VSATs then transmit your purchase information to head office computers, which analyze it and then automatically place orders and provide reports to brand managers and marketing staff concerning sales patterns, problem stores or products, and so on. Summary information will be passed up to senior financial managers showing cash flow, credit sales, and the like. So, while the store managers analyze yesterday's sales of in-line skates in great detail, the corporate finance staff monitor the company's overall cash position. Through IT, the same information at different levels of detail supports different purposes of many different people.

The **downward flow of information** consists of the strategies, goals, objectives, and policies that originate at one level and pass to lower levels. For example, tactical management may order a closeout sale during September and October to reduce inventory. This information passes to operational managers, who generate information concerning percentage discounts and advertising strategies. This information then passes to nonmanagement employees, who carry out the actions.

IT plays a role here mainly to ensure rapid communication. Many companies use IT tools such as videoconferencing to talk directly to people across the company. They also routinely use electronic mail and online bulletin boards and databases to keep staff informed and up to date on company news. When MCI's managers log onto the company's e-mail system every morning, for instance, they get a summary of industry information, MCI's stock price and any new financial results, news of congressional debates concerning the telecommunications industry, and other fast-breaking news. There's no way these managers could compile and track all of this information by themselves. It's IT that makes all this possible.

Businesses such as MCI have to be careful, though. IT has made it possible to provide information to many people throughout the organization quickly and easily, but that information must be carefully assessed for its quality and usefulness. If it's not useful or pertinent, many people may suffer from a form of electronic junk mail—electronic information they don't need. Information overload of this nature is information that has no value. This is what turns off many users of e-mail; they receive too much information that they can't possibly assimilate or that they simply don't need.

Businesses must also make their employees aware of how to use the information they receive. In the MCI example, if a manager doesn't understand the significance of yesterday's stock prices, that information has no value. What would give it value is training the manager to understand what the information means and how to use it. In business, sending the right information to the right people and letting them know its significance gives value to information.

The Characteristics of Information. As information moves through an organization, it takes on different characteristics. First, information can be internal or external. **Internal information** describes specific operational aspects of the organization (for example, total sales yesterday, a list of products that aren't selling, and total employee salaries for last year).

External information describes the environment surrounding the organization (for instance, interest rates for proposed loans, competitors' actions, and new tax proposals for next year). External information is used more frequently in higher levels of the organization, while internal information is found throughout the organization.

Information can also be subjective or objective. **Objective information** quantitatively defines something, such as total sales and telephone expenses for last month. **Subjective information** attempts to describe something currently unknown. For example, if an organization was faced with the decision of whether to build a new warehouse, it might speculate on what interest rates will be for borrowing money or what kind of tax incentives various cities would offer.

Finally, information can be characterized by its level of **granularity**—detailed or summarized. Because lower levels of the organization deal with day-to-day operations, information at that level is usually very detailed. At higher levels of the organization, information becomes more summarized. For instance, operational management may use weekly sales reports, while tactical management focuses more on monthly sales information and strategic management on yearly sales information.

Types of Decision Making. Most information in an organization supports some type of decision-making process (see Table 8-1). Some decisions seem quite simple (How should inquiries at the help desk be recorded?), while others are complicated (What is the best city for our new product distribution center?). The extent to which a decision is simple or complicated is referred to as the *structure* of the decision-making process. The structure of the decision-making process is affected by such factors as the amount of available information, the extent to which the information is objective and subjective, and how often the decision must be made.

The decision-making process can be **structured**, **unstructured**, or in between. Consider determining how much a person's net pay should be—this is a structured decision-making process for many reasons. First, the information you need to make this decision is completely available to you—the person's salary, number of dependents, tax withholdings, deductions for benefits, and so on. Second, all the information is objective. An employee has a specific salary or hourly wage, not a range from which you have to choose. Third, this decision-making process involves clear procedures and rules that can be easily programmed. Finally, this is a decision that must be made frequently.

Determining the best city for a new product distribution center, however, is an unstructured decision-making process. Although a lot of information may be available, much of it is probably subjective, such as the quality of the labor force in each city, projections about demographic changes, the attitudes of state and local government officials toward business, the quality of road and air links, and climate considerations. This is also an unstructured decision because it's not something that an organization would do on a regular basis.

As you can probably guess, IT historically was used mostly to support structured decisions. A computer program can easily calculate payroll information but it cannot as easily choose the best city for a product distribution center. The role of IT in decision making, however, is changing. More and more, businesses are figuring out how to use IT to support unstructured decision making as well as structured decision making. In the next section, you'll see how IT contributes to both.

Types of IT Systems That Support an Organization

IT systems exist at all levels of the organization. Some simply capture and record information concerning transactions, while others provide highly summarized reports or aid in the decision-making process. IT systems within an organization fall into five broad categories: transaction processing systems, management information systems, decision support systems, executive support systems, and communication systems.

Transaction Processing Systems

Transaction processing systems (TPS) are IT systems that support the day-to-day operations of the organization. To provide this support, a TPS captures and records information and produces reports that detail what has happened. For example, TPSs capture and record information about specific sales and seat assignments in an airline reservation system and capture and record information concerning which flight attendants and pilots flew on which flights.

Transaction processing systems are at the very heart of IT in an organization. They are the systems that must capture exactly what has happened, including such occurrences as sales to a customer, the arrival of a shipment, hours worked by each employee, the return of defective products, and changes in the local sales tax. For this reason, TPSs must be capable of handling large volumes of incoming information. After capturing information, a TPS is responsible for updating the organization's database (see Figure 8-5). This information is then used by the entire organization to monitor its activities and make adjustments as necessary.

Table 8-1

Flow and Characteristics of Information and Decision Making in an Organization

Organizational Structure	Flow of Information	Characteristics of Information	Types of Decision Making
Highest Level Strategic management	**Up** How the organization is operating	**External** Describes the surrounding environment **Subjective** Attempts to describe the unknown **Summarized** Describes information in summary form	**Unstructured** Nonrecurring decision making that uses a lot of subjective information
	Side to side Between functional units		
Lowest Level Nonmanagement employees	**Down** Strategies, goals, objectives, and policies	**Detailed** Describes operations in complete form **Objective** Quantitatively describes information **Internal** Describes operational aspects	**Structured** Recurring decision making that uses a lot of objective information

Suppose you were going to open your own video arcade in your town and were trying to find a good location. Below, we've listed many different pieces of information that may help you in your decision. Identify which pieces you think would be helpful and whether that information is objective or subjective. Is your decision concerning where to open a new video arcade a structured or unstructured decision?

	Helpful?	Objective?	Subjective?
Number of parking spaces			
Proximity to schools			
Lease costs			
Licensing costs			
City-imposed curfew times			
Remodeling costs			
Minimum wage			
Number of other arcades			
Proximity of other arcades			
Prime interest rate			
Lease period			
Expected population change			
Proximity to grocery store			
Proximity to bookstore			
Proximity to ATM			
Number of stoplights			
Presence of lighted billboards			
Presence of lighted signs			

Figure 8-5

Transaction Processing Systems at the Heart of Information Technology in an Organization

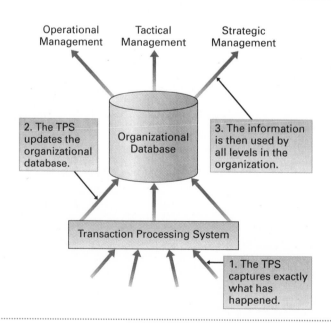

A TPS is also responsible for producing reports that detail what has happened. At Continental Airlines, for instance, a TPS produces a daily report of who purchased a ticket for which flight and what seat the person reserved. Because TPSs capture vast amounts of information and produce detailed reports, you will find that they make extensive use of input and output devices and support a great number of users.

A TPS uses straightforward processing logic that must be completely accurate and reliable. Consider payroll as an example. The processing logic is straightforward because a set of well-defined steps can be easily created for handling all payroll transactions. Additionally, the payroll TPS must be completely accurate and reliable. How would you like to reach your next payday and find that you were shortchanged $100 or did not receive a check at all because the "system was down?"

Management Information Systems

Management information systems (MIS) support the management and control of the day-to-day operations by providing periodic reports that summarize the information captured by TPSs (see Figure 8-6). MISs, therefore, mostly support the operational management level and decisions that have to be made at that level. MISs are often referred to as *management alerting systems* because they alert management to potential problems. For example, a car dealer's sales manager may receive a monthly report that shows salespeople's performance, models of cars by budgeted versus actual sales, and the cost of warranty claims. This information can assist the sales manager in identifying such problems as which salespeople are not producing at the required level, which car models are selling below budgeted sales, and which models require increasing costs through warranty claims.

The report of car models that did not meet budgeted sales is an example of an exception report and a periodic report. An **exception report** provides a subset of

---

Figure 8-6

Management Information Systems

Ⓜanagement information systems (MISs) support the management and control of the day-to-day operations. The first of these two MIS reports is a delinquent customer report or aging schedule (a periodic, exception report), and the second compares actual monthly expenses against budgeted monthly expenses (a periodic, comparative report).

CUSTOMER	ACCOUNT BALANCE	CURRENT	0-30 DAYS	30-60 DAYS	OVER 60 DAYS
ALDRIDGE	$700.00		$700.00		
BARROWS	$300.00	$300.00			
JOHNSON	$750.00				$750.00
CHAN	$290.00	$290.00			
SMITH	$450.00			$450.00	
TOTALS:	$2490.00	$590.00	$700.00	$450.00	$750.00

JOSH'S TREE SERVICE FOR MONTH END 9-31-94 — PAST DUE columns: 0-30 DAYS, 30-60 DAYS, OVER 60 DAYS

EXPENSE ACCOUNT	ACTUAL AMOUNT	BUDGETED AMOUNT	AMOUNT OVER/UNDER
TELEPHONE	$1,734.00	$1,700.00	$34.00
TRAVEL	$9,684.00	$10,000.00	($316.00)
SUPPLIES	$284.00	$192.00	$92.00
SALARIES	$17,384.00	$17,384.00	-0-
TOTAL:	$29,086.00	$29,276.00	($190.00)

JOSH'S TREE SERVICE MARKETING DEPARTMENT FOR MONTH SEPTEMBER 1994

USING INFORMATION TECHNOLOGY TO MAKE PRODUCTS

From Ford Mustangs to Toyota Celicas to Mercedes Benz SLs, automobiles all over the world are being designed, tested, and manufactured by IT through the use of Computer Integrated Manufacturing (CIM). CIM is a concept that focuses on the complete design, testing, and manufacturing of products with the aid of IT. Software tools in CIM include Computer-Aided Design (CAD), Computer-Aided Engineering (CAE), and Computer-Aided Manufacturing (CAM). Manufacturers like the automobile industry have found great advantages in the concept of CIM and its software tools—for example, by using

- **CAD to develop automobile specifications on an IT system so that changes can be made quickly and at a minimal cost.**

- **CAE to extensively test the designs produced during the CAD process. Problems can be fixed on the IT representation of the car as opposed to the prototype.**

- **CAM to use the CAD specifications to instruct the robots how to actually manufacture the automobile.**

CIM is actually an example of a transaction processing system. Why? Because it helps people carry out day-to-day manufacturing operations—designing, testing, and manufacturing products. And automobile manufacturers aren't the only ones using CIM. Besides Bass Brewers (discussed in Chapter 6), a few others and what they make using CIM include:

- **Lepage Bakeries—various breads and English muffins**

- **Pepperidge Farms—snack foods (cookies and so on)**

- **Agripac Inc.—frozen vegetable packaging**

- **Ingersoll Milling Machine—metal cutting and machining systems**

- **Whirlpool International BV—refrigerator and cooking appliance components**

- **Texas Instruments—semiconductors**

- **Boeing—airplanes**

- **Groupe Michelin SA—automobile tires**

- **Collins and Aikman—automobile textiles**

- **Laiteries Reunies de Geneve—yogurt**

available information based on some selection criterion (which cars fell below budgeted sales). Other examples of exception reports include a list of customers who are delinquent in their payments and a list of employees who used sick leave.

A **periodic report** is a report that is received on a predetermined basis. Weekly and monthly reports are examples of periodic reports. MIS reports can also be comparative in nature. **Comparative reports** include a summary of actual expenses compared to budgeted expenses and a comparison of this year's to last year's sales. MISs generally have few direct users who enter large amounts of information because most of the information at this level has already been captured by a TPS. For example, a bank's summary of deposit volumes for each branch is derived from ATM and teller transactions, processed by the relevant TPS.

Decision Support Systems

Decision support systems (DSS) are collections of software tools and information used to assist in the decision-making process. At first glance, you might think MISs and DSSs are the same—not really. MISs help managers make structured decisions that occur frequently (such as how much inventory to have on hand). DSSs, on the other hand, help managers make less frequent, more unstructured decisions. DSSs aid managers in making a decision by helping them recognize that a problem exists, by generating alternative solutions to the problem, and by helping them choose the right alternative.

DSSs also use more subjective and external information than MISs. Let's consider the problem of deciding the best city for a new distribution center. As a manager, you would gather internal information such as product sales and the locations of other distribution centers and add such external information as tax incentives offered by various cities and subjective information like the quality of the labor force in each city.

Then, using a variety of software tools (for example, a spreadsheet, statistical software, and logistical analysis software), you would generate a number of different alternatives based on each city. The process of generating alternatives is called **what-if analysis**. For instance, what happens if sales go flat over the next five years? Will that affect your choice of cities, or should you not build a new distribution center at all? Your product distribution center DSS is an example of a throwaway DSS. A **throwaway decision support system** is one that is used to aid in the decision-making process once and then is literally thrown away because the decision may never be made again.

While decision support systems are designed to help an individual solve a problem, there are also decision support systems that support a group of people working together to solve a problem. A **group decision support system** (GDSS) supports the collaborative efforts of many people by providing hardware and software that facilitates communication and the sharing of information. GDSSs rely on networks of

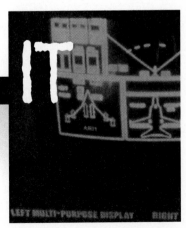

Registration systems at schools are both TPSs and MISs. If you were a department chair or instructor, what type of registration reports would you like to see from the TPS and the MIS? What information would these reports contain? How would the reports be beneficial to you in your efforts to manage a department?

Box 8-1

Choosing a Product Distribution Center

Spreadsheet software is an excellent IT tool for creating a DSS. Here, you can see how spreadsheet software is used to help determine the best location for a new product distribution center.

Spreadsheet 1 helps recognize that a problem exists by estimating required inventory levels based on future sales projections. As you can see, required inventory levels will exceed capacity by 1997.

Spreadsheet 2 helps generate a list of possible alternatives. This spreadsheet includes several options, including leasing space, renovating the existing product distribution center, building a new product distribution center in the same location, and building a product distribution center in one of two new locations.

Spreadsheet 3 helps you choose the right alternative by comparing the two best alternatives (building in St. Louis and Kansas City) according to a simple ranking mechanism.

Spreadsheet 1

SALES FORECASTING AND CAPACITY ANALYSIS REPORT DEC.31, 1996					
				PROJECTED	PROJECTED
SALES	1994	1995	1996	1997	1998
(IN UNITS)	—	—	—	—	—
PRODUCT A	1000	1200	2000	N/A	N/A
PRODUCT B	1000	1700	2000	N/A	N/A
PRODUCT C	2000	2100	2250	N/A	N/A
	—	—	—	—	—
TOTAL:	4500	5000	6250	7812.5	9765.625
% INCREASE	N/A	25%	25%	EST. 25%	EST. 25%
% CAPACITY*	57.14%	71.43%	89.29%	**111.61%**	**139.51%**
* TOTAL STORAGE CAPACITY IS FOR 7000 UNITS.					
SALES WILL EXCEED STORAGE CAPACITY BY 11.61% IN 1997.					

computers and groupware such as videoconferencing, electronic meeting software, and scheduling software to optimize the way a group of people work together.

Executive Support Systems

Executive support systems (ESS) support the information needs of strategic management by providing the most basic summary of information and tools for working with unstructured problems (see Figure 8-7 on page 262). Executive support systems draw on information located within the organization as well as external to it. Strategic management individuals are more concerned with the overall operations of the organization than with specific details about transactions. For example, an ESS may generate a report that shows sales over the last five years. This report may also be in graphical form—an important characteristic of an ESS.

If strategic management were to notice a continuing decline in sales over the last five years, they may incorporate the use of tools (many of which fall into the DSS category) to determine why the decline is occurring and explore several strategies for increasing sales. Information to address the declining sales problem and strategies for increasing sales might come from internal sources in the form of

Box 8-1 cont.

Spreadsheet 2

CAPACITY ANALYSIS REPORT DEC. 31, 1996					
		ALTERNATIVES			
		SAME LOCATION		BUILD IN NEW LOCATION	
				ST. LOUIS	KANSAS CITY
	LEASE	RENOVATE	BUILD		
COSTS:					
LAND PURCHASE:	$0.00	$0.00	$10,000.00	$8,000.00	$12,000.00
LEASE:	$10,000.00	$0.00	$0.00	$0.00	$0.00
LAND IMPROVEMENT:	$0.00	$2,500.00	$12,000.00	$1,000.00	$0.00
BLDG. IMPROVEMENT:	$0.00	$15,000.00	$0.00	$0.00	$0.00
NEW BLDG.	$0.00	$0.00	$15,000.00	$7,000.00	$6,000.00
	—	—	—	—	—
TOTAL:	$10,000.00	$17,500.00	$37,000.00	$15,000.00	$18,000.00
ASSUMPTIONS:					
	LOAN/LEASE TERM (IN YRS): 10				
	INTEREST RATE: 8%				
COST PER YEAR:	$1,000.00	$2,608.05	$5,514.16	$2,235.47	$2,682.56
ADDITIONAL CAPACITY:	4000	5000	8000	15000	17000
COST PER CAPACITY UNIT:	$0.25	$0.52	$0.69	$0.15	$0.16
LABOR FORCE QUALITY:	GOOD	GOOD	GOOD	HIGH	GOOD

Spreadsheet 3

ST. LOUIS AND KANSAS CITY ANALYSIS FOR NEW PRODUCT DISTRIBUTION CENTER DEC. 31, 1996				
	ST. LOUIS	RANKING	KANSAS CITY	RANKING
QUALITY OF LABOR FORCE:	HIGH	1	GOOD	2
ADDITIONAL CAPACITY YIELD:	15,000	2	17,000	1
COST OF RELOCATING EMPLOYEES:	$30,000.00	1	$30,000.00	1
COST PER YEAR:	$2,235.47	1	$2,682.56	2
CENTRALIZED TO U.S.?	YES	1	YES	1
		—		—
AVERAGE RANKING		1.2		1.4
RANKINGS:				
1—BEST CHOICE				
2—SECOND BEST CHOICE				
RECOMMENDATION:	CHOOSE ST. LOUIS AS THE NEW SITE.			

DO-IT-YOURSELF SCANNING AT THE SUPERMARKET

Believe it or not, businesses have been using IT to get you—as a customer—to do the work of their employees. When you use an ATM, you basically take on the role of a teller, entering your account number (your ATM card), specifying how much money to withdraw, and actually getting the cash. What about hotels such as Marriott that give you the capability to check out of your room without ever going to the front desk? What about convenience stores that let you pay by credit card right at the gas pump?

Well, supermarkets are not to be outdone. Several chains in Europe are now letting customers scan their own products. Here's how it works. When you enter the supermarket, you insert your credit card into a slot that causes a dispenser to release a handheld portable bar code reader. As you go up and down the aisles, you scan the products you want and place them in your grocery cart. When you're done shopping, you take the bar code scanner to the checkout clerk, who prints out a receipt and takes your money. It's as simple as that!

What's happening in all these instances is that businesses are letting you do your own transaction processing. As it turns out, it's a win-win situation for everyone. In the supermarket, you'll never wait in another long line, nor will you ever hear "Price check on Aisle 4, please." For the supermarkets, it will mean fewer checkout clerks and faster service, which means happier customers.

Do-it-yourself scanning in supermarkets is now being tested in the United States. Who knows, you may shop for clothes the same way some day.

Figure 8-7

Executive Support Systems

Executive support systems (ESS) support the information needs of strategic management. ESSs provide the most basic summary of information, usually in graphical form.

product line sales and lists of major customers. It could also include external information in the form of sales trends of competitors and the growth of new competitors that offer substitute products or services.

Communication Systems

Communication systems support the flow of information in all forms, including voice, text, graphics, video, and sound. The flow of information may be completely within the organization, or it may be external to the organization.

In Chapter 2, we looked at groupware. Today, groupware is becoming the basis for communication systems within organizations. Groupware supports basic electronic communication between people (electronic mail), scheduling of meetings (scheduling software), virtual meetings (electronic meeting support software), interactive sharing and editing of documents (whiteboard software), interactive face-to-face meetings (videoconferencing), and electronic communication of business documents within the organization and external to it (work flow automation software).

Artificial Intelligence as Decision Support Tools

Decision making is a key part of day-to-day operations and management in an organization. As we discussed, some decisions are simple, while others require a great deal of time and effort. Decisions may also be recurring and nonrecurring. Deciding whether to give a customer a credit card is a recurring decision. Deciding where to build a new product distribution center, on the other hand, is a nonrecurring decision.

DSSs are excellent IT tools for supporting both recurring and nonrecurring decisions. There are also a number of other IT-based tools that can aid in the decision-making process. These IT tools fall into the category of artificial intelligence. **Artificial intelligence** (AI) is the field of study that deals with the capturing, modeling, and storing of human intelligence within an IT system so that the system can facilitate decision-making processes that normally would be undertaken by people. AI tools include neural networks, which we discussed in Chapter 2, genetic software (see Tomorrow's Business Advantage: Software That Mates and Mutates on page 266), and expert systems.

An **expert system** is decision support technology that helps people solve a problem by capturing and using the expertise, logic patterns, and thought processes of an expert. Many expert systems create rules to represent expertise, logic patterns, and thought processes; these are called *rule-based expert systems*. Let's consider deciding what to do when approaching an intersection in a car. Whether you realize it, you go through a series of mental steps (thought processes) when you approach an intersection. The result of these steps becomes the decision you carry out. Table 8-2 shows the rules and actions for deciding what to do when you approach an intersection. If this expert system were actually used, the rules would be displayed to you in questions. Your response (Yes or No) would determine the recommended action, or cause the expert system to ask another question.

Your driving expert system is an example of a simple expert system. It has only five rules and helps make a decision that you probably perform intuitively every day. Although decision making in business is much more complex, expert systems have become invaluable tools for many organizations. For example, the American Stock Exchange uses an expert system called Market Surveillance Expert (MSE) to investigate cases of insider trading. The Securities and Exchange Commission also uses an expert system to investigate possible violations of security laws. In the area of customer service, Whirlpool uses an expert system called

HOW VF BEAT THE PANTS OFF LEVI STRAUSS

Roughly 51 percent of VF Corporation's sales come from its workday jeans lines such as Lee and Wrangler. In 1994, net earnings for VF hit $274.5 million on sales of $4.97 billion. Its $4.97 billion in sales for 1994 represented a 15 percent increase over 1993, and double digits were expected to continue in future years. In the jeans market, VF is literally beating the pants off other competitors such as Levi Strauss.

Why is VF doing so well? You guessed it—VF is using technology to gain an advantage. In 1989, VF began linking its computers to the computers of retailers such as JC Penney, Target, and Wal-Mart. In doing so, VF combines the advantages of a communication system, a transaction processing system, and a decision support system to restock retail outlets within three days.

How does it all work? Let's take a look at Wal-Mart, which sells millions of pairs of Wrangler jeans at over 2,100 retail outlets each year. Each night, the Wal-Mart computers send daily sales information regarding Wrangler jeans to the computers of VF. The VF computers immediately create restocking orders, which arrive at the retail outlets within three days. On the flip side, it sometimes takes up to a month to get in a new order of Levi jeans.

So the connection between the computer systems is a communication system, and the daily handling of sales information is a transaction processing system. Where's the decision support system? It's quite simple. Because of the way inventory is handled, retail outlets only receive shipments of Lee and Wrangler jeans—in both size and style—that are selling. So inventory shipments are totally based on what's selling. No one ever has to try to decide what to order.

The fashion industry changes as often as the weather, and sometimes no one can predict what will happen. Even technology can't always do the right thing, but for VF it has greatly reduced the risk of the fashion trade.[2]

Consumer Appliance Diagnostic System (CADS) to direct customer calls to the appropriate help desk. Prior to using this system, Whirlpool customers were sometimes directed to many different customer service representatives or put on hold for a long time before their questions could be answered.

Expert systems are beneficial because they capture and permanently record human expertise. Suppose, for example, that only one person in an organization

---

Table 8-2

An Expert Driving System

Rule	"Yes" Action	"No" Action
1. Is the light green?	Proceed through the intersection	Go to 2
2. Is the light yellow?	Go to 3	Go to 4
3. Will the light turn red before you can get through the intersection?	Stop	Speed up and proceed through the intersection
4. Do you have time to stop?	Stop	Go to 5
5. Is crossing traffic present?	Proceed into the intersection and prepare for a crash	Speed up and proceed through the intersection

Discovering IT

Interview the manager of your school's bookstore or a manager at a local retail bookstore. Ask him or her to identify the types of IT systems the bookstore uses. Are they TPSs? MISs? DSSs? ESSs? Communication systems? Also ask the manager to explain how a few of the systems work. Which systems share information?

LEFT MULTI-PURPOSE DISPLAY   RIGHT

has the necessary expertise to make a certain decision and that person decides to leave the organization. The departure of a key employee means that the expertise is lost. With an expert system, however, the expertise could be captured, reducing the firm's dependency on that person.

Expert systems are also flexible. Once you have defined the rules and actions, you can change them as new considerations must be taken into account. For example, adding new considerations for the presence of pedestrians and police to your driving expert system would be a relatively easy process. Finally, expert systems are beneficial because they can reconcile the differing views of many experts. Just going through the process of developing an expert system that draws on multiple experts will help to identify and reconcile the ways each expert goes about solving the same problem.

PERSONAL ADVANTAGE

Bridging the Gap

In his book *Techno Vision,* Charles Wang explains, "They're not talking to each other. They're talking at each other. They're talking around each other."[3] What is Charles Wang—the CEO of Computer Associates International—talking about? He's talking about business people and IT people. That gives you an advantage—being able to bridge the communication gap between business and technology.

Business innovation increasingly depends on IT resources. Firms are struggling to bring together in a meaningful dialogue the people with the most insight and experience about business and those with the most knowledge about IT. These two groups of people tend to think on different wavelengths and talk different languages. Smart business people don't feel comfortable addressing IT. State-of-the-art IT people often don't understand business. If you fill the gap, that gives you an advantage.

After all, it took both business experts and IT experts to build the VF system that beat the pants off Levi Strauss. Chances are good that some people traveled between those two groups translating what was being said back and forth. It's unfortunate the IT field has created jargon and buzz words that business people cannot comprehend. For you, though, it represents an opportunity.

SOFTWARE THAT MATES
AND MUTATES

Although it may sound strange, researchers are actually working on a new type of software capable of solving problems that no human can. This new type of software is called *genetic software,* and it is literally growing. Genetic software alters its own code by a process similar to natural selection to create what might be termed the *survival of the cyber-fittest.*

Genetic software is basically a series of modules of code that are given a task. For example, the people at John Deere Tractor developed genetic software to create a production schedule for 90 different models of tractor-sized seed planters. The people at John Deere also provided criteria to guide production scheduling decisions, including minimizing machine setup time, observing the priorities of customer orders, and preventing bottlenecks during production. Within a few seconds, the genetic software created the best possible weekly production schedule—something that used to take several production scheduling specialists an entire day.

Genetic software begins by creating some of the dumbest solutions to a problem and then starts altering itself to create better and better solutions. These changes occur through crossing over, mutating, and competing. Crossover occurs when several of the modules of code come together to form a better module (one that reaches a better solution). Through mutation—in which some modules of code are randomly altered—the genetic software attempts to refine itself to reach better solutions. Finally, through competition, some modules of code that can't seem to produce good solutions become extinct; the ones that produce better and better solutions are the only ones to survive.

Genetic software still has a long way to go before its use becomes widespread, but many companies have obtained an advantage from its use. Here are some examples:

▶ **Texas Instruments used genetic software to design a computer chip on the smallest piece of silicon possible. The genetic software created a design that used 18 percent less space than TI's design team could achieve.**

▶ **Genetic software was used to design a gas turbine engine that went on to become the engine of choice for the Boeing 777.**

▶ **U.S. West uses genetic software to determine the best possible layout of new optical fiber cable systems. The genetic software has reduced the design time from two months to two days and saves U.S. West $1 million to $10 million each time it is used.**

▶ **First Quadrant, an investment firm, uses genetic software to make money in the stock market. The genetic software made over $30 million in 1993 by determining the best possible investment strategies.[4]**

What will they think of next?

Box 8-2

Using Information Technology as a Change Agent in Business

Businesses today are critically evaluating their business processes in hopes of using IT to improve results. This type of critical evaluation is commonly referred to as *business process reengineering, business process improvement,* or *business process investing.* In this chapter and previous ones, you've encountered many examples of process reengineering through IT—self-scanning at grocery stores, in-room checkout system at the Marriott, CIM to design and build automobiles, and so on. In each of these instances, IT has become a change agent for the organization. That is, IT provides a set of tools that allow businesses to rethink and redesign their processes.

In their book, *Reengineering the Corporation,* Michael Hammer and James Champy state that, "information technology plays a critical role in business [process] reengineering. . . . Information technology is part of any reengineering effort, an essential enabler." Those are pretty bold statements about the role of IT as businesses strive to make better use of their time and resources. Let's look at how some companies have used IT to reengineer their processes.

IBM Credit Corporation

Several years ago, when an IBM field salesperson needed credit approval for a purchase by a customer, he or she called in the financing request and impatiently waited, sometimes up to two weeks, for a response. This generally led to dissatisfied customers who eventually found other ways to make their purchases. IBM's credit managers found that the credit approval process took only about 90 minutes, with the many other days consumed by just shuffling papers and passing them from one office to the next. The solution—reengineer the credit approval process using IT so that it now takes only four hours to get an answer.

General Motors and the Saturn Car

Typically, when General Motors needed production parts for automobile assembly, it submitted a purchase order to a supplier, who in turn shipped the necessary parts. It sounds solid, but it doesn't make good business sense because many parts arrived late and slowed work at production facilities. The solution—reengineer the procurement process so that suppliers could access the production schedule of Saturn cars and ship parts long before they would be needed. Hopefully, you noticed that this reengineering example also includes electronic data interchange.

Hallmark Cards, Inc.

Hallmark Cards dominates the U.S. greeting card industry. With hundreds of retail outlets all over the country offering thousands of different products, Hallmark's managers were literally swamped with information. Much of this information took months to assimilate and interpret. The problem—in a seasonal retail environment, months turn into lost profit and old information is meaningless. The solution—reengineer the system for obtaining sales information from retail stores and storing it in the corporate database. Now Hallmark can even tell which products sell better when they are adjacent to other products and suggest changes to retailers overnight.[5]

From these three examples, you can see that IT is indeed a change agent. IT can help firms reengineer processes so that customers are happy (IBM Credit Corporation), so that internal efficiencies are maximized (General Motors), and so that managers can do a better job of managing (Hallmark). Perhaps Michael Hammer and James Champy's statements were accurate.

In this chapter, we've looked at the various types of IT systems that support business organizations. Some IT systems, like TPSs and communication systems, support the day-to-day operations of the organization. Still others, like MISs, DSSs, and ESSs, help managers make decisions. In summary, consider the following.

IT Systems Can Be Used in All Areas of Business

Now you can see that IT systems function in all areas of business. Whether you want to capture sales invoices or figure out what product lines to carry, IT systems can help you. As you do your job every day, ask yourself this question: "Can IT help me do what I'm trying to do?" The answer is probably *yes*. If so, take advantage of IT—it can help you do a better job.

Let IT Help You Solve Problems

People all over the world are using IT systems to help them make decisions. Some of these decisions relate to their personal lives, while others address business-related decisions. IT systems can help you solve problems by helping you identify the problem, by helping you generate alternative solutions, and by recommending possible solutions. Let IT do a lot of the work for you—IT systems work faster than people and will increase your productivity.

The Decision Is Still Yours

You should understand that the final decision rests with you. While it may be nice for a physician to use an expert system to help diagnose a disease, you certainly wouldn't want to be treated by a physician who relied solely on his or her IT system. As you use IT systems to help you make decisions, always remember that IT systems are only tools—you are the real decision maker.

Now You Can . . .

1 Understand the structure of a business organization, how management functions, and the characteristics of information within an organization.

▶ The structure of an organization has four levels:

Nonmanagement employees, who actually carry out the day-to-day operations of the organization.

Operational management, which develops short-range goals and objectives and monitors and controls the day-to-day operations.

Tactical management, which develops medium-range objectives, procedures, and policies to be implemented by operational management.

Strategic management, which develops the long-range goals, objectives, strategies, and policies of the organization.

▶ Management is the process of:

Planning—establishing goals and objectives and developing the required activities to meet those goals and objectives.

Staffing—selecting the appropriate people to meet the goals and objectives of the organization.

Organizing—developing an organizational structure that will allow people to carry out their activities in the best way possible.

Directing—leading the organization through communication, inspiration, and motivation.

Controlling—monitoring the accomplishment of activities to make sure that they are being done correctly.

▶ Characteristics of information include:

Side-to-side flow of information between functional units.

Upward flow of information that describes how the organization is operating.

Downward flow of information that originates at one level and passes to lower levels.

Internal information that describes specific operational aspects of the organization.

External information that describes the environment surrounding the organization.

Objective information that quantitatively defines something.

Subjective information that attempts to describe something currently unknown.

Granularity that describes the level of detail of the information.

2 Describe the five types of IT systems that support an organization.

▶ *Transaction processing systems* support the day-to-day operations of the organization.

▶ *Management information systems* support the management and control of the day-to-day operations by providing periodic reports that summarize the information captured by TPSs.

▶ *Decision support systems* are collections of software tools and information used to assist in the decision-making process.

▶ *Executive support systems* support the information needs of strategic management by providing the most basic summary of information.

▶ *Communication systems* support the flow of information.

3 Describe how decision support systems help you make decisions.

▶ *Decision support systems* can help you make decisions by assisting in one or all of three ways:

By recognizing that a problem exists.

By generating alternative solutions to the problem.

By choosing the right alternative.

4 Define artificial intelligence and describe how expert systems can be used in decision making.

▶ *Artificial intelligence* is the field of study that deals with the capturing, modeling, and storage of human intelligence within an IT system so that the system can facilitate decision-making processes that normally would be undertaken by people.

▶ *An expert system* helps in decision making by capturing and using the expertise, logic patterns, and thought processes of an expert.

Key Terms

Artificial Intelligence (AI)

Communication System

Comparative Report

Controlling

Decision Support System (DSS)

Directing

Downward Flow of Information

Exception Report

Executive Support System (ESS)

Expert System

External Information

Granularity

Group Decision Support System (GDSS)

Internal Information

Management

Management Information System (MIS)

Objective Information

Operational Management

Organizing

Periodic Report

Planning

Side-to-Side Flow of Information

Staffing

Strategic Management

Structured Decision Making

Subjective Information

Tactical Management

Throwaway Decision Support System

Transaction Processing System (TPS)

Unstructured Decision Making

Upward Flow of Information

What-If Analysis

Self-Test

1. The three levels of management are:

   A.

   B.

   C.

2. The process of selecting the appropriate people who can meet the goals and objectives is called:

   A. Planning

   B. Staffing

   C. Organizing

   D. Directing

   E. Controlling

3. _____ rests at the top of the organization and consists of senior or executive management.

4. The level of management that deals with the development of medium-range objectives, procedures, and policies is called:

   A. Strategic management

   B. Tactical management

   C. Operational management

   D. Planning

   E. Directing

5. _____ consists of the strategies, goals, objectives, and policies that originate at one level and pass to lower levels.

6. _____ describes specific operational aspects of the organization.

7. IT systems that support the day-to-day operations of the organization are called:

   A. Transaction processing systems

   B. Management information systems

   C. Decision support systems

   D. Executive support systems

   E. Communication systems

8. What type of reports can management information systems produce?

9. Decision support systems can be used to:

   A.

   B.

   C.

10. IT systems that support the information needs of strategic management by providing summarized information are called:

    A. Transaction processing systems

    B. Management information systems

    C. Decision support systems

D. Executive support systems

E. Communication systems

11. IT systems that support the flow of information are called:

A. Transaction processing systems

B. Management information systems

C. Decision support systems

D. Executive support systems

E. Communication systems

12. _____ capture the expertise, logic patterns, and thought processes of experts.

Short-Answer Questions

1. What are the flow characteristics of information?

2. What is the difference between objective and subjective information?

3. What are the characteristics of transaction processing systems?

4. What is artificial intelligence?

5. What are the benefits of an expert system?

Cruising the Net

1 Connect to the Web page for the Small Business Administration at http://www.sbaonline.sba.gov/. Locate information on how to finance your own business. Describe what you found.

2 Access Web pages published by various corporations or commercial entities (the name of the site usually ends with ".com" such as http://www.apple.com/). Do these organizations publish their corporate news, such as annual reports? Describe how these companies are using the Net to disseminate information.

3 Connect to the Products and Services Web page on the Yahoo directory (connect to http://www.yahoo.com/, then select "Business" and then "Products and Services"). Describe the products and services you can purchase over the Net. How do people pay for these things?

4 Search the Internet for software tools that can help you build your own expert system. What did you find? Were the software tools free? If you were able to download and use any software tools, how good were they?

5 Who are Lewis and Floorwax? Connect to the Web page for the Fox radio station (FM 103.5 in the Denver area) at http://www.rmii.com/thefox and find out. How do you think a Web page on the Internet helps a radio station?

Working in a Group

1. Suppose your group manages a private teaching organization that provides English lessons for immigrant children in your town. You have a pool of 155 volunteer students who work with 32 organizations—schools, churches, and other local groups. Each student has pledged to work 10 hours per week. Using spreadsheet, DBMS, and presentation graphics software, identify an example of a MIS, DSS, and ESS that would help you provide the children with the best possible benefits from the program, schedule your students' time for teaching, and provide you with information for planning.

2. Suppose you and several friends want to set up your own business on the Internet to sell a product out of your home. What would you have to do? As you do your research, be sure to address issues concerning what hardware you need, what software you need, how much it will cost to operate on the Internet, and how people will pay you for your product.

Discussion Questions and Projects

1. Take the expert driving system in Table 8-2 and modify it for the presence of pedestrians and the police.

2. The field of artificial intelligence deals with capturing, modeling, and storing of human intelligence within an IT system. It is so named because the intelligence stored by the IT system is actually artificial. Do you think there will come a time when IT systems are really intelligent? Why or why not?

3. The side-to-side flow of information between functional units in an organization is important. Think about a manufacturing business that has functional units for product research and design, sales/marketing and customer service, manufacturing, accounting, and warehousing and distribution. What do you think information flows would be between these various functional units?

4. In Chapter 2, we looked at many different types of application software. Complete the accompanying matrix by identifying these types of application software according to whether they are used for transaction processing systems, management information systems, decision support systems, executive support systems, or communication systems. Did you find that some types of application software can be used in more than one system?

Application Software	TPS	MIS	DSS	ESS	CS
General business management					
Education					
Word processing					
Desktop publishing					
Spreadsheet					
Database management system					
Hypertext					
Presentation graphics					
Communication					
Personal information management					
Group scheduling					
Electronic meeting support					
Video-conferencing					
Whiteboard					
Work flow automation					
Multimedia					
Virtual reality					
Video capturing and editing					

Reaching the World through IT:

Information Technology as Your Passport to the World

Your Objectives for This Chapter

1 Define the term *global economy*. **2** Describe the four forces shaping today's global economy.

3 Describe the facets of IT that offer you a passport to global citizenship. **4** Explain why the IT

industry is a global industry.

Introduction   Let's think about the many things you do every day. Some of them are probably routine, and you think nothing of them.

- If you wear contacts, you may be putting a "foreign" product in your eye.
- For breakfast, you drink orange juice that includes concentrates from Mexico or Brazil.
- You drink coffee that comes from Colombia.
- If you use sugar, it was probably grown outside the United States, probably in South America.
- You get into your car, no matter whether you consider it "domestic" or "foreign," it has parts that were not made in the United States. If you drive a Ford Fiesta, your car was assembled in Korea. If, on the other hand, you drive a Nissan Quest (a foreign car), it was probably assembled in the United States.
- You may drive to school and pass Italian, Mexican, and Chinese restaurants.
- You use books made from wood harvested outside the United States, probably in Canada. Printing was invented in Germany.
- If you take notes in class with a pencil, it may have come from Japan.
- If you put on a sweater, the wool may have come from Australia or New Zealand.
- If you are sick and get an X-ray, you benefit from a process that was also invented in Germany.
- The American style of government was originally based on the English system of government. The great underlying philosophy of our legal system—that a person is innocent until proven guilty—comes from English law. In many countries, a person who is arrested is assumed to be guilty and must prove his or her innocence.

The worldwide sharing of talents, tastes, and products has increased significantly in the last few decades and shows no sign of slowing down. Indeed, with the fall of the Iron Curtain and the subsequent movement of Warsaw Pact countries to a market-driven economy, combined with the changing attitude in developing countries such as Brazil, it seems the whole world is moving toward a competitive environment. Even Vietnam is promoting the virtues of a market-driven economy.

These world events make it all the more imperative that you prepare to take your place in the new and growing global economy. How can you use IT to do this? IT can help you to communicate with other people around the world, learn about the cultures and workplace issues of other countries, and perhaps conduct business in other countries. In fact, IT may be the single most important force shaping today's global economy. There are many other important forces as well—trade blocs, deregulation, and transnational firms. You'll see discussions concerning these forces throughout this chapter.

In this chapter, we focus on the new global economy that surrounds you and how you can use IT to be a successful part of it (see Figure 9-1). In today's global economy, you encounter IT as:

- A passport for global business
- A passport for your global citizenship
- A global industry

Figure 9-1

Your Focus in This Chapter: Reaching the World through IT

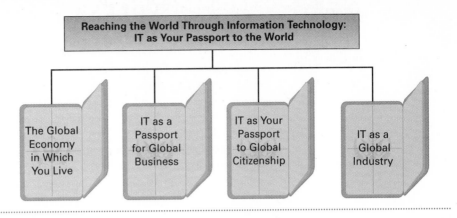

Reaching the World Through Information Technology:
IT as Your Passport to the World

The Global Economy in Which You Live

IT as a Passport for Global Business

IT as Your Passport to Global Citizenship

IT as a Global Industry

The Global Economy in Which You Live

Simply put, a **global economy** is one in which organizations do business all over the world. That includes:

- Selling products and services all over the world
- Producing products and services in countries all over the world
- Buying materials and components from suppliers all over the world
- Acting as a supplier to businesses all over the world
- Forming alliances or partnerships with businesses all over the world

So a global economy does not merely mean selling products and services abroad—it means doing all kinds of business with firms all over the world as if they were your next-door neighbors. The global economy is made possible by the appropriate use of IT. Every firm that operates globally must use IT as a strategic tool.

If you still doubt the significance of the global economy, take a look around your room or apartment and check how many of your own possessions are made abroad. See if you can find, in any industry, a single leading company that is purely domestic. You might think that retailers are, but you'll find Lands' End, Toys 'R' Us, L. L. Bean, and Wal-Mart all using IT to expand overseas. For instance, L. L. Bean uses Japanese-speaking operators in Tokyo to take orders for goods that are immediately shipped to Japan.

How about a workstation made by IBM, Compaq, Dell, or Hewlett-Packard? Each of these U.S. firms' machines typically contain components from Malaysia, the Philippines, Korea, and many other nations. Which firm is the largest seller of workstations in Asia and Latin America and the tenth largest in the United States? It's Acer, a Taiwanese company whose growth has been explosive.

IT in all its forms is helping to shape today's global economy—none probably more so than telecommunications. **Telecommunications** is a general term for everything involved in the electronic movement of information. Telecommunications technology includes communication devices and software (which you studied in Chapters 2 and 6), communication services, and providers of those services (such as AT&T, MCI, and Sprint), and such concepts as electronic data interchange (EDI). In the next two sections, you'll see how global businesses are using telecommunications to gain business advantages and how you can use all types of IT—including telecommunications—to achieve a personal advantage.

VOLKSWAGEN WORLDWIDE

Volkswagen is the fourth-largest automobile manufacturer in the world. Its recent international acquisitions include manufacturing operations in Brazil, the Czech Republic, and Shanghai and Chanchun, in China. According to one Volkswagen manager, telecommunications is a key element in "building a global patchwork of individual plants and sales organizations and making these bodies effective. If we do not accomplish this, we will not be able to integrate the business process and then we will not reach the economies of scale, which is the primary reason we bring companies together."

Building the Volkswagen communications structure is no small task. The firm must overcome not only technological challenges, but social, political, and business hurdles, as well. In Germany, for example, high-speed transmission services can cost up to 20 times more than those in the United States and Japan. In China and most of Europe, Volkswagen must contend with government-owned telecommunications systems that have monopolized transmission services for hundreds of years. It's definitely not easy, but the effort pays off.

Volkswagen now operates in just about every country in the world. Each of these countries offers some business advantage—inexpensive labor, low taxes, proximity to raw materials, quality of natural resources, and so on. Individually, these advantages are not worth the hassle; combined, they define the success of Volkswagen.[1]

IT as a Passport for Global Business

As you prepare to use IT to be a successful part of the global economy, businesses are already doing it. Global business is big business, and global business is not possible without IT. Global businesses coordinate their operations across multiple time zones, and obviously they can do this only if they have first-rate IT capabilities. Electronic mail, fax, videoconferencing, online databases, groupware, and many other IT-based tools that you have studied play essential roles in global business.

We emphasize the word *essential,* and add that people like you who are knowledgeable about these IT tools and comfortable using them, are also essential. Let's consider four global business examples: the World Bank, Irish operations of U.S.-based insurance companies, the London foreign exchange market, and Singapore's use of EDI.

The World Bank

The World Bank has two major operations, one in Washington and one in Jakarta, Indonesia. Jakarta is called "the Washington night shift" because of the way work is coordinated between Jakarta and Washington and the fact that Jakarta is 12 hours ahead of Washington. During a normal workday in Washington, the bank's project managers, economists, and technical specialists carry out complex financial analyses and generate reports. At the end of the Washington day, documents and information are sent by satellite to Jakarta, where the staff are just waking up. When they come in, they work their day, then the process is repeated.

Irish Operations of U.S.-Based Insurance Companies

Many U.S. insurance companies operate like the World Bank by using staff in Ireland to process claims. Ireland offers U.S. insurance companies a combination of well-educated personnel at relatively low wages, tax breaks, and the advantage of the equivalent of the World Bank's night shift. When work starts at 8:00 A.M. in Ireland, New York is asleep. Again, this coordinated work effort would not be possible without such IT-based tools as satellite communications and videoconferencing.

The London Foreign Exchange Market

Today, London uses IT to dominate the world's $400 billion–a–day foreign exchange market. London processes over 40 percent of the world's transactions, an amount equal to that of both New York and Tokyo combined. Because of the deregulation of telecommunications in England and the aggressive movement by British Telecom (England's version of AT&T) to provide the best and fastest telecommunications services, London's phone and data communication costs are a third or more cheaper than those in other European capitals. This lower cost coupled with better quality and availability of telecommunications services has given London the edge in the foreign exchange market.

Singapore's Use of EDI

In spite of its relatively small size (225 square miles), Singapore has become the world's busiest port by using electronic data interchange (EDI). Its EDI system lets

TODAY'S BUSINESS ADVANTAGE

JC PENNEY AND FASHION THROUGH TECHNOLOGY

Ⓨou know how fast fashions go in and out of style. The fashion industry certainly does, and they're using anything and everything they can to turn out fashions as fast as they can. JC Penney, like many others in this very volatile industry, is turning to IT for help.

JC Penney uses telecommunications to greatly shorten the time to design a new item of clothing and have it produced by Far East suppliers. JC Penney faxes high-resolution copies of fashion designs to its suppliers, instead of using a package courier such as FedEx.

More importantly, when the supplier has produced a sample, JC Penney's buyers "meet" with supplier representatives via videoconferencing systems. They can zoom the camera in on, say, a shirt to check the stitching and then discuss changes and agree on delivery schedules, all in a single session.

The average time from design to delivery in the fashion industry is six months, and each party in the chain—manufacturer, wholesaler, and retailer— writes off around 25 percent of its goods due to obsolescence. JC Penney measures its lead time in weeks, however, ensuring fashion apparel that doesn't miss the fashion.

Box 9-1

Another Force Shaping Today's Global Economy ... Transnational Firms

A **transnational firm** is a business that operates worldwide—not only to sell products and services, but also to create them. Essentially, transnational firms are global businesses. Many transnational firms generate most of their revenues from markets outside their home countries. For example, 80 percent of Sony's business comes from outside Japan, just as 80 percent of Xerox's business is outside the United States and 98 percent of the revenues of Hoffman-LaRoche—the giant pharmaceutical company that brought the world Valium—comes from outside Sweden.

Transnational firms operate in all industries, but they are probably most prevalent in the automobile industry. Car manufacturers like Ford and Toyota no longer build cars in one specific country. Rather they use extensive IT networks to coordinate the outsourcing of production across the world, performing design and engineering in several countries and producing parts in other countries. Assembly is handled in still others, so that a given car rolling off the assembly line in Spain may have parts from a dozen countries. In fact, the car made in the United States with the highest percentage of U.S.-made parts is the "Japanese" Honda Accord.

IT is essential to the transnational firm. If you've ever worked in a group, you know how hard it is to coordinate the efforts of a few people to assure the best possible project. Can you imagine how hard it is for a car manufacturer to coordinate the work of thousands of people around the world to design and manufacture a car? It simply would not be possible without good IT.

importers and exporters submit shipping documents electronically. The system has cut the response time for clearing goods through customs from 2 days to about 15 minutes, with an eventual goal of 2 to 3 minutes. In the shipping business, where the cost of handling worldwide shipping documents adds some 7 percent to the cost of world trade, Singapore has used IT to achieve and maintain a competitive edge over other countries that are much larger, but only geographically.

In all these instances, as well as hundreds of others, improving telecommunications costs and quality was a specific aim of the government (see Figure 9-2). Each country saw and still sees telecommunications as a key competitive and economic force. Other countries and governments have realized they must catch up.

Information Technology as Your Passport to Global Citizenship

The global economy in which you now live promises to be a great adventure for you. Just think of what it means to live in an environment composed of diverse cultures and interesting foods, not to mention job opportunities that can take you all over the world. What's really great is that the world and the global economy that await you are not far away—in terms of both time and geographic distances. Your knowledge and use of IT can bring the world to you today without your ever having to leave home.

To be successful using IT in this global economy is certainly an exciting challenge, but not an overwhelming one. In fact, just by reading this book, you already have two advantages. First, it means that you speak English, and English is the language of IT. Consider a very simple example—the word *computer*. It's certainly an English word, but it's recognized around the world as a term synonymous with IT. Second, by reading this book, you already know much about IT. As you have just read, IT is one of the key forces shaping today's global economy.

So the real question facing you is, "How can you use IT as your passport to global citizenship?" In Chapter 1, we discussed the Internet and the World Wide Web,

Figure 9-2

Going Wireless

Thin, narrow countries like Argentina (left) can easily apply fiber optics to provide telecommunications services. Huge, expansive countries like India (right) are choosing wireless technologies such as satellites instead.

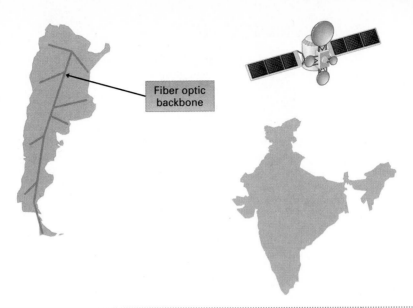

Fiber optic backbone

both of which can help you communicate with people all over the world and find information you need. Let's take a closer look at the Web and other facets of IT that are becoming your passport to global citizenship. This package of features includes utilities for overcoming language differences, Satellite Communications for Learning, the World Radio Network, and broadcasts that originate in individual countries.

The World Wide Web

For you, IT eliminates geographic boundaries between people, countries, and information. Just a few short years ago, if you wanted to do some research for a term paper, you went to the library. If you couldn't find everything you needed, you were forced to go to other sources—perhaps another library in another town or on another campus—or to request copies of the material you needed. Sometimes the copies would arrive too late.

The problem with that scenario is that you were physically forced to go to the source of the material. Also, someone else had to make a physical copy of the material you requested and send it to you. That's not true any more. Today, you can

Discovering IT

Pick an automobile. Now do some research and find out what countries some of its parts come from and where the car is assembled. You may be surprised—there's probably not a car in the world that doesn't contain parts from many countries.

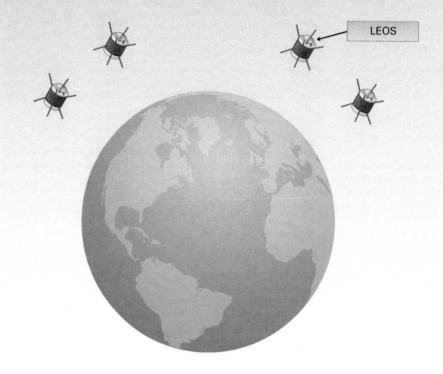

Box 9-2

The Iridium Project

One of the developments in wireless communication technology that could change the entire nature of international communications is Motorola's Iridium Project. The **Iridium Project** involves launching up to 70 low-earth-orbit satellites (LEOS) about 60 miles in the sky. This altitude is low enough for them to pick up signals from digital cellular phones and route them anywhere in the world by passing messages on to the next LEOS, which passes it on to the next and so on. A phone call from, say, Toronto to Bangkok then becomes a local, global call. You can probably guess why the funders of Iridium include the governments of Indonesia and Brazil. How else could they jump to achieve the same global communications reach as Britain and the United States?

LEOS

use the Web to virtually go anywhere you want and immediately get the information you need.

The **World Wide Web**—also known as the Web, W3, or WWW—is a hypertext or hypermedia information service that lets you wander all over the Internet, finding whatever information you want and communicating with people regardless of their location. If you recall, hypertext is a form of software that uses links (usually key words and terms) to connect different modules of information—not only text, but also sound, graphics, and even video. The Web can link modules of information on different servers. Incidentally, the Web was developed by the people at CERN, the European Particle Physics Laboratory in Geneva, Switzerland.

You can use the Web to view great masterpieces of art around the world (the *Mona Lisa,* for example, in the Louvre in Paris), find out about many cities in the world, view maps, and study points of interest, just by clicking. Basically, you can do anything on the Web that you can do on the Internet. The Web, however, makes information access much easier.

The role of hypertext on the Web is basically what makes it different from the use of gophers on the Internet. Using a gopher, you connect to a particular server and retrieve information from it. For example, if you wanted to retrieve information about the *Mona Lisa,* you could connect to the Internet server at the Museum of Arts. If you didn't find everything you needed on that server, you could then connect to the Louvre in Paris.

Using the Web, however, you would simply request information about museums and choose from a list of them regardless of its server location. On the Web, you request, see, and use information by the links that have been established without first having to specify a particular server. If you want, you can also use the Web to connect to a particular server.

What is the Web to you? In short, the Web is the Internet made easier. The Web places the Internet information from all over the world at your fingertips. This is a substantial opportunity for you. Just as the development of Windows made personal computers easier and more fun to use and created a boom in personal computer sales, the Web is making the Internet easier and more fun to use and encouraging more people and information database suppliers to offer information and services on the Internet. In fact, most information database suppliers are moving toward the use of the Web rather than maintaining their own gopher systems.

Consider these examples that could soon be a part of your life:

▶ While writing a term paper on sheep farming in Scotland, instead of doing research in the library why not use IT to actually get information from someone in Scotland who raises sheep?

▶ If you're taking a German course, you can use IT to communicate with someone in Germany and practice your skills.

▶ As you finish your undergraduate degree, you may consider going to graduate school in a foreign country. Instead of relying on material in the library, why not use IT to talk to students at various graduate schools you are considering?

These examples come from an endless list of applications of IT as your passport to global citizenship. The only real limitation is your imagination.

Discovering IT

Suppose you decide to travel around the world and want to identify some good places to visit. Connect to the Virtual Tourist Web site at http://wings.buffalo.edu/world. Did you find any interesting places? Describe the types and amount of information you found. How long do you think it would take you to find the same information in the library?

Box 9-3

Trade Blocs

A **trade bloc** is a group of countries that have pooled their resources to improve delivery of products and services and to reduce, if not eliminate altogether, restrictions on the movement of goods and services between countries. The world's most dominant and visible trade blocs include the General Agreement on Trades and Tariffs (GATT), the North American Free Trade Agreement (NAFTA), and the European Union (EU).

The **General Agreement on Trades and Tariffs** (GATT)—which includes 125 member countries and is now called the *World Trade Organization*—is by far the most complicated effort in human history to forge a worldwide treaty to reduce trade barriers and expand global trade. GATT is the oldest trade bloc, formed by the United States shortly after World War II.

The **North American Free Trade Agreement** (NAFTA) is a trade agreement that was originally ratified between the United States, Canada, and Mexico. It now includes Chile, as well. NAFTA has created an open market of more than 300 million people.

The **European Union** (EU) is a 15-country federation that constitutes the strongest international trade bloc in the world. The EU was created in 1957 by France, West Germany, Italy, Belgium, the Netherlands, and Luxembourg. Since then it has added nine new members and is likely to add others.

How do IT and trade blocs go hand in hand? Let's consider two examples—one for GATT and one for NAFTA.

General Agreement on Trades and Tariffs

Many companies have used GATT to their advantage, but the most successful are using IT as well. Consider ABB Asea Brown Boveri, a widely admired Swedish engineering and manufacturing firm. Its philosophy is total decentralization. Each of its 1,300 companies in 140 countries operates independently, managed as its own entrepreneurial entity. Its chairman protects this spirit aggressively, yet ABB handles the international procurement of goods through a central system.

The individual companies make their own decisions about the volume of coal or steel they want to purchase and when and where they want it delivered. The Geneva head office processes the orders via IT. After receiving the orders electronically, the central procurement group looks for the best price worldwide at the best foreign exchange rate.

This involves complex monitoring of foreign currency rates, swaps and other esoteric financial investments, and so on. None of this would be possible without ABB's global IT network and centralized systems that perform the analysis. In this way, the business unit's decentralized autonomy is fully preserved but the central office of ABB helps it get the best *global* deal possible.

North American Free Trade Agreement

Smart companies in NAFTA countries quickly saw the new role of IT as essential to competing in international markets. For instance, Cemex, the rapidly growing Mexican cement firm, realized that a poor phone system would greatly limit its coordination of operations within Mexico itself, and between Mexican, Spanish, U.S., and Venezuelan operations. Accordingly, the firm's imaginative head of IT leased all of the spare satellite capacity in Mexico, thereby denying Cemex's competitors access to it.

Note how strong an edge this use of IT gives Cemex. Top management has the ability to monitor operations and make quick decisions. Yet the technology involved is relatively simple, and any of Cemex's competitors could have implemented it; sadly for them, they didn't and must now take second place to Cemex.

PERSONAL ADVANTAGE

Putting the World in Your Backyard

Ⓤsing IT, you can literally place the world in your backyard. It could be kind of like having an international barbecue. If you want to give it a try, here are some places to go and where you'll find them:

U.S. State Department (tourist information)	http://www.stolaf.edu/network/travel-advisories.html
Hong Kong	http://www.cuhk.hk/scenery.html
Chile	http://www.dcc.uchile.cl/chile/chile.html
Suriname	http://www.let.rug.nl/~erikt/.Suriname
Singapore and its IT2000 program	http://www.ncb.gov.sg
South Africa, Botswana, Zimbabwe, Namibia, Lesotho, Swaziland (complete with animal sounds)	http://www.travel.co.za/travel.html
Business sites around the world	http://www.cba.uh.edu/ylowpges/ylowpges.html
Museums around the world	http://mistral.enst.fr/wm/net
Information on global demographics	http://www.pop.psu.edu:70/1m
Shopping in Singapore	http://www.ncb.gov.sg/sog/6.shop.html
Shopping in Japan	http://www.ntt.jp/japan/TCJ/SHOPPING/00.html
Slovenian wine shops	http://www.ijs.si/vinoteke
Irish Times newspaper	http://granuaile.IEunet.ie/ois/irishtimes/index.html
St. Petersburg Press (Russian newspaper)	http://www.spb.su/sppress
University of Basque Country, Spain	http://www.sc.ehu.es
University of Auckland, New Zealand	http://www.auckland.ac.nz
Technische Universitaet Berlin, Germany	http://www.cs.tu-berlin.de
Helsinki School of Economics, Finland	http://www.hkkk.fi
Oxford University, England	http://sable.ox.ac.uk

Utilities for Overcoming Language Differences

A major part of your culture has to do with how you perceive signals from other people and how you react. For example, in the Western world, looking someone in the eye often signifies honesty and confidence. In many Asian countries, however, looking someone in the eye could signify a lack of respect.

One of the major manifestations of culture is language. Think about this—according to the 1995 *World Almanac,* there are 222 languages (not to mention thousands of dialects) that are spoken by at least a million people.[2] People usually respond well when a foreign visitor makes an effort to speak even a little of their language. In 1963, John F. Kennedy went to Berlin and said "Ich bin ein Berliner" (I am a Berliner) to express solidarity with the German people in their outrage at the building of the Berlin Wall. His expression of solidarity won him gratitude, but his attempt at speaking German won him great affection. The Pope regularly sends out Christmas and Easter greetings in more than 60 languages, because it gives people a sense of connection and belonging.

Discovering IT

IT can help you overcome language differences in two ways. First, language translation utilities on the Web allow you to translate a message that you receive in a foreign language. These tools make it possible for you to effectively use any information, regardless of its language of origin.

Second, you can buy language translation software for your IT system. So when you write a letter to someone in Italy, you can use language translation software to convert the letter into Italian before sending it overseas. Some day, IT will allow you to speak English on the telephone to someone in Japan who doesn't know English. IT will take in your speech and convert it to Japanese before sending the signal to the person in Japan and reverse the process when the other person speaks Japanese to you.

Satellite Communications for Learning

The **Satellite Communications for Learning** (SCOLA) is the leading distributor of foreign language news programming via satellite to schools, colleges, and businesses. SCOLA is a nonprofit educational consortium that receives and retransmits television programming from more than 30 countries in the original languages. These programs reach more than 10,000 schools, colleges, universities, government and

---

Figure 9-3

How Lotus Handles Numerical Expressions in Different Languages

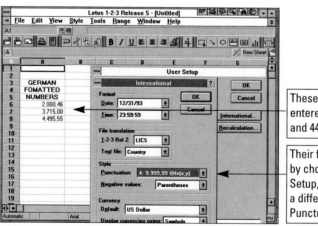

These numbers were entered as 2000.46, 3715, and 4495.55.

Their format was changed by choosing Tools, User Setup, International, and a different form under Punctuation.

Reaching the World through IT: Information Technology as Your Passport to the World

Discovering **IT**

Suppose you need language translation software for your home or business. Do some research to find out about various language translation software packages. If you needed to translate English into Italian, which package would you choose? Greek? Russian? German? Japanese?

military installations, cable TV systems, businesses, and private individuals throughout North America and much of the northern and western hemispheres.

If your school participates in a program such as SCOLA, you have, at your fingertips, the opportunity to view programs that originate from countries that interest you. SCOLA's Channel 1, for example, carries news broadcasts from Bulgaria, China, Croatia, Germany, Greece, Japan, Mexico, Poland, Serbia, Tunisia, and many others. Channel 2 covers variety, entertainment, and the arts. There are also two other channels planned for the future. Channel 3 will transmit courses in many disciplines produced by each country (for example, French philosophy, Russian physics, Chinese Confucianism, and Japanese math). Channel 4 will present classes in less commonly taught languages such as Swahili, Czech, Lakota Indian, and so on.

For you, this type of IT is invaluable as a tool for learning about today's global economy. You can:

▶ Learn about work habits, politics, law, and protocol abroad

▶ Practice modern world languages

PERSONAL ADVANTAGE

Never Be Lost Again around the World

🅣he U.S. government maintains more than 20 low-earth-orbit satellites (LEOS), which can tell you exactly where you are on the earth within 50 feet. Of course, you have to have a way of accessing the satellites; you do so with a global position system (GPS) unit. This handheld device will tell you your exact latitude and longitude by receiving signals sent out by the satellites in orbit around the earth.

The GPS unit will access as many satellites as it can from a particular point on the earth and calculate its own position by determining its position relative to the orbiting satellites. Such devices can also be programmed with the location of other points to determine the direction and distance of those points from your current position. So if you have the location of Dallas, Texas, programmed into your GPS unit and you are currently in New York, your GPS unit will tell you the distance in miles to Dallas and that it is *x* degrees from your current position (0 degrees indicates north). It will even show you your direction and speed if you are in motion.

Commercially, GPS units are widely used by pilots and sailors for navigation. For you, it means always knowing where you are and the direction and distance to where you want to be. You can purchase your own GPS unit for less than $300.

TIMELESS, LOCATIONLESS, CULTURELESS OPERATIONS

Tomorrow's successful businesses will operate in a global environment. It's a simple fact of life. No matter what business you're in, you'll find global customers, global suppliers, global competitors, or some combination of all of these. The *most* successful businesses tomorrow will operate in a global environment in a *timeless, locationless,* and *cultureless* fashion. It's kind of like creating the perfect politically correct business. When, where, and who will not matter.

Timeless businesses must be able to operate not only across multiple time zones, but without regard to time. For example, if you have customers in China, they will probably want to be able to order products at 3:00 in the afternoon. Unfortunately 3 p.m. to them is almost midnight to you. If you have the right technology, your customers will be able to order products 24 hours a day, even while you're at home sleeping the night away.

Locationless businesses will be able to take advantage of opportunities in many different countries. For example, a locationless business might make the best use of software programmers in India, inexpensive labor in China and Brazil, CPU chips in Japan, and mass production in Mexico. At a time when many U.S. businesses are thinking of expanding to the East or West Coasts, the locationless business is thinking in terms of hemispheres and continents.

Finally, cultureless businesses will be able to create seamless operations that combine people and nations with different languages, dialects, backgrounds, religious beliefs, political affiliations, and so on. This is the greatest stumbling block to globalization. Creating and acquiring the technology to work together is not nearly as monumental a task as getting people to work together.

▶ See cultural events as they happen, reported from native perspectives

▶ Learn firsthand the variety of our worldviews

▶ See the customs, conditions, and concerns of the people of the world

SCOLA is described here as an example of a worldwide educational service, but other organizations offer similar services. You should contact your school's Language or Instruction Media Department to find out whether your college or university has this type of service available. If it does, a great opportunity awaits you.

World Radio Network

The **World Radio Network** (WRN) is an audio subcarrier of SCOLA and Superstation TBS in Atlanta. WRN transmits radio programs from 24 countries and describes itself as "News from Its Source." These programs are in English, so you can learn about the events taking place around the world—those each country considers newsworthy and important—and you can do so without understanding a language other than English.

These radio transmissions are not confined to news programs. You can listen to talk shows, music programs, and discussions about local and world events in English. Contributing stations include Radio Netherlands, ABC-Radio Australia, Radio Korea, Israel Radio, YLE Radio Finland, Vatican Radio, Radio Moscow International, and BBC Europe.

Broadcasts That Originate in Individual Countries

Today, national networks don't confine their transmissions to locations within their national boundaries. For example, many millions of people around the world view CNN International. Other U.S. networks are also available on cable outside the United States. Various other countries transmit outside their borders via satellite or cable as well. The German network, Deutsche Welle (German Wave), for example, broadcasts German programming for several hours each day to the United States.

Programs on these types of national networks include news broadcasts, magazine shows, movies, travelogues, and even language classes. Some other national networks include:

▶ Antenna Greece (in Greek)

▶ Arab Network of America (in Arabic)

▶ EDTV Dubai TV (in Arabic)

▶ TV Asia (in Hindi)

▶ Various Mexican stations

▶ Various Canadian stations (some in English and some in French)

The examples we've given you represent just a small sample of the many opportunities that you have to use IT as your passport to global citizenship. Sure, you can go read a book or a newspaper, but you'll learn so much more by using IT as your passport to countries around the world.

What's really exciting is that you don't have to live in a big city or be very close to your country of interest. In fact, you don't even have to have a computer. If your school participates in a program such as SCOLA, all you have to do is take advantage of the resources that are already on your campus. Besides that, you probably have a television, so you may be able to easily tune into the World Radio Network or pick up television broadcasts from other countries.

Information Technology as a Global Industry

The IT industry, like most others, is a global industry. Forces such as deregulation, trade blocs, and transnational firms have influenced the shapes of both today's global economy and the IT industry. Let's consider some facets of IT and see how the global economy is shaping them (see Figure 9-4).

Internal Memory

In memory chips (internal memory or RAM), today's innovation is tomorrow's commodity. Until the late 1970s, U.S. firms dominated the production of memory chips. Japanese firms took over this market by applying the lean production methods created by Toyota, the discipline of total quality management, and a willingness to take a long-term view of business that accepted early losses in the interest of building market share. Slowly but surely, however, U.S. firms have recaptured a portion of the memory market that they once held so strongly.

This competition has generated great strides in the amount of information that memory chips hold. In late 1994, 4-megabit chips—containing 4 million bits— were already standard commodities and 64-megabit chips were routine. In December 1993, Toshiba, IBM, and Siemens (a German firm) announced a joint

Figure 9-4

Information Technology as a Global Industry

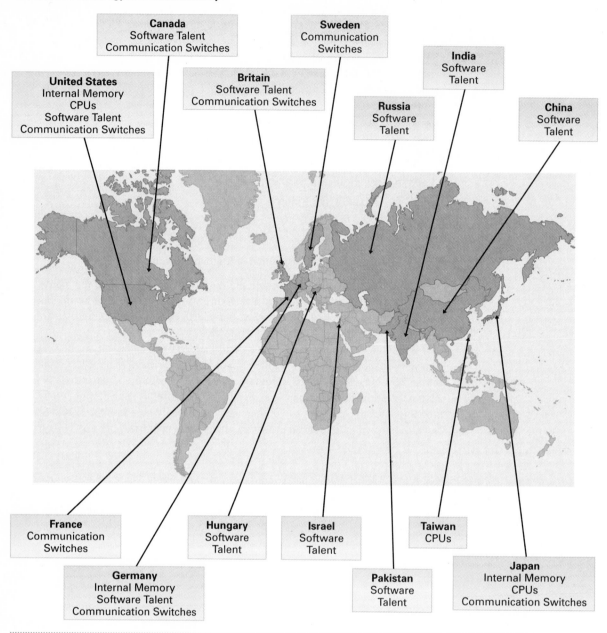

Canada
Software Talent
Communication Switches

Sweden
Communication
Switches

India
Software
Talent

United States
Internal Memory
CPUs
Software Talent
Communication Switches

Britain
Software Talent
Communication Switches

Russia
Software
Talent

China
Software
Talent

France
Communication
Switches

Hungary
Software
Talent

Israel
Software
Talent

Taiwan
CPUs

Germany
Internal Memory
Software Talent
Communication Switches

Pakistan
Software
Talent

Japan
Internal Memory
CPUs
Communication Switches

venture to produce a 256-megabit chip that will store the equivalent of 400,000 typed pages, a stack roughly 130 feet high.

CPUs

Two firms dominate the CPU chip market: Intel and Motorola. Note that both are American and both match the best firms of any country in any industry. Intel has a

75 percent share of the CPU-chip market, while Motorola's 68000 series of chips are used in Apple's Macintosh and its other machines.

Expect that to change. Asia is as dominant in memory chip production as Intel is in CPU chip production. So Asian manufacturers want to copy CPUs and be able to cut their own costs. Asia is full of innovative firms like Acer and giant ones like Hitachi and NEC that can afford the huge capital investments now needed to design and make new chips.

Operating System Software

American firms solidly dominate operating system software, with Microsoft as the central force. Apple holds a strong niche as well through its System 7 series. IBM has a similarly strong niche, mainly in the business use of OS/2 and OS/2 Warp. UNIX, originally developed by Bell Labs, is the other major operating system.

Packaged Software

The leading packages come mostly from American firms, but each country has its own providers. Software for Chinese and Spanish speakers is a rapidly growing market, fueled by China's explosive growth and the opening of Latin America's market through NAFTA. Germany's SAP package has become a popular choice of more and more manufacturers, petrochemical companies, and distribution companies as the basis for integrated information systems.

Custom-Developed Software

This is the software market in which international competition is the hottest. Hungary is a major source of technical talent for scientific applications, with its superb—though traditional—training in engineering and mathematics. British and French skills in systems development are represented by Cap Gemini, the leading European software firm, which also has a strong presence in the United States.

Canada's Systemhouse is just one of the first-rate firms to emerge from this small country (measured in terms of population, not size) in recent decades. India is also a leading provider of well-trained programmers at low cost. Other countries that are major sources of software talent include Pakistan, Israel, India, Russia, and China. The United States, though, still dominates.

Communication Switches

Until the deregulation of telecommunications, each country had its own provider of transmission switches (hardware devices that route communication signals throughout networks). Now competition is wide open and cutthroat. Major competitors include Siemens (Germany), Alcatel (France), NEC (Japan), Motorola (U.S.), Ericcson (Sweden), Northern Telecom (Canada), and AT&T (U.S.).

What does all of this mean to you? The increase in competition means new innovation, lower prices, better capabilities, and technology that seems to change almost every day. It also means that the IT industry offers you significant career opportunities. Even if you major in finance, marketing, or possibly liberal arts, you may end up working for a company that specializes in the development of IT. As these companies get bigger and expand across the globe, you may find yourself working in countries that you cannot find on the map today. Your opportunities are more exciting and challenging than ever before.

You are part of the first global generation, and many of you are the children or grandchildren of immigrants, with roots in all parts of the world. Business is global, but unfortunately the thinking of most managers in large and small companies is not global. That creates a substantial career opportunity for you. The more you think in global terms, keep up with global trends, and understand the global impact of IT, the better prepared you will be for this new world.

Use Information Technology as Your Passport

Not only is IT everywhere, but it can take you everywhere as well. IT gives you access to the World Wide Web, programs such as SCOLA, and radio and television broadcasts from other countries. If someone offered you a round-trip ticket to another country, you'd certainly take it. IT is offering you the same.

Find Ways to Use Information Technology as Your Passport

Many people are not aware of the many worldwide opportunities that IT offers. In fact, this chapter may have been your first introduction to programs such as SCOLA and the WRN. There are many others, too numerous for us to discuss in this chapter. Ask around and explore on your own. You'll quickly find that IT is literally placing the world in your backyard.

Box 9-4

Another Force Shaping Today's Global Economy—Deregulation

Deregulation is the movement to bring open competition and free enterprise into previously restricted areas of business. Examples of deregulation in the United States include the airline and banking industries. The breakup of AT&T and changes in the British telecommunications market are also excellent examples of deregulation. Not long ago (as late as the early 1980s), AT&T controlled the entire spectrum of U.S. telephone service (local and long distance), as did British Telecom in England.

Today, however, deregulation of telephone services in both countries has allowed U.S. Sprint to seek to operate in England, and British Telecom already owns 25 percent of MCI. Most important, prices have dropped dramatically while quality and availability have risen at unbelievable rates. For example, in 1989 it cost 10 times as much to lease a line from Switzerland to New York as it cost to lease a line from New York to Switzerland. Why? Because the U.S. telecommunications industry was deregulated but Switzerland's was not. This type of deregulation leads companies to base their choice of business locations increasingly on the quality, price, and availability of telecommunications.

Chapter 9 Summary

Now You Can . . .

1 Define the term *global economy.*

- A global economy is one in which organizations do business all over the world, including:

  Selling products and services all over the world.

  Producing products and services all over the world.

  Buying materials and components from suppliers all over the world.

  Acting as a supplier to businesses all over the world.

  Forming alliances or partnerships with businesses all over the world.

2 Describe the four forces shaping today's global economy.

- *Telecommunications*—the electronic movement of information—includes communication devices, communication software, communication services, and communication service providers.

- *Deregulation*—the movement to bring open competition and free enterprise into previously restricted areas of business.

- *Trade blocs* are groups of countries that have pooled their resources to improve delivery of products and services and reduce, if not eliminate altogether, restrictions on the movement of goods and services between countries.

- *Transnational firms*—businesses that operate worldwide—not only to sell products and services, but also to create those products and services.

3 Describe the facets of IT that offer you a passport to global citizenship.

- *The World Wide Web*—a hypertext or hypermedia service that lets you wander all over the Internet finding whatever information you want and communicating with people regardless of their location.

- *Utilities for overcoming language differences*—language translation utilities that exist on the Web and language translation software that you can buy for home or business use.

- *Satellite Communications for Learning (SCOLA)*—a nonprofit educational consortium, receives and retransmits television programming from more than 30 countries in the original languages to schools, colleges, and businesses.

- *The World Radio Network*—an audio subcarrier of SCOLA that transmits radio programs from 24 countries in English.

- *Television broadcasts that originate in individual countries*—the television broadcasts of other countries outside their borders via satellite or cable.

4 Explain why the IT industry is a global industry.

- *Internal memory (RAM) production*—includes such countries as the United States, Japan, and Germany.

- *CPU production*—occurs in the United States, Japan, and Taiwan.

- *Software talent*—comes from countries such as the United States, Canada, Hungary, Pakistan, Israel, Germany, Britain, China, India, and Russia.

- *Communication switches*—being produced in countries such as the United States, Canada, Sweden, Japan, France, and Germany.

Key Terms

Deregulation

European Union (EU)

General Agreement on Trades and Tariffs (GATT)

Global economy

Iridium Project

North American Free Trade Agreement (NAFTA)

Satellite Communications for Learning (SCOLA)

Telecommunications

Trade bloc

Transnational firm

World Radio Network

World Wide Web

Self-Test

1. The four forces shaping today's global economy are:

   A.

   B.

   C.

   D.

2. _____ is a general term for the electronic movement of information, which includes communication devices, communication software, communication services, and communication service providers.

3. A _____ is a group of countries that have pooled their resources to improve delivery of products and services and reduce, if not eliminate altogether, restrictions on the movement of goods and services between countries.

4. The trade agreement ratified in 1993 between the United States, Canada, and Mexico is called:

   A. GATT

   B. NAFTA

   C. EU

   D. WTO

   E. EEC

5. The World Trade Organization is now the name for what former trade bloc?

   A. GATT

   B. NAFTA

   C. EU

   D. WTO

   E. EEC

6. The movement to bring open competition and free enterprise into previously restricted areas of business is called:

   A. Free enterprise

   B. Deregulation

   C. International free enterprise

   D. Telecommunications

   E. Free competition

7. A _____ operates worldwide—not only to sell products and services, but also to create those products and services.

8. Transnational firms are most prevalent in the _____ industry.

9. The hypertext or hypermedia information service that lets you wander all over the Internet is called the:

   A. Electronic mail

   B. LEOS

   C. Telecommunications

   D. World Wide Web

   E. Internet Wide Web

10. _____ is the leading distributor of foreign language news programming via satellite to schools, colleges, and businesses.

11. The Iridium Project involves launching up to 70 _____.

12. The strongest international trade bloc is:

   A. NAFTA

   B. EU

   C. GATT

   D. WTO

   E. LEOS

Short-Answer Questions

1. How is today's global economy more than just selling products and services abroad?

2. Why are IT-based tools essential to the transnational firm?

3. Based on where you grew up, what is your culture?

4. What is the Satellite Communications for Learning (SCOLA)?

5. What is the World Radio Network (WRN)?

6. How does the World Wide Web differ from a gopher?

Solutions to Self-Test (1) telecommunications, trade blocs, deregulation, transnational firms—p. 276; (2) telecommunications—p. 277; (3) trade bloc—p. 284; (4) B—p. 284; (5) A—p. 284; (6) B—p. 292; (7) transnational firm—p. 280; (8) automobile—p. 280; (9) D—p. 282; (10) Satellite Communications for Learning—p. 286; (11) low-earth-orbit satellites (LEOS)—p. 282; (12) B—p. 284.

Discussion Questions and Projects

1. Research a big company such as IBM or General Motors and find out the extent to which their operations are global. What sources of information did you use? Did the results of your research surprise you?

2. If we truly are in a global economy, how important is the ability to speak a second language? Do you know another language? What curriculum programs at your school require you to learn another language? If someone asked you what the most important second language to learn was, what would you tell them? Why?

3. One of the drawbacks to doing business in another country is that of nationalization. Nationalization is when a government declares that all business assets located in that country—regardless of who they belong to or the country of origin—now belong to the government. So, in essence, a business investing abroad can lose everything. Find a recent example of nationalization. What country nationalized business assets? Which company (or companies) lost assets located in that country? Do you think that there are times a government should be able to seize assets in this manner? Why or why not?

4. As the economy becomes even more global, what do you think IT's role will be? How does that differ from the role of IT today?

Working in a Group

1. As a group, interview someone from a local business that is part of a transnational firm. Prepare

Cruising the Net

1. Locate a database of the current exchange rates for foreign currencies. What is the current exchange rate for the Japanese yen and the British pound?

2. Connect to the Web page for FinanceNet at http://www.financenet.gov/. What is the FinanceNet? What types of information did you find there? Describe them.

3. Connect to the Web page at the Federal Bureau of Investigation (FBI) at http://naic.nasa.gov/fbi/FBI_homepage.html. What current FBI cases are listed? Describe what you found.

4. Connect to the Web page for FedWorld at http://www.fedworld.gov/. What is FedWorld? What types of information did you find there?

5. Suppose you want to get an internship in Japan for the summer. Connect to the Web site at http:// fuji.stanford.edu/japan_information/japan_ information_guide.html. Did you find any internships that might interest you? How would you apply for these internships?

a short report for the class that details how IT is used in that business.

2. As a group, pick a country that has different workplace habits from the United States. Research that country and prepare a report that details the differences and how you think IT can help to overcome them.

10

Putting IT All Together:

Your Objectives for This Chapter

1 Describe the job opportunities in the field of IT.　**2** Describe the three aspects of IT that you need for any career.　**3** Describe the criminal and ethical considerations in IT.　**4** Understand how IT is going to change.　**5** Understand how changes in IT are going to affect your life.

Jump back to the year 1980. Suppose you had been asked by a local business consortium to give a speech on what to expect in the future. You decided to really impress the group by opening with what you thought would be the wildest but also the most realistic events that would come to pass. Your opening goes like this:

By the year 1995, the following events will occur:

▶ The only country we know of in the entire history of the world that will double its GNP in 10 years (it took the United States 80 years in its expansion in the 19th century) will be Taiwan, a small island with no natural resources.

▶ AT&T will be broken up.

▶ Russia will be in chaos and the communist bloc destroyed.

▶ The most productive automaking plants in the world will be BMW's Frankfurt operation and Ford's in Hermasillo, Mexico.

▶ The United States will have a free trade agreement with one of the most closed economies in the world, Mexico.

▶ There will be 40 million people around the world using the ARPENET computer network, with traffic growing as much as 30 percent a month. ARPENET will be called the Internet and the Information Superhighway.

▶ The kid named Gates whom IBM is using to develop its personal computer operating system will be the richest person in America and his little company, Microsoft, will be worth almost as much as IBM.

▶ You will be able to hold desktop videoconferencing meetings with other people, with the hardware and software costing only around $1,500.

▶ People will be "virtually" shopping in huge malls while sitting in the convenience and luxury of their homes.

▶ CPU chips that fit in the palm of your hand will be able to process over 100 million instructions per second. Complete systems with these chips will cost less than $1,500.

▶ Personal printers that can print in color will cost less than $500.

▶ People will watch "on-demand" first-rate movies in the comfort of their homes.

▶ Compact discs (CDs) will replace cassettes as the primary media for music.

▶ Computer systems in cars will be able to instantly tell people where they are and give directions to the nearest Chinese restaurant.

All these events may seem ordinary to you because they have occurred and have greatly shaped your life over the past 15 years. Unfortunately, you would have been laughed out of the room and recommended for psychiatric treatment had you proposed their coming.

Many of these events have been brought about by IT or are related directly to developments in IT. You're lucky—you're a part of a new culture that will soon become the norm. That culture is based on IT and its use in everyday life. What your generation can and will be able to do with IT is only limited by your imagination and initiative.

In this last chapter, we want to cover three important topics (see Figure 10-1). First, we want to give you a broad overview of the field of IT and the job opportunities available. If you're considering a career in IT, you'll also want to consult friends and professors, who can give you tips for getting a job in IT. And even if you're not considering a career in IT, we provide you with guidelines for what IT knowledge you will be expected to possess in other fields.

Second, we want to discuss the question of ethics. We've alluded to ethical and criminal considerations concerning IT throughout the book, but they deserve

Figure 10-1

Your Focus in This Chapter:
Putting IT All Together

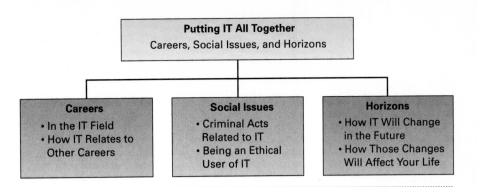

more consideration. You need to be aware of possible criminal actions regarding IT, how you can avoid them, and what your role is in society as an intelligent and ethical user of IT.

And last, we want to leave you with a view of the future of IT and how it can and will impact your life. We don't really know exactly what the future will be, but we have a good idea. We share our view of the future with you so that you can build your own view and do whatever is necessary to be prepared for it.

Information Technology and Your Career: A Question-and-Answer Session

Many people have questions about existing job opportunities in the field of IT or how they can be better prepared for non–IT-related careers by learning more about IT. We've put together a list of questions that people commonly ask. We hope you'll find our answers interesting and stimulating.

Question: What kinds of jobs are available in IT?

Answer: This is the most common question that people ask about the field of IT. Of course, it would be impossible to tell you about every job opportunity in IT; the potential job opportunities in IT are changing just as fast as the industry itself. In many of the other chapters we've discussed various jobs in the IT field; let's now bring them all together. You can also refer to Table 10-1 on page 303 to see salaries for many IT jobs.

Following are the seven jobs that tend to dominate the IT field. And remember, if you're thinking about pursuing a career in the IT field, you don't have to work in the IT industry. IT jobs can be found in all industries, including food and beverage, agriculture, banking, insurance, physical therapy, education, retail, and pharmaceuticals, just to name a few.

▶ **Computer Operators:** Computer operators actually operate the physical IT equipment (hardware). You'll find computer operators in organizations with large IT systems that support many people.

▶ **Hardware Designers and Technicians:** These people design and maintain IT hardware. Their functions range from designing new CPUs, like the Pentium and PowerPC, to repairing printers when something goes wrong.

▶ **Application Programmers:** Application programmers write code for application software. For example, they write accounting software, software that helps managers determine how much inventory to carry, and software that processes ATM transactions.

▶ **System Programmers:** System programmers deal more with operating
system software. These people write code for operating system software such
as DOS, Windows, mainframe operating systems, and utilities that control
such network functions as printing, communicating, and file serving.

▶ **Systems Analysts:** Systems analysts are responsible for determining what a
system must do. These people work with users to determine business requirements and write up formal specifications that programmers follow to write
the code.

▶ **Network Specialists:** Network specialists deal specifically with IT systems
that support many people. Their functions range from determining the appropriate communication media to which local area network (LAN) configuration
is best for a given situation.

▶ **Database Specialists** Database specialists develop, monitor, and maintain databases and database management systems. They determine what information a database must store, what type of database to implement (for example, relational or object-oriented), and software requirements for the DBMS.

Many new and exciting jobs are also opening up in the IT field. Among these are jobs for multimedia designers and authors, virtual reality analysts and designers, video game developers, neural network and genetic software specialists, and Internet application developers. These types of jobs are so new that there is no published information concerning their level of pay or demand. However, accord-

ing to *USA Today,* the 10 best jobs for the future include multimedia software designer (about 30,000 jobs with a potential salary of $100,000), interactive advertising executive, Internet surfer, and cyberdetective.[1] You can bet as these new types of information technology become more prevalent, the need for good, innovative thinkers will skyrocket.

Many companies are already beginning to hire Internet cruiser experts. Net cruiser experts are responsible for finding out what the competition is doing and for keeping up on the new types of information being published on the Net. Sounds like a great job, and it probably is—just playing on the Internet all day.

Question: Okay, you've told me about different jobs in IT, but is there really a demand for people in these areas?

Answer: There is definitely a demand for people in the field of IT. Because the field of IT is changing and growing so rapidly, new people are always needed. In Table 10-2 you can see, according to the March 1994 issue of *Money,* that four IT jobs are among the top 40 jobs in the country—systems analyst (number 1), application and system programmer (number 13), technical writer (number 18), and hardware designer and technician (number 39).

Indeed, throughout the roughly 40 years of IT as a business resource, there's *always* been a shortage of skilled people in these areas. There's no reason to expect the shortage to be reduced. Demand for IT systems greatly exceeds the supply of first-rate people to build them. You should look carefully at Table 10-2, though, and realize that you may have to relocate to find some of these jobs.

Question: What kind of education should I get if I want a career in IT?

Answer: If you're considering a career in IT, think first about the job you want. That choice will help you to determine what type of school you should attend and what your studies should emphasize. Let's look first at the focus of your studies if you choose a four-year program offered by a college, community college, or university. Then we'll look at shorter programs offered by vocational and trade schools.

Colleges and universities offer four-year bachelor's degree programs in IT as well as Master's and Ph.D. programs in IT. If you choose to attend a college or university, some of your studies will also focus on other areas such as liberal arts, math and science, and business. College and university programs are designed to

Table 10-1

A Review of Information Technology Salaries[2]

Position	Salary
Computer operations manager	$56,490
Computer operations supervisor	$40,399
Computer operator	$33,387
Data security administrator	$73,279
Database analyst	$52,844
Database manager	$58,453
Director, IS Operations	$75,196
Director, Networks	$69,374
Director, Systems Development	$74,036
Help desk operator	$30,102
LAN manager	$45,757
Lead computer operator	$34,462
Microcomputer manager	$61,839
Network administrator	$44,492
PC technical support specialist	$33,230
Programmer/analyst	$40,537
Project manager	$58,743
Senior programmer/analyst	$46,235
Senior systems analyst	$51,878
Senior systems programmer	$53,730
Systems analyst	$48,314
Systems programmer	$44,666
Technical specialist	$36,895
Technical support manager	$44,265
Telecommunications manager	$55,811
Telecommunications specialist	$43,253

provide you not only with an education in IT, but also with knowledge in areas that will surround you in your job.

The focus of your studies can be in one of two directions—technical applications or business. For example, the IT specialists who work for NASA on the Space Shuttle program have a technical IT education, while IT specialists who design business systems for large organizations have a business IT education.

Computer science is the area of study most closely associated with a technical IT education. If you get a degree in computer science, you'll probably receive a bachelor of science (B.S.) degree after completing many hours of study in mathematics and science. A degree in computer science will prepare you for jobs in hardware design, system programming, and networking and telecommunications.

Management information systems (MIS) is the field of study associated with a business IT education. If you get a degree in MIS, you'll probably receive a bachelor of business administration (B.B.A.) degree after completing many hours of study in business-related areas such as accounting, organizational behavior, and

Table 10-2

The Top Jobs in the Nation[3]

Job	1994 Rank	1992 Rank	11-Year Job Growth	Where the Jobs Are
Systems analyst	1	31	110%	Silicon Valley, Washington, Boston
Applications and systems programmers	13		30%	Washington, Silicon Valley, Dallas
Technical writers	18	46	23%	Silicon Valley, Boston, Washington
Hardware designers and technicians	39	69	45%	Atlanta, Silicon Valley, Dallas

finance. A degree in MIS will prepare you for jobs in the areas of application programming, networking, and databases.

Notice that we identified job opportunities in networking for both kinds of IT education. In a computer science program, you'll learn all of the technical aspects of how a network works and how to build a network. In an MIS program, your studies will focus, to some extent, on how networks work, but you'll mainly concentrate on how to use networks and IT as an organizational resource.

Which focus you choose is totally up to you. If you prefer math and science, you should consider getting a B.S. in computer science. If you prefer the business side, you should consider getting a B.B.A. in MIS. There are many job opportunities, so pick the one that suits you best.

Vocational and trade schools, on the other hand, offer IT programs that range from six months to two years of study. These programs focus specifically on IT and most often do not require course work in other fields, unlike colleges and universities. Vocational and trade school programs can prepare you for both technical and business careers in IT.

Again, whether you choose to attend a vocational or trade school or a college or university is up to you. The best thing to do is determine what job you want and then find organizations hiring for that position. Take the time to interview these organizations and ask them what type of school you should attend and where to focus your studies.

Question: I now know, in general, what job opportunities are available and something about different IT education programs. Can you tell me some specific skills that I should concentrate on developing during my education?
Answer: As far as non-IT skills are concerned, we encourage you to focus on communication skills and general studies that focus on the environment that will surround you in your job. For example, if you want to be an application program-

Table 10-3

The Five Information Technology Skills Most in Demand in Job Ads[4]

Skill	Percentage of Ads
1. PC/LAN	40.2
2. Relational Database	28.1
3. UNIX	22.0
4. C Programming	19.6
5. COBOL Programming	19.4

Interview one or two students at your school who are about to graduate with a degree in MIS or computer science. With what businesses are they interviewing? What do they think is a reasonable starting salary range? Ask them what you should concentrate on if you're considering a career in IT.

mer for business systems, you should learn as much as you can about business, including accounting, finance, marketing, and human resource management.

For specific IT skills, you can look at Table 10-3 and see that the top five desired skills according to a survey of 1,100 newspaper ads in 10 major cities are PC/LAN, relational database, UNIX, C programming, and COBOL programming. C and COBOL are popular programming languages that are used to write both operating system software (C only) and application software (C and COBOL).

Question: So far you've been focusing on careers in the IT field. What if I don't want a career in IT? I realize that IT is going to be a part of my career. What aspects of IT should I focus on specifically so I can get the best job in another field?

Answer: This is probably the question that applies to most people. Many people are pursuing careers in IT, but many more are pursuing careers in other areas. No matter what career you choose, below is a list of IT skills that you should possess. "Should possess" may sound like a strong way of putting it, but it's no different than telling you that you should know how to add, subtract, multiply, and divide to get any type of job. Just as all employers expect you to have a certain level of knowledge about mathematics, they also expect you to have a certain level of knowledge about IT.

▶ **Personal Productivity Software:** Personal productivity software includes such tools as word processing, DBMSs, presentation graphics, and spreadsheets as well as a host of others. These are the basic IT tools that you'll find in almost any organization. Once you find the perfect job and go to work, your employer will probably expect you to be immediately productive in producing correspondence (word processing software), tracking and maintaining any information you need or for which you are responsible (DBMS software), preparing presentations (presentation graphics), and producing reports that incorporate numbers and graphs (spreadsheet software). Don't sell yourself short by not exploring the vast capabilities of all types of personal productivity software—your knowledge of this type of software is a prerequisite for almost any job.

▶ **Hardware:** Just as you need to know how to use personal productivity software, you also need to know about hardware devices. Not only do you need to know how to use different types of storage devices and input and output devices (such as a keyboard, mouse, and printer), you'll also need to know how to make informed decisions regarding which types of technology are best for a given situation. It would not be in your best interest to prepare a proposal for a new system that includes a dot matrix printer when your printing needs require the high-quality production of text and graphics.

PERSONAL ADVANTAGE

Finding a Job on the Internet

Whether you're considering a career in IT or any one of hundreds of other fields, IT can help you in two ways. First, knowledge of IT is a skill that employers are looking for. Second, you can use your new knowledge of IT to find the right job. How? Simple—use the Internet to advertise yourself and find job announcements.

That's what Bill Smiley did in 1994. As Bill was completing his studies in engineering at a school in south Texas, he began the task of searching for a job. After months of sending out letters and resumes and being continually rejected, he turned to the Internet. Bill placed his resume on one of the many online database services that list people looking for jobs. Four weeks later, he received a phone call from an automobile manufacturer and began his career as an automobile designer. The irony in Bill's story is that he received a rejection letter from that same company two months before they found him on the Internet.

If you think Bill's success in finding a job through the Internet won't happen to you, consider the numbers from three online job and career database services.[5] The first is Online Career Center (OCC). The OCC receives about 80,000 accesses per day. That's 80,000 job seekers and employers cruising OCC for job announcements and potential employees. The second is the Interactive Employment Network (IEM). It claims to have over 2,000 new jobs posted weekly. Finally, there's Career Mosaic. Although it's only about two years old, it receives over 100,000 electronic visits per month.

These numbers only reflect a part of what's really happening. Some analysts estimate that the number of people cruising the Internet for jobs and employees could be as high as 3 million daily. Your advantage is that you now know how to use information technology and the Internet. Is your resume online for thousands of businesses to see? In the accompanying table, we've listed many Web sites for you to consider as you begin your search for a job.

Description	Address
San Francisco Bay Area	http://none.coolware.com/jobs/baymap.html
Contract Technical Employment	http://www.ceweekly.wa.com/
Comprehensive Resource	http://www.careermag.com/careermag/
High-Tech Industry	http://www.mecklerweb.com/careerweb/
Businesses with Job Opportunities	http://www.yahoo.com/business/employment/jobs/companies
Computer Animation Field	http://www.cinenet.net/gweb/lists.html
IT Jobs Around the World	http://www.britain.eu.net/vendor/jobs/main.html
Radio and TV Jobs	http://www.cpb.org/jobline/jobline.htm
Post Your Resume	http://mainsail.com/jobs/htm
Employment Database	http://www.espan.com/cgi-bin/ewais
Health Field	http://www.yahoo.com/health/employment/
Government Jobs	http://www.yahoo.com/business/employment/jobs/government
Employment for Web Developers	http://www.charm.net/~web/jobs.html
National Business Employment Weekly	http://www.occ.com/occ/nbew/nbew01.html
Online Career Center	http://www.occ.com/
International Employment	http://www.britain.eu.net/~idea/
Physics	http://xxx.lanl.gov/announce/jobs
Scientific and Engineering	http://www.spie.org/web/employment/employ_home.html
List of Employment Resources on the Internet	http://www.wpi.edu/~mfriley/jobguide.html

Table 10-4

**How Companies
Use Networks[6]**

Function	Description	Currently Doing	Planning to
Internal communications	Keeping distant offices aware, with e-mail, of changes at headquarters	30%	14%
External communications	Allowing suppliers and contractors to track inventory or production schedules	49%	27%
Advertising	Using a Web page as an information-rich way to advertise	8%	33%
Selling products	Cutting out the intermediary and sell directly to the public	5%	35%

▶ **Networking:** You live in a networked world, in both your personal and your business life. Businesses today depend on networks for the electronic communication among people and the sharing of information, hardware, and software. Don't worry—you won't need to be able to determine the best LAN configuration, but you will need to know what networks can and cannot do. Another important aspect of your networking knowledge should be the Internet. Every day, more and more businesses explore ways to use the Internet as a tool for doing business (see Table 10-4). If you can help your organization gain a business advantage by using the Internet, you'll also have a career advantage.

In short, the more you know about IT the better off you will be when you begin your job search.

Knowing about personal productivity software, different kinds of hardware, and networking applies to all types of jobs. Exactly what IT skills you should focus on for a specific job depends on the career you choose. For example, if you want to be a portfolio investment manager, you'll also want to focus on learning how to build a decision support system. If you're considering a career as a doctor, you'll want to learn more about expert systems. If you're considering a career in retail, you'll want to learn as much as you can about POS systems. The list is endless.

The best thing for you to do is find organizations hiring people in your field and find out what IT skills those organizations want. You can do this by interviewing various people at businesses for which you would like to work or by simply looking through the want ads in newspapers.

Beyond Technology: Ethics and Crime The use of IT in our society has raised many new questions regarding the rights we have as individuals and the obligations that businesses have to individuals. Have you ever received "junk mail" and wondered how the sender got your name and address? Chances are some other organization sold them your name and address. Was that right or wrong? What about when a friend or family member who provides your name and phone number to MCI for its Friends and Family program? How about using your company's computer for personal business? Copying software for a friend? Getting someone else's password and reading his or her e-mail?

The answers to many of these questions are obvious, while others fall into gray areas. All of them, however, deal with ethics. **Ethics** are the standards or set of principles that help guide behavior, actions, and choices. The difficult thing about ethics is that they are often a matter of personal interpretation and not necessarily illegal. For example, when your friend gives MCI your name and phone number it's not illegal, but was it ethical?

These types of ethical and legal considerations regarding IT have been with us since the use of IT began. They have, however, become particularly prevalent with the widespread use of networks. For you, IT ethics mean using your IT system to do things the same way you would do them if you didn't have IT. On the Internet, for instance, you should not use offensive language (this is part of what is called "netiquette"). The laws regulating the use of some forms of language in public should also apply to the Internet. In addition, you should not use IT to intercept and read other people's electronic mail. You certainly wouldn't steal someone's mail from the mailbox in front of his house, so why do it on the Internet?

Information Technology Crimes

Unfortunately, not everyone lives by the same ethical standards, nor does everyone live by the laws that govern us. Kevin Mitnick is a good example of a bad apple. In February 1995, Kevin was caught breaking into an Internet provider computer system and stealing over 20,000 credit card numbers. Not only was he stealing from the Internet provider, he was also invading the privacy of the credit card holders. IT crimes include starting viruses, stealing information, software piracy, and IT destruction.

Computer viruses are software programs that cause an IT system to malfunction. Systems that have a computer virus are said to be "infected." Malfunctions can be as trivial as causing the screen to go blank or as catastrophic as causing a hard disk to reformat itself. What's even worse is that computer viruses migrate from system to system by attaching themselves to other pieces of software or information. If you were working at school, for instance, and used a workstation that was infected, chances are good that you would infect your home system if you used a floppy disk to transfer information from one system to the other (see Figure 10-2). Of course, the Internet makes it even easier for computer viruses to migrate.

How do you protect yourself against viruses? Fortunately, there is software that will help—it's called antivirus software. **Antivirus software** monitors your storage devices to make sure that a computer virus doesn't exist. So when you bring home a floppy disk from school and use it on your home system, the antivirus software will "scan" it to make sure that it doesn't have a virus. If it does, most antivirus software provides utilities for removing the virus. Popular antivirus

Figure 10-2

Where Did You Catch That Virus?[7]

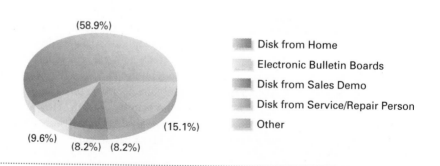

(58.9%)

Disk from Home
Electronic Bulletin Boards
Disk from Sales Demo
Disk from Service/Repair Person
Other

(15.1%)
(9.6%)
(8.2%) (8.2%)

Putting IT All Together: Careers, Social Issues, and Horizons

Suppose you found that some of your disks had a virus. What would be your options for getting rid of the virus? Does your school have antivirus software you can use? If you had to purchase an antivirus software package, which one would you choose and why?

software packages include Anti-Virus by Central Point Software, Norton Anti-Virus by Symantec Corp., and ViruCide by Parsons Technology.

Stealing information is what Kevin Mitnick did. Stealing information is illegally obtaining information. The theft of information is much more difficult to detect than other types of theft. When someone steals, say, your car, you know it. But when someone steals information, he or she takes a copy of it, so you never know it happened. Stealing information amounts to "breaking into" a computer. That is, someone must gain illegal entry into a system and then copy the information. Again, it's very hard to determine when someone has gained illegal entry to a system. In Figure 10-3, you can see the number of reported computer break-ins over the past six years. Most experts, though, believe that these numbers may be as much as 1,000 times too low.

Software piracy, or stealing software, is illegally obtaining and using software. Software piracy is a lot like stealing information—it's hard to detect because someone can steal a copy without leaving a trace. For you, though, purchasing a software package and installing it on two different computers—that is, yours and a friend's—falls into the category of stealing software. In fact, the Software Publishers Association estimated that application software piracy for 1993 alone topped $7.4 billion.[8] Always remember, when you purchase a software package, you have purchased the right to use that package for your own benefit—you have not purchased the right to make copies of the software.

IT destruction is the crime of physically damaging or destroying an IT system that belongs to someone else. For you, this would be like someone breaking into your home and smashing your system. For businesses, IT destruction can be almost catastrophic, which is why businesses with minicomputers, mainframes, and supercomputers go to great lengths to safeguard against IT destruction. Businesses have "computer rooms" that only authorized personnel can enter. These computer rooms have a number of security devices including fireproof walls, security card or key entry only, and site monitoring by surveillance cameras.

The Future of Information Technology and Your Life

IT is changing every day. More important, the changes in IT are changing the way you live your life every day. As you think about the future, we ask you to keep two questions in mind: "How will IT change?" and "How will IT change my life?" No one can really answer

Box 10-1

Help Take a Byte Out of Cyber Crime

Ⓝo matter how hard we try to eliminate it, IT crime will always be around. There are, however, a number of things that you can do to protect yourself against IT crimes. First, and most important, is to be an ethical user of IT. If we all pitch in and do what's right, we can keep IT crime to a minimum. To protect yourself against people who are not ethical, consider doing the following:

▶ **Change your password frequently:** If you have password access to an IT system, change your password frequently. This will help prevent people from trying to figure out what your password is.

▶ **Don't use a password associated with something personal:** Most people use a password that contains some personal association—birth date, name of a friend, favorite sports team, and so on. *Computer hackers,* people who break into systems, find out as much as they can about someone and then try passwords that have some personal association.

▶ **Don't give out vital personal information over the Internet:** While on the Internet, think carefully about giving out your home address and phone number, social security number, and other personal information. Remember, your information travels over a vast network and the wrong people can intercept it.

▶ **Don't leave floppy disks laying around:** Just as you wouldn't leave personal mail laying around, you should not leave floppy disks laying around. Take the time to put them in a desk drawer or somewhere out of view.

▶ **Use antivirus software with automatic scanning:** Always have antivirus software that automatically scans for viruses. Even unsuspecting friends and family members can accidentally give you a virus.

▶ **Know your company's policy regarding e-mail:** Many companies have policies regarding the use of e-mail; some of them even reserve the right to read your e-mail.

▶ **Don't use a business computer to store personal information:** It's unethical to use a business computer for personal purposes. Most important though, many people have access to your system at work. Do your work at work, and leave your personal business at home.

Figure 10-3

Computer Crimes Skyrocket![9]

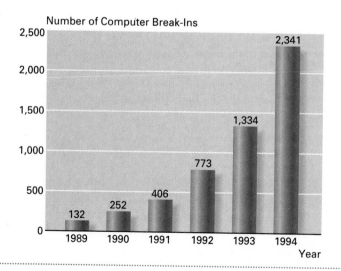

Number of Computer Break-Ins

Putting IT All Together: Careers, Social Issues, and Horizons

these two questions with a great deal of certainty, but let's look at some things we know for certain.

Changes in Information Technology

In the next several years, you can expect to see IT change in four ways:

▶ Through rightsizing

▶ Through integration

▶ Through a restructuring of the IT industry

▶ By incorporating more of the senses

These four key areas will dramatically affect how you view IT and how IT will change your life.

First, IT is rightsizing. Rightsizing means that IT systems are getting smaller, and at the same time, more powerful and less expensive than their larger predecessors. These smaller systems will become more the "right size" and give you greater portability. With this new portability, you'll be able to be productive no matter where you are—on the beach, in an airplane, or driving down the road. In the future, expect to see increased use of and more capabilities in portables, personal digital assistants, and smart cards. You can also expect to see more businesses developing applications for smaller systems including workstations (see Figure 10-4).

Second, IT will change through integration. By integration, we mean that hardware and software manufacturers will work more closely together so that you won't be limited to working with just one type of hardware or with software that works only for a particular operating system. The best example of this change is the working relationship that Apple and IBM are developing. Apple and IBM have long been competitors in the IT market. In earlier years, if you owned an Apple, you were limited to Apple products and could not use any IBM (or IBM-compatible) hardware or software.

Figure 10-4

U.S. Growth in Applications by Platform

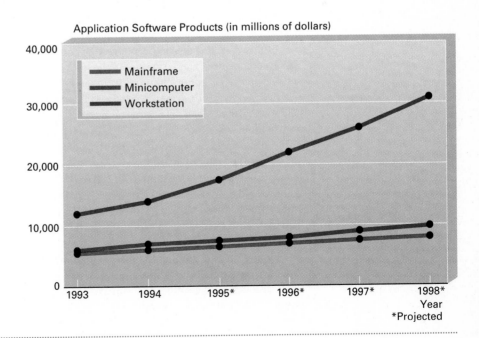

Application Software Products (in millions of dollars)

Putting IT All Together: Careers, Social Issues, and Horizons

3 1 1

CONTROLLING COMPUTERS
WITH YOUR MIND

Many people have a difficult time believing that IT will soon be able to incorporate such senses as smell and taste. They have an even harder time believing that we'll someday be able to control IT with our minds. Well, how about this—a small firm recently introduced a product called *The Mind Drive.* And it does just what its name says. It lets you control movements on the screen without ever touching an input device.

The Mind Drive actually does have an input device, but it works like no other. The input device for The Mind Drive is a sensor that slips over your finger. It measures very, very small physiological responses through your skin and sends them to the CPU. The CPU interprets your physiological responses and causes movement on the screen to occur. And you never lifted a finger—literally!

The Mind Drive will be released in late 1995 or early 1996 for $100 to $200. Applications that will be able to use The Mind Drive include action video games, art and music software (think, and the orchestra changes tempo), lie detector games, and learning enhancement software.

In the movie *Field of Dreams,* the big statement was, "If you build it, they will come." With The Mind Drive, the statement will be, "If you think it, it will happen."[10]

Today, that is changing. Information transfer between IT systems by Apple and IBM is much easier. Apple's ads for its PowerPC machines emphasize their compatibility with Windows. And someday soon, you will be able to connect your IBM-compatible system directly to an Apple printer or scanner. This will not only give you more flexibility, it will allow you to choose the best IBM has to offer and the best Apple has to offer.

Other examples of integration in the IT industry include Novell's acquisition of the WordPefect Corporation, IBM's acquisition of the Lotus Corporation, and Microsoft's ill-fated attempt to acquire Intuit, the maker of Quicken.

Third, the IT industry is in a major state of flux and will change dramatically over the next several years. Some of the acquisitions we already noted are examples of this. You can also expect to see the combining of media, IT, and communications companies. These types of companies are scrambling to bring products and services into your home and provide you with the tools (IT) to access those products and services. For example, MCI recently invested $2 billion in Rupert Murdoch's News Corp. These two companies have combined to develop, market, and distribute electronic information and entertainment. Some possibilities include online news services, video on demand, and electronic commerce.

As the IT industry restructures itself, you can expect other developments to have a great impact. For example, in late 1994 Apple announced for the first time that it would allow the manufacturing of Apple compatibles. Many companies are expected to try (and some will fail) to manufacture and sell Apple compatibles. The great chip race between Motorola, AMD, Cyrix, Intel, and NexGen will also continue and cause major restructuring in the IT industry.

Finally, IT is beginning to incorporate more of the senses. We have already looked at virtual reality—a special system that incorporates movement and the sense of touch. In the future, you can expect great gains to be made in these areas, and possibly in the areas of smell and taste.

How Will Information Technology Change My Life?

The changes in IT over the next several years will be dramatic and mind-boggling. Even more important, though, is how these changes will change your life. As you look to the future and the emerging changes in IT, think about these things in your everyday life:

▶ Home-integrated computing

▶ Education-integrated computing

▶ Travel-integrated computing

▶ Customer-integrated computing

Home-Integrated Computing. IT has permeated all parts of your life. In your home, for example, you can find **intelligent consumer products**—products that have IT as a component. Intelligent consumer products include refrigerators, televisions, VCRs, stereos, toaster ovens, and even breadmakers. All these products use IT to monitor how they function and provide automated responses to your preset requests. For

TODAY'S BUSINESS ADVANTAGE

DELL AND GATEWAY DELIVER TO YOUR DOORSTEP

Throughout 1994, big computer companies such as IBM, Compaq, and Apple all bailed out of the mail-order computer business. Each predicted that the mail-order computer business would go flat, if not decline, over the next few years. Dell Computer and Gateway 2000, however, saw something different—something that made them stay in the mail-order business and abandon any type of selling in retail stores.

This time, companies such as IBM, Compaq, and Apple made the wrong choice, and the small (then) start-up companies such as Dell Computer and Gateway 2000 won in a big way. Gateway's revenues skyrocketed, rising an estimated 50 percent in 1994 to $2.6 billion. Its stock went up almost 150 percent , from 9 to 22 points. Dell, which earned around $3.5 billion in 1994 revenues, did even better in the stock market. Its stock went from 19 points to over 50. Dell and Gateway now own an estimated 50 percent of the $9-billion-a-year mail-order business.

So what's the advantage in selling by mail order? Well, it's not a single advantage—it's actually four advantages rolled into one. First, experienced buyers are ordering more computers through mail order because of the cost savings. These types of buyers know what they want and don't need the handholding that a retail store typically offers. Second, mail-order operations carry far less inventory. Dell, for example, carries only 35 days of inventory, compared to Compaq's 110 days.

Less inventory leads to the third advantage—the ability to react more quickly to technological changes. This translates into less obsolete inventory and expensive write-offs. When the Pentium chip was announced, for instance, Gateway was able to convert 50 percent of its machines in inventory in a matter of a few months, compared to 10 percent in the case of Compaq and IBM. Finally, by selling mail order, the expensive intermediary (the retailer) is eliminated. So Gateway's operating costs are only 5.4 percent of revenue, versus 13 percent for Compaq. And when you're doing $2.6 billion in business, that 7.6 percent adds up fast.

Both Dell and Gateway are projecting growth of 15 to 40 percent over the next several years through mail-order computer retailing. They have found their competitive advantage.[11]

Figure 10-5

Your Future as a Telecommuter

Ⓜ️ore than 8 million people already telecommute. By 1998, that number is expected to exceed 13 million.[12]

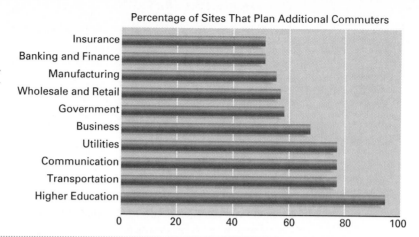

Percentage of Sites That Plan Additional Commuters

example, if you own a multi-CD stereo player and set the music selection for random play, a computer chip takes over and generates a random selection of music from the different CDs. And don't forget our opening example of your integrated home management (IHM) system in Chapter 1. Someday soon, all your electronic devices will be tied together. You may even be able to start the coffee while working at your desk with just a few clicks of the mouse or by voice activation.

Technology in your home will also allow you to do home shopping, view electronic media (for example, newspapers and magazines), and pay your bills while sitting in your favorite recliner. One IT-based product that will help you do this is an interactive television. An **interactive television** is a television with a keyboard, storage, and the ability to respond to your requests to transmit and receive vast amounts of information from all over the world. Interactive TVs will let you view advertisements whenever you want (instead of in the middle of a program), watch videos whenever you want, and do online interactive shopping at such stores as Macy's, Nordstrom's, and Toys 'R' Us.

As technology continues to work its way into your life at home, you can also expect to work at home instead of going to the office. In Chapter 1, we talked

Figure 10-6

Education-Integrated Computing

about telecommuting—being an employee of an organization but working at home instead of going to the office. Telecommuting may happen faster than you think. In fact, at least half of all major business segments plan to add more telecommuters (see Figure 10-5). Don't be surprised if you're in an interview and someone asks you if you would mind working at home instead of slogging through traffic five days a week to get to the office.

Education-Integrated Computing. Education basically provides you with information in the form of instructor lectures and books. Because education is information based, it is a prime candidate for the use of IT. In Chapter 2, we discussed using videoconferencing in the classroom, but it doesn't stop there. Imagine the day when you can be a student in Fort Hays State University in Kansas and live in Denver, Colorado. That day is coming—you will actually have the ability to enroll in any school in the country, live in a completely different area, and attend all your classes via videoconferencing. Just like many people telecommute to work, you will be able to telecommute to school (see Figure 10-6).

Also, imagine the day when you won't go to the bookstore to buy books; instead you'll view a copy using the school's network. These types of virtual books will be achieved through electronic publishing. **Electronic publishing** is the development of material designed specifically for electronic distribution and use. You may even have special IT equipment in the classroom that lets you view a textbook electronically while your instructor presents a lecture.

Travel-Integrated Computing. Earlier, we said that IT was rightsizing—getting smaller, more powerful, and cheaper. In the future, we will all carry around IT systems much the same way we carry around pocket calculators and credit cards today. You see, not only will IT systems be small enough to carry around all the time, it's also becoming necessary that we have our systems with us at all times. Wireless communications plus rightsizing will make this practical and affordable.

As you travel, you'll also find more information technology. Think about airplanes and hotels. The airline industry is responding to the requests of travelers by providing in-plane fax machines, cellular phones, and even individual screens on which you can watch the movie of your choice (of course, for a small fee). Hotels are also beginning to use IT for customer convenience. The year 2000 hotel will have automated facilities that include a smart card to check in; order on-demand movies in your room; and an interactive TV to call home and check messages, open the wet bar, and check out (see Figure 10-7). Your only contact with the hotel personnel may be to order more towels.

Customer-Integrated Computing. Finally, you can expect businesses to use IT to make it faster, easier, and more convenient for you as a customer. We have already discussed many examples of customer-integrated computing in this text, including ATMs, self-scanning at grocery stores, package delivery tracking systems designed specifically for use by customers, and pay-at-the-pump fuel stations. What's coming next is digital cash. **Digital cash** is an electronic form of currency that you can use to purchase products and services at stores as well as make purchases on the Internet.

Digital cash comes in the form of electronic tokens that represent a certain denomination of money. You can store digital cash on a smart card or your system at home. If you want to make a purchase at a store, the store's computer system would automatically deduct the amount of the purchase from your card. When you run out of money, you would simply stop by the digital cash machine and buy more electronic tokens.

If you could build the classroom of the future, what would it look like? What IT would be included? Do you think that students using your classroom of the future will get a better education than you?

The Internet is the major reason we are moving to an electronic form of cash. If you make a purchase on the Internet using your credit card, your credit number and all of the information associated with it travels over a vast network and becomes easily accessible to many people. To overcome this, you can use digital

---

Figure 10-7

The Year 2000 Hotel

To check in, guest inserts personal card into an automated check-in machine (ACM), which provides room number and makes a billing record.

Guest opens room door by using ACM card. Motion detectors cause lights, heat, or air conditioning to turn on automatically upon entry.

Guest can plug notebook computer into TV to connect to office and to read electronic mail. The monitor is touch-sensitive and has an internal CD ROM.

Screen displays map of nearby restaurants. Guest can view menus, make reservations, or request delivery.

Access to on-line shopping services allow guest to order merchandise and have it delivered.

Guest can call home using a videophone connected to the TV. Charge is recorded on ACM card.

Video-on-demand offers large library of movies.

At checkout, guest can call up itemized bill. ACM card is inserted to approve payment.

---

cash. From a provider of digital cash, you simply buy digital cash and then send it out over the Internet to make purchases. The person or organization from whom you made the purchase can then use the digital cash to make other purchases or trade it in to the digital cash provider for paper currency (see Figure 10-8). The obvious advantage to this is that information about you does not travel with your digital cash.

Many disadvantages will have to be overcome, however. First, there are no regulations for how digital cash should be handled and for who can be a provider of digital cash. Second, digital cash is easy to copy, making it easy prey for counterfeiters. Third, you can lose your digital cash if you misplace your smart card or your hard disk crashes at home. This is similar to losing your wallet. Finally, digital cash will make it easy to "launder" money on the Internet. Because no information travels with the digital cash, it cannot be tracked to its origin. Nonetheless, digital cash is coming, and it promises to radically alter the way we do business, not to mention the fact that it will throw the banking industry into chaos.

In all these instances—home, education, travel, and customer-integrated computing—businesses can gain an advantage by using or offering these types of integrated computing services. Most important, in all these instances you can obtain a personal advantage by making them part of your everyday life.

Figure 10-8

Using Digital Cash on the Internet

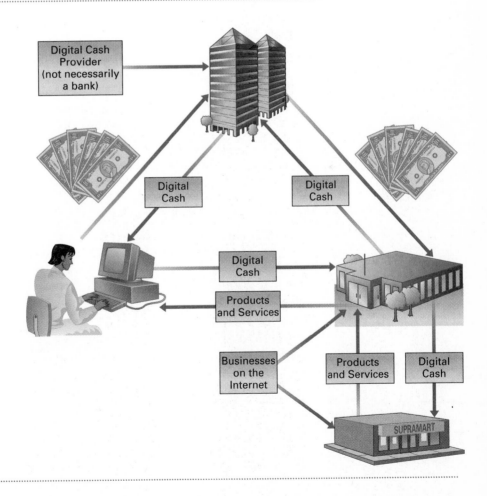

Regardless of your future college education and career, IT will play an integral role. If you're a liberal arts student studying to become an English teacher, you'll need to know how to use IT effectively; you won't need to understand the details of the technology, but you'll need to have a grasp of some fundamentals to increase your overall effectiveness in the classroom.

If you plan to have a computer science or MIS major or minor, you'll need to know the technology in detail but you'll also need to understand its uses—in both business and personal situations—so you can help make the technology valuable to organizations and people. If you plan to have a business career, you'll need to understand how IT affects operations, competition, customer service, and innovation.

This book has given you a starting point, no matter what road you choose to travel. As a general student, it shows you how to understand and apply IT to your own career in terms of productivity, skill, and innovation. As a technical student, it helps you to begin to understand the very broad world of IT and its uses. You will later explore many of the topics you've studied here in much more detail. As a business student in economics, public administration, or finance, this book gives you a sense of IT's role in organizations and what that means to you in your future employment.

As a final note, we'd like to leave you with some parting thoughts concerning IT.

You Are the Most Important Component of an IT System

Perhaps the most important thing to remember about IT is that you are the most important component of an IT system. Without you, IT is just a computer—it is not capable of doing anything without your direction and instruction.

IT Is Changing and Affecting Your Life

IT is probably the fastest-changing field today. The changes in IT are also bringing about rapid and dramatic changes in the way you live your life. When you see IT changing, think about how it will change your life and take every advantage of it that you can. Remember, IT and what you can do with it may determine how good a job you get and how long you keep that job.

Consider a Career in IT

We hope that you have decided to pursue a career in IT. It's an exciting field with many job opportunities just waiting for you. If you're thinking about a career in IT, talk to your instructors to find out what courses you need to take and talk to people who already work in the IT field. Those people can also tell you what knowledge you need to gain while you're in school.

Don't Stop Here—Keep Learning

Whether you decide to pursue a career in IT or some other area, don't stop learning about IT. IT can help you be more productive in any field—medicine, sales, or even criminal justice. Whatever you decide to do, IT will be waiting there for you. It's up to you to take advantage of IT and of what it can do for you.

Look Back to Where You Began

It's the year 2006—you're up early one morning to get a head start on the day. Your integrated home management (IHM) system—which consists of your computer, television, telephone, fax machine, VCR, stereo, and home environmental controls—has already turned on the coffee machine, printed a list of concerts in your town for the weekend, confirmed your airline reservations, and is displaying a message that you need to call Shannon. While sitting in the comfort of your favorite reclining chair, you say, "Call Shannon and send airline information." Your IHM system calls Shannon and sends her a copy of your flight schedule. On your television screen you see Shannon and your flight schedule, and the two of you discuss when Shannon will pick you up at the airport.

It doesn't sound so farfetched now, does it?

Chapter 10 Summary

Now You Can . . .

1. Describe the job opportunities in the field of IT.

    ▶ *Computer operators,* who actually operate the physical IT equipment hardware.

    ▶ *Hardware designers and technicians,* who design and maintain IT hardware.

    ▶ *Application programmers,* who write code for application software.

    ▶ *System programmers,* who write code for operating system software.

    ▶ *Systems analysts,* who determine what an IT system must do.

    ▶ *Network specialists,* who work with IT systems that support many people.

    ▶ *Database specialists,* who develop, monitor, and maintain databases and database management systems.

    ▶ There are also many new opportunities in IT in such areas as multimedia, video games, virtual reality, neural networks, genetic software, and the Internet.

2. Describe the three aspects of IT that you need for any career.

    ▶ *Personal productivity software:* How to use personal productivity software and what the various types of personal productivity software can do.

    ▶ *Hardware:* How to use various types of hardware and make informed decisions regarding which types of technology are best for a given situation.

    ▶ *Networking:* What networks can and cannot do and how to use the Internet.

3. Describe the criminal and ethical considerations in IT.

    ▶ *Ethics* are the standards or set of principles that help guide behavior, actions, or choices.

    ▶ *IT ethics* means using your IT system to do things the same way you would do them if you didn't have IT.

    ▶ *Information technology crimes:*

    Computer viruses are software programs that cause an IT system to malfunction.

    Stealing information is illegally obtaining information.

Software piracy, or stealing software, is illegally obtaining and using software.

IT destruction is the crime of physically damaging or destroying an IT system that belongs to someone else.

4. Understand how IT is going to change.

    ▶ *Through rightsizing:* IT systems are getting smaller, and at the same time, more powerful and less expensive than their larger predecessors.

    ▶ *Through integration:* IT manufacturers working together so that you can choose the best each has to offer.

    ▶ *Through a restructuring of the IT industry:* Through acquisitions, a combining of media, IT, and communications companies, and the continuation of the great chip race.

    ▶ *By incorporating more of the senses:* Greater gains in sound and possibly even in the senses of smell and taste.

5. Understand how changes in IT are going to affect your life.

    ▶ *Home-integrated computing:* Intelligent consumer products, interactive television, and telecommuting.

    ▶ *Education-integrated computing:* Telecommuting to get an education, and electronic publishing.

    ▶ *Travel-integrated computing:* Airplanes and hotels.

    ▶ *Customer-integrated computing:* Businesses providing customers with technology to make it faster, easier, and more convenient to buy products and services. Also, digital cash.

Key Terms

Antivirus Software

Application Programmer

Computer Operator

Computer Science

Computer Virus

Database Specialist

Digital Cash

Electronic Publishing

Ethics

Hardware Designer and Technician

Intelligent Consumer Product

Interactive Television

IT Destruction

Management Information Systems (MIS)

Network Specialist

Software Piracy

System Programmer

Systems Analyst

Self-Test

1. What are seven common jobs in the IT field?

    A.

    B.

    C.

    D.

    E.

    F.

    G.

2. People who actually operate the physical IT equipment are called:

    A. Systems analysts

    B. Application programmers

    C. Computer operators

    D. Database specialists

    E. Network specialists

3. People responsible for determining what an IT system must do are called:

    A. Systems analysts

    B. Application programmers

    C. Computer operators

    D. Database specialists

    E. Network specialists

4. According to *Money* magazine, the number 1 job in the nation is:

    A. Hardware designer and technician

    B. Technical writer

    C. Application and system programmer

    D. Systems analyst

5. _____ is the field of study associated with a technical IT education.

6. _____ is the field of study associated with a business IT education.

7. _____ offer programs in IT that range from six months to two years of study.

8. The five most sought-after skills in IT are:

    A.

    B.

    C.

    D.

    E.

9. What are the three aspects of IT that you should know in order to pursue any career?

    A.

    B.

    C.

10. _____ are the standards or set of principles that help guide behavior, actions, and choices.

11. Software programs that cause an IT system to malfunction are called:

    A. Computer lockouts

    B. Pirates

    C. Hackers

    D. Computer bombs

    E. Computer viruses

12. _____ is the crime of physically damaging or destroying an IT system that belongs to someone else.

13. In what four ways can you expect to see IT change?

    A.

    B.

    C.

    D.

14. _____ are products that have IT as a component of them.

15. _____ is the development of material designed specifically for electronic distribution and use.

Short-Answer Questions

1. What are some of the newer job opportunities that are available in the IT field?

2. Why is networking an important skill to learn for any career?

3. What are the four different types of IT crimes?

4. Why is education a prime candidate for the use of IT?

5. What is digital cash? How does it work?

Discussion Questions and Projects

1. Review your local newspaper and develop a list of the top IT skills that businesses are seeking. How do these correspond to the national survey in Table 10-2? Do the salaries seem consistent with the ones listed in Table 10-1?

2. We stated that IT will change by incorporating all the senses. Can you identify some IT applications that might make use of the senses of smell and taste?

Working in a Group

1. Jobs in the future will increasingly require more IT knowledge. Develop what you think would be the "job ad of the future" for the following fields (be sure to include all IT requirements):

   Marketing research
   Product advertisement
   Radiology
   Petrochemical geology
   Securities analysis
   Stock brokering
   Speech writing

Cruising the Net

1 Locate resources on the Net that list job postings. You can do a Net search on keywords "job posting" or you can connect to one of the many Web pages listing job announcements (such as the one at http://oriole.umd:8000/employ.html). What job opportunities are there in IT? Describe the information you located.

2 Do a Net search on CWIS (Campus Wide Information System) or follow the gopher menu to locate a gopher server for an educational institution of your choice. Describe the types of information you located.

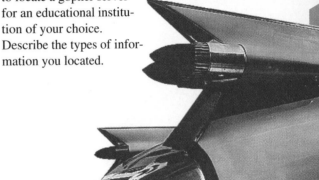

2. In the near future, automobiles will be equipped with more IT than your imagination can possibly conceive. Let your group's imagination run wild anyway and describe what IT the automobile of the future will include and what functions the IT will perform. Don't hesitate to think creatively—it may just happen!

Solutions to Self-Test (1) computer operator, hardware designer and technician, application programmer, system programmer, systems analyst, network specialist, database specialist—p. 299; (2) C—p. 299; (3) A—p. 300; (4) D—p. 302; (5) computer science—p. 303; (6) management information systems—p. 303; (7) vocational and trade schools—p. 304; (8) PC/LAN, relational database, UNIX, C programming, COBOL programming—p. 305; (9) personal productivity software, hardware, networking—p. 305; (10) ethics—p. 308; (11) E—p. 308; (12) IT destruction—p. 309; (13) through rightsizing, through integration, through a restructuring of the IT industry, by incorporating more of the senses—p. 311; (14) intelligent consumer products—p. 313; (15) electronic publishing—p. 315.

Notes

Chapter 1

1. Phillip Fiorini, "Workers say: No place like Home," *USA Today,* September 21, 1994, p. 1B.
2. Mortimer Zuckerman, "America's Silent Revolution," *U.S. News & World Report,* July 18, 1994, p. 90.
3. Bruce Horovitz, "PC sellers targeting home users," *USA Today,* November 28, 1994, p. 1B.
4. *The Financial Times,* "The Key to Competitiveness," March 1, 1995, p. 3.

Chapter 2

1. Nina Burns, "E-Mail Beyond the LAN," *PC Magazine,* April 25, 1995, pp. 102–108.
2. Dataquest, 1994.

Chapter 3

1. Bill Howard, "11th Annual Printer Issue," *PC Magazine,* November 22, 1994, pp. 110–118.

Chapter 5

1. Thomas Stewart, "What Information Cost," *Fortune* July 10, 1995, pp. 119–121.
2. Joan Hamilton, "Medicine's New Weapon: Data," *BusinessWeek,* March 27, 1995, pp. 184–188.
3. Ernest Schell, "How to Make Millions with Database Marketing," *Datamation,* August 1, 1992.
4. "Computerworld's Eighth Annual Salary Survey," *Computerworld,* September 5, 1994.

Chapter 6

1. Peter G.W. Keen and J. Michael Cummins, *Networks in Action: Business Choices and Telecommunications Decisions,* Wadsworth Publishing Company, Belmont, California, 1994, pp. 145–146.
2. *PC Magazine,* "The Versatile Network Operating System, May 30, 1995, pp. 228–258.
3. Peter G.W. Keen and J. Michael Cummins, *Networks in Action,* p. 336.
4. "Computerworld's Eighth Annual Salary Survey," *Computerworld,* September 5, 1994.
5. Bruce Raymar, "All Roads Lead to IT," *Computerworld—The Global 100,* May 1, 1995.

Chapter 7

1. "Computerworld's Eighth Annual Salary Survey," *Computerworld,* September 5, 1994.

Chapter 8

1. Steve Lunce, "An Examination of the Managerial Issues Involved in the Contingency Planning for Information Systems," The University of Texas at Arlington, 1994.
2. Joseph Weber, "Just Get It to the Stores on Time," *BusinessWeek,* March 6, 1995, pp. 66–67.
3. Charles Wang, *Techno Vision,* McGraw-Hill, Inc., New York, 1994.
4. Sharon Begley, "Software au Naturel," *Newsweek,* May 8, 1995, pp. 70–71.
5. Michael Hammer and James Champy, *Reengineering the Corporation: A Manifesto for Business Revolution,* HarperBusiness, New York, 1993.

Chapter 9

1. Peter G.W. Keen and J. Michael Cummins, *Networks in Action: Business Choices and Telecommunications Decisions,* Wadsworth Publishing Company, Belmont, California, 1994, pp. 95–96.
2. *The World Almanac,* Funk and Wagnalls Corporation, New Jersey, 1995.

Chapter 10

1. Craig Wilson, "Where the Work Is in the Computer Era," *USA Today,* March 29, 1995, p. 1D.
2. "Computerworld's Eighth Annual Salary Survey," *Computerworld,* September 5, 1994.
3. Jersey Gilbert, "The Best Jobs in America," *Money,* March 1994, pp. 70–74.
4. Kirk Arnett and Charles Litecky, "Career Path Development for the Most Wanted Skills in the MIS Job Market," *Journal of Systems Management,* February 1994, pp. 6–10.
5. Pam Dixon, "Jobs on the Web," *Sky,* May 1995, pp. 129–138.
6. Paul Eng, "Big Business on the Net? Not Yet," *BusinessWeek,* June 26, 1995, pp. 100–101.
7. Becky Beyers, "Are You Vulnerable to Cybercrime?," *USA Today,* February 20, 1995, p. 3B,
8. Stephen Keating, "Software Sleuths Clean Up," *The Denver Post,* August 21, 1994, pp. 1, 8H.
9. Becky Beyers, "Are You Vulnerable to Cybercrime?" p. 3B.
10. Bruce Schwartz, "A Video Game Accessory that Works by Mind Control," *USA Today,* June 16, 1995, p. 1D.
11. Peter Burrows, "The Computer Is in the Mail (Really)," *BusinessWeek,* January 23, 1995, pp. 76–77.
12. Edward Baig, "Welcome to the Officeless Office," *BusinessWeek,* June 26, 1995, pp. 104–105.

Antivirus software: A type of utility software that protects against viruses.

Application generation subsystem: The subsystem of a DBMS that contains tools that help you create and update other features such as menus, data entry screens, reports, and application software.

Application programmer: A person who writes code for application software.

Application software: The layer of software closest to you that helps you solve specific problems or perform specific tasks.

Arithmetic/logic unit (A/L unit): The hardware that executes application software instructions. It is part of the central processing unit.

Artificial intelligence (AI): The field of study that deals with the capturing, modeling, and storing of human intelligence within an IT system so that the system can facilitate decision-making processes that normally would be undertaken by people.

Asynchronous transfer mode (ATM): A transmission method for sending information that divides a long message into smaller units (called packets).

Audio output device: An output device that lets you hear information.

Automatic speech recognition (ASR system): An input device that not only captures what you are saying but also has the ability to separate your speech into words and sentences.

Bar code reader: An input device that interprets bar codes and passes the corresponding numbers to a system for processing.

Binary digit system: An information scheme that uses base-2. It uses only the digits 0 and 1 to represent all information.

Bit: A digit position in the binary digit system represented by either a 0 or a 1.

Bridge: An internetworking device that connects two networks of the same kind.

Broadcast radio: An unguided communication medium popularly used for digital paging, cellular phone systems, and wireless personal communication networks within a building or in a limited geographic area.

Bus configuration: A network configuration in which the nodes are connected to a single communication medium over which all information, software, and messages must travel.

Byte: A logical grouping of bits (usually 8) that is the same as a character.

Cache memory: Special ultrafast (hence more expensive) RAM that holds frequently used application software instructions and information.

Carrier sense multiple access with collision detection (CSMA/CD): A communications protocol that manages communication in a network by having each node "listen" to the network for communications.

Cathode ray tube (CRT): The category of soft copy output device most often used on workstations and larger IT systems.

CD-recording (CD-R) technology: The hardware and software for creating your own CDs.

Central processing unit (CPU): The hardware that executes instructions, processes information, and directs how all the other hardware components work together. It includes the arithmetic/logic unit and the control unit.

Centralized network: A network with one main CPU that processes all information requests and handles communication.

Client: A workstation in a client/server network that maintains local software and information and does as much of the processing as possible.

Client/server network: A distributed network in which many workstations (clients) are connected to a central workstation (server).

Cluster controller: A communication device that manages a group of devices that share a single high-speed communication medium connected to another location.

Coaxial cable: A guided communication medium that consists of one or more central wires surrounded by thick insulation cable.

Code generator: Software that allows you to specify the desired results of information processing requests without having to detail the steps necessary to obtain the information.

Communication device: The hardware connection between different IT systems.

Communication link: The electronic pathway over which information travels from sender to receiver in a network.

Communication medium: The path over which information travels in a network.

Communication software: Software that helps you electronically send information to and receive it from another person. Often called electronic mail or e-mail.

Communication switch: A hardware device that brings together the communication media and routes communication throughout a network.

Communication system: An IT system that supports the flow of information.

Communications protocol: The set of procedures that define how two devices communicate with each other in a network.

Compact disk read-only memory (CD-ROM): The most popular type of optical disk.

Comparative report: A report that compares two or more sets of similar information.

Complex instruction set computing (CISC): An instruction set for CPUs that has as many built-in instructions as possible. Most prevalent on business workstations and portable systems.

Computer operator: A person who operates the physical IT equipment (hardware).

Computer science: The area of study most closely associated with a technical IT education.

Computer-assisted software engineering tool (CASE tool): Software tools that automate some portion of the system development life cycle.

Context-level diagram: A data flow diagram that shows how your system interacts with the sources and sinks by identifying the flows of data from the sources and the flows of information to the sinks.

Control unit: The hardware that directs how all the hardware components work. It is part of the central processing unit.

Controlling: The process of monitoring people's efforts to accomplish activities to make sure that they move the business toward its objectives.

Custom-developed software: Software that has been written by a specific business for its own use.

Data: A known fact with a singular meaning.

Data administration: The function within an organization responsible for ensuring that the correct information is available to users and applications when needed.

Data administration subsystem: The subsystem of a DBMS that lets you establish users of a database, specify who can update which information, and develop methods for backing up and recovering the database in the event of a failure.

Data communications equipment (DCE): Any communication device that makes the physical connection between the nodes and the actual network.

Data definition subsystem: The subsystem of a DBMS that helps you create and maintain the data dictionary and define the structure of the files in a database.

Data dictionary: Contains the description of the structure of the information found in the files of a database.

Data flow diagram (DFD): A graphical tool that shows the processes that act on data and information as they flow through a system.

Data integrity: The correctness of information as it appears in an IT system.

Data manipulation subsystem: The subsystem of a DBMS that lets you add and delete records, change field contents, and view the database.

Data redundancy: The problem of having the same information stored in many different places.

Data store: A file, which can be paper or computer stored, that contains information.

Database: A group of related files.

Database management system (DBMS) software: Software designed to help you create, store, and manipulate a database.

Database specialist: A person who develops, monitors, and maintains databases and database management systems.

Decision support system (DSS): An IT system that is a collection of software tools and information used to assist in the decision-making process.

Dedicated input device: An input device that handles one specific functional task.

Dedicated IT system: An IT system that performs only one specific task.

Deregulation: The movement to bring open competition and free enterprise into previously restricted areas of business.

Desktop publishing software: Software that extends word processing software to help you create documents that need special features not provided by a word processing package.

Digital cash: An electronic form of currency that you can use to purchase products and services at stores as well as make purchases on the Internet.

Directing: The process of leading the organization through communication, inspiration, and motivation.

Disk operating system (DOS): The oldest operating system in the Microsoft family.

Distributed network: A network that is a collection of workstations connected to each other, along with various shared storage devices and input and output devices.

Dot matrix printer: Non-letter quality impact printers that use matrix pins to strike a printer ribbon on a page.

Downward flow of information: Information that consists of strategies, goals, objectives, and policies that originate at one level and pass to lower levels.

Education software: Software that helps you learn about a specific topic or area of interest.

Electrically erasable programmable read-only memory (EEPROM): ROM internal memory that allows you to use special software to change the set of instructions.

Electronic data interchange (EDI): The direct computer-to-computer transfer of information normally provided by the use of standard business paper documents.

Electronic meeting support software: Software that lets a group have a "virtual" meeting on its computers.

Electronic publishing: The development of material designed specifically for electronic distribution and use.

Embedded IT system: An IT system that is built into another product.

Entity: Something about which you wish to store information that can be uniquely described with a primary key.

Entity class: A grouping of similar entities.

Entity-relationship (E-R) diagram: A graph representing entity classes, attributes, and relationships.

Erasable optical disk (EOD): The storage medium used by magneto-optical storage technologies.

Erasable programmable read-only memory (EPROM): ROM internal memory that allows you, with a special ultraviolet light device, to change the instructions in a matter of minutes.

Ergonomics: The field of study that deals with human physical interaction with equipment.

European Union (EU): A 15-country federation that constitutes the strongest international trade bloc in the world.

Exception report: A report that provides a subset of available information based on some selection criterion.

Executive support system (ESS): An IT system that supports the information needs of strategic management by providing a basic summary of information and tools for working with unstructured problems.

Expert system: A decision support technology that helps people solve a problem by capturing and using the expertise, logic patterns, and thought processes of an expert.

External information: Information that describes the environment surrounding the organization.

Fault-tolerant system: IT systems that have extra hardware, software, and power supply components that can be used to keep a system running in case the primary hardware, software, or power supply components fail.

Fiber distributed data interface (FDDI): A communications protocol that uses token passing with high-speed optical fiber as the communication medium.

Field: A logical grouping of characters.

File: A logical grouping of records.

File management system: The software that maintains the information in a logical grouping of files.

Flash memory: A special permanent memory chip that resembles RAM but does not lose its contents when you turn off your system.

Flat panel display: The category of soft copy output device most often used on portable systems.

Floppy disk: Circular, flexible plastic platter protected by a jacket.

Foreign key: The primary key of one relation that appears as an attribute of another relation in the relational database model.

Front-end processor: A special computer that handles the communications functions for the host computer.

FTP server: A server of the Internet that is an archive of documents and files that can be transferred to your computer.

Gateway: An internetworking device that connects networks that are totally dissimilar.

General Agreement on Trades and Tariffs (GATT): The most complicated effort in human history to forge a worldwide treaty to reduce trade barriers and expand global trade. Now called the World Trade Organization (WTO), it includes 125 member countries.

General business management software: Software that automates specific functions that businesses perform every day such as payroll and accounts receivable.

Gigabyte (GB): 1,073,741,824 characters or bytes (roughly 1 billion).

Global economy: An economy in which organizations do business all over the world selling products and services; producing products and services; buying materials and components from suppliers; acting as suppliers; and forming alliances or partnerships.

Glove input device: A motion input device that captures and records the shape and the strength of the movements of your hand and fingers.

Gopher server: A server on the Internet that lets you access information in a menu-driven format.

Granularity: The level of detail of information.

Graphics adapter card: The interface board that connects the monitor or screen to the rest of the hardware.

Group decision support system (GDSS): A decision support system that supports the collaborative efforts of many people by providing hardware and software that facilitates communication and the sharing of information.

Group scheduling software: Software that helps you schedule meetings.

Groupware: Software that helps people communicate, share information, perform their work more efficiently and effectively, and work together to make decisions using IT.

Guided communication medium: A communication medium over which information travels an enclosed path.

Hard copy output device: Output device that produces output on some tangible medium like paper.

Hard disk: A storage device composed of many rigid platters.

Hard disk cartridge: A disk storage device in which the disk drive is separate from the hard disk storage medium.

Hard disk pack: A hard disk cartridge for larger systems (minicomputers, mainframe computers, and supercomputers).

Hardcard: A type of hard disk that can be added to your system by inserting it into an expansion slot.

Hardware: The physical components of an IT system including input devices, output devices, storage devices, the processing engine, and communication devices.

Hardware designer and technician: A person who designs and maintains IT hardware.

Headset: A motion input device and an output device that captures the movement of your head—side to side and up and down—and generates a screen image that completely covers your vision.

Holographic storage: A storage technology that incorporates depth to store information three-dimensionally on different faces of crystal-like objects.

Hybrid network: A network that combines the central processing capabilities of a centralized network with the distributed processing capabilities of a distributed network.

Hypertext software: Software that lets you create, manage, and retrieve modules of information—in the form of text, pictures, and even video—by logical association such as information topic, key word, or author.

Image scanning: An input device that lets you scan digital images of entire pictures and drawings as well as preprinted and handwritten text.

In-house system development life cycle (in-house SDLC): A set of six stages that an organization goes through to develop an IT system by using its own IT specialists.

Industry-specific software: Software that helps businesses in a specific industry perform a task that is specific to that industry.

Information: A fact known as a result of presenting data in a more meaningful way.

Information retrieval and management software: Software that lets you store, retrieve, and update information by logical association.

Information technology (IT): A set of tools that helps you work with information and perform tasks related to information processing.

Inheritance: A feature of the object-oriented database model that can be used to pass information from one object to another.

Initial feasibility review: The process of determining if the benefits of the proposed system outweigh the expected costs of the development of a new system.

Ink jet printer: Letter quality nonimpact hard copy output device that sprays ink onto the page.

Input device: Hardware device that helps you capture information and commands.

Integrated services digital network (ISDN): The plan and international communications standard for the transition of the world's public telephone system from analog to digital for the purpose of transmitting all types of information simultaneously over twisted-pair telephone lines.

Intelligent consumer product: Products that have IT as a component.

Intelligent network: A special network that basically knows where you are, who you are, and who you want to get in touch with and why.

Interactive television: A television with a keyboard, storage, and the ability to respond to your requests to transmit and receive vast amounts of information from all over the world.

Internal hard disk: A single unit that contains both the disk drive and the storage medium (multiple platters).

Internal information: Information that describes specific operational aspects of the organization.

Internal memory: The hardware that is a temporary storage area that holds information you are working with, application software you are using, and operating system software.

Internet: A network of networked computers that lets you communicate with and obtain information from people all over the world.

Internetworking unit: A special hardware communication device that connects two or more networks.

Iridium project: The launching of up to 70 low-earth-orbit satellites (LEOS) about 60 miles in the sky.

IT destruction: The IT crime of physically damaging or destroying an IT system that belongs to someone else.

IT network: A coordinated group of IT components that support many people working together, including sharing hardware, sharing software, sharing information, and communicating with each other.

Kilobyte (KB): 1,024 characters or bytes.

LAN configuration: Defines the manner in which the various nodes in a network are connected.

Laser printer: Nonimpact letter quality hard copy output device that is the choice of business printing.

Light pen: A special light-producing input device used in conjunction with a light-sensitive screen.

Local area network (LAN): A network that covers a limited geographic area such as an office or office building.

Magnetic disk storage device: A disk storage device that represents information on a disk by creating electromagnetic charges on a metallic oxide film covering the surface of the disk storage medium.

Magnetic-ink character recognition (MICR): An input device that electronically reads a set of preprinted magnetic symbols.

Magneto-optical (MO) storage device: A storage device that uses a laser that allows information to be packed more densely and a form of magnetization that lets you change the stored information.

Management: The process of planning activities, providing the necessary staffing to accomplish activities, organizing the activities and staffing in a meaningful way, and directing and controlling the accomplishment of activities.

Management information system (MIS): An IT system that supports the management and control of day-to-day operations by providing periodic reports that summarize the information captured by a transaction processing system.

Management information systems (MIS): The field of study associated with a business IT education.

Mainframe: Large IT usually found in business environments where many people have information processing requests at the same time.

Megabyte (MB): 1,048,576 characters or bytes.

Megahertz (MHz): Millions of cycles per second. The number of cycles that an internal clock makes.

Mesh configuration: A network configuration in which node connections are made according to transmission traffic.

Method: Services or actions that can be used to add, change, or delete records and fields in the object-oriented database model.

Method dictionary: The place where methods are stored in the object-oriented database model.

Metropolitan area network (MAN): A network that covers a large area such as a city, but usually a distance no greater than 10 to 20 miles.

Microwave: An unguided communication medium that uses a high-frequency band of radio broadcast transmission.

Minicomputer: Large IT usually found in business environments where many people have information processing requests at the same time.

Modem: A communication device that converts the digital signal of your IT system into an analog form that can be transmitted over a telephone network and then converts the analog signals back to digital signals at the other end of the transmission.

Monitor: See soft copy output device.

Motion input device: An input device that records physical movement.

Mouse: A small handheld input device that causes the cursor to move on the screen as you move the mouse across a flat surface.

Multimedia: Software that combines information in all forms in a way that users can navigate through the information in any order they wish.

Multiplexer: A communication device that aggregates several communication media and allows them to share a single communication medium that usually operates at a much higher capacity and greater speed.

Multiprocessing: The ability of an operating system to spread your work over several CPUs at the same time.

Network administration team: Responsible for ensuring that the network matches the structural and operational characteristics of the organization and meets people's day-to-day processing and communication needs.

Network interface card: A special network card that connects a node (usually a workstation) to a network.

Network manager: Coordinates the overall efforts of the network administration team and acts as a liaison to the strategic task force of the organization.

Network operating system (NOS) software: The software in a network that is responsible for managing (1) the communication within a network, (2) any multiprocessing that takes place, (3) the sharing of hardware devices, and (4) any communication external to another network.

Network specialist: A person who deals specifically with IT systems that support many people.

Node: Any IT device in a network.

North American Free Trade Agreement (NAFTA): A trade agreement originally ratified between the United States, Canada, and Mexico and now includes Chile.

Notebook: The most common type of portable system. Basically, carry-around, battery-powered systems that offer you the capabilities of a workstation, but to a lesser degree.

Object: Contains fields that describe each record and a list of services or actions that can be used to add, change, or delete records and fields in the object-oriented database model.

Object linking and embedding (OLE): The ability of an operating system that supports the sharing of information between applications.

Object-oriented database model: A database model that uses objects to store information.

Objective information: Information that quantitatively defines something.

Operating system software: The part of the system software that controls application software execution and manages how the hardware works together.

Operating system/2 (OS/2): IBM's contribution to the operating system environment.

Operational management: The level of management that develops short-range goals and objectives that will meet the medium-range goals and objectives of tactical management.

Optical character recognition (OCR): An input device that works with both formatted and unformatted input. With formatted input, OCR devices read preprinted information that has been standardized by ANSI. With unformatted input, OCR devices convert a digital picture of text into actual text that can be edited.

Optical disk storage device: A storage device that uses a laser beam device to read and write information to an optical disk medium.

Optical fiber: A guided communication medium that transmits information in the form of light pulses through a thin glass or plastic fiber.

Optical mark recognition (OMR): An input device that detects the presence of absence of a mark in a predetermined place.

Organizing: The development of an organizational structure that will allow people to carry out their activities in the best possible way.

Output device: Hardware device that lets you receive the results of your requests.

Outsourcing: When an organization decides to let someone else take over and develop, operate, and/or maintain part of its operations.

Parallel conversion: A conversion method that involves using both the old and new system until the project development team determines that the new system works correctly.

Parallel processing: The use of multiple CPUs in a single IT system to process many instructions in parallel, or simultaneously.

Path: All communication links over which information travels in a network.

Peer-to-peer network: A distributed network in which many workstations are connected to each other and do not rely on a server for global software and information, information processing tasks, or communication within the network.

Pen mouse: A mouse-like input device that resembles a fountain pen connected to your computer.

Pen-based computer: A special IT system built around the use of unformatted OCR and a special writing stylus used to write on the screen.

Periodic report: A report that is received on a predetermined basis.

Personal digital assistant (PDA): The smallest of the portable systems. Designed mostly for personal information management, limited note taking, document manipulation (word processing), and spreadsheet work.

Personal information management software: Software that helps you manage information relating to contacts, schedules, tasks, and finances.

Personal productivity software: Software designed to help do things that you could probably do manually.

Piecemeal conversion: A conversion method that involves implementing only a portion of the new system before other portions are implemented.

Piloting conversion: A conversion method that involves using only a portion of the users to test a new system.

Pixel: The smallest display unit on a screen that can be turned on or off and made different shades of colors.

Planning: The process of establishing goals and objectives and developing the required activities to meet those goals and objectives.

Plotter: Special hard copy output devices for creating nontext images like architectural drawings, maps, diagrams, and charts.

Plug and play: The ability of an operating system that lets you add input, output, and storage devices to your system while it's actually running.

Plunge conversion: A conversion method that involves totally discarding the old system and immediately beginning to use the new system.

Point-of-sale (POS) system: IT-based system that captures information at the point of a sale and then transmits that information to another system for processing.

Pointing input device: An input device that lets you literally "point" to choose information and/or commands that you want to enter.

Pointing stick: A small rubber-like input device that causes the cursor to move on the screen as you apply directional pressure.

Portability: The ability of an operating system to run application software designed for another operating system.

Portable IT system: Small, battery-powered system that you can take with you wherever you go.

Premastering software: The software in CD-recording for simulating a CD on your magnetic hard disk.

Presentation graphics software: Software that helps you to create high-quality presentations of information, including transparencies, handouts for presentations, on-screen presentations, and even 35mm slides.

Primary key: The field in a given file that uniquely describes each record.

Printer: The most popular type of hard copy output device.

Private network: Networks in which an organization has the exclusive rights to use the communication facility.

Process: Transforms inputs into outputs.

Processing engine: The hardware that handles the behind-the-scenes work in an IT system. It includes the central processing unit and the internal memory.

Program-to-data dependency: The problem of having to store the structure of information in a file with the software that maintains the file.

Programmable read-only memory (PROM): ROM internal memory specifically programmed by the manufacturer for a particular use.

Programmer: An IT specialist responsible for writing the software code.

Programming language: The set of rules that define the syntax for how software must be written.

Project development team: The group of people—including a project manager, several IT specialists, management individuals, users, and customers—who are responsible for the development of a new system.

Project plan: A plan that includes proposed dates for completing major tasks and a budget for the development of a new system.

Proof-of-concept prototype: A prototype that proves something can be done.

Prototype: A simulation or experimental model of a proposed system or product.

Public network: Communication facilities owned and operated by a common carrier such as AT&T and MCI that serves a large number of subscribers, usually on a pay-as-you-go basis.

Random access memory (RAM): The area of internal memory where your information, application, and operating system software reside while you're using them.

Read-only memory (ROM): The part of the internal memory that comes with certain system software instructions already built in.

Record: A logical grouping of fields.

Reduced instruction set computing (RISC): An instruction set for CPUs that has as few built-in instructions as possible. Dominate engineering and scientific workstation environments.

Relation: A file or table in the relational database model.

Relational database model: A database model that uses a series of tables or files called relations to store information.

Request for proposal (RFP): A document that outlines the necessary requirements for a new system and solicits bids from other organizations or individuals.

Resolution: The sharpness of the image produced on a screen.

Ring configuration: A network configuration in which the connections of nodes (usually through a common communication medium) form a closed loop.

Router: An internetworking device that connects networks that are dissimilar with respect to some operations like node addressing and message size.

Satellite: An unguided communication medium that receives information from a node on earth, repeats the information, and sends it to one or more receiving nodes on earth.

Satellite Communications for Learning (SCOLA): The leading nonprofit educational consortium that distributes foreign language news programming via satellite to schools, colleges, and businesses.

Scanning input device: An input device that provides a way of entering information already recorded on paper.

Screen: See soft copy output device.

Selling prototype: A prototype that helps sell the idea of a proposed system.

Server: A workstation in a client/server network that is responsible for file control, printer control, communications control, and network control.

Side-to-side flow of information: Information that defines the communications between various functional units.

Sink: A person or organization that receives information from a system.

Site license agreement: A contract between an organization that a software manufacturer grants your organization the right to let many people access and use a software copy on a network.

Smart card: Special IT system about the size of a credit card that includes a CPU, an operating system (on ROM), and a small amount of internal memory (about 64 KB).

Soft copy output device: The most popular type of output device and includes screens or monitors.

Software: The set of instructions that your central processing unit executes to perform a particular intellectual task for you.

Software development: The process of specifying, designing, writing, and testing software.

Software piracy: Illegally obtaining and using software.

Software suite: A collection of software applications that work together in an integrated fashion.

Sound input device: An input device that lets you capture and record sounds so that you can change them if you wish and reproduce them at a later time.

Sound output device: An output device that reproduces recorded sounds such as music and speech.

Source: A person or organization from which data originates.

Speech synthesis output device: An output device that actually creates speech output.

Spreadsheet software: Software that works with rows and columns and lets you enter and change information in cells (the intersection of a row and column) and specify how the cell contents are related to each other.

Staffing: The process of selecting the appropriate people to meet the goals and objectives of the organization by accomplishing required activities.

Star configuration: A network configuration which has a central workstation from which all other nodes radiate.

Storage device: Hardware component that permanently stores information and software.

Strategic management: The level of management that is responsible for developing the overall goals, objectives, strategies, and policies of an organization.

Structured decision making: A decision-making process in which information is complete and objective that an organization makes on a regular basis.

Subjective information: Information that attempts to describe something currently unknown.

Subnotebook: Combines many of the rich capabilities of notebooks with the small size and portability of personal digital assistants.

Supercomputer: High-speed special purpose systems designed to perform billions of instructions per second in a research environment.

Superscalar CPU: CPUs that can execute more than one instruction per clock cycle.

System 7: The most recent operating system for the Apple line of personal computers.

System development life cycle (SDLC): The process an organization goes through to develop a new system.

System programmer: A person who deals with operating system software.

System software: The layer of software closest to the CPU that coordinates the interaction of all the hardware while you use the application software.

Systems analyst: An IT specialist who works with users to define how the current system works, what changes need to be made, and how the new system will work.

Tactical management: The level of management that deals with the development of medium-range objectives, procedures, and policies that will ensure that strategic management goals and objectives are met.

Taligent: A joint-venture operating system developed by IBM, Apple, and Hewlett-Packard that uses an interface based on "people, places, and things."

Tape storage device: A storage device that uses a magnetic method of storage and a sequential method of access to read and write information to and from a magnetic tape.

Telecommunications: Everything involved in the electronic movement of information including communication devices and software, communication services, and providers of those services, and such concepts as electronic data interchange (EDI).

Terminal: A hardware device combining a keyboard and monitor.

Throwaway decision support system: A decision support system that is used to aid in the decision-making process once and then is literally thrown away because the decision may never be made again.

Token passing: A communications protocol that literally "passes" around an electronic token or message board that each node in a network gets to use in turn.

Touch screen: An input device that lets you point at and touch a particular function on a screen.

Trackball: An upside-down, stationary mouse-like input device in which you move the ball instead of the device.

Trade bloc: A group of countries that have pooled their resources to improve delivery of products and services and to reduce, if not eliminate altogether, restrictions on the movement of goods and services between countries.

Transaction processing system (TPS): An IT system that supports the day-to-day operations of an organization.

Transmission speed: The measure of how much information—usually in bits—can be passed through a communication link in a single second.

Transnational firm: A firm that operates worldwide—not only to sell products and services, but also to create them.

Twisted-pair cable: A guided communication medium which consists of two insulated copper wires twisted in a spiral.

Unguided communication medium: Any communication medium that radiates information in many directions.

UNIX: An operating system first developed for use on minicomputers; the workhorse of business rather than personal computing.

Unstructured decision making: A decision-making process in which information is subjective and not completely available and that an organization may not make frequently.

Upward flow of information: Information that describes how the organization is operating.

Value-added network (VAN): Public networks that provide information and software in addition to communication facilities.

Video capturing and editing software: Software that allows you to store and edit videos.

Videoconferencing software: Software that supports interactive face-to-face meetings through computers.

Virtual memory: Permanent disk storage used as "pseudo" RAM.

Virtual reality: A three-dimensional computer simulation in which you actively participate.

Virus: A software program that causes your computer to malfunction.

Walker: A motion input device that records the movement of your legs, including speed of travel.

Web: A server on the Internet that uses a hypertext format to present information to you. Some of the information is underlined or in the form of a button that you can click on and have more related information appear.

Whiteboard software: Software that lets people in a group interactively share and edit documents.

Wide area network (WAN): A network that covers a large geographic area such as a county, state, country, or even the entire world.

Windows: A graphical user interface shell that is laid on top of DOS.

Windows '95: The operating system software successor to Windows that is designed for primarily general business management, personal productivity, personal information management, and education software.

Windows NT: Microsoft's most powerful operating system that focuses on advanced engineering applications, large financial applications, and any other tasks that involve intense number-crunching and the ability to provide networking for a large number of computers.

Word: The number of bytes that can be manipulated at one time by the arithmetic/logic unit.

Word processing software: Software that helps you create, edit, save, and print documents that primarily consist of text.

Work flow automation software: Software designed to help you electronically create, distribute, and store standard business documents such as sales order forms.

Workstation: IT system that fits easily on a desktop and is designed mostly for use by one person. Alternative terms include personal computer, PC, and microcomputer.

World Radio Network (WRN): An audio subcarrier or SCOLA and Superstation TBS in Atlanta that transmits radio programs from 24 countries in English.

Index

Index